International Kierkegaard
Commentary

D1597952

International Kierkegaard Commentary

The Concept of Irony

edited by
Robert L. Perkins

MERCER UNIVERSITY PRESS

ISBN 0-86554-742-4   MUP/H559

B
4373
.043
P73
2001

International Kierkegaard Commentary
The Concept of Irony
Copyright ©2001
Mercer University Press, Macon, Georgia 31210-3960 USA
All rights reserved
Printed in the United States of America

The paper used in this publication meets the minimum requirements
of American National Standard for Information Sciences—
Permanence of Paper for Printed Library Materials, ANSI Z39.48-1984.

Library of Congress Cataloging-in-Publication Data

The concept of irony / edited by Robert L. Perkins.
pp. cm. — (International Kierkegaard commentary ; 2)
Includes bibliographical references and index.
ISBN 0-86554-742-4 (alk. paper).
1. Kierkegaard, Søren, 1813–1855. Om begrebet ironi.
2. Irony.   3. Socrates.
I. Perkins, Robert L., 1930–   . II. Series.
B4376.I58 1984 vol. 2
[B4373.043]
198'9s—dc21
[128]
                                                    2001004752
                                                    CIP

Contents

Acknowledgments

All the contributors to the volume would desire to make acknowledgments, but it is a privilege reserved for the editor. Those whom the contributors would have named will be content to have served their friends and colleagues.

I also have the privilege of thanking two persons at Stetson University who have supported my work in general and the International Kierkegaard Commentary in particular: H. Douglas Lee, president of Stetson University, and Grady Ballenger, dean of the College of Arts and Sciences.

The advisory board and the volume consultant read all the contributions, offered valuable insights into the articles, and also made some recommendations for changes. Dr. Julia Watkin of the University of Tasmania continues to be particularly helpful in suggesting possible authors and tracking down obscure allusions in Kierkegaard's texts. The interest of Mercer University Press and especially the efforts of Senior Editor Edmon L. Rowell, Jr. are deeply appreciated. Princeton University Press gave permission to quote from *The Concept of Irony* and other translations to which they hold copyright.

The several contributors and I also thank our families for the lost evenings and other scattered hours while we pursued these tasks. Finally, I wish to thank my wife, Sylvia Walsh, for assistance at every stage of this project and for making our life together an unutterable joy.

Robert L. Perkins

Sigla

AN   "Armed Neutrality". See PV.

BA   *The Book on Adler*, trans. Howard V. Hong and Edna H. Hong. Princeton NJ: Princeton University Press, 1995.

C   *The Crisis and a Crisis in the Life of an Actress*. See *Christian Discourses*.

CA   *The Concept of Anxiety*, trans. Reidar Thomte in collaboration with Albert B. Anderson. Princeton NJ: Princeton University Press, 1980.

CD   *Christian Discourses* and *The Crisis and a Crisis in the Life of an Actress*,
C   trans. Howard V. Hong and Edna H. Hong. Princeton NJ: Princeton University Press, 1997.

CI   *The Concept of Irony* together with "Notes on Schelling's Berlin NSBL Lectures" trans. Howard V. Hong and Edna H. Hong. Princeton NJ: Princeton University Press, 1989.

COR   *The Corsair Affair*, trans. Howard V. Hong and Edna H. Hong. Princeton NJ: Princeton University Press, 1982.

CUP   *Concluding Unscientific Postscript to 'Philosophical Fragments'*, two vols. trans. Howard V. Hong and Edna H. Hong. Princeton NJ: Princeton University Press, 1992.

EO, 1   *Either/Or*, trans. Howard V. Hong and Edna H. Hong. Princeton NJ:
EO, 2   Princeton University Press, 1987.

EPW   *Early Polemical Writings*, trans. Julia Watkin. Princeton NJ: Princeton Uni-
FPOSL   versity Press, 1990.

EUD   *Eighteen Upbuilding Discourses*, trans. Howard H. Hong and Edna H. Hong. Princeton NJ: Princeton University Press, 1990.

FPOSL   *From the Papers of One Still Living*. See EPW.

FSE   *For Self-Examination* and *Judge for Yourself!*, trans. Howard V. Hong and
JFY   Edna H. Hong. Princeton NJ: Princeton University Press, 1990.

FT   *Fear and Trembling* and *Repetition*, trans. Howard V. Hong and Edna H.
R   Hong. Princeton NJ: Princeton University Press, 1983.

JC   Johannes Climacus or De omnibus dubitandum est, See PF.

JFY   *Judge for Yourself!* See FSE.

JP   *Søren Kierkegaard's Journals and Papers*, Ed. and trans. Howard V. Hong and Edna H. Hong, assisted by Gregor Malantschuk. Bloomington: Indiana University Press, 1, 1967; 2, 1970; 3 and 4, 1975; 5-7, 1978.

LD   *Letters and Documents*, trans. Hendrik Rosenmeier. Princeton NJ: Princeton University Press, 1978.

NA   Newspaper Articles, 1854–1855. See TM.

NSBL "Notes on Schelling's Berlin Lectures." See CI.

OMWA On My Work as an Author. See PV.

P   *Prefaces* and "Writing Sampler", trans. Todd W. Nichol. Princeton NJ:
WS   Princeton University Press, 1998.

PC   *Practice in Christianity,* trans. Howard V. Hong and Edna H. Hong.
       Princeton NJ: Princeton University Press, 1991.

PF   *Philosophical Fragments* and "Johannes Climacus," trans. Howard V. Hong
JC   and Edna H. Hong. Princeton NJ: Princeton University Press, 1985.

PV   *On My Work as an Author,* "The Point of View for My Work as an
OMWA   Author" and "Armed Neutrality", trans. Howard V. Hong and Edna H.
AN   Hong. Princeton NJ: Princeton University Press, 1998.

R   *Repetition.* See FT.

SLW   *Stages on Life's Way,* trans. Howard V. Hong and Edna H. Hong.
       Princeton NJ: Princeton University Press, 1988.

SUD   *The Sickness unto Death,* trans. Howard V. Hong and Edna Hong.
       Princeton NJ: Princeton University Press, 1980.

TA   *Two Ages: the Age of Revolution and the Present Age.* A Literary *Review,*
       trans. Howard V. Hong and Edna H. Hong. Princeton NJ: Princeton
       University Press, 1978.

TDIO   *Three Discourses on Imagined Occasions,* trans. Howard V. Hong and Edna
       H. Hong. Princeton NJ: Princeton University Press, 1993.

TM   *'The Moment' and Late Writings,* trans. Howard V. Hong and Edna H.
       Hong. Princeton NJ: Princeton University Press, 1998.

UDVS   *Upbuilding Discourses in Various Spirits,* trans. Howard V. Hong and Edna
       H.Hong. Princeton NJ: Princeton University Press, 1993.

WA   *Without Authority,* trans. Howard V. Hong and Edna H. Hong. Princeton
       NJ: Princeton University Press, 1997.

WL   *Works of Love,* trans. Howard V. Hong and Edna H. Hong. Princeton NJ:
       Princeton University Press, 1995.

WS   "Writing Sampler" See P.

SKS   *Søren Kierkegaards Skrifter,* ed. Niels Jørgen Cappelørn, Joakim Graff, Jette
       Knudson, Johnny Kondrup, and Alastair McKinnon. Published by the
       Søren Kierkegaard Forskningscenteret. Copenhagen: Gads Forlag, 1997ff.

SKS, K *Kommentar til Søren Kierkegaards Skrifter,* ed. Niels Jørgen Cappelørn,
       Joachim Garff, Jette Knudson, Johnny Kondrup, Alastair McKinnon, and
       Finn Hauberg Mortensen. Published by the Søren Kierkegaards
       Forskningscenteret. Copenhagen: Gads Forlag, 1997ff.

Introduction

Kierkegaard's master's thesis, *The Concept of Irony with Constant Reference to Socrates*, is the last of the youthful publications that began with the ironic "Another Defense of Woman's Great Abilities," continued through a series of newspaper articles critical of the National Liberals, and became more intellectually serious with the appraisal of Hans Christian Andersen's work as a novelist in *From the Papers of One Still Living*. During this period Kierkegaard also wrote the famous Socratic self-examination we call the "Gilleleie Journal," dated 1 August 1935, and a satire in the form of a play, *The Battle between the Old and the New Soap-Cellars*—the date being uncertain—in which he continued his ironic interpretation of the social, political, and intellectual environment in nineteenth-century Denmark. A brief resume of this sequence will, to some extent, prepare us for the thesis but will also provoke new puzzlements about its nature and philosophic significance.

Kierkegaard's Irony before The Concept of Irony

Kierkegaard's very first publication, a satire entitled "Another Defense of Woman's Great Abilities", was published 17 December 1834 in *Kjøbenhavns flyvende Post* (*Copenhagen's Flying Post*). It is as callous as a man of cultured intelligence and literary talent could write at that time. His irony borders on sarcasm about the social issue of woman's emancipation, a sarcasm made socially and politically irresponsible by its complete silence on the actual condition of women.[1] In this supercilious context Kierkegaard elaborates the bromide from the ancient writers about Xanthippe's shrewishness to the effect that she "is still remembered as a pattern

---

[1] See Julia Watkin, "Serious Jest? Kierkegaard as Young Polemicist in 'Defense' of Women" in *International Kierkegaard Commentary: "Early Polemical Writings,"* ed. Robert L. Perkins (Macon GA: Mercer University Press, 1999) 7-25.

of feminine eloquence and as a founder of a school that has lasted to this very day, whereas Socrates' school has long since disappeared" (EPW, [3], 231n6).

To be sure, this first mention of Socrates was not auspicious, but Kierkegaard ironizes himself: he would soon enroll in Socrates' school and adopt the latter's ironic cross-examination as the model by which he would analyze the pretensions and conventional truths of his age. Not only did the Socratic elenchus become the method of Kierkegaard's by which he examined the pretensions of his age (CI, 34-37; TA, 10), but it also became the model of his self-criticism and self-understanding (JP, 4:4260).

Kierkegaard was also attracted to politics and developed swiftly as a critic. During the year after the first essay on women's emancipation he closely followed the struggle over the freedom of the press and thought seriously about the nature of politics and its relation to historical research and writing. In this polemical and highly charged context he also began to think seriously about what we would call his "self-identity."[2] The tone of his lecture at the student union (28 November 1835), "Our Journalistic Literature", and the series of newspaper articles regarding the National Liberals (18 February–10 April 1836) was consistently ironic, but there are identifiable serious purposes in these efforts.

First, he sided with the liberals on the issue of the freedom of the press. This fact should, but did not, forever rebut the charge that Kierkegaard was an unqualified supporter of the absolute monarchy. Second, Kierkegaard caught the National Liberals red-handed in the creation of what we today would call "ideological history," a view that history led inexorably to the present crisis and also that the party writing the history is or has the solution of the problem or issue in question. "History is on our side." Third, in the student union lecture, Kierkegaard attempted briefly to present himself as a *réflecteur*, a thinker, critic, and/or commentator. This is the first public claim by Kierkegaard that he perceived himself as dedicated to the life of the mind, and one

---

[2]For considerable more detail on the issues in these writings consult Robert L. Perkins, "Power, Politics, and Media Critique" in *International Kierkegaard Commentary: "Early Polemical Writings,"* 27-44. See also his references to previous secondary literature on these early polemical writings.

wonders what the listeners thought of this confession, particularly if they recalled his first publication.

However, had the audience at the student union had access to the document we call the "Gilleleie Journal" (1 August 1835; JP, 5:5100), they would not have been so puzzled by Kierkegaard's precocious self-understanding.[3] The Journal contains a deep meditation on Socrates, and they would have perceived how much detailed thought underlay the self-designation as a *réflecteur* and how deeply the spirit of the Platonic Socrates had entered into Kierkegaard's consciousness. For instance, he translates the Socratic sense of divine vocation (Plato, *Apology* 21, 28) into the search for "the idea for which I am willing to live and to die" (JP, 5:5100, cited EO, 2:361), silently recalling that Socrates both lived and died for his idea. Further,

> One must first learn to know oneself before knowing anything else (γνῶθι σεαυτον). Not until a man has inwardly understood *himself* and then sees the course he is to take does his life gain peace and meaning; only then is he free of that irksome, sinister traveling companion—that irony of life that manifests itself in the sphere of knowledge and invites true knowing to begin with a not-knowing. (Socrates) (JP, 5:5100; cited EO, 2:364)

This passage demonstrates that irony is central to his thought about knowing and that such knowledge is the basis of a sustain-

---

[3]One of the most interesting contributions to the understanding of the Gilleleie Journal is Henning Fenger's *Kierkegaard, the Myths and their Origins*, trans. George C. Schoolfield (New Haven CT: Yale University Press, 1980) 69-122. Fenger's claim that the journal "may be" part of an incomplete epistolary novel is not securely based, because, for one reason, no notes of such a plan survive, and for another, Kierkegaard does not discuss the plan in his journals. However, Fenger's analysis of the circumstances of the trip to Gilleleie is detailed and helpful. Focusing in exhaustive detail on Danish literary history, Fenger's study mentions Socrates only once (p. 99) in his analysis of the journal and provides no interpretation of the importance, or lack thereof, of Socrates in the letter. Whether the letter is fictive or not is philosophically uninteresting, for the fact is that in the journal Kierkegaard laid the foundations of the view of Socrates he never repudiated but rather developed through many permutations into the high interpretation of Socrates we find in *Philosophical Fragments*, *Concluding Unscientific Postscript to "Philosophical Fragments"* and *The Sickness unto Death*.

able human life. Conceptually, there is no great distance from the "Gilleleie Journal" to the closing chapter of the thesis (CI, 324-29).

The "Gilleleie Journal" suggests Kierkegaard had already begun to cultivate his own self-reflection and critical powers rather profoundly and to act on their bases directly by writing and indirectly by the use of irony in his writing. The lighthearted fun he pokes at the successive revisions of Danish history in the exchange with the National Liberals, far from being conservative cant, is founded on the perception that they had not gone through the period of not-knowing before expressing the ideological bias of their view of history. Kierkegaard's irony in these pieces is clearly a weapon wielded on behalf of the Socratic view that an acknowledgement of ignorance is the beginning of wisdom. Such an existential skepticism lies at the basis of the many either/ors that characterize his authorship. Methodologically the examination of aestheticism, bourgeois ethical complacency and conformity, the various forms of idealism, and the cultural establishment is interestingly similar to the Socratic examination of the power establishment of Athens (Plato, *Apology* 21a-23b).

Further evidence of the pertinence of the Socratic is evident in Kierkegaard's first book, a short literary critique of Hans Christian Anderson as a novelist, *From the Papers of One Still Living*. The real significance of Socrates in this work is not the short reference made to him in a passage quoted from the novel (EPW, 99), but rather in the development of two concepts, life-development and life-view.[4] Although both terms are borrowed from Poul Martin Møller, the notion of life-development is directly rooted in Goethe, the German neoclassicists, and the romantic views of self-cultivation (*Bildung*). German intellectual life, whether classic or romantic, was at the time inspired by the views of Plato and the importance of an ideal moral and personal development evident primarily in the middle dialogues.

Life-development is the requisite "to becom[ing] a personality" (EPW, 70) and is a

---

[4]Sylvia Walsh is the first to emphasize the concept of life-development as a necessary element before the development of the life-view, which has often been treated in the literature. See her *Living Poetically: Kierkegaard's Existential Aesthetics* (University Park PA: Pennsylvania State University Press, 1994) 30-41.

deep and earnest embracing of a given actuality, no matter how one loses oneself in it, as a life-strengthening rest in it and admiration of it, without the necessity of its ever coming to expression as such, but which can never have anything but the highest importance for the individual, even though it all went so unnoticed that the mood itself seemed born in secrecy and buried in silence.[5] (EPW, 71)

Life-development is then, like the ethical stage of life, "reflective, active, and teleological, having the choice and development of the self in the context of the social environment as its goal."[6]

A life-view is the outcome of life-development; it is to conceptualize oneself as this particular self in this environment at this time. "A life view thus provides a comprehensive center of orientation that enables one to take a firm, positive stance toward life, with a sense of self-confidence in meeting the challenges of life rather than being overcome by them."[7] A life-view, then, is the guiding interpretative and teleological principle of one's life, a less "religious" version of Socrates' divine vocation. The concepts of life-development and life-view are not ironic in the least; rather they are a rebuttal to the irony of life. Of course, irony can be used as a tool on behalf of a life-view or critically of a life-view. Kierkegaard uses irony as a literary tool once more before he writes the thesis.

---

[5]Few passages in Kierkegaard's work so vividly demonstrate the qualifications he does not have to make in developing this concept. First, Ann Frank could have explained a few things to Kierkegaard about relating to one's environment and experiencing a profound life-development and life-view in an environment which was anything but admirable. In Kierkegaard's defense, however, there is no reason why life-development and life-view cannot be provoked in an environment such as 1940s Amsterdam. Second, by contrast, it is indicative of the truth of Kierkegaard's view of Andersen's limits that he could only seethe over Kierkegaard's criticism for years and criticize him only after his death in a self-serving fairy tale. See Bruce Kirmmse, "A Rose with Thorns: Hans Christian Andersen's Relation to Kierkegaard" in *International Kierkegaard Commentary: "Early Polemical Writings,"* ed. Robert L. Perkins (Macon GA: Mercer University Press, 1999) 69-85.

[6]Walsh, *Living Poetically*, 36.

[7]Walsh, *Living Poetically*, 37.

The final experiment of his youth before the thesis is the composition of a farce,[8] *The Battle between the Old and the New Soap-Cellars* (EPW, 103-24).[9] The objects of the farce are well-known characters in the university and among the National Liberals. However, to make Kierkegaard's negative views clear, we need note only the major Socratic allusion in the piece: residence in the Prytaneum. All the accumulated motley crew of idiots in the cast are publicly cared for in the New Prytaneum. The irony could hardly be more cutting, given the fate of Socrates' request that he be given free meals in the "Old" Prytaneum (Plato, *Apology*, 36e). By this undetermined time, Socrates had become not only Kierkegaard's model of self-knowledge, the basis for understanding life-development and how to transform that into a life-view, he is also the model antagonist of the whole cultural and political establishment. It is also clear to those of us who have the advantage of afterthought and a careful review of this early literature that Socrates, whose position is irony, defined as "infinite, absolute negativity" in the thesis, will become the limit of Kierkegaard's own social and political criticism. He will become neither a sophist nor a romantic.

The Concept of Irony was both a culmination and a beginning: It was both the end of a voyage of discovery, the last of several youthful experiments, and the launching of the journey of Kierkegaard's adult life and work. The thesis, lying at the end of the various exercises in writing, intellectual and moral postures, and vocational experiments, is then crucial to the understanding of both Kierkegaard's intellectual and personal development. As the official readers of the thesis noted, Kierkegaard's thesis fulfilled the requirements of *"insight and knowledge"* requisite for the degree. However, there was a consistently repeated criticism from all the readers that the thesis frequently violated standards of good taste

---

[8]As a subgenre of the comic, Kierkegaard had a sustained interest in farce. See R, 158-67, and Walsh, *Living Poetically*, 133-34.

[9]Recent analyses of the "Soap-Cellars" are authored by David Cain, "Kierkegaard's Anticipation of Authorship: 'Where Shall I Find a Foothold?' " and David Law, "The Literary Sources of Kierkegaard's 'The Battle between the Old and the New Soap-Cellars.' " Both are in *International Kierkegaard Commentary: "Early Polemical Writings."*

and that its style was objectionable. After the requisite final oral examination on 29 September 1841, the M.A. degree was issued on 20 October 1841.[10]

In *The Concept of Irony* Kierkegaard distinguishes two levels of irony. First, irony appears as a rhetorical tool to be used and, perhaps, abused (as by the Sophists or by an effete literary experimenter in a "defense" of woman). Second, irony is Socrates' position (CI, 6, 9, 12, and many other references). Nowhere does Kierkegaard take it as his own standpoint, though he found Socrates' position historically justified (CI, 198-218). The image of Socrates which he developed, along with a renewal of religious conviction (JP, 5:5324), preclude his ever becoming a sophist or a romantic. Given that the lecture at the student union followed the intense period of self-examination reflected in the "Gilleleie Journal," there is every reason to think that Socrates is the model of Kierkegaard's self-identification as a réflecteur and also the source of the concepts of life-development and life-view developed in the critique of Andersen. Moreover, it is clear that Kierkegaard already perceives the gap between the ideal of Socratism and the cultural realities of his own time.

But there are difficulties. Two examples must suffice.

Socrates' irony is characterized as "infinite, absolute negativity" (CI, 26, 474-75n.64). The expression is not clarified when introduced and is never clearly analyzed but only slowly shown through its uses. Infinite, absolute negativity is a position and more polemical toward the social and political environment than the irony of life that accompanies the person who has not made the grounding decision about the nature of his/her own person (JP, 5:5100). How these two forms of irony are related remains unclear.

Another and perhaps worse difficulty lies in the fact that Kierkegaard values Aristophanes' view of Socrates over that of Plato.

---

[10]CI, xii. See also the article of Bruce Kirmmse, "Socrates in the Fast Lane: Kierkegaard's *Concept of Irony* on the University's *Velocifère*. Documents, Context, Commentary, and Interpretation," in this volume. The master's degree was abandoned in 1854, and those holding the degree were declared to be doctors of Philosophy, thereby conforming the practice of the faculty of Philosophy to that of the other faculties of the university (CI, xiii).

Thesis VII states that "Aristophanes has come very close to the truth in his depiction of Socrates" while "Plato raised him too high" according to Thesis III (CI, 6, 474-75n.64). These two readings seem problematic in view of the review of the experimental writings discussed above, especially the "Gilleleie Journal," and the historic understanding of Socrates as the martyr of philosophy. It may turn out that Kierkegaard at the very beginning of his writing career understood Socrates quite differently from the hagiographic tradition that has characterized so much Platonic scholarship. Is it possible to render a consistent reading of the authorship from this point of view?

These and many other complexities in *The Concept of Irony* are addressed from the several perspectives of the authors of this volume. *The Concept of Irony* remains to this day among the least understood of Kierkegaard's texts. So to the articles we now turn.

Introducing the Commentators

Bruce Kirmmse translates the official records relative to the thesis and examines the official regulations, the comments of the readers, their personal relations, the power plays, the evasions of responsibility, and the tensions provoked by Kierkegaard's thesis in his article, "Socrates in the Fast Lane: Kierkegaard's *The Concept of Irony* on the University's *Velocifère*. Documents, Context, Commentary, and Interpretation." Kirmmse points out that this is "the first and last time that Kierkegaard submitted his work to the direct criticism of the scholarly community in such a manner that he was obliged to defend it." The final oral examination occupied an afternoon and an evening, the common practice at the time. Kirmmse provides an exhaustive "official history" of the thesis. Yet, many of the presences and absences from the examination, the comments on the thesis, and other details suggest portents of things to come.

Tonny Aagaard Olesen in his article, "Kierkegaard's Socratic Hermeneutic in *The Concept of Irony*," claims that *The Concept of Irony* is a "gold mine of hermeneutic reflection", which he proceeds to demonstrate by presenting three readings of the text, the first being the most general and each subsequent one being more specific than its predecessor. First, he discusses the composition and methodology of the dissertation as a whole. Most problematic for Olesen is the unbalanced proportion of the two parts of the thesis. Focusing more specifically, he then examines the first part of the thesis for a closer analysis of the hermeneutic question associated with it: Can Socrates be understood without contradiction unless his position is taken to be infinite, absolute negativity? Olesen concentrates finally on the first chapter of the first part which is "the most original in the dissertation from a hermeneutical point of view," where he finds behind the anti-Hegelianism a Socratic midwife and eroticist, or "amorist," following the Hongs' translation. In addition to Olesen's interesting formulation of some hermeneutic issues, his article introduces the reader to a wide range of Danish commentary on and critique of Kierkegaard's thesis.

Identifying Kierkegaard's hermeneutic as an erotic hermeneutics, Sylvia Walsh's article, "Ironic Love: An Amorist Interpretation of Socratic Eros," provides an erotic reading of *The Concept of Irony*. While recognizing that Kierkegaard's erotic hermeneutics constitutes an advance over patriarchal modes of interpretation, Walsh argues that it is still debatable "whether Kierkegaard's erotic hermeneutics really abandons [the] patriarchal framework or merely tempers it." Walsh further finds that the love embodied in Socrates is for Kierkegaard an ironic and negative love with the result that nothing can be learned from it about the true nature of love. Basing his reading on Socrates' rejection of Alcibiades, Kierkegaard thinks that Socratic eros "turns back into itself in ironic satisfaction" (CI, 165). "No relationship was strong enough to bind him" (CI, 182), for his irony required that he "separate [him]self from the other" (CI, 177). Alcibiades was correct: Socrates reversed the roles of pederasty, the latter becoming the beloved and the youth the lover. The same irony closed Socrates off from the other claims of traditional society (CI, 165). However, his irony did create a new dimension, subjectivity, and thus he is world-historically justified. Still, Walsh thinks Kierkegaard's thesis is far from embracing the Socratic form of irony and eros, for it ends with a concept of controlled irony that includes a "sound and healthy love" (CI, 328-29) that embraces others and historic actuality, a point developed throughout the subsequent authorship.

Anthony J. Burgess in his article, "The Upbuilding in the Irony of Kierkegaard's *The Concept of Irony*," addresses the question of the possible irony of the thesis itself: Is the declared and emphasized adherence in the dissertation to much of the letter of Hegel's view of Socrates an ironic and comic way to undermine Hegel's philosophy? To answer this question Burgess undertakes three readings of the thesis. The first reading reveals a Hegelian reading of Socrates; the second reveals a version of romantic irony as presented by Solger that denies the possibility of moving beyond the finite (CI, 320); and the third reading reveals something that is not irony at all, which, following the Hong translation and the common roots between English and Danish, we call "the upbuilding." Negativity, having undercut the vanity of the world and the emptiness of our concepts of the infinite, posits "the lightest and weakest indication of subjectivity" (thesis VIII). This thin truth of irony affords the basis of edification, and the cue is, ironically, based on Hegel's characterization of Solger.

Two articles focus on thesis VII, "Aristophanes has come very close to the truth in his depiction of Socrates" (CI, 6). This statement seems outrageous, but Martin Andic and Eric Ziolkowski both attempt, in very different ways, to make the case that Kierkegaard has correctly understood Socrates by valorizing Aristophanes' view. Plato, by contrast, has not so much misunderstood Socrates as he has "raised him too high" (CI, 6).

In his essay, "Clouds of Irony," Martin Andic attempts to answer several questions: (1) Does Aristophanes contradict Plato? (2) Is *Clouds* a malicious slander? (3) Who or what are the Clouds? (4) Is irony essentially negative? The answers to these questions, Andic claims, demonstrate that "Kierkegaard got Aristophanes right, because he got Socrates right and saw how Aristophanes did too." Kierkegaard read *Clouds* accurately because he read Socrates entirely negatively and because he so sharply distinguishes Plato from Socrates. The charges against Socrates are trivially true, but in the philosophical and "world-historical" view of things, utterly false. Thus *Clouds*, if properly understood, is not malicious but undiluted and truthful irony.

Eric Ziolkowski undertakes an entirely different kind of investigation in his article, "From *Clouds* to *Corsair*: Kierkegaard, Aristophanes, and the Problem of Socrates," the problem being, of course, the latter's identity: Who/What was Socrates? Ziolkowski divides his study into three parts. First, he provides a history of Socrates' portrait from antiquity to the present; second, he discusses the relation of *Clouds* to the trial, a subject Kierkegaard completely neglects, and, third, he traces Kierkegaard's treatment of Aristophanes and his play throughout the authorship. The problem of the identity of the historical Socrates parallels that of discussion of the historical Jesus at all times, the picture of the one influencing that of the other, from Justin Martyr's "a Christian before Christ" to Baur's determination to insert an "or" between their names. The second issue, the relation, if any, between the historic Socrates' trial and *Clouds,* is particularly vexing because of the explicit criticism of the play uttered by the Platonic Socrates (*Apology* 18b-c; CI, 6, thesis V). Kierkegaard's agreement with Hegel's rehabilitation of Aristophanes and his play sounds false and strained in our ears. Moreover, as Ziolkowski shows, thesis VII puts Kierkegaard clearly in conflict with the view dominant since his death, the view definitively enunciated by John Burnet and A. E. Taylor, that the Platonic view of Socrates is the truer one. Finally, Ziolkowski shows the subsequent history of Aristophanes in Kierkegaard's authorship, how he continued to hold to the view expressed in the thesis through his conflict with the *Corsair,* attempting to be loyal to both Aristophanes and to Socrates, no mean trick. Then Ziolkowski finds one text more, one that suggests that finally Kierkegaard questioned thesis VII.

Adriaan van Heerden in his article, "Was the Death of Socrates a Tragedy? Kierkegaard versus Hegel on the Possibility of the Mediation of the Tragic in Ethics," sets the familiar antagonists face to face again. Van Heerden argues that finally the death of Socrates is a tragedy for Hegel and not a tragedy for Kierkegaard. Van Heerden finds that their contrasting judgments say a lot about their views of the importance of subjectivity as it relates to moral existence as well as about views of the role of the tragic in Kierkegaard's later moral philosophy. Van Heerden concludes that Kierkegaard is a "Christian-Socratic" moral philosopher and that the foundation of Kierkegaard's moral project in the subsequent authorship is laid here in *The Concept of Irony.* Even more important, however, is that though Hegel, with his attempt to reconcile subjectivity with objective spirit, may have considered his project to be the completion of Socrates' aborted effort, Kierkegaard's understanding goes in exactly the opposite direction. For him there must be a rebirth of tragedy in the religious sphere of existence through resignation (with regard to the objective) and irony (with regard to the subjective). Van Heerden offers a powerful interpretation of the thesis as the first expression of Kierkegaard's subsequent anti-Hegelian polemic.

Pia Søltoft examines the relation of "Ethics and Irony" in her essay of that name and also claims that the views of ethics found in the thesis underlie many of the nuances of Kierkegaard's later ethical thought. From the very first, she claims, his ethical thought reflected a deep sense of intersubjectivity, that is, that personal and social ethics are mirror images of each other. As presented in the dissertation, Socratic irony, by contrast, means finally that one should separate oneself from the other, and this raises many questions, such as, for instance, What is Socrates' responsibility for and to his students? Romantic irony, moreover, leads to a total acosmism in which the very possibility of an intersubjective ethic is impossible. Socrates' irony was "the lightest and weakest indication of subjectivity" (thesis VIII), but romantic irony is the subjectivity of subjectivity, or subjectivity raised to an infinite degree. Forgetting that the ego of Fichte only posits the world in a metaphysical sense, the romantics attempted to posit a world of historical actuality, but they managed only to seduce themselves and those who followed them into a life denuded of social and ethical relations. As opposed to this effort to live poetically, Kierkegaard urged that we should allow ourselves to be poetically composed, clearly a metaphor of a fundamental Christian insight. But the major source of Kierkegaard's ethical insight in the thesis is nonetheless Hegel, about whom he expressed strong reservations.

Several articles are directed to the last, all too brief, but absolutely crucial chapter of the thesis entitled, "Irony as a Controlled Element, the Truth of Irony."

Richard M. Summers in his article, " 'Controlled Irony' and the Emergence of the Self in Kierkegaard's Dissertation," first provides the intellectual and literary context for the hopelessness and nihilism in European literature current at the time, particularly in the Young Germany movement. That this literary development is explicitly only a minor presence in the thesis should not mislead one into thinking that it is a minor motive for either the selection of irony as Kierkegaard's topic or the conceptual development of the thesis itself. In strong expository sections of his article Summers develops the relation of Socrates and the romantics to "historical actuality," finding the former to test Greek life and culture by its own idealized self-characterization, and the latter to deny all actuality and to substitute for it a poetic invention. Socrates' irony secures an ideal view even as it criticizes historical actuality while, by contrast, the irony of the romantics is enslaved to their own caprice and sensuality because they lose touch with actuality. Mastered or controlled irony, Kierkegaard's own view, enables the objective to dominate the terms and limits of literature and life (CI, 324), rather than the poet's ironic subjectivity. Summers exegetes in detail how Kierkegaard used Goethe and Shakespeare, comparing H. C. Anderson to them negatively. However, the principal use of irony is a tool that will enable us to "live poetically," an art any and all can master in his or her own historical actuality, which is itself both a gift and a task. Irony enables us to live without the weight of actuality crushing us and to avoid getting lost in possibility and our dreams.

Ronald L. Hall in his article, "The Irony of Irony," examines the notion of "standpoint": What does it mean to have a standpoint? He argues that the positive existential standpoint (which he calls "faith") must exclude the negative standpoint of irony, despite the fact that Socrates' irony served him well, because the modern romantic standpoint undercuts the psychological pre-suppositions of faith. At the same time, faith must include the dialectical "*play* of irony", but only as a controlled element. To sustain this complex position, Hall examines the Socratic standpoint of irony understood as "infinite, absolute negativity." Socrates' negativity enabled him to engage the Greek state and culture and to uncover the first rudiments of human subjectivity. The negativity of romantic irony, by contrast, undercuts the actuality of the very conditions of subjectivity itself and so must be repudiated altogether. The back side of this counterfeit coin is that romantic irony, having repudiated historical actuality, became intoxicated with its own negative freedom and took flight from the finite world into a spurious infinity created by the romantic's own imaginations. Finally, Hall argues that controlled irony, the negative qualification of subjectivity itself, enables spirit to take up its proper place in the world.

The ambiguity and possible irony of the last sentence in the thesis is the theme of George Pattison's article, "Beyond the Grasp of Irony." Surely one of the most impenetrable last sentences in an academic dissertation ever written, it reads, "Yet all this lies beyond the scope of this study, and if anyone should wish food for thought, I recommend Prof. Martensen's review of Heiberg's *Nye Digte*" (CI, 329). Does the sentence throw doubt on the seriousness of the thesis, that is, does this sentence demand we consider the thesis itself to be ironic? Or could it mean that the major representatives of the philosophy of Hegel in Copenhagen, J. L. Heiberg and Hans Lassen Martensen, are themselves possessed of the same skepticism and irony that both they and their mentor condemned in romanticism? Pattison is convinced by the last position, but that does not mean there are not many huge ironic chunks and vastly more small ironic innuendoes in the thesis. Nor does it mean that aesthetic irony is without its proper uses and aesthetic pleasures. It means, rather, that irony is not overcome by either aesthetics (Heiberg) or theology (Martensen) or philosophy (Hegel). It is overcome only by suffering and by "one's utter dependence on God's creating and saving grace." The last sentence of the dissertation is no mere smarty exit from a complex thesis; rather it is a gauntlet that serves notice of the difference between the reigning intellectual lights and the newest *magister*. Working out the challenge embedded in this sentence would require the full use of Kierkegaard's genius, would focus the authorship, would use up his strength, and exhaust his life.

The seminal importance of the thesis is apparent anywhere irony is deeply thought about, and Merold Westphal's essay, "Kierkegaard, Socratic Irony, and Deconstruction," attempts to extend Plato's and Kierkegaard's distinctions between Socrates and the sophists to show how Derrida is a "direct descendent of Socrates," and not a sophist at all. That being the case, we can discover how "postmodernism—if there is such a thing—can have a Kierkegaardian and not only a Nietzschean inspiration." Westphal's essay is an important contribution to, as well as an encapsulation of, his ongoing project to stress the Kierkegaardian origin of deconstruction in his concepts of irony and subjectivity, and in his criticism of the established order.

The last essay in this volume, "The Irony of Revelation: The Young Kierkegaard Listens to the Old Schelling," by Peter Fenves attempts to read the thesis from the standpoint of the notes (CI, 333-412) Kierkegaard took at the lectures given by Schelling in Berlin, where Kierkegaard traveled immediately after the final defense of the thesis. Fenves attempts to determine how problematic the seriousness of the thesis itself is: Is the thesis itself an exercise in irony? Or, did Kierkegaard unconsciously ironize himself and his thesis by not recognizing it as ironic? Or is the thesis ironic at our expense, that is, does Kierkegaard leave us wondering, though he offers many hints on both sides of this issue? Schelling's lectures become poignant for Kierkegaard, because instead of Hegel's system being "positive," as Kierkegaard had declared in his thesis (CI, 323), Schelling finds it to be negative. Needless to say, the old Schelling had the full attention of the young *magister*, at least for some weeks. Fenves discusses the two places where the issues of *The Concept of Irony* and Schelling's lectures diverge, positivity and "divine irony," and the point where these two converge: sin (CI, 255). Thus, there is a sense in which the thesis is ironic, for "Just as philosophy begins with doubt, so also a life that may be called human begins with irony" (CI, 6, thesis XV). According to Fenves, even philosophy begins with irony. Every beginning, even the beginning of the god of Schelling's theogonic mythology of beginnings, is subject to irony.

The Concept of Irony is an important work in its own right in addition to being a fertile seedbed of many of the fundamental insights of the later authorship. I suspect it has been neglected primarily because Kierkegaard left it out of all his remarks about and reviews of his authorship. It is also a very complex work, many passages being, for want of a better word, dense. The combination of density and its reputed (but disputed) irony has not served to make it an attractive work. The reader must give due consideration to the issue of the irony of the dissertation as a whole and distinguish that from the irony of many turns of speech and arguments that affect only the immediate context. We, the readers, give such close attention to these matters because we think that with, in, and by the irony, most of the time, Kierkegaard says exactly what he means. However, this volume of essays is offered our readers, who by their superior erudition and better thinking we invite to become our teachers.

Robert L. Perkins

1

Socrates in the Fast Lane: Kierkegaard's The Concept of Irony on the University's Velocifère. Documents, Context, Commentary, and Interpretation

Bruce H. Kirmmse[1]

In considering Kierkegaard's *On the Concept of Irony, with Continual Reference to Socrates*, it is important to keep in mind some facts which are well-known but sometimes not fully appreciated, namely, that it was a *dissertation for an academic degree*; that it was the portal to any possible academic career; that the submission and defense of the dissertation was the first and last time that Kierkegaard exposed his work to the direct criticism of the scholarly community in such a manner that he was obliged to defend it; and that the entire affair was an academic exercise (in both the positive and negative senses of the term), governed by the procedures of the University of Copenhagen. Thus the *magister* dissertation provides a unique window into the life and thought of Søren Kierkegaard the ordinary citizen, who had to play by the rules that governed all others in his situation, rather than Søren Kierkegaard the independently wealthy eccentric, the Socrates of Strøget who published his own works and was beholden to no one. This is the

[1]This essay was written with support from the R. Francis Johnson Fund for Faculty Development of Connecticut College and is dedicated to the memory of the late R. Francis Johnson, who was my dean, my colleague, my advisor, and my friend for almost a quarter century. I am thankful to Rigsarkivet (the Danish National Archives) and to the Søren Kierkegaard Research Centre in Copenhagen for providing excellent work environments; to Birgit Christensen and Tinne Vammen for help in deciphering obscure passages in several manuscripts; and to Margaret Hellman for her careful editorial eye.

last glimpse we get *before* Kierkegaard becomes this figure, when he was still a Socrates in the making. And perhaps for this reason, Kierkegaard often excluded his dissertation from what he considered his "authorship" proper.

The present essay is prefaced by a translation of all the archival materials touching on Søren Kierkegaard's *magister* dissertation for the University of Copenhagen, *The Concept of Irony*. In providing the documentary material in full I have included some items which may appear to be mere bureaucratic pettifoggery or which repeat matter contained in other documents. Nonetheless, there is much material of extraordinary interest which has never previously appeared in English (nor, in most cases, in Danish). Some apparently bureaucratic details, when viewed in the chronological context of the entire archival file, may clarify the manner in which Kierkegaard's case was handled, why it was handled that way, and, finally, the sort of person Kierkegaard's teachers and colleagues believed him to be.

The structure of this essay is as follows: *I. Documents*, that is, all the archival materials, arranged in chronological order; *II. Context*, that is, an overall view of the University of Copenhagen, with specific attention given to the two faculties with which Kierkegaard was associated, Theology and Philosophy, as well as an explanation of the procedural matters associated with obtaining the *magister* degree; *III. Commentary on the Documents*, that is, an examination of several important matters which form the focal points of these documents, namely, Kierkegaard's petition for dispensation from the requirement to submit his dissertation in Latin, the comments made by faculty members on the style and substance of Kierkegaard's dissertation, the comments pertaining to the Latin theses Kierkegaard appended to his work, and matters pertaining to the oral defense; *IV. Interpretation and Summary*, an interpretative finale, in which an attempt is made to relate the events surrounding the dissertation to a larger biographical understanding of Kierkegaard.

I. Documents Relating to Kierkegaard's Magister Dissertation

Document 1. June 2, 1841—Kierkegaard's petition to the King to submit a dissertation in Danish[2]

Copenhagen, 2 June 1841

Søren Aabye Kierkegaard, *Cand. theol. cum laude* from June 1840, most humbly petitions for permission to submit his dissertation for the *magister* degree, *On the Concept of Irony, With Continual Reference to Socrates,* in the mother tongue, though with the stipulation that Latin theses[3] be appended to it and that the oral defense be conducted in Latin.

To the King!

The undersigned hereby ventures to come before Your Majesty with this most humble petition for permission to submit his dissertation for the *magister* degree, *On the Concept of Irony, With Continual Reference to Socrates,* in the mother tongue, though with the stipulation that Latin theses be appended to it and that the oral defense be conducted in Latin.

In daring most humbly to direct Your Majesty's most exalted attention to my present petition, it is primarily the thought that through royal grace similar favor has been shown both to *Magister* Hammerich and to *Magister* Adler, that gives me the courage to hope, and this all the more so because the external circumstances appear to be entirely identical. With respect to the particular subject matter I treat, it is true that irony does in a way belong to classical antiquity, but really only insofar as the modern era has its beginning at this very point, so that the modern era may lay claim to grasping this concept in the strictest sense. Furthermore, in the recent past this concept has made its presence felt in a rich multiplicity of individual cases. Real attention must also be paid to the appearance of this concept in our own time. In view of this, I most humbly take the liberty of directing Your Majesty's most exalted attention to how difficult—indeed, impossible—it would be to treat this subject exhaustively in the language which was formerly that of the learned without overmuch injury to free, personal expression. But just as my petition is supported by the nature of the subject

---

[2]Rigsarkivet, Dansk Kancelli, Direktionen for Universitetet og de lærde Skoler, Forestillinger 1841, nr. 2194 [National Archives, Danish Chancery, Supervisors of the University and Learned Schools, Proposals 1841, no. 2194]. Another translation is available in LD, 23-25.

[3]Note that the published English translation (LD, 23) renders the Danish *latinske Theses* as "Latin summary," which is clearly an error. A look at the wording of several dispensations from the Latin dissertation requirement, which we will examine subsequently, makes this clear. What Kierkegaard appended to his Danish-language dissertation was thus a set of Latin theses, not a Latin summary.

matter, so also do I hope that by my examinations—which were all completed with the highest grades, and the philological-philosophical examination with distinction—I have proven that I possess sufficient knowledge of the learned languages that I cannot be regarded as undeserving of such favor. To this must be added that over a long period of time I have been engaged in teaching the Latin language and have thus had occasion not to forget what I have learned and perhaps to learn more. In this connection I most humbly take the liberty of enclosing a copy of a recommendation from the headmaster of the Borgerdyd School, Professor Nielsen:

Mr. S. Aabye Kirkegaard [sic], *Cand. theol.*, excelled as a student in this school because of his hard work and intelligence and his brilliant understanding of the subjects taught in general and of the form and spirit of languages in particular. Already at that time he gave us cause to expect great things of his integrity, self-reliance, and ability; his acute, clear, and comprehensive vision; his profound, lively, and serious mind; and his generally excellent gift for exposition, which he has subsequently demonstrated. Circumstances have not made it necessary for him to teach, but he has nonetheless frequently felt a need to do so. Thus for several years, at my request, he has helped me with students who were weak in Latin composition, and he has successfully motivated them to do the sort of thinking which is not merely directed at passing their examinations but which will continue to have an effect in their later lives. For a couple of years, when my own weak eyesight prevented me from correcting the essays of the most advanced class, he did this in my stead, displaying, now in a more mature fashion, the insight into language that I had recognized in him when he was a student at this school. At his request, during one academic year he taught Latin to the students in the second form and helped them progress a great deal, both in their Latin and in their general intellectual development. Several of them were graduated this year, when he again was kind enough to assist me with Latin and composition for the advanced class, and he performed just as well as I myself could have done.

Therefore, so far as I can judge, he has an uncommon mastery of the Latin language, both orally and in writing.

Borgerdyd School in Copenhagen   M. Nielsen
          Nov.   , 1840

That this be most graciously approved, petitions

Most humbly,
Søren Aabye Kirkegaard
Cand. theol.

Document 2. June 3, 1841—Journal of the Philosophy Faculty: Kierkegaard delivers his dissertation to the faculty[4]

As a dissertation for the *magister* degree, *Cand. theol.* Kierkegaard *personally* delivered a treatise written in the Danish language (in 6 quarto volumes) *On the Concept of Irony, with Continual Reference to Socrates* and also informed the Dean that he had sent a petition to the Supervisors that he might be permitted to obtain the *magister* degree with a Danish dissertation instead of a Latin one, although he would defend it, with appended theses, in Latin. Cf. no. 55.

After[5] having been gone through by the Dean, as the first reader, the dissertation was sent, on the 15th of June, first to Prof. Madvig and thereafter, together with the petition which had arrived in the meanwhile (cf. no. 55), to Prof. Petersen.

Document 3. June 15, 1841—Supervisors of the University request an opinion from the University Consistory regarding Kierkegaard's petition to submit his dissertation in Danish[6]

To the Consistory
15 June 1841
Before further action is taken with respect to the enclosed petition, in which *Cand. theol.* Søren Aabye Kierkegaard petitions to be permitted to submit his dissertation for the *magister* degree, *On the Concept of Irony, With Continual Reference to Socrates*, in the mother tongue, though with the stipulation that Latin theses be appended to it and that the oral defense be conducted in Latin, the Supervisors must officially request that the Rector and Professors kindly communicate their considered opinion, returning same with the enclosed material.

Document 4. June 16, 1841—Comment sheet with Dean Sibbern's evaluation, as first reader, of Kierkegaard's dissertation[7]

The enclosed dissertation in 6 large quarto booklets, *On the Concept of Irony, with Continual Reference to Socrates*, was brought to me during the early days of June by its author, *Cand. theol.* Søren Kierkegaard, as a dissertation for the *magister*

[4]Rigsarkivet, Københavns Universitets arkiv, Det filosofiske Fakultet, Diarium [Archives of the University of Copenhagen, Philosophy Faculty, Journal] 1836–1856, 1841, no. 50, June 3, 1841.
[5]Same Philosophy faculty journal item, under "Resolutions and Transactions."
[6]See note to document 1 above, insert in 2194.
[7]Rigsarkivet, Københavns Universitets arkiv, Det filosofiske Fakultet, 1841, no. 50, KU 35. 02. 17. From F. C. Sibbern, on a folio sheet of paper which was circulated to the faculty readers of Kierkegaard's dissertation; each subsequent reader was thus able to read the remarks of all previous readers.

degree. In addition, he told me that he had sent in a petition, via the Supervisors of the University, that he might be permitted to submit a dissertation of this type *in Danish* and have it printed in the same language, with the stipulation that if it is found worthy of being accepted for defense, he would defend it, along with appended theses, *in Latin*. Inasmuch as dispensations of this sort have now been granted to a number of people, and inasmuch as the subject matter—in the manner in which the author has treated it with reference to the most recent philosophy—is poorly suited to be dealt with in Danish [in the margin, in another hand: *Latin*], I hope that nothing will be stand in the way of recommending that the aforementioned person's petition be granted when it comes before the faculty for an official opinion, which has not yet happened, and I wish to be authorized by my gentlemen colleagues to make such a recommendation. As for the dissertation itself, which I have gone through in my capacity as first reader, the point of the first and largest part is to present an idea which to the best of my knowledge is the author's original conception but which has been inspired by the spate of material written about Socrates in recent years: namely, to see Socrates' greatest significance in his role as a principal representative of the sort of irony which is related to the scepticism that subsequently developed in Greece and which, in combatting the Sophists, appears to have been a natural transition to a more profound sort of philosophizing. When it is borne in mind that, as is well known, even Schleiermacher believed that Socrates ought principally be viewed as *a dialectician* and that it was as such that Socrates practiced his famous maieutics, or art of midwifery, so it may now be added that Socrates was a dialectician *in a negative direction* because, as is well known, he of course allowed his knowledge to consist of the fact that he knew nothing, and his art consisted in convincing others that *they*, too, knew nothing. And when a number of things to which Hegel in particular has referred are added to the above, one readily becomes conversant with our author's idea that Socrates was a master of irony and functioned primarily in that role. Indeed, one might wish that our author's idea had been carried through with even more rigor than seems to me to be present in this work of his, which has taken on large proportions through overmuch effort to summon up and explain everything. With respect to various details, it would certainly be desirable that in the final revision of the dissertation a few things which are appropriate to a lower sort of genre could be trimmed away as luxuriant growths. But otherwise, *from the point of view of style*, the dissertation reads easily. The principal exposition of the author's idea with respect to its significance in the history of philosophy is in booklet 4, pages 28 to 34, to which I wish to direct your attention.[8] Incidentally, the author has not limited himself only to Socrates, but in the second principal part of the dissertation he treats irony in our age, with particular reference to the *Shlegel* [sic] brothers, *Tiek* [sic], and *Solger*. But undoubtedly the title of the dissertation ought to be changed so that it reads

---

[8]Because the original manuscript of Kierkegaard's dissertation has not survived, it is not possible accurately to link this and subsequent references in the readers' reports to specific passages in the published version.

"Socrates as an Ironist, With Contributions to the Development of the Concept of Irony in General, Particularly with Reference to the Most Recent Times."

I ask that the matter be expedited in such a way that the dissertation, with readers' comments, can be returned to the author before the beginning of the summer holidays. That the dissertation be accepted for defense is, I hope, beyond doubt. Despite its length, it reads easily and fairly quickly, as the language flows well and the handwriting is very legible.

Copenhagen, 16 June 1841

F. C. Sibbern

Dean, Faculty of Philosophy

Document 5. June 19, 1841—University Rector Ørsted requests an opinion from the Philosophy Faculty regarding Kierkegaard's petition[9]

In accordance with the enclosed official communiqué from the Royal Supervisors of the University and the Learned Schools (with enclosure) concerning a petition from *Cand. theol.* Kirkegaard [*sic*] to be permitted to write a *magister* dissertation in Danish, the Philosophy Faculty is hereby requested to give its opinion.

19 July 1841   H. C. Ørsted

To the Philosophy Faculty

Document 6. June 19, 1841—Journal of the Philosophy Faculty: Rector Ørsted forwards to the faculty an official communiqué from the Supervisors plus Kierkegaard's petition[10]

The Rector forwarded to the faculty an official communiqué from the Supervisors with a petition from *Candidat* Kierkegaard that he might be permitted to submit for the *magister* degree his dissertation written in *Danish*. Cf. no. 50. See no. 67.

Was[11] placed together with the dissertation itself, which was recently put in circulation. The professors involved recommended granting the petition, though with the stipulation that the dissertation be accompanied by Latin theses which comprise its principal points and which are submitted for approval prior to being printed. The Consistory was written in this connection on July 7th.

---

[9]As head of the Consistory, H. C. Ørsted here contacts the Philosophy Faculty pursuant to the Supervisors' request for an opinion in document 3 above; in Rigsarkivet, Københavns Universitets arkiv, Det filosofiske Fakultet, 1841, no. 55, KU 35. 02. 17.

[10]See note to document 2 above. Journal item no. 55, dated June 19, 1841.

[11]Same Philosophy Faculty journal item, under "Resolutions and Transactions."

Document 7. June 20, 1841—Prof. Madvig's comments on Kierkegaard's dissertation, added to Dean Sibbern's comment sheet[12]

In analogy with a couple of earlier cases, I vote that the Faculty recommend that the petition to accept the author's dissertation in Danish be granted. With respect to the dissertation itself (a large portion of which I am already familiar with), it bears the stamp of such intellectual liveliness and fresh thought, and of multifaceted studies, both of Greek literature and of modern philosophy and aesthetics, that it seems to me entirely to qualify the author for the *magister* degree. Yet on the other hand, not only is it burdened with a certain free and easy carelessness of composition, but even the exposition of concepts lacks scholarly order, form, and firm focus. This is particularly clear in the arrangement of the dissertation's two principal parts and the connection between them. The exposition suffers from a self-satisfied pursuit of the piquant and the witty, which not infrequently lapses into the outright vulgar and tasteless. (A little sample of this can be seen in the remarks—noted by the Dean in pencil—seventeen pages from the end of the fifth booklet, as well as the sixth booklet, p. 10, where, as chance would have it, the author describes a period which had already been shaken out of its old ways by the French Revolution as a stagnant "still life.") One could be tempted to make the removal of the worst [crossed out in the original: *crudest*] of these excrescences a *condition* for acceptance, were it not for the fact that negotiations about this would be difficult and awkward. Given the particular nature of the author and his preference for these elements, it would be fruitless to express a *wish* regarding this if not even the Dean will see the dissertation after it has been trimmed a bit in this respect.

20 June 1841   J. N. Madvig

Document 8. June 21, 1841—Dean Sibbern forwards the comment sheet (plus Kierkegaard's petition, received meanwhile from the Rector) to Professors Petersen and Brøndsted, adding to the sheet this note[13]

After having received this dissertation (and the present letter) back from Professor Madvig, to whom I had sent it first because he was already familiar with a portion of it and could thus render a judgment on it more quickly, I now enclose the petition (which I have in the meanwhile received from the Exalted Rector) from Mr. *Candidat* Kierkegaard for permission to submit the dissertation in Danish.

    I am now forwarding this matter to the gentlemen Professors of Greek literature, one of whom, I assume, will be an official opponent along with myself.

21 June 1841   Sibbern

---

[12]See note to document 4 above. Item no. 2, from J. N. Madvig, continued on the same folio sheet.

[13]See note to document 4 above. Item no. 3, from F. C. Sibbern, continued on the same folio sheet.

Document 9. July 4, 1841—Prof. Petersen's comments, added to Dean Sibbern's comment sheet, evaluating Kierkegaard's dissertation[14]

I received this dissertation on the 21st or 22nd of June and am sending it further on the 4th of July. Despite the Dean's wishes I have been unable to forward it any earlier; this can be explained by the unusual length of the dissertation, and it can be excused by the fact that I had a great deal of other urgent business with which it conflicted.

So as not to delay the matter any more than absolutely necessary, I have limited myself to a quick inspection, which did, however, allow me to come to a judgment on the present piece of work. I concur with the vote of my gentlemen colleagues (Professors Sibbern and Madvig) that this dissertation qualifies the author for the *magister* degree under the condition that he append Latin theses which will form the basis of the oral arguments. In connection with this I suggest that it be required that these theses state as completely as possible the dissertation's principal points. Similarly, it goes without saying that these theses are to be submitted for approval prior to being printed with the dissertation.

This piece would profit a great deal by being reworked in order to gain more order and compression. But since I, too, share the view that this probably cannot be attained because, given his personality, the author neither can nor will undertake such changes, we must probably limit ourselves to suggesting what is lacking in this respect while still requesting that various excesses of the sarcastic or mocking sort be removed as inappropriate in a piece of academic writing. Conferring with the author about this could certainly be left to the Dean, who has already noted in the margins the worst instances of this sort of thing.

I concur with the change of title suggested by Prof. Sibbern. Given the circumstances, and under the conditions noted above, we can certainly agree to recommend that the requested permission to submit the dissertation in Danish be granted.

> Regensen 4th July 1841   F. C. Petersen

Document 10. July 7, 1841—Prof. Brøndsted's comments, added to Dean Sibbern's comment sheet, evaluating Kierkegaard's dissertation[15]

I am forwarding this significant piece of work of Mr. Kierkegaard after having had it in my possession for only one day and despite the fact that I feel a great inclination to read the whole of it with studied attention. But since the Most Excellent Dean wants to have this lengthy dissertation returned to the author "before the beginning of the summer holidays," there is nothing to do but to let

---

[14]See note to document 4 above. Item no. 4, from F. C. Petersen, continued on the same folio sheet.

[15]See note to document 4 above. Item no. 5, from P. O. Brøndsted, continued on the same folio sheet.

it go down the Faculty's railroad in a *velocifère* [express coach] (I mean its fastest possible conveyance) so that it can reach its destination in good time. It might be unduly delayed were I—overburdened as I now am with the task of completing the reading I am supposed to finish before the summer holidays—to keep this remarkable treatise until I had read it properly. I have looked into it at many points, however, and I certainly believe that I, too, can vote that the dissertation be accepted for defense and that, in keeping with previous instances, the petition for submitting it in Danish be supported, though, as in similar cases, with the addition of Latin theses which are to be submitted to the Dean and the Faculty prior to being printed. But I must postpone a closer acquaintance with this book until it is printed and the time for the formal arguments has been scheduled.

Nevertheless, I cannot refrain from expressing the same wish already expressed by my colleagues, that the Most Excellent Dean will endeavor to have the author trim away certain excrescences, which indeed in some places—e.g., the passage pointed out by Prof. Madvig on pages 10-11 in the sixth booklet—burgeon into quite large growths and testify to the author's occasional inability to resist the inner temptation to leap over the boundary which separates both genuine irony and reasonable satire from the unrefreshing territory of vulgar exaggeration. Passages of this sort are many and crude. If a personal preference for tidbits of this sort prevents the author from following advice in this regard, we can certainly take comfort in the fact that it is the task of the Faculty *only* to recognize *knowledge* and *abilities*, but *not in any way* to bring about better taste in those who, in keeping with their knowledge and their abilities, *ought* to have better taste.

Received Monday evening, the 5th, forwarded Wednesday morning, the 7th of July 1841.

> *Brøndsted.*

Document 11. July 7, 1841—Letter from Dean Sibbern to the Consistory, recommending that Kierkegaard's petition be granted[16]

Now that the professors of this Faculty most concerned in this matter, namely, the three professors of philology and myself, (Prof. Nielsen did not wish to have the dissertation), have had a chance to read or to look through Mr. *Cand. theol.* Kierkegaard's dissertation on Socrates as an ironist (three of the four of us have actually been through this large [*in the margin*: In print it will undoubtedly take up 20 arks [320 octavo pages]] but interesting dissertation in its entirety), and they have all agreed both to accept the dissertation for defense and to recommend the approval of the author's petition (which I return along with the official communiqué received from the Supervisors) to be permitted to submit it in Danish, I have not deemed it necessary to let this lengthy dissertation circulate further until the question which has been raised [concerning the acceptability of a dissertation

---

[16]See note to document 1 above. Number 3 of 5 inserts in 2194.

written in Danish] is resolved. Rather, in keeping with what has been done in similar cases, I have judged that I could send the petition back to the Consistory with the declaration that we are unanimous that *the petition be approved* though with the stipulation that the author must supplement the dissertation *with Latin theses* which *state its principal points* and which *are to be presented to the appropriate professors for approval prior to being printed.*

Copenhagen, 7 July 1841.   Sibbern

To the Consistory

Document 12. Undated, between July 7 and 11, 1841 (most probably July 9 or 10)—Rector Ørsted's reaction to Kierkegaard's dissertation, private letter to Dean Sibbern[17]

Thanks, dear friend and colleague, for letting me have a look at Kirkegaard's [sic] dissertation. Time constraints and many other items of business have limited me to an extremely fleeting acquaintance with it. Despite the fact that I certainly see in it the expression of significant intellectual strengths, I nevertheless cannot deny that it makes a generally unpleasant impression on me, particularly because of two things, both of which I detest: verbosity and affectation.

Even though I have no doubt that this dissertation is more deserving of acceptance than many another, and that having more people read it will not alter the judgment already reached, it seems to me necessary for the sake of form that either Marthensen [sic], as outgoing acting lecturer in philosophy, or Nielsen, who is now the only professor in that field, read it as well. Nielsen can scarcely recuse himself. It is obvious that someone who submits a dissertation of this length must resign himself to the fact that it takes time for people to read it.

Your letter to the Consistory will probably also give rise to objections concerning this point; I am therefore returning it to you confidentially. Should you not share my reservations, I request that you return to me the letter addressed to the Consistory (with enclosure) tomorrow or early the day after tomorrow. It should then be included in the next dossier. N. [*meaning unclear*], had already gone out this morning.

Yours
H. C. Ørsted

To Mr. Professor Sibbern, Knight and Dannebrogsmand

---

[17]See note to document 4 above. Letter from H. C. Ørsted to F. C. Sibbern, inserted on a small sheet of paper.

Document 13. July 12, 1841—Prof. H. L. Martensen's comments, added to Dean Sibbern's comment sheet, evaluating Kierkegaard's dissertation[18]

Since Professor Sibbern has requested that I cast a vote in this matter, I hereby declare that I concur with the views already voiced and thus vote for the acceptance of the dissertation.

Monday, 12 July 1841   H. Martensen

Document 14. July 17, 1841—Rector Ørsted and the Consistory recommend to the Supervisors that Kierkegaard's petition be granted[19]

Herewith in reply to the petition, received together with the Royal Supervisors' very esteemed communication of the 15th of last month—in which *Cand. theol.* Søren Aabye Kjerkegaard [*sic*] petitions to be permitted to submit his dissertation for the *magister* degree, *On the Concept of Irony, With Continual Reference to Socrates,* in the mother tongue, though with the stipulation that Latin theses be appended to it and that the oral defense be conducted in Latin—and in accordance with the requested and herewith enclosed declaration concerning this matter, dated the 7th of this month, from the Dean of the Philosophy Faculty, Professor Sibbern, one must most respectfully recommend that the petition be granted.
Copenhagen, 17 July 1841.
H. C. Ørsted
Algreen Ussing
/J Reinhardt
To The Royal Supervisors of the University and the Learned Schools

Document 15. July 29, 1841—A "humble proposal" (i.e., a draft for the King to sign) from the Supervisors that Kierkegaard's petition be granted[20]

Most Humble Proposal
for permission for *Cand. theol.* Kierkegaard to acquire the *magister* degree with a dissertation in the Danish language.

The Supervisors have received from *Cand. theol.* S. A. Kierkegaard a most humble petition for permission to submit his dissertation for the *magister* degree, *On the Concept of Irony, With Continual Reference to Socrates,* in the mother tongue, though with the stipulation that Latin theses be appended to it and that the oral

---

[18]See note to document 4 above. Item no. 6, from H. L. Martensen, continued on the same folio sheet.
[19]See note to document 1 above. Insert no. 4 in 2194.
[20]See note to document 1 above. This document and the next constitute the main document numbered 2194.

defense be conducted in Latin. He has supported his petition by referring to the fact that through royal grace similar favor has previously been shown to others in cases which appear to be entirely identical to the case in point and for reasons which are also present here. In this connection he has observed that it is true that irony does in a way belong to classical antiquity, but that the modern era may lay claim to grasping this concept in the strictest sense, and that it would be difficult—indeed, impossible—to treat this subject exhaustively in the language which was formerly that of the learned without overmuch injury to free, personal expression. In addition to this he believes that, given the manner in which he has completed his studies, having come through all his examinations with the highest grades, and the philological-philosophical examination with distinction, and because he has taught Latin at the Borgerdyd School in Copenhagen with excellent results, he has presented such proof of his knowledge of the learned languages that there does not appear to be anything here that would stand in the way of granting his request.

Whereas the Consistory and the Philosophy Faculty, whose declarations the Supervisors have solicited, have been in agreement that this petition be granted—and inasmuch as the Faculty has also noted that it has found the dissertation entirely deserving of being accepted for defense—so the Supervisors as well cannot but agree that the same reasons are present in this case that in a number of previous cases occasioned a similar most gracious permission, namely, most recently, pursuant to a most exalted resolution of the 8th of May last year, in the case of *Cand. theol. Magister* A. P. Adler, at present a parish pastor. And since the Supervisors must most humbly be of the opinion that it would be very anomalous and inexpedient if philosophical topics which could not be successfully treated in Latin were to be as good as totally excluded from competition for academic honors in the very Faculty which bears the name of Philosophy, the Supervisors believe—both in view of this and in view of what has been noted with respect to Candidate Kierkegaard's extensive studies and his extraordinary erudition, particularly with respect to the philological sciences—that they ought most humbly recommend that he be granted the permission he has requested, which, however, must be subject to the proviso that the author supplement the dissertation with Latin theses which state its principal points and which are to be presented to the appropriate professors for approval prior to being printed, and that the oral arguments be in the Latin language.

The Supervisors thus recommend, in profoundest humility:

> that *Cand. theol.* Søren Aabye Kierkegaard may most graciously be granted permission to acquire the *magister* degree with the philosophical dissertation submitted by him and written in the Danish language, though with the stipulation that the oral arguments be in the Latin language and be based upon Latin theses which state its principal points and which are to be appended to it after having been approved by the Philosophy Faculty.

Document 16. July 30, 1841—King Christian VIII's resolution granting Kierkegaard's petition[21]

Royal Resolution

We will most graciously have *Cand. theol.* Søren Aabye Kierkegaard granted permission to acquire the *magister* degree with the philosophical dissertation submitted by him and written in the Danish language, though with the stipulation that the oral arguments be in the [crossed out in the original: Danish] Latin language and be based upon Latin theses which state its principal points and which are to be appended to it after having been approved by the Philosophy Faculty.

Copenhagen, 30 July 1841

Christian R.

Document 17. August 28, 1841—Papers of the Philosophy Faculty: a verbatim account of the message from the Supervisors to the Consistory, transmitting the King's resolution of July 30, 1841, granting Kierkegaard's petition[22]

Dated the 10th of this month, the Royal Supervisors of the University and the Learned Schools have written the Consistory as follows:

"After having received the opinion furnished by Messrs. Rector and Professors, dated the 17th of last month, concerning *Cand. theol.* Kjerkegaard's [sic] petition for permission to acquire the *magister* degree with a dissertation in the Danish language, the Supervisors have put forward a most humble proposal in this connection, and it has subsequently pleased His Majesty the King, on the 30th of that month, most graciously to resolve as follows:

"We will most graciously have *Cand. theol.* Søren Aabye Kjerkegaard [sic] granted permission to acquire the *magister* degree with the philosophical dissertation submitted by him and written in the Danish language, though with the stipulation that the oral arguments be in the Latin language and be based upon Latin theses which state its principal points and which are to be appended to it after having been approved by the Philosophy Faculty."

The above is transmitted to the Faculty for its own information and is to be made known to the petitioner.

---

[21]See note to document 15 above. This royal resolution is in the left-hand column of the folio-sized sheet on which "humble proposal" no. 2194 is written.

[22]Rigsarkivet, Københavns Universitets arkiv, Det filosofiske Fakultet, 1841, no. 67, KU 35. 02. 17. Note from Rector Ørsted and the supervisors to the Philosophy faculty.

Copenhagen, 28 August 1841
       H. C. Ørsted
       Algreen Ussing
       /J Reinhardt
[in Kierkegaard's hand] *vidi* S. A. Kierkegaard[23]
To the Philosophy Faculty

Document 18. August 28, 1841—Journal of the Philosophy Faculty: receipt of royal resolution granting Kierkegaard's petition noted[24]

The Consistory transmits royal permission for Søren Kierkegaard to submit a dissertation written in Danish for the *magister degree*, et al. Cf. no. 55.

Document 19. September 7 and 8, 1841—Journal of the Philosophy Faculty: receipt and circulation of Kierkegaard's Latin theses, etc. noted[25]

Cand. theol. Søren Kierkegaard submitted his theses for his inaugural dissertation. On September 7th they were sent to Professors Brøndsted, Petersen, Madvig.

They[26] returned [the theses] the next day. The comments made [about the theses] were communicated to Kierkegaard orally. Councillor of State Brøndsted will be one official opponent and Prof. Sibbern the other. The formal public arguments were later scheduled for Wednesday, September 29th.

Document 20. September 7, 1841—Dean Sibbern's comment sheet accompanying Kierkegaard's Latin theses[27]

To those of my gentlemen colleagues whom it concerns, I enclose *Candidat* Søren Kierkegaard's theses, which are to accompany his inaugural dissertation, and submit them for your approval, unless someone wishes to require that any of them be altered. In addition, I request my gentlemen to consider which of you will serve as official opponent. I will be one of the official opponents, and the other might best be one of the professors of Greek philology, though perhaps also Professor Madvig, who is most familiar with the dissertation, could take it on.

---

[23]"I have seen it. [signed] S. A. Kierkegaard."

[24]See note to document 2 above. Journal item no. 67, dated August 28, 1841.

[25]See note to document 2 above. Journal item no. 74; no date, but refers to September 7 and September 8, 1841.

[26]Same Philosophy Faculty journal item, under "Resolutions and Transactions."

[27]Rigsarkivet, Københavns Universitets arkiv, Det filosofiske Fakultet, 1841, no. 74, KU 35. 02. 17.

Copenhagen 7 September 1841
Sibbern
P.S.: Mr. Kierkegaard hopes to have his dissertation from the printer soon enough
to be able, without undue haste, to defend before the university entrance examinations begin on October 1st.

*Document 21. September 7, 1841—Prof. Brøndsted's comments, added to
Dean Sibbern's comment sheet accompanying Kierkegaard's Latin theses*[28]

I have only two things two say with respect to these theses. *The first thing* is that
it seems to me that the author would do better to omit nos. I and XV. Number
I, because it concerns sensitive matters which it would be very difficult to discuss
publicly without giving offense. And with respect to no. XV, because treating the
subject matter in Latin will without fail lead to a fruitless battle of terms which
will probably focus on what the author means by *humana vita*. The *second* thing
I will take the liberty of noting is that the author ought to be urged to phrase no.
IX somewhat differently. The reason for this is that if the purpose of having *Latin*
theses in addition to a printed book (which for good reasons could not have been
written in Latin), is of course to present something about which one can converse
in that language, then this purpose is not served by offering a thesis in which
substantialitas, realitas, and *idealitas* are the principal points.

If the public arguments are not scheduled to take place any earlier than a few
days after the conclusion of lectures and are set for one of the last days of this
month, I have nothing against being appointed as one of the official opponents.
But it would be better if one of my gentlemen colleagues would take on the
assignment, since surely both of them already know the book better than I do.
When it circulated in the Faculty, I was not able to have the lengthy manuscript
for more than one day, as the Most Excellent Dean will surely remember.

Received Tuesday evening, the 7th, forwarded Wednesday morning, the 8th of
September 1841.   Most respectfully
Brøndsted.

*Document 22. September 8, 1841—Prof. Petersen's comments, added to
Dean Sibbern's comment sheet accompanying Kierkegaard's Latin theses*[29]

I have nothing to say with respect to Mr. *Candidat* Kierkegaard's theses other than
to note that I dare say that no. XIII could use some close editing. There do not

---

[28]See note to document 20 above. Comments from P. O. Brøndsted, continued
on the same folio sheet. Kierkegaard's Latin theses, with English translations, are
in CI, 5-6.
[29]See note to document 20 above. Comments from F. C. Petersen, continued
on the same folio sheet.

seem to me to be sufficient reasons to require that anything be left out, particularly since there are so many theses that there are plenty among which to choose. With respect to no. IX, with this sort of subject matter there must be freedom to use the terminology complained of [by Prof. Brøndsted], and the author would likely reply that he could not substitute other words for the ones used without resorting to complicated and vague circumlocutions.

Since my colleague, Mr. Privy Councillor Brøndsted (under the conditions he cites, which as far as I know will be met) is willing to serve as an official opponent, it is my wish that he do so, unless Prof. Madvig takes on that assignment. Furthermore, at present I am very poorly acquainted with the dissertation, and I take the liberty of adding that this time it will probably be my turn to serve as examiner at the final examinations in philosophy. Is the change in no. XII by the author?

Received and forwarded the 9th[30] of September 1841.

F. C. Petersen

Document 23. September 8, 1841—Prof. Madvig's comments, added to Dean Sibbern's comment sheet accompanying Kierkegaard's Latin theses[31]

I have no comment with respect to the acceptability of the theses submitted. Because the dissertation from which they are extracted is focused so much on Plato, Aristophanes, and Xenophon, my gentlemen colleagues are certainly those most suited to be official opponents. And because this summer I have been (still am, and for several weeks will continue to be) very pressed with work from which, if I get the chance, I would like to tear myself away for a couple of days at the end of this month, I would prefer to be relieved of the *duty* to serve as opponent on this occasion. If I am present and have a bit of time, I will contribute to the formal arguments as an opponent *ex auditorio*.

8 September 1841   J. N. Madvig

---

[30]There appears to be an error in the date Petersen assigns to his comments. Petersen's date of September 9, 1841 is probably an error for September 8, as the journal of the Philosophy Faculty notes that this comment sheet was returned on that day.

[31]See note to document 20 above. Comments by J. N. Madvig, continued on the same folio sheet.

Document 24. October 1, 1841—Letter from Prof. Brøndsted and Dean Sibbern to the Supervisors, informing them of Kierkegaard's successful oral defense of his dissertation[32]

Wednesday the 29th of September *Candidat* Kierkegaard publicly defended, in Latin, his inaugural dissertation *On the Concept of Irony, With Continual Reference to Socrates* plus the 15 Latin theses appended to it. The official opponents were the undersigned. In addition, the opponents *ex auditorio* were: Professor Petersen, Professor Heiberg, Dr. Kierkegaard (brother of the above-mentioned), *Lic. theol.* Dr. Beck, Senior Master Dahl, *Cand. mag.* Thue from Norway, *Cand. theol.* Christens. The oral arguments lasted from 10 until 2 in the first part of the day and from 4 to 7 in the afternoon. The intelligence and intellectual liveliness, the proficiency and dialectical skill, which are so much in evidence in *Candidat* Kierkegaard's dissertation, were also prominent in his defense of it, and we must regard him as entirely deserving of the honor of the *magister* degree to which he aspires. We now hereby recommend that that degree be authorized.

Copenhagen, 1 October 1841

Brøndsted.   F. C. Sibbern

To the Exalted Royal Supervisors of the University and the Learned Schools

Document 25. October 12, 1841—A "humble proposal" (i.e., a draft for the King to sign) from the Supervisors, asking that the Philosophy Faculty be authorized to confer the magister *degree on Kierkegaard*[33]

Most Humble Proposal
concerning that two academic degrees may be conferred.

The Supervisors have received a report from the Philosophy Faculty that on the 29th of last month *Cand. theol.* Søren Aabye Kierkegaard defended in Latin his dissertation for the *magister* degree in philosophy, *On The Concept of Irony, With Continual Reference to Socrates*, plus 15 Latin theses appended to it; the dissertation was written by him in the Danish language in accordance with the permission granted him pursuant to a most exalted resolution communicated to him on the 30th of July this year; and the Faculty has declared that whereas the lively intelligence, proficiency, and dialectical skill to which *Candidat* Kierkegaard's dissertation testifies were also prominent in his defense of it, it must regard him as entirely deserving of the desired academic honor.

---

[32]From Rigsarkivet, Dansk Kancelli, Direktionen for Universitetet og de lærde Skoler, Forestillinger 1841, no. 2216 (three documents in all). This first document, an insert in 2216, is a letter from P. O. Brøndsted and F. C. Sibbern to the supervisors.

[33]See note to document 24 above. This "humble proposal" no. 2216 is written in the right-hand column of a folio-sized sheet, leaving room for the royal resolution in the left-hand column of the same sheet.

[The proposal continues by explaining why Andreas Frederik Krieger ought to receive a law degree from the University of Copenhagen.]
In accordance with this, the Supervisors must request, in profoundest humility,
Your Majesty's most exalted authority for the appropriate Faculty to confer upon *Cand. theol.* Søren Aabye Kierkegaard the *magister* degree [...] from the University of Copenhagen.

Document 26. October 14, 1841—King Christian VIII's resolution authorizing the Philosophy Faculty to grant Kierkegaard the magister degree[34]

Royal Resolution
We will most graciously have the appropriate Faculty authorized to confer upon *Cand. theol.* Søren Aabye Kjerkegaard [sic] the *magister* degree [...] from the University of Copenhagen.
Sorgenfrie 14 October 1841

Christian R.

Document 27. October 26, 1841—Notification from the Supervisors that the King has issued a resolution authorizing the Philosophy Faculty to confer the magister *degree on Kierkegaard*[35]

Pursuant to the Supervisors' most humble proposal, on the 14th of this month it has pleased His Majesty the King most graciously to authorize the Faculty to confer upon *Cand. theol.* Søren Aabye Kjerkegaard [sic] the *magister* degree from the University of Copenhagen—
Which most exalted resolution ought without fail be transmitted officially to the Faculty for its requisite information and measures.

The Royal Supervisors of the University and the Learned Schools, the 26th of October 1841
Engelstoft   J. Hansen   Kolderup Rosenvinge   /Selmer
To the Philosophy Faculty

---

[34]See note to document 24 above. This royal resolution is written in the left-hand column of the folio-sized sheet on which "humble proposal" no. 2216 (see document 25 above) is written.
[35]Rigsarkivet, Københavns Universitets arkiv, Det filosofiske Fakultet, 1841, no. 124b, KU 35. 02. 17.

Document 28. October 26, 1841—Journal of the Philosophy Faculty : receipt from the Supervisors of authorization to grant the magister *degree noted; diploma issued and sent.*[36]

Official communiqué from the Supervisors, reporting that on October 14th the King authorized the Faculty to confer the *magister* degree on Kierkegaard. The diploma was issued and sent to him.

II. Context. The University of Copenhagen

A. The University of Copenhagen in the 1830s and 1840s: An Overview

Founded in 1479, the University of Copenhagen had scarcely got off the ground when it was reestablished in 1537 as part of the general reorganization of religious and educational institutions in the wake of the Reformation. Always the creature of royal power and of the church, in the course of the seventeenth century the university was graven even more indelibly with the marks of royal absolutism, and graduates were granted the degree of *candidatus*, which signified that a person was a candidate for employment by the state or the state church in the fields of theology, law, or medicine. During the eighteenth and early nineteenth centuries, the university was subjected to further reforms in the name of enlightenment and of the more efficient use of state resources.

Things had of course changed somewhat by the time Kierkegaard attended the university.[37] But it is remarkable how much had not changed. The University was composed of four faculties: the three "higher" faculties (theology, law, and medicine) and a newer one, "philosophy," a catchall designation which had to cover everything else taught at the university: philosophy (in the narrow, modern sense); literature; classical, Semitic, and modern philology; history; geography; economics; mathematics; and all the natural sciences.

---

[36]Rigsarkivet, Københavns Universitets arkiv, Diarium 1836–1856, 1841, no. 124b, October 26, 1841.

[37]Kierkegaard enrolled as a theology student in 1830, received his degree of *Cand. theol.* in 1840, and his formal relationship with the University of Copenhagen ended with his successful defense of his dissertation and the receipt of the *magister* degree in philosophy in 1841.

Among the reasons for Søren Kierkegaard's decision to enroll as a theological student was the wish of his father that he, like his elder brother Peter Christian, pursue a career in the State Church (which constituted the largest market for university graduates), a path which appeared to hold out the promise both of divine approval and of a secure, comfortable livelihood. And Michael Pedersen Kierkegaard was not alone in perceiving the advantages of studying theology: In Søren Kierkegaard's time the Theology Faculty was still by far the one which enrolled the greatest number of new students, accounting for approximately half of the about 1,000 students at the University of Copenhagen.[38] Despite the number of students, the Theology Faculty had only five full-time instructors. This radical imbalance between the numbers of students and professors was also found, to a greater or lesser extent, on the other faculties[39] and was the result of a steady growth in the size of the student body at at time of serious budgetary constraints. Furthermore, the professors were in general quite poorly paid, with the consequence that many of them offered private lecture series and were financially dependent upon the fees from such lectures.[40] Although students from poorer families were often exempted from such fees, many students often had to take jobs, not only to support themselves while at the university but

---

[38]See Leif Grane, "Det teologiske Fakultet 1830–1925" in Leif Grane, ed., *Det teologiske Fakultet*, vol. V of *Københavns Universitet 1479–1979*, 14 vols. (Copenhagen: G. E. C. Gads Forlag, 1980) 325. For a detailed table of the number of matriculated students by faculty, see Jette Kjærulff Hellesen and Ole Tuxen, "Københavns Universitet 1788–1848" (hereafter "KU 1788–1848") in Leif Grane and Kai Hørby, eds., *Almindelig Historie, 1788–1936*, vol. 2 of *Københavns Universitet 1479–1979*, (Copenhagen: G. E. C. Gads Forlag, 1993) 153. At a bit more than 1,000 students, the University of Copenhagen was fairly large by contemporary European standards. In northern Germany only Berlin was larger, and the universities in Kiel and Kristiania (now Oslo) were much smaller.

[39]According to the *Kongelig Dansk Hof- og Stats-Calender for Aar 1835* (Copenhagen: Schultz, 1835), the official governmental yearbook and almanac of the day, the University of Copenhagen had a professoriate which was very small by current standards: the Theology faculty had four members, the Law faculty had five, as did the Medical Faculty; and the Philosophy Faculty, covering everything else taught at the university, had only twenty-three members.

[40]See Kjærulff Hellesen and Tuxen, "KU 1788–1848," 121-22.

also in order to earn the money needed to attend their professors' private lectures or to pay private tutors, who were widely used.

Each of the university's four faculties was governed by a Dean, a post which rotated annually among the faculty's members. The internal affairs of the university as a whole were governed by the Consistory, a council consisting of the three most senior members of each of the three "higher" faculties and the four most senior members of the Philosophy faculty. The Consistory was presided over by the Rector, who was chosen annually (though the Philosophy Faculty's representative served a two-year term), on a rotating basis, from the most senior member of the delegations from each of the various faculties. In addition to convening the Consistory (where he had two votes) and supervising its work, the Rector also served as the external representative of the university, in particular to the Supervisors of the University and the Learned Schools, which was the independent government agency charged with oversight of the university and other institutions of higher learning. There were three Supervisors, typically a conservative jurist, a senior professor (e.g., J. L. A. Kolderup-Rosenvinge, professor of law and a friend of Kierkegaard), and often a high churchman (e.g., J. P. Mynster, who was a member until he became bishop in 1834). The Supervisors were appointed by the monarch and reported directly to him; in general their views tended to be the final word on matters pertaining to the university.

Students generally prepared for the university at private preparatory or "Latin" schools, although some prepared with private tutors. An account of a would-be university student's character, his course of study, and his performance on the examinations administered at the preparatory school was forwarded to the university by the headmaster of the school, accompanied by a formal letter in Latin. The incoming student then took his university entrance examination (*examen artium*) on a wide variety of subjects, normally administered during four days in October, with examination periods of four hours each morning and four hours each afternoon. The possible grades were *laudabilis* (praiseworthy) or occasionally *laudabilis præ ceteris* (outstanding); *haud illaudabilis* (not unpraiseworthy); and *non contemnendus* (not to be looked down upon). Greek, Latin, and Danish counted double in computing the final grade, and one could not pass with more than

six *nons*. During the first year at the university, the student was
expected to attend lectures and prepare himself for the so-called
"second examination," (the *examen philologicum-philosophicum*, often
simply called the *philosophicum*) which was divided into "philological" (Latin, Greek, history, mathematics, and, for theologians,
Hebrew) and "philosophical" (philosophy, physics, and astronomy)
parts. The examinations were oral, with all the subjects for each
part administered on the same day, typically in April or October;
the first or philological part had to be passed before the second,
philosophical part could be taken. The possible grades were the
same as for the entrance examination.

The student body of the university was extremely atypical of
the population of Denmark as a whole, which was an overwhelm-
ingly rural society. Two-thirds of the student body of the University of Copenhagen was drawn from towns, while only one-fifth of
the Danish population lived in towns. And fifty percent of
students had fathers who had had a higher education or held a
position normally filled by someone with a university education,
while at most a few percent of Danish families were in this
situation. In sum, although the great majority of Danes came from
peasant families, "by and large there were no sons of peasants at
the university in the 1830s and 1840s," and indeed there is
evidence that the social base of the university was narrower in the
nineteenth century than it had been in the eighteenth.[41]

As in other European countries, there was considerable unrest
among university students in the period 1830–1848. Some of this
can be attributed to high unemployment among recent university
graduates, and some of it can be attributed to the general European and Danish movement toward political liberalism. For example,
on the night of December 3-4, 1839, when the conservative old
King Frederik VI died, some 250 students, following the lead of
Orla Lehmann, signed a petition asking the new monarch Christian
VIII to grant freedom of the press and a liberal constitution. This
was not a monolithic movement, and a group of ca. 400 students

---

[41]Kjærulff Hellesen and Tuxen, "KU 1788–1848," 161-63. The other statistics
cited here and much of the description of the university and student life are
drawn from this and from other volumes of the massive 14-volume work
Københavns Universitet, 1479–1979.

signed a counterpetition in which they voiced their opposition to the student body expressing itself as a class, while a third group, positioning itself between the other two, gathered 71 signatures on its petition.[42]

Approximately one-third of the students enrolled at the university did not attend classes regularly and in 1834 Prof. H. N. Clausen of the Theology Faculty proposed that the seats in the lecture halls of the new university building be numbered, with students assigned to particular places, so that their diligence could be monitored, but a storm of student protest caused the plan to be dropped.[43] Similarly, in 1837 Clausen proposed that first-year students should attend five hours of lectures a day and other students three hours a day, but nothing seems to have come of these proposals. It was not unusual for lectures that had a bearing on examinations to be attended by as many as 100 students, though this varied widely from professor to professor, with Clausen's lectures, and later Martensen's, among the most well attended on the Theology Faculty. The style of lecturing was not unusual for universities of the time: Often the professor read from his notes at a slow, steady pace while the students copied down his remarks, word for word. There was also considerable traffic in purchased sets of notes, taken down by others.[44]

The library facilities available to university students were quite limited. The University Library was in a period of considerable growth, tripling in size from the 1830s to the early 1850s, when it reached 120,000 volumes. But the opening hours were restricted, and there was only one hour a day when students could use the library undisturbed by the comings and goings of borrowers. Thus in the early 1840s circulation was only 12,000 volumes a year. The Royal Library was larger, with ca. 400,000 volumes by the late

---

[42]Kjærulff Hellesen and Tuxen, "KU 1788–1848," 184.

[43]Søren Kierkegaard was one of the protesters. See Bruce H. Kirmmse, *Encounters with Kierkegaard* (Princeton University Press: Princeton, NJ, 1996), 20.

[44]Kierkegaard's own notes on Martensen's lectures on the history of modern philosophy, held in the winter of 1838–1839, are of this type. They are not in Kierkegaard's hand, though they appear to bear his interlinear and marginal markings. See *Søren Kierkegaards Papirer*, 2nd ed., (hereafter "SKP") II C 25, published in SKP, XII, 280-331.

1840s, but service was poor and waiting periods were long, so that during this same period the Royal Library had a circulation of only ca. 5,000 volumes a year. Better service was available at various private libraries, of which the Athenæum, established in 1820, was the largest, and by the late 1840s it had an annual circulation of 28,000 volumes, larger than the University and Royal Libraries combined.[45] But the Athenæum was expensive and many less well-to-do students could not afford it (though Søren Kierkegaard could and was a member).

The university year was divided into two semesters, one running from the beginning of November through the end of March, the other from the first of May through the end of August. Academic examinations were given in April and October, and there were vacations from December 25 to January 6 and again from mid-July to mid-August. Lectures were held every day excepting Sunday, from 8:00 a.m. to 8:00 p.m. Starting in 1831 the Theology Faculty instituted a three-year cycle during which all the material necessary for the *candidat* examinations was supposed to be covered, but in fact absences of faculty members and other departures from the schedule meant that it could often take as long as six years for the entire cycle to be completed. Theology Faculty brochures from the 1830s made the claim that the normal duration of the theological education was three years, but the actual time was closer to five years.[46] During the period 1788–1848 there was also a general tendency for the time spent on a university education to increase. By the 1830s, durations of the three to six years became more and more frequent, and it was almost as common for a university education to last seven to nine years, with theology students tending to have somewhat longer educations than law students. During the 1840s the average length of time a student spent at the university, whether or not he completed his studies, grew to almost eight years. The completion rate for university educations during the period seems to have been close to 70%,

[45]For these and other details regarding the academic libraries, see Kjærulff Hellesen and Tuxen, "KU 1788–1848," 215-17.
[46]See Grane, "Det teologiske Fakultet," 333.

however, a much larger proportion than in the late eighteenth century.[47]

As a result of the state bankruptcy and hard times that accompanied the Napoleonic wars, the annual production of university graduates reached a low point of ca. 70 in 1815, but thereafter this number increased, reaching a high of ca. 130 in 1840.[48] As noted, of the possible curricula, "theology was the traditional favorite. In the public mind, a theological education and a university education were still synonymous. Furthermore, a theological graduate had much better employment prospects than graduates from the other faculties."[49] Thus, the number of theological graduates increased from an annual average of 46 in the 1820s to an average of 67 per year in the period 1830–1847. The problem was that during the 1830s only an average of 43 theological graduates per year found positions, and that number increased only slightly, to 47, in the 1840s, so that the surplus of unemployed theological graduates ballooned from 169 in 1830 to 481 in 1845.[50]

The examination process for the *candidat* degree was gruelling. Examinations were held at fixed times, four times a year. Written examinations came first, and only if they were judged satisfactory could one proceed to the oral examinations, which were public, supposedly to guarantee impartial treatment. The use of Latin as the language of debate in oral examinations was in continual retreat from the late eighteenth century through the mid-nineteenth. Contrary to what one might expect, forces within the university, and particularly such highly respected classicists as the world-renowned Latinist J. N. Madvig, repeatedly pushed for eliminating or at least reducing the Latin requirement in academic settings, complaining that Latin led to a cramped style of expression in teaching and debate and that it permitted otherwise mediocre students who were capable Latinists to slip through their

---

[47]See Kjærulff Hellesen and Tuxen, "KU 1788–1848," 236-38, and Niels Petersen, "Københavns Universitet 1848–1902" in Leif Grane and Kai Hørby, eds., *Almindelig Historie, 1788–1936*, vol. 2 of *Københavns Universitet 1479–1979* (Copenhagen: G. E. C. Gads Forlag, 1993) 284.

[48]Kjærulff Hellesen and Tuxen, "KU 1788–1848," 238.

[49]Kjærulff Hellesen and Tuxen, "KU 1788–1848," 240-41.

[50]Kjærulff Hellesen and Tuxen, "KU 1788–1848," 240-41.

examinations, while placing at a disadvantage others who were in the opposite situation. These university-based reformers were opposed with some success by the more conservative members of the University Supervisors, such as J. P. Mynster, and indeed by King Frederik VI himself.[51] Nonetheless, by the late 1830s the use of Latin as the language of instruction and examination had been reduced so that even in its greatest stronghold, the Theology Faculty, it was restricted to exegetical subjects.[52]

The possible grades on the examination for the *candidat* degree were the same as for the *artium* and *philosophicum* examinations: *laud*, *haud*, and *non*. The distinguished church historian Leif Grane writes that "particularly in the 1830s and 1840s, when Denmark was crawling with theological graduates, the overall grade [on one's *candidat* examination] was of decisive significance with respect to the possibility of landing a pastoral position within a foreseeable period of time."[53] A graduate with a *non* on his final examination had virtually no chance of finding a position, and less desirable positions came to be called *haud* positions. Thus many aspiring pastors retook their final examinations repeatedly in the hope of improving their grade and thus their employment chances, a tactic which placed considerable strain on the university's examination system.

The names of the degrees granted by the various faculties varied somewhat, though the basic degree indicating that one was university-educated was the *candidat*. The next highest degree from the three "higher" faculties was the *licentiat*, and from the Philosophy Faculty the *magister*;[54] access to the right to dispute for this degree was limited to those who had gotten the highest grades on their *candidat* examinations. For all four faculties, the highest

---

[51]See Fritze Smith, *Bidrag til Doktordisputatsens Historie ved Københavns Universitet* (Ejnar Munksgaard: Copenhagen, 1950) 81-82; see also Kjærulff Hellesen and Tuxen, "KU 1788–1848," 206, 228-30.

[52]See Kjærulff Hellesen and Tuxen, "KU 1788–1848," 205 and Grane, "Det teologiske Fakultet," 336-37.

[53]Grane, "Det teologiske Fakultet," 338.

[54]In 1854 the dissertation-based *magister* degree from the Philosophy Faculty was abolished, and those with that degree (e.g., Søren Kierkegaard) were officially designated as *doktor*, a usage which by then was already current in common parlance.

academic degree was the *doktor*, though in the faculties of theology and law the right to dispute for this degree was reserved for individuals who occupied high positions or were already known for their learning. Throughout the first half of the nineteenth century there was an increasing tendency to seek advanced academic degrees: At the beginning of the century the number of advanced degrees granted annually averaged 2.8, and by the period 1837–1848 that number had increased to 6.3.[55]

B. The Theology Faculty

The historian Leif Grane points out that there was a sea change in the personnel of the Theology Faculty in the early 1830s, and by 1833 the faculty took on the form which would largely characterize it during Kierkegaard's time at the University.[56] It was a young faculty, dominated by the intellect and personality of H. N. Clausen (1793–1877), a respected New Testament scholar who was appointed *lektor* (closest approximation: "assistant professor") in 1821 and was promoted to *professor extraordinarius* ("associate professor") the following year. After emerging victorious from a notorious libel suit with Grundtvig in 1826, Clausen was appointed *professor ordinarius* ("full professor") in 1830, having made quite a name for himself as a learned and eloquent defender of a moderate middle position on the theological landscape, mediating between Enlightenment rationalism and orthodox literalism. Grane, who is not uncritical of Clausen, sums up Clausen's standpoint under the slogan " 'Reason and the Bible': that is, the philological-historical study of the Bible as the foundation of theology," a standpoint that Grane believes to be irreconcilable with Lutheran confessionalism or with the Grundtvigian position, although it was acceptable to the three younger colleagues who had joined Clausen on the faculty by the early 1830s.[57] Indeed, "Even though he was far from being in theological agreement with the others, [H. L.] Martensen could also concur with this Clausenian centrist position, which was as opposed to radical critique [of the Bible] as it was to ortho-

[55]Kjærulff Hellesen and Tuxen, "KU 1788–1848," 267-68.
[56]See Leif Grane, "Det teologiske Fakultet," 328-29.
[57]Grane, "Det teologiske Fakultet," 330-31.

doxy."[58] It is worth noting that by virtue of his seat on the all-powerful University Supervisors, which he retained until 1834, Mynster, though certainly no ally of Clausen in theological matters, most likely played a key role in the molding the Theology faculty in this period, favoring non-Grundtvigian candidates over those who, though arguably better qualified, were unacceptable because of their association with Grundtvig.[59] Thus the *licentiat* dissertation submitted by Peter Christian Kierkegaard in 1835, just after he had thrown in his lot with Grundtvig, was vigorously opposed by every member of the faculty and was only accepted, grudgingly, when it was pointed out by Clausen that rejection by the Theology Faculty might be misconstrued by the public, making P. C. Kierkegaard appear a martyr and the faculty appear narrow-minded.[60] Sharing a common enemy can partially outweigh the lack of agreement in other areas, and Grane notes that despite their disagreements on both theology and politics, Mynster and Clausen had an important common ground in their shared distaste for Grundtvig.[61]

The three new faculty members appointed in the late 1820s and early 1830s were M. H. Hohlenberg, an Old Testament scholar, appointed 1826; C. T. Engelstoft, a church historian, appointed 1833; and C. E. Scharling, who taught introduction to New Testament (while Clausen taught hermeneutics), appointed 1833. This Theology Faculty was a youthful group. In 1833 Clausen was only 41 years old, while Hohlenberg was 32, Engelstoft was 30, and Scharling was a mere 26. The three younger men had neither the scholarly reputation nor the personal force to challenge the leadership of Clausen, the respected centrist. During the political ferment of the 1830s and 1840s, Clausen, already well known as a moderate liberal on theological matters, emerged as a national spokesman for the same position in the political and constitutional

---

[58]Grane, "Det teologiske Fakultet," 330-31.

[59]Grane cites the examples of the failure of the eminently well-qualified A. G. Rudelbach to find a position in the late 1820s and the choice of church historian C. T. Engelstoft over J. F. Fenger in 1833; see Grane, "Det teologiske Fakultet," 329-31.

[60]See the discussion of P. C. Kierkegaard's dissertation later in this essay.

[61]Grane, "Det teologiske Fakultet," 349-50.

debate. But despite his impressive learning and his fashionable views on politics, there was a vagueness to Clausen's middle-of-the-road theological position, and he failed to attract the bright lights among the students who were searching for a clear-cut "school," be it Hegelianism, the radical criticism of Strauss or Feuerbach, or the liturgical theology of Grundtvig. Furthermore, Clausen's personality had a cool, distant air, which kept him from winning many genuine adherents among the younger theologians. Indeed, Grane points out that the Theological Faculty of the late 1820s and early 1830s was in general so dry and uninspiring that there were a good many theological students who sought spiritual nourishment not from the theologians but from members of the Philosophical Faculty, particularly F. C. Sibbern and Poul Martin xMøller. Speaking of Sibbern in this connection, Grane notes that "his attitude was connected with a warm and untiring spirit of helpfulness, which caused him to have personal contact even with rather young students in a quite unconventional manner. There could be no talk of self-importance, neither for the sake of his position nor for the sake of 'scholarship'."[62]

The landscape of the Theology Faculty then underwent a significant change with the appointment of H. L. Martensen as a *lektor* in theology in 1838. (Martensen became *professor extraordinarius* in 1840 and *professor ordinarius* in 1850.) Martensen had passed through an early Grundtvigian phase and had subsequently studied with Clausen (as well as with Sibbern of the Philosophy faculty), but in the mid-1830s he had been profoundly influenced by the philosophy of Hegel and had formed a deep personal and intellectual alliance with the leading Danish Hegelian, J. L. Heiberg.

Martensen and Clausen were the stars of the Theology Faculty. The other three professors—Hohlenberg, Engelstoft, and Scharling—were competent but run-of-the-mill and attracted little attention. Clausen was uniformly seen as a clear and accomplished lecturer and attracted many listeners, "at any rate when his lectures were relevant to the examinations," and his popularity

---

[62]Grane, "Det teologiske Fakultet," 344. See also Kjærulff Hellesen and Tuxen, "KU 1788–1848," 202.

was only surpassed in the late 1830s and 1840s, when larger numbers of students flocked to hear Martensen "for the sake of the lectures themselves."[63] Martensen was a man of intellectual vigor and personal dynamism, and this made him Clausen's rival, first within the Theology Faculty, then for the favor of students, and ultimately for leadership of the Danish Church. Like Clausen, Martensen wrote and lectured on dogmatics, and his area of expertise could be described broadly as philosophy of religion, that is, the history of "modern" (i.e., post-Kantian) philosophy, plus systematics and ethics. Not long after joining the Theology Faculty Martensen began to moderate his Hegelianism, possibly influenced by the exclusion of the Left Hegelian Hans Brøchner from theological study in 1841 and by the appearance of Brøchner's translation of D. F. Strauss' *Christliche Glaubenslehre* (Doctrines of the Christian Faith) in 1842–1843. Whether out of a concern for his career or for the matter itself, Martensen, like the other members of the Theology faculty, quickly and quietly surrendered to the all-engulfing tide of moderation.

One of Martensen's responsibilities after his initial appointment in April 1838 was to take over the survey lecture course on moral philosophy, required of all beginning university students and usually offered by the Philosophy Faculty, most recently by the well loved (and now lamented) Poul Martin Møller, who had died a month earlier at the age of 43. (This is of particular interest in connection with the study of Kierkegaard's intellectual and personal development. As will be noted subsequently in this essay, Kierkegaard had a reverential relationship to Møller and was highly critical of attempts by anyone—Martensen on the Theology Faculty and, as we will see, Rasmus Nielsen on the Philosophy Faculty—to fill the empty place left by Møller's premature death.)

It will readily be appreciated that there was a mismatch between young Søren Kierkegaard and the Theology Faculty. Kierkegaard's intellectual interests were wide-ranging, shot through with unusual combinations and juxtapositions, and he sought existential intensity and authenticity in his teachers. The Theology Faculty, by contrast—with the exception, at least initially, of

---

[63]Grane, "Det teologiske Fakultet," 334-35, 341.

Martensen—was characterized by a rather flat and cautious conventionality. Thus Kierkegaard's involvement with most of the members of the Theology Faculty was unremarkable, while his relations with Martensen were fraught with difficulty, perhaps with rivalry. It is not surprising that after he had fulfilled his obligation to his father by taking his *candidat* degree in theology—and probably well before he actually completed his examinations for that degree—Kierkegaard decided to pursue a higher degree, not with the Theology Faculty, but with the Philosophy Faculty, and to seek guidance from the decent and affable Sibbern, with whom he was already well acquainted, and scholarly assistance from J. N. Madvig, who was one of Denmark's most famous scholars.

C. The Philosophy Faculty

As has been noted, the Philosophy faculty was an *omnium gatherum*, but the members who are of interest in connection with Kierkegaard's *magister* dissertation are of course those concerned with philosophy and with classical philology. There were five professors in this category: P. O. Brøndsted and F. C. Petersen, professors of Greek; J. N. Madvig, professor of Latin; and F. C. Sibbern and Rasmus Nielsen, professors of philosophy. When Kierkegaard's dissertation came before the faculty in June 1841, Nielsen had just been appointed to the position previously held by the late Poul Martin Møller, a position that had remained open since Møller's death in March 1838. Nielsen declined to participate in judging Kierkegaard's work, and his relationship to Kierkegaard will be considered in a subsequent section of this essay.

Professor Peder Oluf Brøndsted (1780–1842), a philologist and archaeologist, was the greatest Danish neo-Hellenist of the nineteenth century. Brøndsted was an enthusiast for living in "the Greek spirit," i.e., total immersion in the aesthetic and moral universe of ancient Greece, and he appeared as such to his contemporaries: a romantic, well-travelled figure who could impart to others the feelings and the lifeview of the ancients. He was a formidable interpreter of ancient monuments, a talent grounded on his remarkable knowledge of classical literature, and his brilliant interpretation of the Parthenon as an aesthetic whole was widely acknowledged. Furthermore, Brøndsted had a very independent relationship to the university, and this contributed to his image as a free spirit and an uncompromising seeker of the truth. From his first appointment on 1813 to his death in 1842 (age 62) Brøndsted was in Copenhagen only about half the time, spending the rest of the time in Rome, Paris, and London, communicating to other scholars the results of his pioneering field work in Greece and Asia Minor.[64]

Frederik Christian Petersen (1786–1859) was a much less prominent figure than Brøndsted, for whom he first served as a replacement in 1818, during one of Brøndsted's many absences from the university. Petersen was not a particularly original thinker and was more a teacher than a scholar. He wrote some useful but dry textbooks and a couple of good articles on classical art, but after he was named provost of Regensen, a residential college of the university, even this modest scholarly production came to an end. Petersen never took leaves to pursue research, and after his initial appointment in 1818 he remained in Copenhagen without interruption until his death in 1859. He was known to be an extreme political conservative, and when he feared that a student reading society, founded at the college of which he was provost, might assert too much independence, he caused it to be disbanded. Indeed, Petersen served as "an out-and-out police spy against the students at Regensen."[65]

Johan Nicolai Madvig (1804–1886) was a brilliant and original mind, one of the world's greatest classicists of the nineteenth century. In 1828 he accepted a post as *lektor* in classical philology at the University of Copenhagen and was promoted to professor the following year. With the exception of an interruption during the turbulent years 1848–1851, when he served as a member of parliament and as Minister of Culture, Madvig continued in his professorship until his retirement in 1879 at age 75. Madvig's greatest achievement was his work on Cicero, but he was also revered for his work on Latin grammar, and his grammar text remained in use over much of the world well into the twentieth

---

[64]This information as well as the information on F. C. Petersen and J. N. Madvig is gleaned from Ivan Boserup's excellent essay "Klassisk filologi efter 1800," in Povl Johs. Jensen and Leif Grane, eds., *Det filosofiske Fakultet*, 1. del, vol. 8 of *Københavns Universitet 1479–1979* (Copenhagen: G. E. C. Gad: 1992) 295-334.

[65]Kjærulff Hellesen and Tuxen, "KU 1788–1848," 136.

century. Later in his career Madvig turned his attention to producing a scholarly edition of Livy's history of Rome, and in his old age he produced a major work on Roman politics and administration. Madvig had no truck with romantic views of the Greeks and Romans or with the notion that the viewpoint of classical antiquity can or ought to be reappropriated by the present. He believed that classical studies were to serve the present and that only by honestly admitting the gap by which the present is separated from antiquity can we ourselves be free. Madvig was not uncritical of the shortcomings of ancient civilization, e.g., with respect to slavery and the status of women, and his views on these matters fit in nicely with his general political outlook, which was a thoughtful liberalism. As noted, Madvig also took the lead in pushing for the abolition of the mandatory academic use of Latin as the language of dissertation and debate, arguing that only when it was freed from this bondage could the study of Latin truly come into its own as a modern scholarly discipline.

Frederik Christian Sibbern (1785–1872) was the senior philosopher on the faculty. As a young man Sibbern studied law and philosophy at the University of Copenhagen and numbered the brothers H. C. and A. S. Ørsted among his friends. After defending his doctorate on the philosophy of law in 1811, Sibbern went on the customary grand tour, seeking out Henrich Steffens (whom he had first seen but disliked at his famous lectures in Copenhagen in 1802) in Halle; attending the lectures of Fichte the elder, Schleiermacher, Solger, and, most important, Schelling; and even seeking out an audience with Goethe. Sibbern was called back to Denmark in 1813 and despite his youth (age 28) was asked to take up the philosophy chair at the University of Copenhagen, a position he held until his retirement in 1870 at age 85. Sibbern wrote a great many works in various fields, including philosophical psychology, logic, aesthetics, metaphysics, ethics, and even fiction. His most important works were those in psychology, particularly the early works *Menneskets aandelige Natur og Væsen. Et Udkast til en Psychologie* (Man's Spiritual Nature and Essence: A Draft of a Psychology) (1819) and *Psychologisk Pathologie* (Psychological Pathology) (1828) which constituted his principal contribution to this field. Like many of his contemporaries, Sibbern had a period of infatuation with Hegel, followed by a firm rejection.

As time went on, Sibbern's lively writing style became increasingly dense and almost unreadable. Sibbern's religious views developed over the years, and after the mid-1840s he more and more distanced himself from anything resembling ordinary Christianity, which he regarded as narrow-minded and judgmental. This is most apparent in his long and unfinished futuristic-utopian work, *Meddelelser af Indholdet af et Skrift fra Aaret 2135* (*Accounts of the Contents of a Text from the Year 2135*), published in installments 1858–1872, in which he proposed a nondoctrinal variant of Christianity, purged of such notions as eternal damnation, the Holy Trinity, and even the divinity of Christ. Sibbern's political views underwent a similar development, from a faith in patriarchal absolutism to a hope for some sort of utopian communism.

It was Sibbern's personality and his teaching, however, and not his published works which created his reputation and mediated his influence. As mentioned earlier, theology students migrated to the Philosophy Faculty in order to study with Sibbern, who was an extraordinarily sympathetic personality. He radiated charm, an almost childlike enthusiasm, and an inextinguishable optimism, and he was known for his remarkable ability to support others in times of need and crisis. There were those, however, who felt that there was a certain naiveté at the heart or core of Sibbern's character and believed that he lacked the subtlety needed to penetrate to the core of the self, and as we will see, Søren Kierkegaard was among those who shared this sense of Sibbern's limitations. (Sibbern's role as Kierkegaard's friend and ally in shepherding *The Concept of Irony* through the Philosophy Faculty—as well as his service as middleman in Kierkegaard's relationships to Poul Martin Møller and to Rasmus Nielsen—will be discussed in a subsequent section of this essay.)

D. The Magister Degree: Procedural Matters

As has been noted, the *magister* degree in philosophy was available only to those who had done well on their *candidat* examinations. (This posed no problem for Kierkegaard, whose performance on his examinations had been judged *laudabilis*.) An aspirant for the *magister* degree had to submit a copy of the proposed dissertation to the Dean of the faculty, who would then circulate it among faculty members, specifically among those upon

whose area of expertise the dissertation touched most directly, and
the faculty would then arrive at a consensual judgment about
whether or not to allow the matter to proceed by accepting the
dissertation for oral defense. If a dissertation was accepted for
defense, the faculty members' comments and requests for alterations would be sent in writing or conveyed orally to the aspiring
magister, who was expected to be guided by these comments in
preparing the final version, which would then be resubmitted for
approval by the faculty before being printed for distribution prior
to a public oral defense. A minimum of 250 copies of the dissertation were to be made publicly available, normally three or four
days in advance of the scheduled public defense. Approximately
200 copies were for university teachers, students, and others with
an interest in the matter, e.g., the Copenhagen clergy, so that those
who wished to serve as opponents *ex auditorio* could familiarize
themselves with the dissertation ahead of time. An additional fifty
copies were given to the Rector of the university, presumably to be
exchanged for dissertations from other European universities.[66]

The public defense took place in a university auditorium and
normally lasted several hours with an intermission. Unless a
dispensation had been granted, the language of the written
dissertation was Latin. The language of the oral defense was Latin
in any case. The faculty put forward two official opponents, and
opponents *ex auditorio* could also come forward during the
proceedings. Normally—that is, unless there was a debacle—the
official opponents reported to the University Supervisors that the
defense was successful, described the character of the debate and
of the aspirant's defense, and recommended that the granting of
the degree be authorized. Following this, the Supervisors would
request that the monarch authorize the appropriate faculty of the
university to confer the degree upon the aspirant, whereupon the
monarch complied and granted the authorization. Word of the
monarch's authorization was then conveyed by the Supervisors
back to the appropriate faculty, which issued the diploma.

There could be minor variations from this formula, most
notably in those cases (such as Søren Kierkegaard's), increasingly

---

[66]See Kjærulff Hellesen and Tuxen, "KU 1788–1848," 260.

frequent after the late 1830s, in which the degree aspirant requested dispensation from the requirement that the dissertation submitted be written in Latin. In these cases, the aspirant made direct application to the Crown via the Supervisors, who referred the case back down to the Rector and the Consistory, who then asked the Dean of the appropriate faculty to supply the faculty's opinion and recommendation on the matter. The faculty's views were then conveyed back up the bureaucratic ladder, via the Rector and Consistory, to the Supervisors, who generally accepted the faculty's recommendation, perhaps modifying or supplementing whatever conditions and stipulations the faculty had attached, and formulated it as a "humble proposal" to the absolute monarch. This done, the permission thus granted was conveyed back down the same channels to the appropriate faculty and finally to the degree aspirant himself. This accounts for the parallel sets of communications in Kierkegaard's file, as in the files of other degree aspirants who sought dispensation from the Latin requirement: one set of papers pertained to the dispensation petition, the other to the degree itself. Because each set of documents assumes the existence of the other, and documents dealing with the substance of the dissertation sometimes refer to the Latin-requirement documents, in the present essay the two series of documents have been merged and arranged in chronological sequence for the sake of clarity. The language used in these documents was formulaic, and the specific qualitative wording appropriate to each case was often borrowed from the aspirant's original petition, perhaps modified by the relevant faculty and possibly modified again by the Supervisors. This accounts for the recurrence of various phrases and usages.

III. Commentary on Documents
Relating to Kierkegaard's Magister Dissertation

A. Documents Pertaining to Kierkegaard's Petition
for Dispensation from the Latin Dissertation Requirement

Kierkegaard's request to be released from the requirement of writing his dissertation in Latin was nothing new. As will be seen, several others, starting with Martin Hammerich in 1835, had petitioned successfully in this connection. But even before this, in 1832, at the request of the Consistory, the classicist J. N. Madvig and his colleague H. C. Ørsted had produced a recommendation concerning the use of Latin, in which they suggested that—with the exception of classical philology, where Latin would still be required—all academic dissertations above the level of the *candidat* (i.e., those for the *licentiat, magister*, and *doktor* degrees) could be submitted either in Danish or Latin, and that the same freedom of choice pertain to the language of the oral defense. Despite the fact that it was authored by the prestigious Latinist Madvig, the proposal failed to win the approval of the Supervisors, and the right of free choice between Latin and Danish was not introduced until 1854. Nonetheless, freedom of choice was introduced by dispensation, on a case-by-case basis, and at an accelerating rate. Of 82 dissertations submitted in the period 1836–1841, only 4% were in Danish; of 38 dissertations in the period 1842–1854, 29% were in Danish.[67] The historian Fritze Smith has gathered an entire bouquet of testimonials against the compulsory use of Latin from such famed lights as the classicist P. O. Brøndsted; the poet Adam Oehlenschlæger; the geologist J. G. Forchhammer, whose complaint was that forcing the language requirement upon his subject matter would result in "very imperfect and barbarous Latin," full of circumlocutions and direct translations—a criticism which would soon be echoed by such petitioners as Adler, Martensen, and Kierkegaard; the physicist H. C. Ørsted; and of course, the classicist J. N. Madvig, who explained that he had switched in 1840 to lecturing in Danish because "the Latin form naturally hindered . . . a freer and lighter movement, a more profound and clear expression of certain ideas, e.g., in aesthetics."[68]

Despite the views of these established academics (who had already earned their advanced degrees with dissertations submitted in Latin), the real trailblazer was the young Martin J. Hammerich (1811–1881) who in 1835 petitioned to be permitted to submit a Danish dissertation on the subject of "The Ragnarok

---

[67]See Martin Hammerich, "Om Disputerøvelser ved Universitetet," *Nordisk Universitets-Tidsskrift*, I, 1854, 114, and Kjærulff Hellesen and Tuxen, "KU 1788–1848," 262.

[68]Fritze Smith, *Doktordisputatsens Historie*, 77-82.

Myth and its Significance for Old Norse Religion." The treasure trove of Sanskrit sources had just been opened for many European researchers, and Hammerich had taught himself that language in order to do comparative and historical research on the body of Indo-European mythology. In his petition Hammerich pointed out that both the ancient sources of Norse mythology and the modern portion of his dissertation, which gives an overview of mythology, "move in a circle of ideas which belongs to the present, and which has not found expression in the ancient Latin language."[69] Hammerich's petition was sent back to the university for comment, and it found its way to the Philosophy Faculty, whose Dean, F. C. Sibbern, immediately and wholeheartedly favored recommending that the petition be granted. Sibbern was seconded by H. C. Ørsted and others, including Oehlenschlæger, the classicist F. C. Petersen, and Poul Martin Møller. The philologist Christian Molbech pointed out, however, that Hammerich had asked only for permission to submit a dissertation *written* in Danish, and that the oral defense was another matter. The oral defense could very well take place in Latin, Molbech insisted, and for the purpose of facilitating such a debate, it would be helpful and appropriate "to extract from the dissertation several theses which were best suited for the purpose, and to publish them in Latin and let them serve as the subjects of the oral defense."[70] Finally, the great Madvig favored Hammerich's petition in principle, but was opposed in practice to granting exceptions to a bad rule instead of changing the rule itself. Madvig favored holding an excellent piece of scholarship, like Hammerich's, hostage in order to force the Supervisors to change the rule, rather than offer them the easy way out by granting Hammerich a dispensation only because of the excellence of this particular

---

[69]From Martin J. Hammerich's petition, dated November 7, 1835, to the king (i.e., to the Supervisors) that he be granted a dispensation from the requirement of submitting a Latin dissertation; in Rigsarkivet, Dansk Kancelli, Directionen for Universitetet og de lærde Skoler, Forestillingsprotokoller, 1836, no. 1662.

[70]Christian Molbech's remarks, dated December 1, 1835, on a sheet of comments circulated among the Philosophy Faculty's members; in Rigsarkivet, Dansk Kancelli, Directionen for Universitetet og de lærde Skoler, Forestillinger 1845, nos. 2608-78; originally from 1835, but filed together with other cases concerning Danish-language dissertations under no. 2652.

piece of work.[71] The recommendation transmitted by Dean F. C. Sibbern to the Rector and the Consistory reflected the differences of opinion within his own faculty, and the recommendation transmitted by the Consistory and the Rector to the Supervisors reproduced and ramified these divisions.[72] The diversity of views within the Philosophy Faculty made it easier for the Supervisors and the moderate conservative Molbech to have their way. In the end the rule was not changed. Instead, at the request of the Supervisors, the king ordered that Hammerich be granted a dispensation whereby he was permitted, as an exception from the rule, to submit a dissertation *written* in Danish because, as the Supervisors put it, "there can be scholarly topics whose treatment in print is of great interest, but whose treatment in the Latin language would lead to significant, sometimes insuperable difficulties, and also make the work less useful." The oral defense was to be in Latin, however, and in order to facilitate this, the king (i.e., the Supervisors) added the requirement, originally suggested by Molbech, that the aspirant supply a number of Latin theses drawn from the dissertation itself.[73]

Hammerich's case created the blueprint followed by Kierkegaard five years later when he sought a similar dispensation for *The Concept of Irony*, and the various university authorities—the Rector, the Consistory, and in particular the Philosophy Faculty, where F. C. Sibbern was once again serving as Dean—followed a by-then familiar routine. Meanwhile there had been two other cases of requests for dispensations from the Latin requirement, both of them of considerable interest.

---

[71]As in the preceding note, dated December 3, 1835.

[72]Sibbern's recommendation to the rector and the consistory, dated December 14, 1835, and the recommendation from the rector and the consistory to the supervisors of the university, dated December 28, 1835. Both documents are in Rigsarkivet, Dansk Kancelli, Directionen for Universitetet og de lærde Skoler, Forestillinger, nos. 2608-78; originally from 1836, but filed together with other cases concerning Danish-language dissertations under no. 2652.

[73]The recommendation by the supervisors is dated January 14, 1836, and the resolution by King Frederik VI is dated January 15, 1836; in Rigsarkivet, Dansk Kancelli, Directionen for Universitetet og de lærde Skoler, Forestillingsprotokoller, 1836, no. 1662.

Lektor H. L. Martensen, the most junior member of the Theology faculty, had needed to acquire a doctoral degree in order to be promoted to the rank of *professor extraordinarius*, an advancement which was expected of him. In February 1840 Martensen petitioned the Supervisors for permission to submit a Danish-language dissertation, taking the liberty also to send his "most highly esteemed colleagues" on the Theology Faculty a copy of the petition in order to speed the process on its way.[74] Martensen wished to write on fourteenth- and fifteenth-century German mysticism both as "the forerunner of the Reformation" and also as "containing rich philosophical contents which offer many points of comparison with the philosophical theology of our day" (i.e., with Hegelian theology). The problem was that the texts of German mysticism "are written in the Old German language, . . . and it is a part of the historical significance of that literature that its authors wrested themselves from the petrified usages of Latin and created a new expression of life in the mother tongue, thereby paving the way for the Reformation."[75] Furthermore, Martensen explained that "throughout the dissertation I must presuppose, as my point of departure, views which are a part of the present day and which are peculiar to modern *videnskabelig* (scientific or scholarly) thought, while in a dead language one searches in vain for words which are a part of the new life of the sciences."[76] In other words, Hegel does not translate into Latin very well. Martensen, not unaware of the precedent already set by the Supervisors in the case of Hammerich's *licentiat* dissertation for the Philosophy Faculty, stated that he wished to conduct the oral defense in Latin, based on Latin theses extracted from the dissertation, which was of course Molbech's compromise formula that had been employed in Hammerich's case.

[74]H. L. Martensen's letter of transmittal to the Theology Faculty, dated February 22, 1840; in Rigsarkivet, Københavns Universitets arkiv, Det teologiske Fakultet, Dekanatssager 1840–1843, KU 31. 021.10.

[75]H. L. Martensen's petition to the king (i.e., to the supervisors), dated February 22, 1840; in Rigsarkivet, Dansk Kancelli, Directionen for Universitetet og de lærde Skoler, Forestillinger, 1840, nos. 2018-2102, no. 2033, supplement.

[76]As in the preceding note.

Through the Rector and the Consistory, the Theology Faculty was asked for its reaction to Martensen's petition, and its response is quite revealing. The general tone of that rather conservative faculty was one of unease. Surely, it was argued, if the particular topic favored by *Lektor* Martensen or any other aspirant is not suitable for treatment in Latin, that is no reason to change the rule because the would-be doctor could easily choose another topic more amenable to that language. Still, although unwilling to change the rule, Martensen's colleagues did not want to be uncollegial. They were aware that the university itself had imposed on Martensen the obligation to acquire the doctorate; that the time before the coming round of doctoral promotions was short (typically, advanced academic degrees were conferred on the occasion of some major event, in this case, the approaching coronation of Christian VIII, scheduled for June 1840); and that their colleague was thus obliged to make use of a scholarly manuscript he already had on hand. So, rather than compel Martensen to choose between "abandoning his intention of acquiring the doctorate during the approaching academic festival or presenting for public judgment [another] piece of work which he himself would find unsatisfactory," the majority of the Theology Faculty recommended that he be permitted to submit a Danish dissertation, provided, of course, that the oral defense was in Latin and was based upon Latin theses extracted from the dissertation.[77]

Martensen seems to have had a weaker case than Hammerich. Medieval German mysticism and Hegelian philosophy were not nearly as foreign to Latin as were Old Norse and Sanskrit. But Martensen's case sailed through the university authorities to the Supervisors, who cited the precedent they had created in granting the exception to Hammerich four years earlier and granted Martensen his dispensation with extraordinary speed: Martensen's original petition had been dated February 22, 1840; the Supervisors' recommendation to the king was dated March 19; and the king signed the empowering resolution the next day. This was not

---

[77]Recommendation of the Theology Faculty, dated March 5, 1840; in Rigsarkivet, Københavns Universitets arkiv, Det teologiske Fakultet, Dekanatssager 1840–1843, KU 31. 021. 10.

fast enough for Martensen, however. He was well known and well respected in international academic circles and managed to secure an honorary doctorate from the University of Kiel. (Kiel was a part of the composite Danish monarchy and also held an academic festival on the occasion of Christian VIII's coronation.) Thus Martensen never made use of the dispensation granted him with such remarkable celerity, and because the doctorate he received was an *honorary* one, he never had to defend it orally in any language. The University of Copenhagen promoted Martensen to *professor extraordinarius* later in 1840.

Immediately after Martensen was granted a dispensation allowing him to submit a Danish-language dissertation, Adolph Peter Adler—another young Hegelian whose path would cross fatefully with Søren Kierkegaard's—petitioned for permission to do exactly the same thing. On April 11, 1840, Adler asked the Supervisors that he be allowed to submit in Danish his Hegel-inspired dissertation *Den isolerede Subjectivetet i dens vigtigste Skikkelser* (*Isolated Subjectivity in its Principal Forms*) to the Philosophy Faculty. Adler motivated his request by pointing out that "the topic of the dissertation is in an area which was foreign to antiquity, leading one to believe that it could only be written in the Latin language with great difficulty and not without loss both in form and content."[78] Clearly aware of the Hammerich and Martensen precedents, Adler stated his intention to conduct his oral defense in Latin. The Philosophy Faculty, asked for its views, was aware both of its own earlier position in Hammerich's case and of the circumstance that less than a month earlier the Supervisors had approved the Theology Faculty's recommendation in Martensen's weaker case. Thus not surprisingly the faculty unanimously recommended in favor of Adler's petition, though several members, led by Madvig, still wanted a new rule rather than continual exceptions, and a majority was in favor of permitting the oral defense to take place in Danish as well.[79] Adler was under the same time con-

[78]Adolph Peter Adler's petition to the king (i.e., to the supervisors), dated April 11, 1840; in Rigsarkivet, Dansk Kancelli, Directionen for Universitetet og de lærde Skoler, Forestillinger 1840, nos. 2018-2102, no. 2055, supplement.

[79]Rigsarkivet, Københavns Universitets arkiv, Det filosofiske Fakultet, Dekanatssager, 1840, ad 39; KU 35. 02. 16.

straints as Martensen if he was to defend his dissertation at the June 1840 coronation festival. Therefore the Supervisors expedited Adler's case as they had Martensen's, and on May 7, 1840, citing their own earlier precedents in the cases of Hammerich and Martensen, they recommended approval of Adler's petition, albeit under the same conditions attached to the earlier dispensations, namely, that the oral defense be conducted in Latin and be based upon Latin theses appended to the dissertation.[80]

This was the state of affairs in June 1841 when Kierkegaard petitioned to be permitted to submit his *magister* dissertation in Danish. By this time these "exceptions" were on the way to becoming the rule. In granting the petition of each subsequent petitioner, the authorities cited all the previous exceptions: In Martensen's case, Hammerich's case was cited; in Adler's case, both Martensen's and Hammerich's were cited. Everyone in academic circles knew of these cases. Thus it is not at all surprising that Kierkegaard cited Hammerich's and Adler's cases in his petition. Kierkegaard was personally acquainted with both men. He had known Hammerich from childhood because both the Kierkegaard and Hammerich families (along with the families of Kierkegaard's fiancée Regine Olsen and his lifelong friend Emil Boesen, whose mother was Hammerich's aunt) were members of the Herrnhut (i.e., Moravian) Congregation of Brothers on Stormgade in Copenhagen, and he probably saw Hammerich from time to time during their years at the university. Kierkegaard also knew Adler from his university years, as we know from Hans Brøchner's account of a conversation between Kierkegaard and Adler dating from that period (which of course antedated Kierkegaard's later fascination with Adler's claims of special religious knowledge).[81] Both Hammerich and Adler could have given Kierkegaard detailed accounts of their petitions to submit Danish-language dissertations, along with specific advice about what wording to include, e.g., the offer to append Latin theses and to conduct the oral debate in Latin, something which would scarcely

---

[80]Rigsarkivet, Dansk Kancelli, Directionen for Universitetet of de lærde Skoler, Forestillingsprotokoller, 1840, no. 2055.

[81]See Kirmmse, *Encounters*, 228.

have occurred to Kierkegaard on his own. (Alternatively or additionally, Kierkegaard's friend and advisor F. C. Sibbern could have provided him with the same information.)

What *is* surprising, on the other hand, is that in citing precedents Kierkegaard did *not* mention Martensen's case. Perhaps Howard and Edna Hong have the whole answer (CI, xi) when they surmise that Kierkegaard "probably" did not cite the Martensen precedent because Martensen had not actually made use of the dispensation granted him and because Kierkegaard thought Martensen might sit in judgment of his dissertation (though, in the event, Martensen's role in this capacity was marginal). But the Martensen precedent did not seem irrelevant in other, later cases, e.g., the case of *Cand. theol.* K. W. Wiborg, whose successful petition in 1842 for permission to submit a Danish-language *magister* dissertation on Scandinavian mythology explicitly cited a list of all previous successful petitioners, including Hammerich, Martensen, Adler, and S. A. Kierkegaard.[82]

So perhaps there is also something else at work in Kierkegaard's neglect of the Martensen precedent. Perhaps Kierkegaard's failure to include Martensen along with his mention of Hammerich and Adler stems from some early animus he felt toward Martensen, and which he may have felt was reciprocated. There are reasonable grounds for this conjecture. We know that in his early years as a theological student (most probably 1833–1834) Kierkegaard employed Martensen as a tutor and that he subsequently attended Martensen's lectures at the university in the winter of 1838–1839, not long after Martensen had taken over this responsibility from the late Poul Martin Møller. Since we know that Kierkegaard had an almost worshipful, disciple-like relationship to Møller, and that at some point in 1841 he expressed to Sibbern his caustic resentment at Rasmus Nielsen's temerity in thinking that he could step into Møller's shoes,[83] it is not unreasonable to surmise that Kierkegaard may well have harbored similar feelings about what he would have perceived as Martensen's presumptu-

---

[82]The case of K. W. Wiborg is in Rigsarkivet, Dansk Kancelli, Directionen for Universitetet og de lærde Skoler, Forestillinger 1842 (filed together with Forestillinger 1845), no. 2318.

[83]See the account of this incident in the final section of the present essay.

ousness with respect to the late Møller. For Martensen's part, we know from his memoirs (which, it is true, are very jaundiced and written long after the fact) that Kierkegaard did not make a pleasant impression on his tutor.[84] And we also know that Kierkegaard had come to Martensen during the writing of *The Concept of Irony*, had read him portions of it aloud, and that Martensen had not been impressed, a fact which can hardly have been lost on Kierkegaard.[85]

And finally, although this may not relate directly to Kierkegaard's decision to omit mention of Martensen in his dispensation petition of June 1841, the following ought to be mentioned here in connection with the rest of our examination of the Kierkegaard-Martensen relationship in the context of *The Concept of Irony*: With the very last words of his dissertation Kierkegaard referred directly to Martensen's glowing review (actually more an encomium than a review) of J. L. Heiberg's *Nye Digte* (New Poems).[86] By the end

---

[84]Martensen:

He [Søren Kierkegaard] had his own way of arranging his tutoring. He did not follow any set syllabus, but only asked that I lecture to him and converse with him. I chose to lecture to him on the main points of Schleiermacher's dogmatics and then discuss them. I recognized immediately that his was not an ordinary intellect but that he also had an irresistible urge to sophistry, to hairsplitting games, which showed itself at every opportunity and was often tiresome. I recollect in particular that it surfaced when we examined the doctrine of divine election, where there is, so to speak, an open door for sophists. (Cited in Kirmmse, *Encounters*, 196.)

[85]Martensen:

He once came to me in my home and wished to read me part of his treatise on the concept of irony—as far as I remember, a polemic against Friedrich Schlegel's one-sided aestheticism. I let him read, but only expressed appreciation rather coolly. A contributing factor was his language and style, with its intolerable discursiveness. The many, tiring repetitions, the unendingly long sentences, and the affected and mannered expressions were unpleasant to me, just as they have always disturbed me when I read his works. But he appears not to have forgotten that I failed to display a greater enthusiasm for his opus. (Cited in Kirmmse, *Encounters*, 198-99.)

[86]H. L. Martensen, review of *Nye Digte* by J. L. Heiberg, in *Fædrelandet*, 2. Aargang, nos. 398-400, Sunday–Tuesday, January 10-12, 1841. The last lines of Martensen's review are: "In the present case we must therefore hope that the author [J. L. Heiberg] is granted new and fresh recognition, because with his work he has raised himself and our literature to previously unknown heights."

of *The Concept of Irony*, any suspicious reader with a sense of Kierkegaard's wit might well already have come to the conclusion that Kierkegaard's dissertation was not only *about* irony, but was *itself* ironic and that Kierkegaard's praise of Martensen's fawning relationship to Heiberg might plausibly be construed as ironic mockery. We cannot discount the possibility, or even the likelihood, that what seems plausible to us may also have dawned on Martensen. There appear to have been a number of good reasons for Kierkegaard and Martensen to give one another a wide berth.

B. Readers' Comments on Kierkegaard's Dissertation

It is clear that Kierkegaard was regarded by the Philosophy Faculty as a brilliant but difficult and intractable young man who must be handled with care. It is also clear that there were no doubts about his intellectual abilities or about the quality of what he had submitted to the faculty for acceptance as a dissertation for the *magister* degree. This is why all the criticism of Kierkegaard seems to be just so much nibbling at the edges, wheel spinning, letting off steam. And, finally, it is clear that Kierkegaard had a firm friend and ally in F. C. Sibbern, who, fortunately for Kierkegaard, was then serving as Dean of the Philosophy Faculty and was thus in an ideal position to guide Kierkegaard's somewhat unwieldy and unconventional work through the very conventional machinery of the University of Copenhagen.

Sibbern's evaluation of *The Concept of Irony* is not only positive, but insightful, particularly when he views Kierkegaard's Socrates as a further development along the lines that had recently been adumbrated by Schleiermacher. Sibbern's suggested title change is also very apt, though he undoubtedly knew better than anyone how little likely it was that Kierkegaard would change the title—or anything else. Hence Sibbern's criticisms of the work and of Kierkegaard's sarcastic exuberance are very modest and not terribly specific, expressing the desire that "in the final revision of the dissertation a few things appropriate to a lower sort of genre be trimmed away as luxuriant growths." This was a concession to the criticisms that were sure to follow when Kierkegaard's dissertation made its rounds of the appropriate readers (Madvig, Petersen, and Brøndsted), accompanied by the comment sheet on which Sibbern had made his remarks and on which and the others would record theirs sequentially. But the horticultural figure about trimming away "luxuriant growths" was not merely a concession, it was also a lightning rod, as it turned out, with each successive reader building upon the botanical language, thereby venting his frustration with Kierkegaard's alternately adolescent and magisterial manner—and himself not yet a *magister!*—without actually daring to make any real, substantive requirements for alterations or even offering any concrete suggestions. The gadfly Kierkegaard was as maddening and elusive at the very start of his career as he would be at the end. Sibbern closes his remarks by urging, as he will repeatedly throughout the affair, that the matter be handled as expeditiously as possible. One might ask whether Sibbern is behaving more like the Dean of the Philosophy Faculty or like Kierkegaard's personal lieutenant. (Kierkegaard's relation to Sibbern will be investigated further in the concluding section of this essay.)

J. N. Madvig, it is clear, was in touch with Kierkegaard during the writing of the dissertation, and he immediately starts out with such a positive assessment—"it bears the stamp of such intellectual liveliness and fresh thought, and of multifaceted studies both of Greek literature and of modern philosophy and aesthetics that it seems to me entirely to qualify the author for the *magister* degree"—that his subsequent harsh criticisms lose all their force and fall dead to the floor. They are there for form's sake, so that no one could accuse Madvig of failing to uphold good taste and the proper tone. At the end of his remarks, Madvig's tirade breaks off as abruptly as it began, and he closes with a whimper, saying in effect "What's the use? The 'particular nature' of the author, which is the source of his 'tasteless and vulgar excrescences,' is also what would make negotiations about removing them awkward and fruitless—and anyway, the final version of the dissertation will not be reviewed by anyone, not even the Dean." Did Madvig and the others suspect that there was complicity here? that the cunning Kierkegaard was exploiting the faithful Dean, bending the man to his own purposes? At any rate, for all his vehement criticisms, Madvig is not willing to stipulate a single *condition* for the acceptance of Kierkegaard's work. And now the rest of the faculty reviewers, each of whom could read the remarks of the previous readers, would follow the lead of Madvig, their most illustrious colleague (and the only one who had *actually read* the manuscript) who from now on would drop entirely out of sight in the matter of Kierkegaard.

F. C. Petersen, complaining about the shortness of the time he has had to read this lengthy dissertation (though he has had it for two weeks), begins his remarks by agreeing with Sibbern and Madvig that Kierkegaard's work qualifies him for the *magister* degree. Seeming to take a slightly tougher stand, Petersen conditions his approval upon Kierkegaard appending Latin theses to the dissertation—a condition which is altogether toothless inasmuch as Kierkegaard in his petition of more than a month earlier had already stipulated his willingness to append just such theses. Thereafter Petersen airs his pique with Kierkegaard's "excesses of the sarcastic or mocking sort," but then shrugs his shoulders because "the author's personality" makes him neither willing nor able to undertake such changes. And finally, in a logical *non sequitur*, Petersen leaves negotiations concerning these unattainable changes to Dean Sibbern, who Madvig has already noted will not see the final version in any event!

The great Hellenist P. O. Brøndsted begins his comments on the dissertation with the complaint that he has not had time "to read the whole of it with studied attention," which seems reasonable enough because he only had it for a single day. Brøndsted then goes on to complain of "the Most Excellent Dean's" desire to rush the matter through "before the beginning of the summer holidays," and concludes, with some annoyance, that "there is nothing to do but let it go down the faculty's railroad in a *velocifère* [express coach] (I mean its fastest possible conveyance)." Thus Brøndsted states rather than implies that Sibbern is literally *railroading* Kierkegaard's dissertation through the faculty. But then, despite—or perhaps because of—his scanty acquaintance with the manuscript, Brøndsted accedes with respect to the principal issue: He "can vote that the dissertation be accepted for defense," with the condition, of course, that Kierkegaard supply Latin theses, which as we have repeatedly seen, is no condition at all, since Kierkegaard had already yielded on this point. Brøndsted then repeats that he will have to "postpone a closer acquaintance with this book until it is printed," but his allegedly fleeting look at the work had not prevented him from taking umbrage, like his colleagues before him, at Kierkegaard's stylistic "excrescences" which "testify to the author's occasional inability to resist the inner temptation to leap over the boundary which separates both genuine irony and reasonable satire from the unrefreshing territory of vulgar exaggeration." Brøndsted concludes by noting, rather huffily, that since Kierkegaard, because of his "personal preference," will not take advice on matters of this sort, it is appropriate and salutary that the faculty, having ascertained the adequacy of the work as a piece of scholarship, wash its hands of the matter and walk away from it with a clear conscience.

Kierkegaard's dossier went next to H. C. Ørsted, who received it as part of his duties as Rector of the university. Ørsted was also a member of the Philosophy Faculty and thus normally entitled to read Kierkegaard's dissertation, though, as he had not been put on the evaluation committee by Dean Sibbern, his opinion was not required and in any event not binding. Nonetheless Ørsted took the time to read, or at least glance through, Kierkegaard's work, and like the others he focused on what he found offensive in it: Despite "significant intellectual strengths, I nevertheless cannot deny that it makes a generally unpleasant impression on me, particularly because of two things, both of which I detest: verbosity and affectation." Ørsted admitted that he did not doubt that the dissertation was worthy of acceptance, but still, as Rector, he felt that he could more or less require that Sibbern add yet another reader, either H. L. Martensen, who had until recently served as a *lektor* in philosophy, or Rasmus Nielsen, who was the newly appointed professor of philosophy. Perhaps Ørsted's reasoning was that, as outsiders/newcomers, Martensen and Nielsen would bring a perspective that the seasoned veterans of the Philosophy Faculty lacked—or perhaps merely that Nielsen and Martensen had not yet been cowed into submission by unique strengths of Kierkegaard's character.

In any event, Ørsted's hopes for an "outside" opinion were not fulfilled. Sibbern had noted in his letter of transmittal to the Consistory (which Ørsted ought to have seen) that "Prof. Nielsen did not wish to have the dissertation." Why Nielsen did not wish to have it is not known, but perhaps he knew that Kierkegaard had been very sarcastic and critical to Sibbern with respect to his own appointment to Poul Martin Møller's old philosophy chair, which had taken place only a couple of months earlier.[87] In his introduction to his translation of *The Concept of Irony*, Lee M. Capel states that "Kierkegaard's attack on Nielsen for accepting his appointment without being prepared to fill it [was] an attack made to Sibbern personally and known to Nielsen,"[88] implying that Sibbern had repeated Kierkegaard's words. Although Capel provides no documentation for this, Sibbern was such an honest and naive soul that one can imagine that in an unguarded moment he could simply have blurted out Kierkegaard's criticisms, which had certainly rankled Sibbern, either directly to Nielsen himself or to a third party who took them further to Nielsen. At any rate, Nielsen refused to have anything to do with Kierkegaard's dissertation. So Sibbern was forced to turn to Martensen who, as we have seen, probably had his own reasons to be wary of Kierkegaard. Still, Martensen was a junior colleague, and this was a direct request from the venerable Dean of the faculty he had served until recently, a request, moreover, which had originated with Rector Ørsted, head of the university. So Martensen complied, but just barely, and satisfied the letter of the law with a one-sentence reply: "Since Professor Sibbern has requested that I cast a vote in this matter, I hereby declare that I concur with the views already voiced and thus vote for the acceptance of the dissertation." The evaluation process was complete.

But in considering the reactions of his teachers, perhaps we ought not be too quick to overplay the uniqueness of Kierkegaard's force of character, tempting as it may be to do so, before considering a bit more of the documentary evidence. Just as Kierkegaard was not the first or the only aspiring degree candidate to wish to write a Danish dissertation and to agree to the compromise of adding Latin theses to his work, so the documentary record teaches us that Kierkegaard was quite normal in other aspects as well. Like Kierkegaard, Martin Hammerich was apparently capable of including in his work tendentious asides and jibes which appeared tasteless to his teachers on the Philosophy Faculty, and

---

[87]The account of this incident is in the final section of this essay.
[88]Søren Kierkegaard, *The Concept of Irony*, translated and with an introduction and notes by Lee M. Capel (Collins: London, 1966) "Introduction," 12.

the comment sheet which circulated through the faculty bears this out.[89] E. C. Werlauff, a professor of Scandinavian history on the Philosophy Faculty, found Hammerich's diction "perhaps inappropriate for an academic piece" and his tone "petulant." Prof. Molbech, a Nordic philologist, agreed with his colleagues that certain of Hammerich's "polemical expressions" were "inappropriate" but he attributed them to "the author's peculiar style and manner of expression," and Molbech would at most be party "to directing the author's attention to what we believe we have discovered of this sort of thing, without *requiring* [emphasis in original] any changes as an absolute condition."

One could almost think that Hammerich was being handled with the same kid gloves that were subsequently used with Kierkegaard, but then J. N. Madvig weighed in and the situation changed entirely. Although he begins by agreeing that Hammerich's dissertation, by virtue of its "brilliant perceptions and thoughtful working-through of the material as well as by virtue of the original points of view it develops" is "*completely deserving* [emphasis in original] of acceptance," Madvig goes on to complain of "a certain verbosity." And then, when he gets to Hammerich's thoughtless and brash sarcasm, Madvig puts his foot down: "One can certainly allow the author a number of almost youthful expressions, but a couple of them are of the type that I think *we must require* [emphasis in original] altered in a dissertation."

Madvig's elder colleague F. C. Petersen is a bit more lenient but he agrees that "it could be *required* [emphasis in original] . . . that certain 'unnecessary and merely annoying' remarks be removed or modified." H. C. Ørsted also finds "the changes required by Professors Madvig and Petersen to be necessary." And the historian Laurids Engelstoft also makes it "an *absolute and unalterable* [emphasis in original] condition that the author excise *all* [emphasis in original] inappropriate and inadmissable expres-

---

[89]The remarks in this and the two subsequent paragraphs are from the comment sheet circulated by F. C. Sibbern, dean of the Philosophy Faculty in connection with Martin J. Hammerich's *magister* dissertation, dated November 24, 1835 through February 25, 1836; in Rigsarkivet, Københavns Universitets arkiv, Det filosofiske Fakultet, Dekanatssager 1835–1836, I; KU 35. 02. 01.

sions and formulations . . . which have been noted and labelled as such by Professors Madvig and Petersen."

So what was unique about Kierkegaard was not the desire to slip free of the Latin dissertation requirement, nor even the penchant for including youthfully brash and sarcastic writing in a supposedly academic work, a brashness which was just as capable of inciting the faculty against him as it had been incited against Hammerich. What was unique about Kierkegaard was the *something else* in his character that made the faculty afraid to follow through: something that frustrated the intentions of his professors, vexed as they were, to discipline him; something that caused the illustrious Madvig to beat a quiet retreat; something that made the great Brøndsted want to get rid of Kierkegaard by sending him on his way in an "express coach."

Søren Kierkegaard was a tease, "the Fork." His writing could make his professors fume, but so could Martin Hammerich's. There is a temptation to misplace the emphasis by focussing on the vexation Kierkegaard caused his elders. It is not unusual for bright young minds to vex their elders, and it is not unusual for the elders to fume, sometimes at length and in writing. But there is fuming and there is fuming. In Hammerich's case, the fuming of his professors was *a prelude to action*, to the imposition of the *"absolute and unalterable condition"* that he omit some parts and alter others of what he had written, and the record shows that these criticisms were communicated directly to Hammerich.[90] In Kierkegaard's case, the fuming of his professors was *a substitute for action*: They were merely letting off steam for their private relief and mutual reassurance; they knew before committing their frustrations to paper that they would make no demands on Kierkegaard. There is nothing in the documentary record that indicates that the professors' critical remarks were ever communicated to Kierkegaard. (Indeed, the record shows that the only official critique ever communicated to Kierkegaard concerned the Latin theses, and he seems to have blithely ignored it.) What was

---

[90]"Journal of the Philosophy Faculty," entries of February 26 and March 4, 1836; in Rigsarkivet, Københavns Universitets arkiv, Det filosofiske Fakultet, Diarium 1835–1836, KU 35. 01. 04.

unusual about Søren Kierkegaard was his talent for *getting away with it*, for spellbinding and disarming the opposition.

C. The Latin Theses

The communiqué of the Consistory to the Philosophy Faculty, dated August 28, 1841 (document 17) was Søren Kierkegaard's official notification that the Supervisors of the University had secured the king's assent to his petition for a dispensation from the Latin dissertation requirement. It was also the official notification to Kierkegaard of his obligation (to which he had already agreed) to append to his dissertation Latin theses which would serve as the basis of oral arguments. Kierkegaard was shown the communiqué and was required to sign it as proof that he had been notified of its contents. Since the document itself was dated August 28, and Kierkegaard delivered the required Latin theses to the faculty on September 6 or 7, it seems likely that he had already prepared them, at least in draft form. In any event, Kierkegaard knew the rules of the game from the cases of Hammerich, Martensen, and Adler. He had offered to produce the theses in early June and had had plenty of time to prepare them.

The Philosophy Faculty journal for September 7-8, 1841 notes the receipt of Kierkegaard's Latin theses, which were then circulated to Professors Brøndsted, Petersen, and Madvig. At the top of the comment sheet he circulated to the readers, Dean Sibbern included a note stating that he was "submitting them for your approval, unless someone wishes to require any of them be altered." The readers' written comments on the theses were returned the next day, and their substance was communicated to Kierkegaard orally. As it turned out, two of the readers did want several theses altered or omitted. Brøndsted wished to see thesis I ("The similarity between Christ and Socrates consists essentially in their dissimilarity") omitted because of the "offensive" nature of the public discussion it would probably entail. And he wished to see thesis XV ("Just as philosophy begins with doubt, so also a life that may be called human begins with irony") omitted because it would inevitably lead to a fruitless conflict about what constitutes "human life." Finally, Brøndsted also wished to see alterations in thesis IX ("Socrates drove all his contemporaries out of substantiality as if naked from a shipwreck, undermined actuality, envisioned ideality in the distance, touched it, but did not take possession of it") because he did not believe it would be possible to converse in Latin about "substantiality," "actuality," and "ideality." F. C. Petersen favored alterations in thesis XIII ("Irony is not so much apathy, devoid of the more tender emotions of the soul; instead, it must rather be regarded as vexation at the possession also by others of that which it desires for itself") but did not specify what they ought to be. On the other hand, Petersen opposed Brøndsted with respect to thesis IX, which he favored leaving as it was. Madvig had no comment whatever with respect to the theses. On balance then, if we may disregard Petersen's vague suggestion of alterations to thesis XIII, and if we regard Petersen's support for the original text of thesis IX as canceling out Brøndsted's call for alterations in it, the changes "required" come down to Brøndsted's call for the omission of Theses I and XV. If, as the journal of the faculty claims, the substance of these remarks was transmitted to Kierkegaard orally, this was most probably done by Dean Sibbern. One wonders what the good man made of such a vague and partially conflicting set of comments in communicating them to Kierkegaard. We do not have the original text which Kierkegaard submitted to the faculty (or virtually any other "draft" material for *The Concept of Irony*), and thus we cannot be certain that Kierkegaard did not make small changes to some of the theses, perhaps in the direction requested by his readers. But he certainly did not omit theses I and XV, and judging from the dissertation in its published form and from what survives of the readers' comments, it seems likely that Kierkegaard made no changes whatever, and that the faculty members acquiesced in his stubbornness. That would be typical of both parties.

D. The Oral Defense

On the comment sheet for reactions to Kierkegaard's Latin theses that was circulated to Professors Brøndsted, Madvig, and Petersen on September 7, 1841, Dean F. C. Sibbern states that Kierkegaard hopes to have his dissertation back from the printer in time for an oral defense by the end of September. Sibbern further states that he will be one of the two official opponents and that—presumably because the dissertation is "with continual reference to Socrates"—he would expect that one of the two professors of Greek (Brøndsted or Petersen) would be the other opponent, or, failing that, Madvig, because he is the one "who is most familiar with the dissertation." Brøndsted, the first recipient of the theses and of Sibbern's note, still insists that his knowledge of the book is scanty and that "my gentlemen colleagues . . . know the book better than I do." But even though he makes this demurrer, Brøndsted grants that if the proceedings "are set for one of the last days of the month, I have nothing against being appointed as one of the official opponents." This was all the other two readers needed in order to escape the burden of being Kierkegaard's official opponent. Madvig notes that he has been terribly busy and that the subject matter of the dissertation makes it more appropriate for the two Hellenists, but he does say that if he gets a chance he might yet serve as an opponent *ex auditorio*. Petersen insists that he is still "very poorly acquainted with the dissertation," that he is too busy because he must soon serve as examiner in final examinations, and that therefore, since Prof. Brøndsted has offered to serve if the timing is right (and Petersen believes that the timing *will* be right), he will defer to Brøndsted—or, failing him, to Madvig (which is odd, since on the same sheet of paper, immediately preceding Petersen's remarks, Madvig had flatly stated that he would *not* serve as an official opponent). An entry in the journal of the Philosophy Faculty dated September 8, 1841 notes the outcome—Sibbern and Brøndsted will be the official opponents—and sets a date for the public defense: Wednesday, September 29, 1841.

Unfortunately no record survives of what was said at the oral defense, but we do have the official letter which reports the names of the opponents, both official and *ex auditorio*, and which agrees with the two brief newspaper accounts of the event.[91] The proceed-

---

[91]The two newspaper accounts are those in *Berlingske Tidende* and *Dagen* for Wednesday and Thursday, September 29 and 30, 1841. The only way in which the newspaper accounts differ from the official letter sent by Profs. Brøndsted and Sibbern to the Supervisors of the University (document 24) is that the account in *Dagen* states that the second session proceedings lasted from 4:00 PM in the afternoon until 7:30 PM in the evening, while the official letter states that the proceedings lasted until 7:00 PM, as does the account in *Berlingske Tidende*. Beyond listing the official and *ex auditorio* opponents, neither newspaper account

ings were held in an auditorium at the University of Copenhagen and "an unusually large audience" was in attendance. The high level of interest may have been stirred up by the reputation as a polemicist Kierkegaard had already earned by dint of his various newspaper articles and his critique of Hans Christian Andersen. Perhaps, as well, word had got out that Søren Kierkegaard's dissertation was controversial and that his defense might possibly ignite the same sort of fireworks as those touched off by his brother Peter Christian's defense four and one-half years earlier. (P. C. Kierkegaard's famous dissertation defense will be dealt with below.) It should also be remembered that the sizable audience turned out fully aware that all the proceedings would be in *Latin*, but this was not quite as off-putting as it might sound to modern ears, as Latin occupied a position in the academic world something like that occupied *de facto* by English today.

As is still customary with such proceedings, the first to speak was one of the official opponents, namely, Prof. Brøndsted. Normally, as in this instance, the other official opponent would speak at the conclusion of the proceedings. This position was reserved for Dean Sibbern, who was in charge of the entire affair and had the responsibility for leading them to an orderly conclusion. It is not known what Brøndsted queried Kierkegaard about, but it is reasonable to assume that he was generally positive and did not make much, if anything, out of the sort of criticisms he had raised (but not acted upon) in his reader's report. As the faculty had already voted to accept the dissertation for defense, the faculty's official opponents would not normally have offered radical criticism in any case.

After Brøndsted came the series of *ex auditorio* opponents, the first of whom was Prof. F. C. Petersen, who had said that he was too busy with final examinations to serve as an official opponent. It is conceivable that Petersen, since he was not an official opponent, may have given vent to some of the peeve he had displayed during the in-house judgment of Kierkegaard's dissertation, but it is not terribly likely. Like Sibbern, Brøndsted, and the

---

characterizes the proceedings, with the exception that the *Berlingske Tidende* version says that "an unusually large audience" was present.

others, Petersen had voted to accept the dissertation. In any case, if Petersen's presence was somewhat unexpected, the same could be said of the *absence* of Madvig, who in begging off had held out the hope of attending the proceedings and making an appearance *ex auditorio*. The failure of Madvig to appear may not have been terribly surprising to Kierkegaard. Hans Brøchner tells a story of Kierkegaard being let down by Madvig on another occasion (unfortunately, we do not know if it was before or after the dissertation defense):

> On the occasion of my lectures he once spoke to me about the definition of virtue in Aristotelian metaphysics as μεσότης. He had correctly seen that this definition was not valid for virtue in general, but only for ethical virtue—something which by no means was generally accepted at that time. He told me that he had sought enlightenment from Madvig and Sibbern on this point and on several others in the *Nichomachean Ethics*. Madvig had told him that it was so long since he had read that work that he no longer could recall it. "And Madvig is otherwise a brick," added S. K. Sibbern, on the other hand, had immediately been able to provide him with the information he sought.[92]

After Prof. Petersen came Johan Ludvig Heiberg, a titular professor at the Royal Military College, an important aesthetician, and the undisputed king of the Danish theatre. In addition, Heiberg was Denmark's leading Hegelian, though by the early 1840s Hegel's star had begun to set in Denmark. Heiberg had also recently published his finest work, *Nye Digte*, which, as noted, had been the subject of Martensen's glowing review earlier in the year, a review which Kierkegaard pointedly mentioned in the last lines of *The Concept of Irony*. Furthermore, near the beginning of the dissertation (CI, 26) Kierkegaard had mentioned by name a work by Heiberg, *Alferne* (The Elves), and there are a number of tangential or possible references to Heiberg scattered throughout the book. And of course Hegel was a major focus of the dissertation as well. So there were ample reasons for Heiberg to show up and debate with Kierkegaard.

Of interest equal to Heiberg's decision to attend the proceedings and step forth as an opponent *ex auditorio*, however, is the

---

[92]Kirmmse, *Encounters*, 241.

likelihood that his good friend H. L. Martensen did not attend at all. For the reasons set forth earlier in this essay, it is reasonable to assume that Martensen and Kierkegaard were wary of one another. When forced to comment on Kierkegaard's dissertation, Martensen had been laconic in the extreme. Were he now to attend the public defense, people would expect him to come forward as an opponent. It was wiser and safer to stay away. Martensen and Madvig are the only faculty members with whom Kierkegaard is known to have discussed his dissertation prior to its submission to the faculty in June 1841, but neither came forward as opponents *ex auditorio*, and almost certainly neither attended the defense at all.

Heiberg was followed by Kierkegaard's elder brother, Peter Christian Kierkegaard, without doubt a "friendly" opponent. In their "Historical Introduction" to their translation of *The Concept of Irony* (CI, xi), the Hongs mention (though without documentation) that Peter Christian had served as his younger brother's "official advocate" during the public defense. This sort of aide was entitled a *respondens*, and it was not uncommon for degree aspirants whose Latin was weak to have such assistance.[93] Søren Kierkegaard's Latin was excellent, but that does not mean that he might not have used his elder brother as support in this technical sense, though I am not aware of any documentary evidence of this.

As mentioned in the discussion of the Theology Faculty earlier in this essay, Peter Christian had defended his theological *licentiat* degree in January 1836 in a public debate which became legendary for its contentiousness and controversy, a debate in which P. C. Kierkegaard, ponderous in print, had had an opportunity to demonstrate his dexterity and strength as a dialectician in verbal combat. Not long before the elder Kierkegaard submitted his *licentiat* dissertation to the Theology Faculty in August 1835, he had publicly indicated his sympathy with the Grundtvigian camp in the theological wars of the day. Instantly his stock fell with the established theologians who dominated the Theology Faculty. His dissertation was almost rejected by the faculty, but they sensed that that would be a political disaster and instead agreed to accept it for defense, "although not without misgivings both with respect

[93]Kjærulff Hellesen and Tuxen, "KU 1788–1848," 260-61.

to its contents and form"[94]—an extraordinarily negative remark, bordering on the uncivil. (Whatever the Philosophy Faculty's feelings about the excesses in *Søren* Kierkegaard's dissertation, it would never have dared to address him in this manner.) As it turned out, the public defense was a *tour de force* in which P. C. Kierkegaard put his opponents to flight, and even the official description of the event sent by the Theology Faculty to the Supervisors of the University grudgingly conceded the elder Kierkegaard's brilliance in debate: "In view of its inferior scholarly worth, the faculty had not been without misgivings in accepting the dissertation for defense, but in the oral defense the author displayed unusual talent and skill in the art of debate."[95]

Incidentally, it was on this occasion of his oral defense in 1836 that *Peter Christian* Kierkegaard was described as having "played toss-in-a-blanket with the faculty and the other opponents,"[96] and not *Søren* Kierkegaard in 1841, as the Hongs have it their Historical Introduction (CI, xi).[97] Lee M. Capel makes almost the same error, again taking a phrase from the same 1836 letter describing Peter Christian Kierkegaard's famous victory and using it to describe

---

[94]Letter from Prof. M. H. Hohlenberg, Dean of the Theology Faculty to P. C. Kierkegaard, dated October 25, 1835; in Rigsarkivet, Københavns Universitets arkiv, Det teologiske Fakultet, Dekanatssager 1835–1837, KU 31. 02. 08: 1835, løbenr. 167.

[95]Resolution from the University Supervisors to the king, dated February 17, 1836, recommending the granting of the *licentiat* degree in theology to P. C. Kierkegaard; in Rigsarkivet, Dansk Kancelli, Directionen for Universitetet og de lærde Skoler, Forestillingsprotokoller, 1836, no. 1667. The entire affair of P. C. Kierkegaard's *licentiat* degree is the subject of a fine article by the church historian Leif Grane, "Omkring Peter Christian Kierkegaards teologiske disputats," *Kirkehistoriske Samlinger*, 1976, 122-49.

[96]Peter Rørdam, letter to his brother, dated February 23, 1836, in H. F. Rørdam, ed., *Peter Rørdam. Blade af hans Levnedsbog og Brevvexling fra 1806 til 1844* (Copenhagen: Schoenberg, 1891) 17.

[97]The Hongs have the reference to the source of this phrase in Peter Rørdam's letters correct, but apparently did not check it, taking it directly from a misreading of Carl Weltzer's pioneering article, "Omkring Søren Kierkegaards Disputats," in *Kirkehistoriske Samlinger*, 6. række, 6. bind (1948–1950), 284-311. Rørdam's phrase about "playing toss-in-a-blanket with the faculty" appears on page 309 of Weltzer's article.

Søren Kierkegaard's dissertation defense in 1841.⁹⁸ These lapses by previous commentators are not entirely trivial, because without the material erroneously cited by the Hongs and Capel we are forced to admit that we really have no idea of how Søren Kierkegaard's oral defense actually went. In any case, it is reasonable to assume that Søren Kierkegaard had conferred with his brother at least occasionally during the composition of *The Concept of Irony*, and that when the elder Kierkegaard came forward as an opponent he did so as a famous debater and as his younger brother's nestor. Indeed, P. C. Kierkegaard may well have been there as much to intimidate other actual or potential opponents *ex auditorio* as actually to debate his brother Søren.

Next after Peter Christian Kierkegaard came Dr. Andreas Frederik Beck, an eccentric theologian whose Left-Hegelian (Straussian) views prevented him from having a career in the Danish Church. Although we have no record of what Beck said to Kierkegaard during the public debate, he published a rather lengthy review of *The Concept of Irony* in May and June 1842 in the newspaper *Fædrelandet*,⁹⁹ and Kierkegaard replied to him in the columns of the same newspaper.¹⁰⁰ So it is not unreasonable to attempt to reconstruct their exchange during the public debate of September 1841 on the basis of their printed words of 1842. Beck's review is generally positive and in places quite insightful. Early in his review he uses his praise of Kierkegaard's "speculative-critical" writing as a tool with which to criticize the work of Rasmus Nielsen: "Here we do not encounter vague and diffuse reasoning, as we do in Professor Nielsen, about essence and phenomenon, phenomenon and essence, in complete abstraction from the historical."¹⁰¹ On a number of occasions Beck permits his own

⁹⁸See Capel, "Introduction," 12, where he cites Weltzer as stating that *Søren* Kierkegaard was "able to hold his own" [*en Karl for sin Hat*]. Weltzer does indeed use these words, but when he does so, he is citing Peter Rørdam's description of *Peter Christian* Kierkegaard's performance *in 1836*.

⁹⁹*Fædrelandet*, Sunday, May 29, 1842, no. 890, cols. 7133-40, and Sunday, June 5, 1842, no. 897, cols. 7189-91.

¹⁰⁰*Fædrelandet*, Sunday, June 12, 1842, no. 904, cols. 7245-52; English translation in COR, 3-12.

¹⁰¹Beck, cols. 7133-34.

affinities for the Tübingen school to shine through, e.g.: "Xenophon has failed to realize what is essential about the Socratic dialogue, namely, the idea of ironic negativity's soft echo throughout apparently ordinary everyday talk. This or similar insights are asserted in similar fashion by Bruno Bauer with respect to the Gospel of John."[102] But in fairness to Kierkegaard, Beck is quick to point out that Kierkegaard does not share this theological line: "Naturally no notion of this appears in our author, who more frequently makes clear his own preference for traditional theology."[103]

Beck does find some fault with Kierkegaard's dissertation, however, citing the alleged failure to show "the inner relationship" of the ironic to the comic, which "imparts to this part of the investigation a somewhat uncertain character."[104] The only other criticism Beck voices in his otherwise appreciative review comes at the very end, where he is unhappy with "a number of allusions and references in the book, which probably only a very few people will understand and in which this reviewer did not have the honor of following the author."[105] Worse, however, Beck concludes by censuring the dissertation for displaying just the same sort of informal wit which was condemned by Kierkegaard's faculty readers: "The author seems to have been less than fortunate when he has wished to let his wit sparkle in a more positive fashion. Because that which can be pleasing or acceptable in an informal chat or when walking in the street makes a quite different impression when it is expressed with the pretensions that accompany the printed page. It can certainly be amusing, it cannot be denied—but it is not to the author's advantage."[106] If Beck actually expressed some of these sentiments during the public proceedings of September 29, 1841, one wonders how Kierkegaard would have responded, and one can speculate what glee this criticism might have brought to Kierkegaard's professors!

---

[102]Beck, col. 7137.
[103]Beck, col. 7137.
[104]Beck, col. 7139.
[105]Beck, col. 7191.
[106]Beck, col. 7191.

Kierkegaard's response to Beck is included in a short article entitled "Public Confession." The tone of the piece is one of wry and ironic raillery, mockery, a bobbing-and-weaving attack on targets of opportunity, though the underlying theme is alarmed criticism of the regimentation of the age, in general, and of the triumph of "the System" (i.e., Hegel and his epigones), in particular. Though the specific response to Beck is in an appendix to the article, Kierkegaard misses no chance to tease and criticize quite a number of other figures along the way. Rasmus Nielsen is portrayed as a hack, Hegelian system-grinder: "The age is working its way toward the system. Prof. Nielsen has already published 21 sections of his logic, which form the first portion of a *Logic*, which in turn form the first part of an all-encompassing *Encyclopedia* . . . [which] one dares to conclude will be of infinite size" (COR, 5-6, my translation). Also Martensen, who had promised to "go beyond Hegel," comes in for criticism, though not by name: "We have Hegelians. These have in turn divided themselves into two parties. The one party is those who have not got into Hegel, yet are nonetheless Hegelians. The other party are those who have gone beyond Hegel, yet are nonetheless Hegelians" (COR, 6, my translation). No wonder Nielsen and Martensen stayed away from the public defense! Kierkegaard also mentions Heiberg, who is handled ambiguously: "Professor Heiberg has become insignificant" (COR, 7-8, my translation). This is apparently Kierkegaard's indictment of the age for refusing to recognize quality when it encounters it, but of course the sentence also admits of the opposite reading.

And naturally Kierkegaard focuses on Beck. Even in the first part of "Public Confession," Beck, whose Left-Hegelian opus, *Begrebet Mythus eller den religiøse Aands Form* (The Concept of Myth, or the Form of the Religious Spirit), had been published since Kierkegaard's dissertation defense, comes in for abuse: "Has anyone failed to notice that Dr. Beck has abolished religion in order to make room for the System?" (COR, 7-8, my translation). When Kierkegaard finally turns to Beck's review, his tone is even harsher. Kierkegaard is far less generous to Beck than Beck had been to him:

> In a review in *Fædrelandet* Dr. Beck has rescued my dissertation from the oblivion of the reading public. The honored reviewer

provides an overview of the book's contents from which I have
really not learned anything new. Toward the end he believes that
I deserve to be criticized because there are a number of allusions
he does not understand. . . . It is punishment enough for me that
Dr. Beck has not understood me, and all the more so because it
was already burdensome to me that Dr. Beck believed he had understood me in a number of passages. (COR, 10, my translation)

What Kierkegaard particularly objects to, it is clear, is not so much
Beck's review in *Fædrelandet* as what he perceives as Beck's attempt
in his recent book, *Begrebet Mythus*, to assimilate Kierkegaard to
the Left Hegelians Strauss, Feuerbach, Vatke, and Bruno Bauer.
Since this part of Kierkegaard's criticism is not really a response to
Beck's review of his dissertation, a review in which Beck was
actually quite careful to dissociate Kierkegaard from the Left
Hegelians and from his own views, it is unlikely that this issue
entered into the oral debate in September 1841, but the debate
between Kierkegaard and Beck was certainly sharp and almost
undoubtedly focused on the role of Hegel in *The Concept of Irony*.

The exchange with A. F. Beck was followed by a two-hour
intermission, from 2:00 to 4:00 PM. When the public defense
resumed, the first opponent *ex auditorio* was Senior Master (i.e.,
head teacher) Frederik Peter Jacob Dahl (1788–1864). An expert in
Scandinavian philology, Dahl had left Copenhagen briefly to teach
philosophy at the University of Christiania (now Oslo) and had
then returned to take charge of his old preparatory school,
Frederiksborg School in northern Zealand. Dahl had been J. N.
Madvig's teacher of Danish language and literature when Madvig
had been a pupil there. It is conceivable that Dahl had been told
by Madvig that Kierkegaard's defense would be an interesting one.

Dahl was followed by *Cand. mag.* H. J. Thue (erroneously
labelled a university student in the *Berlingske Tidende* account) from
Norway, who had recently arrived at the University of Copenhagen with the support of a fellowship to study classical mythology
and archaeology.[107] Next came Christian Fenger Christens (1819–
1855), who had been a theological student with Kierkegaard at the

---

[107]Some of the information on Thue is from the excellent introduction to the
commentary volume that accompanies *Om Begrebet Ironi* in *Søren Kierkegaards
Skrifter* (SKS, K1:144). No source is given.

university. The two young men had been friends as students, and when they took their final examinations, Christens finished third in the class, Kierkegaard fourth.[108] The two remained close during the year following Kierkegaard's oral defense, when both were studying in Berlin. Hans Brøchner writes:

> S. K. met many Danes in the winter [of 1841–1842] he spent in Berlin. Many of them had gone there in order to hear Schelling. Among them was my late friend Christian Fenger Christens. S. K. spoke of him with great appreciation; later he told me that Christens was the brightest of all the Danes who had been in Berlin that winter.[109]

During the winter Kierkegaard and Christens were in Berlin, the latter passed Brøchner's greetings on to Kierkegaard and conveyed Kierkegaard's regards back to Brøchner.[110] Given the mutual respect that Kierkegaard and Christens had for one another and the cordiality of their relationship, it is reasonable to surmise that Kierkegaard had discussed part or all of his dissertation with Christens during the writing of it, and it is certain that Christens was a "friendly" opponent.

Last came Sibbern, who as Dean of the Philosophy Faculty was an official opponent. His task was to wrap up the proceedings and bring them to an appropriate end. It is not unlikely that Sibbern took into account some of the remarks of the earlier opponents, and it is certain that he was a decorous and amicable critic. Sibbern was warm and open toward even younger students, and he had been a friend of Kierkegaard since the latter's early years at the university. (Sibbern's relation to Kierkegaard will be examined further in the next and final section of this essay.) Sibbern's concluding remarks may also have included some of the points he made in his written assessment on the comment sheet he had circulated among the various faculty members prior to the acceptance of Kierkegaard's dissertation for defense, but it is pretty certain that those oral remarks would not have included any

---

[108]Kirmmse, *Encounters*, 228.
[109]Kirmmse, *Encounters*, 230.
[110]Kirmmse, *Encounters*, 229.

mention of his one minor complaint about "luxuriant growths" of material that was "appropriate to a lower sort of genre."

Sibbern was Kierkegaard's protector and undoubtedly had a controlling hand in drafting the final letter (document 24) from the Philosophy faculty to the Supervisors of the University, in which Kierkegaard's performance at his oral defense was summed up: "The intelligence and intellectual liveliness, the proficiency and dialectical skill, which are so much in evidence in *Candidat* Kierkegaard's dissertation, were also prominent in his defense of it." In sum, there can be no doubt that Søren Kierkegaard's oral defense of his dissertation, if it perhaps lacked the pyrotechnics attendant upon his elder brother's more politically charged performance several years earlier, was nonetheless a triumph.

On October 1, two days after Kierkegaard's defense, the Supervisors were notified and were asked to recommend the granting of the *magister* degree; they transmitted a resolution to this effect to the king on October 12. On October 14, 1841 King Christian VIII authorized the granting of the *magister* degree to Søren Kierkegaard, but the Supervisors did not notify university officials of this until October 26, which was one day after Søren Kierkegaard, his engagement to Regine Olsen finally and definitively ended, had departed for Berlin. The *magister* diploma was sent to him by university functionaries.

IV. Interpretation and Summary

The particular circumstances concerning Kierkegaard's *magister* dissertation will here be viewed in the context of Kierkegaard's entire life. The events surrounding Kierkegaard's dissertation tell us a good deal about how Kierkegaard came to be the person he was and about what became of him subsequently.

A. Sibbern on Kierkegaard

Central to this larger, synoptic understanding of the place of the dissertation in Kierkegaard's life is an understanding of his relation to F. C. Sibbern, who was a great deal more than a university Dean in this drama. We know from Sibbern's account that the two had a fairly close and friendly relationship almost from the beginning of Kierkegaard's career as a university student:

"Early on, he looked to me for advice and not infrequently came to my house, and I visited him. I often walked with him or rode with him in a carriage."[111] They discussed, among other things, philosophical matters, including Hegel.[112] We know as well that Sibbern's relationship with Kierkegaard encompassed more than academic and intellectual concerns, and that it extended, specifically, to Kierkegaard's love life. Regine Olsen Schlegel testified that Sibbern "had been a frequent guest on [her] carriage rides with Kierkegaard," and Sibbern recollected that "when [Kierkegaard] became engaged, he brought me along to visit his sweetheart."[113]

Thus, during the period that Kierkegaard's dissertation was in the works, in addition to serving as Kierkegaard's professor and to providing the guidance expected of a Dean, Sibbern was also privy to Kierkegaard's personal life and quite plausibly either knew about or strongly suspected that Kierkegaard was in the process of breaking off his engagement with Regine. Indeed, Sibbern was subsequently angry about the manner in which Kierkegaard had treated his fiancée:

> When he wanted to break off with her—but by compelling her to break off with him—he behaved in such a way that Miss O. said he had mistreated her soul. She used that expression, and she felt deep indignation about it, but she could not stand it when people spoke ill of him, as they did in her parents' home. That she was able to speak otherwise in my presence meant that I became the person who had to give her support. I told her, however, that I must view the fact that she did not become K.'s [wife] as a good thing for her. This was because Kierkegaard's spirit was continually preoccupied with itself, and this man, confined as he was in self-reflection, would either have tormented her with jealousy or have lived with her as if he were totally unconcerned with her. When the engagement was broken off, I said to K. that he was the sort of person who ought never be engaged at all, and that the sort of thing which had happened to him should not have happened to a man of his age.[114]

---

[111]Kirmmse, *Encounters*, 216; see also 19, 215, 217.
[112]Kirmmse, *Encounters*, 215, 217.
[113]Kirmmse, *Encounters*, 37, 213.
[114]Kirmmse, *Encounters*, 213-14.

Even after the engagement between Kierkegaard and Regine Olsen
had been definitively broken off, Sibbern continued to play a role
in their relationship. In addition to serving as a spiritual or
psychological counselor to the jilted Regine ("I became the person
who had to give her support") Sibbern also made himself available
as a sort of a go-between for the erstwhile lovers, relaying
Kierkegaard's religious discourses to his ex-fiancée.[115]

In the years following the Kierkegaard's return to Denmark
from his 1841–1842 sojourn in Berlin, after the furor surrounding
the broken engagement had subsided and Kierkegaard began his
career as a writer, Sibbern and Kierkegaard continued to have a
friendly relationship and continued to see one another, but
apparently not as often as previously. Contact between the two
seems to have stopped well before Kierkegaard's final attack on
the Church,[116] though that attack would of course have made
continuing any sort of relationship impossible. Sibbern's proper
bourgeois sensibilities were shocked by Kierkegaard's conduct in
the attack, and Martensen reported, with evident glee, that Sibbern
had said to him that "Kierkegaard had here revealed himself to be
a philistine"[117]—which was one of the worst epithets available to
the Danish Golden Age.

Yet even here all may not be quite as it seems. Sibbern had a
lady correspondent in the provinces, a certain Miss Petronella
Ross, who had been in the habit of reading Kierkegaard's works
for edification. When Kierkegaard unleashed his attack, Miss Ross
was very upset and turned to Sibbern, stating that despite her
admiration for Kierkegaard's religious writings, he ought to be
"whipped with a vengeance" and have his "wings . . . clipped a
little."[118] Later she wrote Sibbern again, wanting to know why he
had not taken up his pen to oppose Kierkegaard publicly.[119] But
Sibbern begged off, stating that "just about everything that there

---

[115]Kirmmse, *Encounters*, 37.
[116]Sibbern: "I did not see him again during the years before his death." Cited
in Kirmmse, *Encounters*, 215.
[117]Kirmmse, *Encounters*, 201.
[118]Kirmmse, *Encounters*, 101.
[119]Kirmmse, *Encounters*, 103.

was to say [had been] said," and that in order to express himself properly he would have to have written an entire essay on the subject and that he had therefore decided to let the matter go.[120] And at the height of Kierkegaard's assault, in July 1855, in an aside included in a newspaper review of an another author, Sibbern could find something nice to say about the man all polite Copenhagen loved to hate, referring to Kierkegaard as "one of our young men, an acute dialectical thinker."[121]

So there may be something else at work here as well: Perhaps Sibbern, although offended by Kierkegaard on behalf of the norms of propriety, softened his stance a bit because he himself had begun to have serious scruples about the established church and was well on his way toward developing his own idiosyncratic religion. The fruit of Sibbern's unorthodoxy—touched upon earlier in this essay—was the interminable and unreadable futuristic novel, *Meddelelser af Indholdet af et Skrift fra Aaret 2135*, the concluding portions of which were published posthumously, in which Sibbern displayed his familiar, almost boyishly buoyant humanity and his ever-present optimism. In the novel Sibbern retrospectively shed crocodile tears about the unseemly behavior of Søren Kierkegaard way back then in 1855, while making it clear that by the year 2135 Christianity's importance had faded for him. Thus for Sibbern, Kierkegaard's crime was against good taste, not against religion.

B. Kierkegaard on Sibbern

But what did Kierkegaard think of Sibbern? Kierkegaard's attitude toward Sibbern seems to have been one of genuine affection which, however, was not quite matched by an equal measure of respect. Kierkegaard was certainly not unaware of Sibbern's tilt toward Regine Olsen during the termination of their engagement, and writing from Berlin, he expressed his evident displeasure to his friend Emil Boesen. Kierkegaard writes, in a letter dated October 31, 1841, that he has heard that Sibbern had come looking for him "the day before I left [for Berlin] 'in order to give me a

---

[120]Kirmmse, *Encounters*, 103.
[121]F. C. Sibbern, review of Axel Nyblæus, *Är en practisk philosophie möjlig efter Hegels verldsåsikt?*, in *Fædrelandet*, July 7, 1855, from Jens Himmelstrup, *Sibbern* (Copenhagen: Schultz, 1934) 263.

thorough dressing down,' since he too had now become convinced
that I was an egotistical and vain man, an ironist in the worst
sense" (LD, 90). A couple of weeks later, on November 18,
Kierkegaard writes to another friend, Pastor P. J. Spang:

> When I left, the sluice gates of conversation opened, and it is
> probably still dripping from the roofs. What is Sibbern doing?
> For I do assume that what is sane and lofty in him has prevailed
> once more, or has he really placed himself at the head of the
> gossipmongers at tea parties? If so, what danger is there in that?
> I am no longer in town, and if I were, Sibbern would be man
> enough to prevent my approaching any girl, at least according to
> his own conceited idea of himself. And should there be more of
> my evil kind, Sibbern might of course resign his chair and let
> himself be hired as an "uncle" or family protector for a small fee.
> He might be mounted on horseback to enable him to get around
> more quickly. Then he could let me have his chair, and thus all
> of us would be well served, and I rendered harmless, for as
> Sibbern knows, a professor of philosophy ought not to do that
> sort of thing. If he has come to his senses, please give him my
> regards. (LD, 96)

Brøchner gives us a picture of Kierkegaard's overall assessment of
Sibbern:

> S. K. appreciated Sibbern greatly, even though he was not blind
> to his weaknesses. Among these he once emphasized Sibbern's
> complete lack of irony, and, from a psychological point of view,
> his lack of an awareness of the disguised passions, the reduplica-
> tion [Fordobbling] by which the one passion assumes the form of
> another. In his opinion, this was why Sibbern was often taken in
> when many people, ladies, in particular, turned to him to consult
> him as a sort of psychological and spiritual adviser.[122]

However annoyed he may have been at what he viewed as the
older man's interference in his personal life, Kierkegaard certainly
did not want to break off his relationship with Sibbern, and he
wrote him a perhaps disingenuously friendly (or even sycophantic)
letter from Berlin, dated December 15, 1841:

> Today, through my nephew Henrich Lund, I received the
> greetings you expressly requested him to convey. I am so pleased
> to have those greetings that it would never occur to me to return

---

[122]Kirmmse, *Encounters*, 241.

my own greetings by the same medium. On the contrary, I consider them a poetic summons to reply in what may be a rather discursive manner.

Even now when I cannot personally ascertain it for myself every day, I have never doubted that you would maintain some of that interest with which you have always honored me, especially after Poul Møller's death. Therefore, when I did not receive greetings of any kind until now, I easily explained this to myself by saying that circumstances had not brought you into contact with anybody whom you knew to be writing to me. . . .

The longer I live here in Berlin the more I realize the truth of the advice you have given me again and again out of regard for both me and my dissertation: that it be translated into German. I will wait and see about that. If it does happen, I can honestly say that you are responsible. If any good comes of this, it will be a pleasure for me to think that in this I have once more an occasion to think of you. . . .

From my native country I hear little. The Danes here do get the newspapers, but I do not read them as I do not have enough time, yet time enough and time sufficient to think about a man like you, dear Professor, who by your conduct towards me have always obliged me and entitled me to call myself
                         Your devoted
                         S. Kierkegaard (LD, 106-108)

In sum, Kierkegaard certainly felt bemusement, impatience, and even some anger at the older man's simpleminded righteousness and his pretensions. And Kierkegaard must reasonably also have felt embarrassment: All during 1841, not only did Sibbern likely know a good deal about the personal troubles from which Kierkegaard so desperately wanted to flee, but Kierkegaard *knew* that Sibbern knew this, and this cannot have failed to make Kierkegaard uncomfortable. Still, Kierkegaard could make use of Sibbern's involvement in his affairs, and he was not above taking advantage of what he knew was Sibbern's soft spot for him. Thus Kierkegaard had been able to rely on Sibbern in 1841, when the latter was serving his turn as Dean of the Philosophy Faculty, to guide—or indeed, to use Brøndsted's huffy expression, to *railroad*—his dissertation (and the requisite dispensation from the obligation that it be written in Latin) through the university machinery as expeditiously as possible, and in so doing further Kierkegaard's plan to break his engagement and flee to Berlin. The sort of double role in which Sibbern was situated had the effect of placing him in just the sort of conflict-of-interest situation which made him more compliant with Kierkegaard's wishes. And, as has been noted, Sibbern continued to be used in this way, even after the breakup, ferrying Kierkegaard's works to Regine Olsen and news of Regine back to Kierkegaard. To put it a bit cruelly, unhappy as he was with Sibbern's "goodness," Kierkegaard was content to use him as beast of burden, and Sibbern uncomplainingly (and perhaps somewhat unwittingly) complied.

C. The Ghost of Poul Martin Møller

But there was something else, something more important, binding Kierkegaard to Sibbern, and in Kierkegaard's December 1841 letter to Sibbern, it can be sensed in the odd, *en passant* mention of the late Poul Møller. Why Møller? Why mention him to Sibbern? As noted earlier, we know that as a young university student, after his *philosophicum* examinations in April and October 1831, Kierkegaard set to work studying theology, but was soon put off by the aridity of the Theology Faculty and, like many young theologians, gravitated toward the Philosophy Faculty, and specifically toward the multifaceted, affable Sibbern and his younger colleague Poul Martin Møller, who was by all accounts a very magnetic personality. Kierkegaard attended Sibbern's lectures on aesthetics and poetics in the summer semester (May–September) of 1833 and on the philosophy of Christianity in the following winter semester of 1833–1834 (November 1833–May 1834). According to Sibbern's testimony, it was at this time, if not earlier, that Kierkegaard began calling on him at home.

In the latter part of 1834 Kierkegaard's attention seems to have focused increasingly on a number of aesthetic projects, e.g., first, the "Master Thief" and subsequently Don Juan, Faust, and Ahasuerus (the Wandering Jew). Theology fell more and more by the wayside, and by the spring of 1836 it seems to have been entirely eclipsed. Still, whatever else was going on in Kierkegaard's life—and this has been a subject of great speculation among his biographers—he certainly remained very much engaged with Poul Møller. From at least as early as 1835, Kierkegaard's journals contain sketches and ideas concerning irony, and by the latter part of 1836 Socrates makes his initial appearance as the representative of irony, already placed in dialogue with Christianity.[123] Conversations with Poul Møller were probably a part of these developments; this can be glimpsed in an interesting entry, dated July 6, 1837. Embedded in this lengthy entry, which concerns the boundaries between irony and humor, between Socrates and Christianity, is the following: "Poul Møller in an extremely interesting conversation, the evening of June 30th [1837]" (SKP, II A 102, my translation; JP, 2:1690).

Møller was himself interested in "the concept of irony" and was the author of a fragment bearing that name, which, although it was published only posthumously (and after Kierkegaard had published his own On the Concept of Irony), most likely formed part of the underpinnings of their conversations. Møller's fragment On the Concept of Irony lies in the same philosophical and intellectual province as Kierkegaard's work. Although Møller writes straightforwardly, and not ironically (as Kierkegaard did) of irony, he shares the point of view which would soon be Kierkegaard's, taking modern irony (Frederick Schlegel, et al.) to task for promoting the excessive emphasis on subjective freedom that has led to the antinomianism and nihilism of the present day.[124] Indeed, so strong is the parallel that Himmelstrup states flatly in his Søren Kierkegaards Opfattelse af Socrates (Søren Kierkegaard's Conception of Socrates) that "On the whole, Kierkegaard's exposition is almost a continuation and further development of the essay on 'moral irony' which Poul Møller had started writing."[125] Thus Kierkegaard's The Concept of Irony certainly has its origins as early as his conversations with Møller of 1837, and probably a couple of years earlier. (Incidentally, Møller also produced a fragment on Ahasuerus, the Wandering Jew— published posthumously in the same collection in which his irony fragment appeared—which may well have formed the basis of his conversations with Kierkegaard on

---

[123]"Irony, the ignorance with which Socrates began—the world created from nothing—the pure virgin of whom Christ was born." SKP, I A 190, my translation; JP 2:1673.

[124]Poul M. Møller, "Om Begrebet Ironie" in Efterladte Skrifter, 3rd ed., vol. 3 (Copenhagen: C. A. Reitzel, 1856) 152-58.

[125]Jens Himmelstrup, Søren Kierkegaards Opfattelse af Sokrates. En Studie i dansk Filosofis Historie (Copenhagen: Arnold Busck, 1924) 73.

this topic, a subject which we know was also of great interest to Kierkegaard.)[126]

Whatever the specifics of Poul Martin Møller's influence on Kierkegaard, it is incontestable that the relationship was very strong, bordering on the "spiritual pederasty" with which Hamann says Socrates encompassed his pupils—a phrase which Kierkegaard mentions in the above-mentioned journal entry of July 1837, immediately after alluding to his conversation of the previous month with Møller. When Møller died the following spring, still a fairly young man, Kierkegaard was crushed: "April [1838]. Once again a long time has passed in which I have not been able to pull myself together to do the least thing. Now I must make another little attempt. Poul Møller is dead" (SKP, II A 309, my translation; JP, 2:5302). These are strong words in a journal in which, as is well known, Kierkegaard does not even record the deaths of his mother or his favorite siblings. The memory of Møller was a strong motivating force, a spirit which guided and goaded Kierkegaard for much of his life.

Furthermore, Møller, who, this essay argues, was present at the very origin of Kierkegaard's *The Concept of Irony*, was also viewed by Kierkegaard as the fount of his other "concept" book, *The Concept of Anxiety*, published in 1844. That book is dedicated to Møller, and the original draft of the dedication is extraordinarily revealing:

> To the late
> Professor *Poul Martin Møller*
> the happy lover of Greek culture, the admirer of Homer, the confidant of Socrates, the interpreter of Aristotle—Denmark's joy in "Joy over Denmark"—the enthusiasm of my youth; the confidant of my beginnings; my lost friend; my sadly missed reader, though "widely traveled, yet always remembered in the Danish summer,"
> The mighty trumpet of my awakening; the desired object of my feelings,
> this work is dedicated. (SKP, V B 46; translation from CA, 178)

This gives us a vivid impression of the sense of devotion, of reverence and awe, with which Kierkegaard viewed Poul Møller. Therefore it is all the more interesting when Kierkegaard informs

---

[126]Poul M. Møller, "Ahasverus" in *Efterladte Skrifter*, vol. 3, 159-62.

us in his journals of Møller's last words to him and of how he
came to know of them:

The Extraordinary

Oh, to be the extraordinary on the polemical terms of the
Christian extraordinary: It is in one sense terrible, almost fatal.
Not only is it the greatest possible, almost superhuman, effort,
but this relationship of opposition to others, and the degree of
opposition: It is fatal for all merely human sympathy.

See—sympathy is my passion—this is why I have always
wanted merely to point out the extraordinary.

I recall the words of the dying Poul Møller, which he often
said to me while he lived, and which, if my memory is not
mistaken (in addition to the words, "Tell little K. to be careful
not to set himself too large a plan of study, because doing so has
caused me much harm"), he enjoined Sibbern to repeat to me
again and again: "You are so polemical through and through,
that it is quite frightful."

Oh, despite having been so polemical through and through,
even in my youth: Christianity is still almost too polemical for
me.

[marginal note to the above entry] I cannot definitely remember whether the dying P. M. enjoined upon Sibbern to say those
words to me ("You are so polemical through and through, etc."),
and I am almost inclined to doubt it. On the other hand, I remember very well that the last time S. talked with him before his
death he enjoined S. to say the other words to me. And as for the
first words ("You are so polemical through and through"), when
he was alive, that was his expression again and again, and S.,
too, has followed him in using the words against me many times.
(SKP, XI,1 A 275 and 276, my translation; JP, 6:6888 and 6889)

Thus, not only did Poul Møller have an important deathbed
message for Kierkegaard, namely, that he not take on too ambitious a work plan (advice which Kierkegaard apparently ignored),
but of great importance is the fact that he sent the message *via*
Sibbern. Sibbern was the intermediary between Kierkegaard and
the teacher Kierkegaard most loved and respected, Poul Martin
Møller. And Møller's monitory words about Kierkegaard being too
polemical apparently hit their mark because Kierkegaard clearly
admits to being hyperpolemical—but seems to excuse it by saying
that Christianity is even more so. Thus, even if Poul Møller was
not on his deathbed when he uttered his critical words about
Kierkegaard's polemical nature, he definitely did say them, and in

front of Sibbern, who never tired of repeating them to Kierkegaard. All this is very revealing about the matrix which constituted the Kierkegaard-Møller-Sibbern relationship.

But there is yet another revealing aspect to this journal entry, namely, that it is *from 1854*. Kierkegaard had heard these words from Sibbern (and/or directly from Møller) in 1838—and of course they were so important that he did not need to write them down— and he treasured them and pondered them and agonized over them for the rest of his life. And now, in 1854 when the final furious assault on the Church was about to begin, Kierkegaard brought them forth once again, this time committing them to paper because he wanted to situate his own polemical nature, for which Møller had chided him, in relation to the larger polemic he believed to be Christianity. In Kierkegaard's journals, as well as in his memory, Kierkegaard was present at the end of Møller's life, and Møller was present at the end of Kierkegaard's. And Sibbern was present as well, the attendant, the faithful messenger.

D. The Other Death in 1838: Michael Pedersen Kierkegaard

This vignette, then, constitutes Kierkegaard's story of the death of Poul Martin Møller: (1) a young man, now no longer young; (2) a revered older figure, now many years dead; and (3) words spoken at the time of the older man's death, words which are remembered by the younger man many years later, on the eve his own final battle. Almost parallel to this is Kierkegaard's story of the death of his *father*, Michael Pedersen Kierkegaard, who likewise died in 1838—when, incidentally, Søren Kierkegaard was 25 years old, the legal age of majority in nineteenth-century Denmark. Møller died in April of 1838, the elder Kierkegaard in August. Møller was the teacher Kierkegaard loved and respected above all others. Michael Pedersen Kierkegaard was the greatest man in Søren Kierkegaard's life. Kierkegaard says he brought the news of his father's death straight to Bishop Mynster, supposedly a close friend of the family, the person old Kierkegaard had respected most in the world, and that when the bishop was informed of the death he seemed at first unable to recollect who Michael Pedersen Kierkegaard was! (SKP, XI,2 A 419, p. 409). Interestingly, we know about this purported incident from 1838 only because Søren Kierkegaard wrote about it in his journal—*in 1854*. Just as with the last words Kierkegaard attributed to Poul Møller, these words touching upon his father's passing were uttered, Kierkegaard says, *in 1838*, but they smoldered until he wrote them down just prior to the great battle at the end of his life.

Indeed, Søren Kierkegaard lived the whole of his adult life—including the period during which he wrote his first "real" work, *The Concept of Irony*—in the shadow of the 1838 deaths of these two men: Poul Martin Møller, his teacher and mentor; and Michael Pedersen Kierkegaard, Søren's father, who represented to his son, if not God Himself, then certainly Christianity in its truest form, what the son would come to call "the Christianity of the New Testament." Søren Kierkegaard would spend the rest of his life in the continuing presence of these absences, this double loss, and he would have to contend with the people who would stand in for these lost figures—only, of course, to dismiss those stand-ins as laughably inadequate. Most famous, of course, was Kierkegaard's relationship to Mynster, "my father's pastor," whom Kierkegaard says he did his best to revere, only ultimately to reject him, heaping scorn upon him in the attack on the Church. This of course is why Kierkegaard's open attack on Mynster, which began on December 18, 1854, included the otherwise apparently inexplicable references to Kierkegaard's *father*, references which seem out of place until one understands Kierkegaard's mental terrain.[127] Our Hamlet could not tolerate such a satyr ("weak, pleasure-mad, and great only as a declaimer" [TM, 8, my translation]) as a replacement for the Hyperion who had been his father.

---

[127]The implication of the discovery of Mynster's lack of genuine engagement with Michael Pedersen Kierkegaard would of course have been clear to Søren Kierkegaard as early as 1838, but he did not take action to avenge the family's wounded honor until other events and injuries propelled him in that direction. Most notorious, certainly, were Kierkegaard's coarse attacks upon the office and the person of Mynster that finally surfaced in 1854–1855, but traces of his vendetta can be seen well before that time, at least as early as *Christian Discourses* (1848) and unmistakably in *Practice in Christianity* (1850). I have discussed the implications of Søren Kierkegaard/Michael Pedersen Kierkegaard/Mynster triangle in more detail in "Out with It!: The Modern Breakthrough, Kierkegaard, and Denmark" in Alastair Hannay and Gordon D. Marino, eds., *The Cambridge Companion to Kierkegaard* (Cambridge University Press: Cambridge and New York, 1998) 15–47.

E. Two Hamlets

The allusion to Hamlet is not chosen capriciously. It is the contention of this essay that the Hamlet story is the configuration which best represents Søren Kierkegaard's situation both with respect to the two heroes he lost in 1838 and to the inadequate stand-ins who would replace them. Kierkegaard in fact had a lifelong fascination with Shakespeare and especially with *Hamlet*. In addition to the well-known "Side-glance at Shakespeare's *Hamlet*" in *Stages on Life's Way* (SLW, 452-54), Kierkegaard's journals contain numerous entries about the play, beginning as early as 1836 and continuing through late 1854. Kierkegaard views the Hamlet figure variously, e.g., as the modern individual paralyzed by reflection and as the self-enclosed and misunderstood hero whose suffering consists largely in the misunderstanding with which he has enveloped himself.[128] There can scarcely be much doubt that some of these understandings of Hamlet were also in part self-understandings. This notion is supported, for example, by the memoirs of Kierkegaard's niece, Henriette Lund, which strongly imply that there was a powerful strain of identification between Kierkegaard and Shakespeare's melancholy Dane.[129]

But in concerning himself with *Hamlet* Kierkegaard can scarcely have confined his interest only to problems associated with the main character's sense of self. The play, after all, is about the death of a heroic father and the obligation of the son to prevent a lesser man, who was apparently complicit in the father's demise, from taking his place unchallenged. The triangle of Hamlet/the Ghost

---

[128]See, e.g., SKP, V A 90 (JP, 2:1247) and VII,1 A 113 (JP, 5:5900). There is an interesting entry from late 1854, entitled "Two Aesthetic Comments, Which I Will Nonetheless Note Down" (SKP, XI,1 A 501; JP, 2:1562). The first comment is about whether Hamlet's love affair with Ophelia was feigned or genuine, while the second part concerns the aesthetic blunder in allowing Don Quixote to die, thus making him a character in "a sort of a moral tale." Kierkegaard argues that if, on the other hand, Don Quixote had been given another fantastic obsession, he could have gone on forever as the embodiment of "the infinite fantastic," and his character would have been placed where it belongs, namely, in the category of the "romantic comic." This "aesthetic" entry, coming as it does just prior to Kierkegaard's final campaign, invites all sorts of readings.

[129]Kirmmse, *Encounters*, 171-72.

of Hamlet's Father/Claudius is uncannily close to the *two* triangles
that dominated Kierkegaard's life after 1838. We have already had
a cursory look at the *first* triangle: Kierkegaard/Kierkegaard's
father/Bishop Mynster. Of more interest here is the *second* triangle:
Kierkegaard/Poul Møller/H. L. Martensen. Or, alternatively: Kier-
kegaard/Poul Møller/Rasmus Nielsen. Martensen was the stand-in
for Møller on the Theology Faculty and Nielsen was Møller's
stand-in on the Philosophy faculty. And of course, neither Hamlet
nor Søren Kierkegaard viewed replacement figures under the
harmless dramatic category of "stand-ins": Like the evil King
Claudius, Nielsen and Martensen were *usurpers*, pure and simple.
No one could replace Poul Martin Møller.

As has been noted earlier, upon Poul Møller's death in 1838,
Martensen immediately took over Møller's lectures on moral
philosophy. Martensen summarized his lectures in *Grundrids til
Moralphilosophiens System* (Outline of the System of Moral Philosophy) (1841), which was written to be used in conjunction with the
course and which provides us a basis upon which to estimate the
content of Martensen's actual lectures. One notices immediately
that Martensen's work is markedly Hegelian in tone. This contrasts
sharply with Møller, who had flirted with Hegel but had then conceived a great distaste for him and had attacked him in the only
philosophical work he managed to publish in his brief lifetime,
Tanker over Muligheden af Beviser for Menneskets Udødelighed
(Thoughts on the Possibility of Proofs of Human Immortality).[130]
Of course the radical mismatch between Møller and Martensen
cannot have escaped Søren Kierkegaard's notice. For Kierkegaard,
Martensen's attempt to step in and take over Møller's lectures
must have been added to the catalogue of other outstanding differences between Martensen and himself which have been mentioned
earlier in this essay. After 1838 the breach with Martensen would
never be healed and would only worsen with time.

Rasmus Nielsen's crime was of course identical to Martensen's:
He had tried to replace Poul Martin Møller. It is interesting to note
that Nielsen, later a bitter enemy of Martensen, had started on his

---

[130]Originally published in *Maanedsskrift for Litteratur*, XVII, 1836, 1-72 and 422-
53.

Hegelian path with the support and encouragement of Martensen. (Nielsen's 1840 *licentiat* dissertation in theology was entitled "On the Employment of the Speculative Method in the Examination of the Sacred History.") In the winter of 1840–1841 Nielsen lectured at the university as a private tutor; his subjects were church history and New Testament exegesis. On April 22, 1841 he accepted appointment to the Philosophy Faculty, filling Møller's vacant chair in moral philosophy, which had remained empty for three years for want of a suitable candidate. In the summer of 1841, his first summer as a professor, Nielsen lectured on metaphysics. He cannot have had much time to prepare for these lectures. In his recollections of Kierkegaard, Hans Brøchner relates the following exchange between Sibbern and Kierkegaard, which apparently took place while Kierkegaard was still a degree candidate:

> Once [Kierkegaard] told me that Sibbern had suggested that he apply for a position as a lecturer in philosophy. K. had replied that in that case he would have to insist on a couple of years in which to prepare himself. "Oh! How can you imagine that they would hire you under such conditions?" asked Sibbern. "Yes, of course, I could do like Rasmus Nielsen and let them hire me unprepared." Sibbern became cross and said: "You always have to pick on Nielsen!" This was shortly after Nielsen had been appointed to the university.[131]

The purported impact of this conversation upon Nielsen has already been noted in connection with our examination of readers' comments on Kierkegaard's dissertation. In any event, as we have seen, whether or not he had direct knowledge of Kierkegaard's (apparently repeated) ridicule, Nielsen refused to read Kierkegaard's dissertation and almost undoubtedly stayed away from the public defense. And as we have also seen from a brief look at Kierkegaard's 1842 article, "Public Confession," Nielsen fared no better at Kierkegaard's hands subsequently.

Yet the two would-be replacements for Poul Møller reacted differently to Kierkegaard. Martensen, as we know from his memoirs, put Kierkegaard permanently on his "watch list." He kept his distance, and relations between the two never improved.

---

[131]Kirmmse, *Encounters*, 235.

In the course of the 1840s, Nielsen, on the other hand, became intrigued, perhaps even converted, by Kierkegaard's work. Nielsen was a muddled, indeed execrable, writer and not a terribly original thinker, but he possessed a certain inner unrest which impelled him toward the genius of Søren Kierkegaard. And, for reasons that scholarship has not yet fully interpreted or explained, in the later 1840s Kierkegaard decided to make use of Rasmus Nielsen, to take him on as a disciple and a popularizer of his work, who could carry on were Kierkegaard to die. (As is well known, quite a number of times before his actual death, Kierkegaard had the recurrent conviction that his death was imminent.) In a journal entry from the summer of 1848, Kierkegaard writes: "So just one wish for these efforts of mine, if I am parted from them. . . . My wish is that now R. Nielsen might be someone to depend upon" (SKP, IX A 227, my translation; JP, 6:6238). But it was not long before Kierkegaard regretted his attempt at a rapprochement, and the on-again, off-again relationship between the two men ended in bitterness for Kierkegaard, who as early as 1849 came to believe that Nielsen was merely interested in plagiarizing his ideas in order to advance his own career.[132]

Worse still, Kierkegaard could not shake off his original estimate of Nielsen as a mediocrity; to Brøchner he said: "Nielsen is a windbag!"[133] Nielsen was a second-rater, a man who could simply be written off. Kierkegaard heaped scorn on Nielsen's efforts, both privately to Nielsen himself and not so privately, to those of his friends and associates who would listen. How Nielsen felt about this second wave of rejection by Kierkegaard is not of concern to this essay, but publicly he continued to soldier on, plodding along in what he said were Kierkegaard's footsteps, whether Kierkegaard wanted him there or not. And the stolid Nielsen was among the few "dignitaries" [Honoratiores] who attended Kierkegaard's funeral, though H. L. Martensen, by then a bishop, harrumphed that "there were no dignitaries in attendance, unless one wishes to include R. Nielsen . . . in this category."[134]

---

[132]Cf., e.g., SKP, X,6 B 84-102 (partially reproduced in JP 6404, 6405, 6406, 6663), where Nielsen is labelled, among other things, "a plagiarist."

[133]Kirmmse, Encounters, 235.

[134]Kirmmse, Encounters, 135.

F. Hamlet . . . and Polonius

If we have assigned Kierkegaard the role of Hamlet; the ghost of Poul Martin Møller the role of Hamlet's father's ghost; and H. L. Martensen (and Rasmus Nielsen) the role of King Claudius the usurper, what role remains for F. C. Sibbern? Why of course that of *Polonius*, the Lord Chamberlain, the bumbling, sententious, amiable, well-meaning middleman. As we have seen, Sibbern was a warm, generous, diffuse man, soft-edged in every way that Kierkegaard was hard. And, as noted, despite his affection for Sibbern, Kierkegaard was not above making use of him. At dissertation time, when irony had to become academic and Socrates had to get on the fast track—on an "express coach" through the university and out of town—Kierkegaard rode Sibbern like a horse to the train station: loving him, patronizing him, pitying him, despising him a little for his lack of dialectical sharpness and psychological insight, yet cherishing him again for his childlike simplicity of character. Poor Sibbern, a decent, friendly man, who in 1841 had been embarrassed when he had had to listen to young Kierkegaard's ridicule of Rasmus Nielsen and had tried to make the sarcastic genius express himself more politely; poor Sibbern, who in 1855, despite his continuing affection for Kierkegaard and his own growing doubts about Christianity, had been unable to resist the temptation to tattle on him, confiding to Martensen his belief that in attacking Mynster, Kierkegaard had shown himself to be "a philistine." To poor Sibbern, as sprawling and untidy in his intellectual habits as he was endearing as a person, was given the role of the ever so slightly pitiable Polonius in both of the parallel *Hamlet* dramas in which Søren Kierkegaard was willy-nilly engaged.

G. The End: Socrates, Through and Through

Whether or not Poul Møller actually said it on his deathbed—Kierkegaard admits that his memory is unclear on this point—during his life he had repeatedly upbraided Kierkegaard for being "so polemical through and through, that it is quite frightful." Nonetheless, even before Møller's death in 1838 Kierkegaard had already identified himself with the ironic, polemical Socrates. And in July 1840, when he was presumably in the middle of writing his dissertation, whose full title is *On the Concept of Irony, With Continual Reference to Socrates*, Kierkegaard wrote in his journal of Socrates' "polemical use" of the art of questioning, concluding with this assertion: "What modern philosophy busies itself with so much—the removing of every presupposition in order to begin with nothing—was also done by Socrates in his way, in order to end with nothing" (SKP, III A 7, my translation; JP, 1:754). So, too, with the polemical, ironic Kierkegaard: He began with Socrates, in his dissertation and even before. And, at the end of his life, he explained himself by way of analogy to the polemical, ironic Socrates. When Kierkegaard lay on *his* deathbed, he was satisfied in the knowledge that he had completed his life's work and had placed a torpedo under the ark of the Established Church. He knew that the final issue of *The Moment*, number 10, lay ready for publication, and he knew that the most incisive and troubling article in that issue was the one entitled "My Task,"[135] in which Kierkegaard repeatedly states, "I am not a Christian," explaining his position by stating that "the only analogy I hold before myself is Socrates" (TM, 340-41). *Of course* Kierkegaard was "polemical through and through." His hero was *Socrates*, whom he consistently viewed as polemical and as an ironist. And although his understanding of Socrates evolved over the course of his career, the Greek gadfly remained Kierkegaard's polemical-ironic *daimon*, emblematic of the highest *human* relationship. The elusive Kierkegaard remained Socratic through and through, from his dissertation to his deathbed.[136]

---

[135]I discuss Kierkegaard's "My Task"—and develop further the position adumbrated in this concluding paragraph—in " 'I am not a Christian'—A 'Sublime Lie'? or 'Without Authority,' Playing Desdemona to Christendom's Othello," in *Anthropology and Authority: Essays on Søren Kierkegaard*, ed. Poul Houe, Gordon Marino, and Sven Rossel (Amsterdam and Atlanta: Rodopi Press, 2000) 129-36.

[136]Original manuscript copyright ©2000, Bruce H. Kirmmse. All rights reserved. May not be reproduced in any form without written permission of the author. The present pages—copyedited, designed, composed, and published by Mercer University Press—are copyrighted ©2001 by Mercer University Press. All rights reserved. See volume copyrights, page iv above.

2

Kierkegaard's Socratic Hermeneutic
in The Concept of Irony

Tonny Aagaard Olesen

Kierkegaard's works are a gold mine of hermeneutic reflection. Even in places where the dialectic of understanding is not discussed, the theme is constantly present in the formal aspects of his writing. These aspects are the result of an applied hermeneutic and therefore inextricably bound up with the process of understanding. In the pseudonymous works, this hermeneutic is often discussed under headings such as "double reflection," "the dialectic of communication," or "reduplication." The aim of this article is to focus on this hermeneutic. The question I will address is whether there is a special methodological or hermeneutical reflection in *The Concept of Irony*, and if so, where and in what capacity.

This investigation is divided into three parts. First, I will discuss the thematic composition and methodology of the dissertation *in toto*. Secondly, this overview will lead to a closer inspection of "Part One" of *The Concept of Irony* and the hermeneutic problems associated with it. Thirdly, I will concentrate on "Chapter One" in "Part One," which, I will argue, is the most original in the dissertation from a hermeneutical perspective. That is, I will begin with an overview of *The Concept of Irony* as a whole, then narrow my focus to "Part One," and from there, I will proceed to an even closer examination of "Chapter One." The title of this article reflects the hermeneutical theory and practice which is unfolded in this chapter.

The movement and thematic focus of my article implies that it ought to be read as an introductory meditation on *The Concept of Irony* rather than a distillation of detailed results. First and foremost, the article aims to direct attention to a specific kind of methodological self-reflection, which is not just a condition for a satisfactory understanding the dissertation, but also points forward to a fundamental hermeneutical theme in the later pseudonymous and edifying works. Finally, in the fourth and concluding section, I will provide a brief illustration of the later significance of this theme. In order to remain in the context of the dissertation, I will include Kierkegaard's response to one of his critics, first in relation to *The Concept of Irony*, and then in response to a review of *Philosophical Fragments*. My aim here is to illustrate that Kierkegaard's well-known "Socratic hermeneutic" is located in his text in theory as well as in practice.

The first time an interpreter claimed that *The Concept of Irony* is of central importance for Kierkegaard's authorship was shortly after Kierkegaard's death in 1855. This claim appeared in an article which was a kind of obituary for both Hegelianism and Kierkegaard since the former was said to end with the latter.[1] The author of the article, theologian Hans Frederik Helveg (1816–1901) who was well acquainted with Kierkegaard's thinking,[2] paints an intriguing portrait of Kierkegaard's project, emphasizing especially Kierkegaard's interest in reconfiguring the results of speculative objectivity to existential understanding via personal appropriation. Helveg finds this project already fully sketched in *The Concept of Irony*. He writes of the work:

> It also includes much more of the author's later views and assertions than one would think (. . .). It gives an image of its author which resembles the well-known [engraving] "Napoleon on his own Grave." The contours show up after a short time, but only after one has the image in mind oneself. One can also say that the work in question not only treats irony but is an irony, specifically its aim, for it contains something quite different and contains much more than the recipient could imagine. The members of the Department of Philosophy who evaluated the piece could hardly have imagined that the work of the young

---

[1]Hans Frederik Helveg, "Hegelianismen i Danmark," in *Dansk Kirketidende* 51-52 (1855): 825-37, 841-52.

[2]Helveg had already written several articles on Kierkegaard. Among these were a pair of articles comparing Kierkegaard with the Hegelian priest Adolph Peter Adler (1812–1869). For Helveg's bibliography, see Søren Jensen, *H. F. Helvegs forfatterskab—en bibliografi* (Copenhagen: private publisher, 1987).

author was not as much a requirement for a Magister degree as it was a program for life; it was not the solution to a scholarly problem but a *life task*.[3]

This life task Helveg speaks of is a very important aspect of Kierkegaard's hermeneutic. We could call this the task of self-understanding. Accordingly, he uses Socrates as a model and irony as the measure of self-development. Self-understanding is the condition of possibility for every concrete application of understanding. The center of gravity in the following article, however, lies more in an objective dialectical problem, namely, determining to what degree *The Concept of Irony* contains a special methodological self-reflection which has self-understanding as its object and its concrete presupposition. In effect, I am asking how we best should understand Kierkegaard's dissertation.

1. *The Dissertation in toto*

1.1 The First Evaluation

Kierkegaard entitled his dissertation *The Concept of Irony with Continual Reference to Socrates* at his own insistence. Philosophy professor Frederik Christian Sibbern (1785–1872), the director of the dissertation committee, commented on the title in his evaluation: "Without a doubt," he wrote, "it ought to be changed to *Socrates as Ironist with a Contribution to the Development of the Concept of Irony in General, Particularly with Regard to the Most Recent Times*.[4] When one considers the two parts of the dissertation, it is easy to understand Sibbern's objection: the first part, entitled "The Position of Socrates Viewed as Irony," is not only the most comprehensive section, but also the area where Kierkegaard's original philological-exegetical readings shine. The second part, called "On the Concept of Irony," seems less scholarly by comparison. Not only the conceptual framework, but also the portrayal of Romantic irony by Ludwig Tieck (1773–1853), Friedrich Schlegel (1772–1829), and Karl Wilhelm Ferdinand Solger (1780–1819) seems in many ways unoriginal—that is, Hegelian—insofar as a moral evaluation

---

[3]Helveg, *Dansk Kirketidende* 51:829-30.
[4]SKS, K1:134.

founds the basis of his criticism. And with regard to the section on Romanticism, Kierkegaard proceeds completely without the presence of supporting documentation: in the chapter on Tieck not a single one of Tieck's works is named; in the chapter on Schlegel, he reads *Lucinde*[5] closely, but Schlegel's groundbreaking new formulation of irony is not even mentioned; the chapter on Solger is based primarily on two letters. Finally, the presentation of the final section in the development of the concept, "Irony as a Controlled Element, the Truth of Irony," does not seem to live up to the expectation that a promise of truth naturally creates. Kierkegaard merely posits—without demonstration—that Johann Wolfgang Goethe (1749–1832) and Johan Ludvig Heiberg (1791–1860) represent controlled irony. This postulating stance is not sufficient in a scholarly dissertation regardless of how true it may be.[6]

---

[5]Furthermore, as I have shown in the new Danish commentary to the chapter, Kierkegaard not only makes a close reading, but several long passages in Kierkegaard's text are direct translations of the novel—but without quotation marks.

[6]Since interpreters have often considered the chapter on true irony represented by Goethe and J. L. Heiberg to be pure irony, it is important to note here a piece of evidence that testifies for the seriousness of Kierkegaard's characterization. A few years after Heiberg's death, Ernst Bojesen (1803–1863), Kierkegaard's Greek teacher from *Borgerdydskolen* and later rector at Sorø Academy, published the only speculative aesthetic in Danish literature called *Forstudier til en Afhandling om den Æsthetiske Idees Udvikling hos Grækerne i videnskabelig Retning* (Sorø: Sorø Akademi, 1862). Bojesen, who demonstrates a close familiarity with Kierkegaard's works, also mentions true irony, which controls and limits everything, including itself. In this context, he repeats Kierkegaard's characterization of Heiberg. He adds:

> Genuinely controlled irony appears throughout Heiberg both as a poet and as a polemical critic. As such, he fought with great energy against every exaggeration and one-sided tendency among the poets, as well as against false enthusiasm, blind excitement, and idolatry with names that our compatriots do not always keep themselves completely free of, even if they otherwise want spiritual health and moderation, and an open sense for the comic to be an essential feature of the national character. But from a superficial point of view, unlimited enthusiasm and zeal seem to bespeak a sensitive and warm heart, while irony is cold. He was therefore constantly the object of suspicion by the enthusiasts. But those who knew that they ought to read his writings, and those who knew him personally, know well that his poetic and human personality provided proof for the above mentioned assertion that a consistently carried out irony can very well be united with distinguished sensitivity, a warm heart, and a soft disposition. (120)

Sibbern's advice to move the emphasis from the second half to the first was not followed, of course, even though most of the theses in the dissertation deal with the section on Socrates. The second member of the committee to submit an evaluation, philologist Johan Nicolai Madvig (1804–1886), writes that "the development of the concept itself" suffers from "a lack of scholarly order, form, and concentrated steadiness which appears not least in the arrangement and correspondence of the two major sections of the dissertation."[7] But this otherwise serious objection does not seem to cause Kierkegaard to make any changes either: he neither changes the title nor writes an introduction which would better unite the two parts. As the dissertation stands, each part has its own introduction. If Kierkegaard's overall project is the dialectical development of the concept, then the project itself is not defined or summarized before the introduction to the second part.

1.2 Concept and Phenomenon

In "Part Two" of the dissertation, the concept irony is developed in three stages: "The World-Historical Validity of Irony, the Irony of Socrates," "Irony after Fichte," and "Irony as a Controlled Element, the Truth of Irony." The concept of irony is defined as "infinite absolute negativity." This indicates a point of view which regards absolute ideality as "nothing." That is, this point of view has reflected itself out of a positive, immediately given finitude. As known, Kierkegaard appropriates this formulaic definition from Hegel's characterization of Solger.[8] Viewed philosophically, however, this subverts the development of the concept itself. For he writes: "I am assuming, of course, that the eternal is older than the temporal, and even though philosophy in many ways comes later than history, it in fact instantly makes such a monumental step that it passes the temporal."[9] It is another question whether the historical Socrates incarnated this perspective at all, that is,

---

[7]SKS, K1:134.
[8]The passage is located in the introduction to Hegel's *Lectures on Aesthetics*. See CI, 475n.64. Even though Kierkegaard uses this formula early in the dissertation (cf. CI, 26), he develops the content of this formula for the first time in the section, "The World-Historical Validity of Irony, the Irony of Socrates."
[9]CI, 10; SKS, 1:72.

whether the concept entered into the world with Socrates and not for example, with Solger or Schlegel.

This question is answered in "Part One" of the dissertation when the first stage of the concept is the object of study. Here Kierkegaard demonstrates that the historical Socrates can only be understood without contradiction if Socrates' position is taken to be that of irony. But given that this is demonstrated so elaborately, one could ask if the other stages of the concept do not demand a similar type of proof with evidence derived from historical sources. Kierkegaard notes in his second introduction, which deals with the description of Socrates, that "the main thing is that no factor or feature has been slighted, also that all the factors and features have grouped themselves into a totality."[10] Why is this not the case with the concept of irony found in Tieck, Schlegel, Solger, or the concept represented by Goethe and Heiberg? A distribution of the material in three symmetrical sections corresponding to the stages and their representative historical figures would surely have provided the clarity which Madvig requested. One must admit, however, that this would have required either a dissertation of frightening proportions or a significant editorial reduction of the first section. Perhaps Sibbern's pragmatic suggestion to change the title was in the final analysis a reasonable solution to this *aut-aut*.

The problem of whether Kierkegaard is fundamentally engaged in a treatment of Socrates or of irony itself reflects the metaphysical presuppositions of the dissertation, namely, the distinction between the phenomenon and the concept. The dialectical relationship between these elements grounds the specific methodologies employed in each part, as the respective introductions make evident. In the introduction to the second part, Kierkegaard formulates the relationship as follows:

> But just as I dealt in the first part of the dissertation solely with Socrates, so in the development of the concept it will become apparent in what sense he is a factor in the development of the concept—in other words, it will become apparent whether the concept of irony is absolutely exhausted in him, or whether there are other modes to be inspected before we can say that the concept has been adequately interpreted.

---

[10]CI, 241; SKS, 1:281.

Therefore, just as in the first part of the dissertation the concept always hovered in the background with a continual craving to take shape in the phenomenon, just so in this part of the dissertation the phenomenal manifestation of the concept, as a continual possibility to take up residence among us, will accompany the progress of the discussion. These two factors are inseparable, because if the concept were not in the phenomenon or, more correctly, if the phenomenon were not understandable, actual, only in and with the concept, and if the phenomenon were not in the concept or, more correctly, if from the outset the concept were not understandable, actual, in and with the phenomenon, then all knowledge would be impossible, inasmuch as I in the first case would be lacking the truth, and in the second case the actuality.[11]

When the unity of the phenomenon and the concept is presupposed, two positions lose their validity. On the one hand, historical empiricism, which pays attention to the available phenomenon as the only object of knowledge, is excluded from the essential truth. On the other hand, a one-sided philosophical abstraction of concepts is ontologically invalid. The unity of the phenomenon and the concept signals a unity of the historical and the philosophical perspectives: "Concepts, just like individuals, have their history."[12] The concept is made actual in history just as the historical individual expresses the truth only to the degree to which he or she appropriates and actualizes ideality. This dialectical duality makes possible the methodological difference between the two sections since the first part, which proceeds with the concept hypothetically in mind, takes the historical phenomenon as point of departure; it moves from Socrates to the concept irony. In the second part, meanwhile, the phenomenon follows in the wake of the development of the concept; it moves from the concept to the historical appearance. If the unity of the dissertation consists in the fact that the two parts presuppose each other as dialectical elements in a hermeneutic circle, there is then a decisive methodological difference between the perspective which observes the historical Socrates "under the form of contemplation," and a more philosophical perspective, which places the emphasis on the

---

[11]CI, 241-42; SKS, 1:281.
[12]CI, 9; SKS, 1:71.

development of the concept and then judges the historical appearances. Only in the first case, when the concept is present merely as an intuition in the background while the phenomenon is the primary focus, does Kierkegaard develop the hermeneutical dialectic we are looking for.

2. Part One of The Concept of Irony

If the first part of the dissertation is considered exclusively as the supportive argumentation for the second part, it will be unfairly underestimated and misconstrued. It is just as legitimately a comprehensive, highly qualified contribution to the scholarly discussion of Socrates in its own right. This debate was instituted when modern research on Socrates with its new hermeneutical consciousness began just a few decades prior to Kierkegaard's dissertation.

2.1 Research on Socrates in the Contemporary Context

This effort to critically understand Socrates within his own contemporary context was borne partially by historical-philological interests, and partially by historical-philosophical concerns. To the former belong the large editions of Plato's works: one published in German translation, with commentary, by Friedrich Schleiermacher (published 1804–1828), and one in Danish by Carl Johan Heise (1830–1859). Original language editions were published as well by Friedrich Ast (1819–1832) and Gottfried Stallbaum (1827–1860). Employing source-critical methods, the editors attempted to arrange the individual dialogues according to historical criteria such that it became possible to mark a difference between the historical Socrates and Plato. Included in this debate was the question of how to rank the records of Socrates' contemporaries: Xenophon, Plato, and the more controversial Aristophanes. The nature of the issue gave rise to a lively debate. The latter group, interested in historical-philosophical issues, is represented first and foremost by Georg Wilhelm Friedrich Hegel (1770–1831) who exemplifies this approach most specifically in his posthumously published Lectures on the History of Philosophy (1833). From an almost bird's-eye perspective, Hegel offers a comprehensive account of Socrates' philosophical position and his epoch-making significance in the development of world history. According to Hegel, Socrates instituted "subjective inwardness" which brought him into a tragic conflict with his contemporaries. Since Hegel considers subjectivity in itself to be an invalid position,[13] he gives priority to Aristophanes as a source and he views the trial of Socrates as entirely justified. This is reflected in the research of Hegel's contemporaries as well: the preference of Aristophanes' account of Socrates is comprehensively demonstrated by Heinrich Theodor Rötscher in his *Aristophanes und sein Zeitalter*, while the justification of Socrates' trial is radically developed in Peter Wilhelm Forchhammer's (1803–1894) *Die Athener und Socrates* (1837). As is evident in the first part of the dissertation, Kierkegaard was fully aware of all this research literature.[14]

Kierkegaard's demonstration that Socrates' position is irony stands first and foremost in opposition to Hegel's conception of Socrates. This is unambiguously evident in the "appendix" which concludes the first part. There, the newly developed conception of irony is compared with the common, widespread conceptions which are all then reduced to a single position: "I shall begin with Hegel and end with Hegel, without giving any attention to his predecessors, since they, insofar as they have any significance, have been corroborated by his view, or to his successors, since they have only relative value in comparison with Hegel."[15] Hegel's concept of "subjectivity" is the orienting point for Kierkegaard's concept of "irony," since it is defined as a middle step in the development of Spirit. Irony inserts itself between individuality, which lacks the idea (the sophist), and genuine subjectivity (Plato). Irony is only subjectivity in a negative sense, inasmuch as irony

---

[13]Compare §140 in Hegel's *Philosophy of Right*, in which the moral forms of evil are developed. Here, moral evil is understood as an increasing degree of subjectivity with irony at the pinnacle.

[14]A bibliographic overview of the literature used by Kierkegaard is listed in SKS, K1:377-83. A short treatment of the research literature on Socrates from the nineteenth century is found in Lars O. Lundgren's dissertation (which includes a summary in English), *Socratesbilden. Från Aristophanes till Nietzsche* (Stockholm: Almqvist & Wiksell, 1978). See also Wolfdietrich v. Kloeden's article, "Sokrates," in *Kierkegaard's Classical Inspiration. Bibliotheca Kierkegaardiana* 14, ed. Niels and Marie Mikulová Thulstrup (Copenhagen: Reitzel, 1985) 104-81.

[15]CI, 220; SKS, 1:264.

has reached ideality, but only as an empty form without any positive content. The irony of Socrates is the absolute "freedom-from." It is an "intermediate being" (Mellemvæsen)[16] like Diotima's Eros in Plato's *Symposium* (203 b), which hovers between the human and the divine. With this point of departure, it is up to Kierkegaard to show that the positivity that has been attributed to Socrates is based on a misunderstanding.

2.2 The Strategy of Part One

Kierkegaard's investigation of Socrates' position is divided into three chapters, "The View Made Possible," "The Actualization of the View," and "The View Made Necessary." These titles, which have the ring of a metaphysical history through modal logical categories, state immediately what the chapters do with the concept, but not how they do it via a changing perspective, theme, and method. In the chapter "The View Made Possible," a philological source-critical method is put to work, and strictly speaking, when he speaks of becoming oriented in Socrates as the phenomenon "in the form of contemplation," this is the only chapter to which he refers. Through a close reading of Xenophon, Plato, and Aristophanes, he develops in this chapter, which is virtually free of Hegel, the "hermeneutic of misunderstanding" which we are looking for in this investigation.

At the outset of "The Actualization of the View," he remarks that "I have now entered another sphere."[17] This remark likewise serves notice that the "form of investigation" itself is different;[18] his method becomes more inclined to history inasmuch as the investigation merely explains the immediate "historical facts." In this case, the historical facts Kierkegaard refers to are "Socrates' daimon" and "the trial of Socrates." The desired result of this naive approach to history is that the "possible view" now "actualizes itself through all these historical data."[19] Finally, when we come to "The View Made Necessary," we again move to new territory, namely, the historical-philosophical. Here the view of

---

[16]CI, 106; SKS, 1:159.
[17]CI, 157; SKS, 1:207.
[18]CI, 156; SKS, 1:206.
[19]CI, 156; SKS, 1:206.

Socrates is marshaled as a necessary element in the development of world history. Concerning this new strategy, we are told the following: "If in the first section of this dissertation I tried to apprehend Socrates through *via negationis*, in the second section I shall try to apprehend him through *via eminentia*.[20] That is, while the method in the chapter on "possibility" was to negatively define Socrates' sublime position by denying him every relative, unperfected positivity, now the strategy is the opposite. To an extraordinary degree, every human virtue is attributed to him. Considered positively and world historically, Socrates' irony expresses itself as an "infinite ambiguity."[21]

I will now turn to the most hermeneutically complex chapter in Kierkegaard's dissertation, the first chapter in "Part One." This is also the most thoroughly Socratic chapter, though it also appears as a controlled element in a clever kind of three-step argumentation, which again shows up in the presupposed dialectic between the two main sections.[22]

3. Chapter One of Part One

3.1 The Hermeneutic of Misunderstanding

The introduction to "Part One" is in large part a prelude to "The View Made Possible." As Kierkegaard says, the issue is to ensure that one has a "reliable and authentic view of Socrates' his-

---

[20]CI, 198-99; SKS, 1:262.

[21]CI, 198; SKS, 1:262.

[22]One might add here that it is specifically the first chapter of Kierkegaard's dissertation that is referred to in the following statements about Kierkegaard's dissertation: Norwegian Socrates scholar Egil A. Wyller claims that Kierkegaard completes "a substantial study based on source research which belongs with the best that has been seen and said about the phenomenon Socrates," "Sokrates-skikkelsen, En presentasjon" in *Sokrates i historiens lys. En samling nordiske studier* (Oslo: Solum Forlag, 1985) 13. The Danish professor of classical philology, Povl Johannes Jensen, has said of the living image of Socrates: "It makes no difference that the image in the dissertation rests on a solid scholarly foundation, it is an erudite work which because of its philological method has always been an inspiration for Danish and Norwegian philologists. It is less appreciated out in the world where one does not always relish the light tone of Holberg's fatherland," "Kierkegaards Socrates" in *Sokrates i historiens lys*, 106.

torical-actual, phenomenological existence with respect to the question of the possible relation to the transformed view that was his fate through enthusiastic or envious contemporaries."[23] In order to procure such a view, the observer must familiarize him- or herself with Socrates and his contemporaries. As far as possible, the observer should use an unbiased perspective in order to view first one side of the issue, then the other. Since the concept is already present as a possible horizon of understanding, it is particularly important to avoid the problems of the "the newer philosophical effort," that is, the Hegelians, who project this understanding onto the phenomenon such that the manifold expressions of the phenomenon become distorted. Rather, the observer must be attentive to the smallest detail—as only an "eroticist" can—so that the phenomenon remains "unviolated." The art is "to help the phenomenon to its full expression," so that the concept is seen as coming into existence with the phenomenon.[24] It should be clear enough that behind this kind of anti-Hegelian hermeneutic,[25] one finds an authentic Socratic eroticist and midwife. The conditions for understanding, however, are different than those of the historical Socrates, who worked with the unmediated form of conversation.

An initial stage of such an understanding is to imagine oneself as a contemporary of Socrates. This already presents the first difficulty: "he belonged to the breed of persons with whom the outer as such is not the stopping point.... The outer was not at all in harmony with the inner, but was rather its opposite and only under this angle of refraction is he to be comprehended."[26] No one understands Socrates without understanding his irony; not even his contemporaries "could apprehend him in his immediacy."[27] This dialectical view admittedly presupposes that the later observer has a certain kind of personality, but for the contempo-

[23]CI, 9; SKS, 1:71.
[24]CI, 9; SKS, 1:71.
[25]See also CI, 221; SKS, 1:265: "The difficulty implicit in the establishment of *certainty* about the *phenomenal* aspects of Socrates' existence does not bother Hegel. He generally does not acknowledge such trivial concerns."
[26]CI, 12; SKS, 1:74.
[27]CI, 12; SKS, 1:74.

rary the misunderstanding is unavoidable, since irony "made its entry into the world" for the first time with Socrates.[28]

Every later observer faces the added difficulty that Socrates left no written work behind. We know the historical Socrates primarily through three surviving testimonies which, in their fullness, belong to the classical texts of our literature. This hermeneutical problem had an important parallel in the research into the historical Jesus, which made a breakthrough with David Friedrich Strauss (1808–1878) during Kierkegaard's time,[29] and not least in Ferdinand Christian Baur's (1792–1860) *Das Christliche des Platonismus oder Sokrates und Christus* (1837). Here the relationship is directly thematized. Against Baur, who is also the target for the first thesis in the dissertation, Kierkegaard emphasizes the decisive difference: "Christ's immediate existence" did not mean anything other than what it was, which is why the synoptic gospels could also reproduce his "immediate, accurate" image.[30]

3.2 Sources for Understanding Socrates

In order to understand Socrates, Kierkegaard must abandon himself, to the surviving records but without going into the problems connected with their historical reception. These records include fictional elements and thus include the question of how they in fact reflect the historical Socrates. To use these writings as historical source material about Socrates already intensifies a mere historical possibility, though without this possibility our knowledge of the historical Socrates would be meaningless. The first possible source, and only contemporary source, is Aristophanes'

---

[28]CI, 9; SKS, 1:71.

[29]In the only critical review of Kierkegaard's dissertation we know of—to which I will return—Andreas Frederik Beck (1816–1861) accentuates this connection which at the time was so controversial. By way of introduction, he remarks that the speculative-critical character of the dissertation "provides an interesting parallel to the critique of evangelical history, which in the most recent times has set the theological world in motion," *Fædrelandet*, 890-97, (May 29 and July 5, 1842) 890, column 7133. Despite Kierkegaard's sarcastic attack on the review in the article "Revealed Confession," *Fædrelandet* 904 (June 12, 1842), Beck let the review be printed in German, almost unchanged, in *Deutsche Jahrbücher für Wissenschaft und Kunst* 223-24 (September 1842), 19-20.

[30]CI, 14; SKS, 1:76.

comedy, *The Clouds*, produced 423 BCE when Socrates was approximately 47 years old. In Kierkegaard's investigation of this comedy, it is implicit in the argumentation that Aristophanes' caricature deals with the historical Socrates, though recent research headed by Kenneth Dover has called this assumption into question.[31] The next two possible authorial sources are Xenophon and Plato, both of whom were contemporaries of Socrates, but authored their accounts shortly after his death. Of interest in Xenophon's authorship are the four so-called Socratic writings. Kierkegaard refers primarily to Xenophon's *Memorabilia*, fewer times to *The Apology*, and only a single time to *The Symposium*. Xenophon's writings traditionally appear in Kierkegaard as the most immediately historical; they were composed just after the execution of Socrates clearly for the purpose of defending his reputation against the fatal accusations. One question which Kierkegaard does not ask though, is to what degree Xenophon himself can be considered a eyewitness. Did he belong to Socrates' circle or are his accounts primarily founded on the witness of others, including Plato, as most current scholars would claim? Without question this last point changes the hermeneutic situation, though as Kierkegaard reads Xenophon, the result would presumably be the same.

A third possible source for Kierkegaard are Plato's dialogues whose immortal Socrates certainly belongs to the most essential literary productions in our culture. As already mentioned, Schleiermacher and Ast introduced the study of the classification and chronology of these dialogues.[32] This led to the now familiar classification of the dramatic works, the aporetic (i.e. without result) early dialogues, the great classic middle dialogues in which Socrates seems to have a positive doctrine, and finally, the more speculative late dialogues in which Socrates often remains in the background. This means that in the early dialogues, Plato gives a

---

[31]See Knut Kleve's lively, Kierkegaardian argumentation against Dover in the article "Anti-Dover or Socrates in the Clouds" in *Symbolæ Osloensis* LVIII (1983): 23-37.

[32]On the traditional classification by Diogenes Laertius, see SKS, K1:92. On Schleiermacher's classification in the introduction to his translation, see SKS, K1:202. On Ast's introduction to *Platon's Leben und Schriften* (1816) see SKS, K1:208.

direct account of the historical Socrates in all his dialectical negativity, while in the middle dialogues, Socrates is more of a spokesman for Plato's own philosophical positions (since he imparts to
ideality its positive content). The late dialogues are considered
pure Plato.[33] Accordingly, Kierkegaard concentrates on those
dialogues in which the historical Socrates seems closest. He looks
primarily at the *Gorgias*—which, however, does not receive an
independent chapter—the *Symposium* and *Phaedo*, which make up
a thematically oppositional pairing, the *Protagoras* with a dialectic
without any result, the *Apology*, which Ast declared to be inauthen-
tic, and the first book of the *Republic*, the youthful aspects of which
had been demonstrated by Schleiermacher. According to Kierkegaard's own account, the choice of precisely these six unique
source materials was based on "common opinion."[34]

3.3 Understanding the Sources

On the basis of this source material, Kierkegaard wants to
reconstruct Socrates' existence, and if such a project is possible at
all, it can only happen through something which Kierkegaard
originally calls a "combined reckoning."[35] If the historical Socrates
was an ironist, he must necessarily have been misunderstood. But
"the discrepancy between the three views"[36] can also be explained
by the fact that the three misunderstandings can be traced back to
the points of view, the biases, and the intentions of the three
authors. If Socrates' position was empty ideality, it could not be
reproduced but only viewed or conceived of.[37] Thus, the positivity
in the conceptions of the three authors, as misconceptions, must
accordingly stem from the authors themselves. Kierkegaard formulates the methodological problem as follows:

[33]For a modern discussion of the this classification, see the section on Plato's
authorship in Karsten Friis Johansen's *A History of Ancient Philosophy: From the
Beginnings to Augustine*, trans. Henrik Rosenmeier (London and New York:
Routledge, 1998).
[34]CI, 119; SKS, 1:171.
[35]CI, 12, SKS, 1:74.
[36]CI, 155; SKS, 1:205.
[37]CI, 155; SKS, 1:205.

> Wherever it is a matter of reconstructing a phenomenon by
> means of what could be a view in the stricter sense of the word,
> there is a double task: one must indeed explain the phenomenon
> and in doing so explain the misunderstanding, and through the
> misunderstanding one must attain the phenomenon and through
> the phenomenon break the spell of the misunderstanding.[38]

Through a brilliant close reading of the source texts, Kierkegaard
is able to successfully eliminate all positivities by explaining them
as misunderstandings characteristic of the authors. Instead of
ordering the views historically, he arranges them according to their
relationship to the Idea, that is, to truth. He thus begins with
Xenophon, "the purely historical view," then treats Plato, "the
ideal view," and finally moves to Aristophanes, "the comical
view." According to Kierkegaard and his contemporaries, the
comical was considered highest in the epistemological hierarchy.[39]

In Xenophon, Kierkegaard sees the greatest misunderstanding
of Socrates inasmuch as Xenophon lacked all sense for ideality and
with his apologetic purpose had to transform Socrates into a bourgeois paragon of virtue. Here Socrates appears "busily functioning
as an apostle of finitude, as officious bagman for mediocrity, tire-
lessly recommending his one and only saving secular gospel that
here we found the useful rather than the good, the useful rather
than the beautiful, the established rather than the true, the lucra-
tive rather than the sympathetic, pedestrianism rather than harmonious unity."[40] With this, Xenophon's horizon is already given
from a perspective of misunderstanding, through which we can
just catch a glimpse of the contours of another, more ideal
Socrates.

The situation is completely different with Plato, whose Socrates
is the direct opposite of Xenophon's. Plato's misunderstanding
stems from his great artistic and philosophical abilities which were
developed directly from personal contact with Socrates. Kierkegaard's psychological portrait includes the claim that Plato was a

---

[38]CI, 155; SKS, 1:205.
[39]See my article "Das komische Pathos. Eine Einführung in Kierkegaards Theorie der
Komik" in Kierkegaardiana 20 (1999): 111-36.
[40]CI, 127; SKS, 1:178.

devoted, youthfully imaginative disciple who after Socrates' death believed himself to be indebted to him and wanted to attribute everything to him "because he cherished nothing unless it came from Socrates."[41] But by doing so, Plato attributed to Socrates more than the master deserved. With Plato, one can certainly find negative aspects in the character of Socrates, but they are often framed by Plato's own agenda so that Socrates is represented essentially as a philosophical hero. With a conception of irony up his sleeve, and an interpretation attentive to the details of the dialogues, Kierkegaard tries now to "break the spell of misunderstanding."

3.4 Understanding Socrates

While Xenophon underestimates Socrates, Plato manages to lift him up to the "supramundane regions of the ideas."[42] But Socrates is neither a sophist of finitude, even though he shares traits with him (emptiness), or a philosopher of the idea, with whom he shares ideality. Socrates hovers between them with his irony.

Aristophanes saw this, which is why "he comes closest to the truth" as Kierkegaard says in the seventh thesis: "Aristophanes has come very close to the truth in his depiction of Socrates." The highly, detailed and intensely empathetic reading of The Clouds[43] rests on a peculiar hypothetical presupposition, however. First, one must be clear about the unique characteristic of the Old Comedy, namely, that it was required to be "comically true." Here Kierke-

---

[41]CI, 30; SKS, 1:91.

[42]CI, 128; SKS, 1:179.

[43]One can read about this in the translation of The Clouds by the Danish comedy and Aristophanes expert, Ole Thomsen, Skyerne (Copenhagen: Akademisk Forlag, 1982). He remarks in a chapter on Kierkegaard's interpretation of Aristophanes that Kierkegaard's pages in The Clouds "are of the greatest interest and would be regardless of who had written them. One must understand that the comedy was read for one thing, namely, the light is sheds on Socrates; but as is apparent in my commentary to the individual verses, the book contains a wealth of observations and life." And a bit later: "more than any other Aristophanes interpreter I am familiar with, he presupposes that Aristophanes has a great knowledge of Socrates. He takes him seriously, with humor and a sense for comedy." See also Thomsen's dissertation (which includes an English summary), Komediens kraft: en bog om en genre (Copenhagen: Akademisk Forlag, 1986), in which there is an enlightening chapter on the Romantic rediscovery of Aristophanes.

gaard follows Rötcher's unavoidable dissertation. But if comic truth consists in the contradiction that transcendent ideality reveals its emptiness, then Rötcher (and Hegel) cannot be right about both the fact that Socrates' view or position is subjectivity, and that Aristophanes is a great poet.[44] The argument is as follows: if Socrates is something (i.e., subjectivity, inwardness), then Aristophanes' comedy is nothing (i.e., unjustified, unpoetic, a "satirical poem"). Or the opposite: if Socrates is nothing (i.e., absolute infinite negativity, irony), then Aristophanes' comedy is something (i.e., a masterpiece). Luckily, one might say, Kierkegaard is able to show with his allegorical reading that Aristophanes was a true master whose comedy originated in poetic ideality. Likewise, Kierkegaard shows that Aristophanes did not make the historical Socrates ridiculous with a satirical demonstration of power, but contemplatively saw instead the objective contradiction in Socrates' position. Kierkegaard finds a fixed image of this contradiction in the depiction of Socrates floating below the ceiling, yet supported by the basket: "for the basket is in a way the basis for the empirical actuality that the ironist needs, whereas subjectivity in its infinity gravitates to itself—that is, it is infinitely in suspension."[45] Inasmuch as Aristophanes' misunderstanding is related to comic ideality, he has come closest to the truth since Socrates, as nothing, is more comic than tragic (Hegel).

Through his original hermeneutic, Kierkegaard is able to overcome the apparent contradictions. He relates to the phenomenon contemplatively, erotically, i.e., he keeps moral considerations from arising. He disentangles the dialectical relationship between the author, the work, and the genre; between character, reply, and situation; between the author, the fictional Socrates, and the actual Socrates; between what is said, how it is said, and who says it. To this one must add the relationship between the phenomenon and

---

[44]In his own copy of *The Concept of Irony*, next to the seventh thesis, Kierkegaard—against Hegel—has written a reference to this note in the chapter on Aristophanes: "But, of course, if there had been a Platonic positivity in Socrates, then, however much freedom the Greeks allowed their comedy writers, Aristophanes undeniably overstepped the boundary, the boundary the comic itself possesses: the requirement that it be true to the comic point of view." See SKS, K1:202.

[45]CI, 152; SKS, 1:202.

the concept which presuppose each other as a part of a whole. Kierkegaard's point is not, however, that he presupposes the very concept that will then be demonstrated, but rather the opposite. Through observation of the phenomenon, he wants to demonstrate the very possibility of the presupposition. Or better still, he wants to show that only with this presupposition can we understand Socrates and the contradictions of the surviving texts. Kierkegaard says the following about this unusual strategy:

> I hope, however, that the fair and reasonable reader will recognize this as circumspection on my part, even though the form of the whole treatise thereby departs somewhat from the widespread and in so many ways meritorious scholarly method. If I had posed the final view first of all and in each particular portion had assigned each of these three considerations its place, then I would easily have lost the element of contemplation, which is always important but here doubly so, because by no other way, not by immediate observation, can I gain the phenomenon.[46]

As shown, the first chapter of *The Concept of Irony* sets itself apart from the rest of the dissertation with its unique dialectical hermeneutic and methodological reflection. The fundamental aim of my article has been to focus upon this hermeneutic, that is, to identify it and build a case for claiming that the most original part of the dissertation lies hidden in this hermeneutic. By contrast, it has not been my aim to give a detailed description and explanation of this method; this task belongs to future studies.

4. A Further Perspective

As a concluding perspective, I will offer an illustration of the way in which the hermeneutical focus of *The Concept of Irony* can be applied to Kierkegaard's later authorship and, at the same time, show that the way Andreas Frederik Beck—who was an opponent *ex auditorio* at Kierkegaard's defense—reads Kierkegaard is similar to the way Hegel reads Socrates. Kierkegaard employs irony against both Beck and Hegel since their objective dialectics exclude the subjective aspect of understanding instead of including it.

---

[46]CI, 156; SKS, 1:206.

In the beginning of his article, Helveg said that Kierkegaard's dissertation "not only treats irony, but is an irony." It is evident here that *what* a text treats internally does not capture the way in which it is said. The hermeneutic which Kierkegaard develops in the first chapter of his dissertation requires double reflection. Beck seems not to have lived up to this hermeneutical requirement.

When Beck reviewed *The Concept of Irony* in 1842, he was not able to consult commentaries to assist his *immediate* understanding of the text as readers have been able to do with all later editions.[47] After praising Kierkegaard's humorous form, Beck concludes: "On the other hand, it must be critically stated that there are a number of allusions and references in the book which certainly only the fewest people understand. The reviewer, to name one, does not have the honor of following Herr Author."[48] Kierkegaard seizes ironically on this statement in his response to Beck. He writes that Beck, "who otherwise is a dialectician and an expert in categories" (COR, 10) could well enough have reached other conclusions: when Beck did not understand the allusions, for example, it was Beck himself who deserves the criticism. "It is incredible how much can be drawn from the fact Dr. B. has not understood; would that one might conclude as much from what Dr. B has understood" (COR, 10). He continues, "Moreover, it is sufficient punishment for me that Dr. B has not understood me, and all the more so since it already was grievous enough for me that Dr. B believed that he had understood me in several passages" (COR, 10). Beck does not understand the allusions. But does he have the capacity to understand at all? That is, does he have what we might call a doubly reflected understanding, which is, for example, a condition for understanding irony?

---

[47]See my article, "On Annotating *The Concept of Irony* with Reference to the Editorial History," in *Kierkegaard Studies. Yearbook 2000*, ed. Niels Jørgen Cappelørn, Hermann Deuser, and Jon Stewart (Berlin and New York: de Gruyter, 2000).

[48]See reference in n. 11, no. 897, col. 7191. In the German version, it was changed to "Es muss dagegen getadelt werden, dass sich im Buche eine Menge Anspielungen und Hindeutungen auf (Gott weiss, welche) Verhältnisse, Zustände, Vorgänge meistens wohl in Dänemark oder vielmehr in Kopenhagen finden, die nicht als allbekannt vorausgesetzt werden dürfen, und in denen namentlich der Ref. dem Hrn. Verf. zu folgen die Freude nicht haben konnte."

Beck did not lose his nerve, but later wrote in German a review of *Philosophical Fragments*,[49] though this time anonymously. This review did not escape Kierkegaard's satire either, since in the *Concluding Unscientific Postscript* he allows Johannes Climacus to comment upon it in an extensive note, which, incidentally, is in itself a complete lecture on a doubly reflected hermeneutic. The problem with Beck's review resides not in the immediate factual reading: "His report is accurate, and on the whole, dialectically reliable" (CUP, 1:274). It is the double reflection of understanding which Beck has not managed to reproduce: "The report is didactic, purely and simply didactic; consequently, the reader then will receive the impression that the pamphlet is also didactic" (CUP, 1:275).

Beck's didactic attitude corresponds well to an immediate, factually oriented hermeneutic—one could call it Hegelian—and the review is a prime example of how such a hermeneutic leads to fundamental misunderstanding:

> The contrast of form, the teasing resistance of the imaginary construction of the content, the inventive audacity (which even invents Christianity), the only attempt made to go further (that is, further than the so-called speculative constructing), the indefatigable activity of irony, the parody of speculative thought in the entire plan, the satire in making efforts as if something *was ganz Auszerordentliches und zwar Neues* [altogether extraordinary, that is, new] were to come from them, whereas what always emerges is old-fashioned orthodoxy in its rightful severity—of all this the reader finds no hint in the report. (CUP, 1:275)

It is precisely an eye for "all this" which makes a proper understanding possible. This appeared clearly in the erotic hermeneutic in *The Concept of Irony*. The naive hermeneutic presupposes this understanding in order to get to the issue, but it becomes powerless in every case in which understanding is an essential part of the issue itself. Irony is just such a case.

---

[49]The review is printed in *Neues Repertorium für theologische Literatur und Kirchliche Statistik* 2/1 (1845): 44-48. Reprinted in *Kierkegaardiana* VIII (1971): 212-16; and in *Materialien zur Philosophie Søren Kierkegaards*, ed. Michael Theunissen and Wilfried Greve (Frankfurt am Main: Suhrkamp, 1979). Beck acknowledged his authorship of the article in his book *Theologiske Tilstande i Danmark i Aarene 1842-46* (Copenhagen, 1847) 28.

Kierkegaard concludes his commentary to Beck's review by calling Socrates to mind:

> Suppose that someone had been present at one of Socrates' ironic conversations; suppose that he later gives a report of it to someone but leaves out the irony and says: God knows whether talk like that is irony or earnestness—then he is satirizing himself. But the presence of irony does not necessarily mean that the earnestness is excluded: Only assistant professors assume that. That is, while they otherwise do away with the disjunctive *aut* [or] and fear neither God nor the devil, since they mediate everything—they make an exception of irony; they are unable to mediate that. (CUP, 1:277)

The last thesis in *The Concept of Irony* claims that "a life that may be called human begins with irony" (CI, 6), that is, that an individual must overcome his or her (first) immediacy through reflection. Through irony, one obtains a hermeneutical competence which immediately understands an issue as doubly reflected or, in other words, understands that the outer is not always the inner. That which cannot be mediated is a personal certainty, which is a presupposition of all understanding. When Helveg mentioned that with *The Concept of Irony* Kierkegaard had written a draft for a life task, he was thinking of the task which consists of a personal appropriation. The capacity for understanding belongs to this process of personal appropriation and a sure sign of the depth of understanding is the sense for irony. Formulated as a task, the imperative of understanding can be expressed with the words of the ancient oracle of Delphi: "Know thyself!" Was it not "all this" that Kierkegaard wanted to communicate in the last issue of *The Moment*, when he wrote: "The only analogy I have before me is Socrates; my task is a Socratic task" (TM, 341)?

Ironic Love:
An Amorist Interpretation of Socratic Eros

Sylvia Walsh

In Plato's *Symposium* Socrates makes the remarkable claim that the only thing he understands is "the art of love" (*ta erōtica*) (177d-e). Since Socrates generally professes to know nothing at all, this pronouncement comes as a surprise and should perhaps be taken ironically, with the implication that no more than truth, goodness, or beauty can love be adequately defined and understood by finite human beings.[1] The art of love as exemplified in the person of Socrates nevertheless forms the phenomenological starting point for the formulation of a concept of love in Kierkegaard's doctoral dissertation, *The Concept of Irony*. Although this work is primarily concerned, as its title suggests, with an exposition of the concept of irony, I hope to show that the hermeneutical method employed to illumine that concept in the text also yields a concept of love. But it is an abstract concept of only the negative element in love, and hence an ironic concept of love that is really no concept inasmuch as the positive nature of love remains undisclosed and indefinable in its Socratic manifestation.

That there is a close, even integral connection between interpretation and the erotic is apparent in the hermeneutical method set forth and followed by Kierkegaard in *The Concept of Irony*. In fact, this method may aptly be described as an *erotic hermeneutics* inasmuch as in it the observer/interpreter or "philo-

---

[1] An ironical reading of Socrates' claim is reinforced by the fact that he later retracts it (198D); still later in the text, however, he claims that Diotima "is the one who taught me the art of love" (201D), with the result that the claim remains ambiguous.

sophical knight," as Kierkegaard calls him, is understood as an *amorist (Erotiker)*, that is, an interpreter who pays close attention, in a deferential and enthusiastic fashion, to every feature and factor of the phenomenon (CI, 9). In this way the philosophical concept is allowed to come into existence in and with the phenomenon rather than being imposed upon it by the interpreter in a violent and domineering fashion. The erotic character of Kierkegaard's hermeneutic is heightened by the fact that the phenomenon, identified as feminine in gender, surrenders itself by nature to the stronger, masculine power of the amorist interpreter, whose predominance over the phenomenon is to be used only "to help the phenomenon obtain its full disclosure" (CI, 9).

This way of construing the relation between phenomenon and interpreter undoubtedly constitutes an advance over patriarchal modes of interpretation which, in Kierkegaard's estimation, rely too much on "the jingling of spurs and the voice of the master" (with an obvious allusion to the phenomenological method of Hegel). But it is debateable, from a feminist point of view at least, whether Kierkegaard's erotic hermeneutics really abandons this patriarchal framework or merely tempers it. For on the one hand, stereotyped notions of gender and male/female relations endemic to patriarchy are preserved and perpetuated in his method, which does not appear to go beyond a paternalistic understanding of the relation between the phenomenon and interpreter. Thus one could conclude that while Kierkegaard's erotic hermeneutic does away with intellectual rape and incest on the part of the interpreter/father, it falls short of a radical revisioning of the hermeneutical method itself (CI, 9).[2]

On the other hand, the assistance of the amorist interpreter in the self-disclosure of the phenomenon bears a close likeness to Socratic midwifery, in which Socrates metaphorically assumes the same role as his mother, Phaenarete, who is reported to be a midwife—"like mother, like son," one might say (*Theaetetus*, 149a-

---

[2]An example of the intellectual violence Kierkegaard associates with Hegelian interpretation may be noted in a footnote to the text where Kierkegaard accuses Hegel of "a bold act of rape" in interpreting the Sophistic thesis that man is the measure of all things as meaning "that man is the goal toward which everything strives" (CI, 207n.).

b, 150b-d). Thus the masculine interpreter may be said to appropriate the feminine in a kind of gender reversal on his part. On this
basis one could argue that Kierkegaard's erotic hermeneutic not
only transcends the worst features of patriarchy but is actually
revolutionary in its conception of the erotic and the feminine as
constituting the very essence of philosophic interpretation.[3]

Just as there is an integral connection between the erotic and
interpretation in *The Concept of Irony*, so too one may observe an
intimate relation between the erotic and irony as exemplified in the
figure of Socrates in this text. Not only is Socrates described as an
ironist who sustains a negative relation to the established order, or
the state, but also as "an amorist (*Erotiker*) of the highest order"
who is ironic in his personal relations as well (CI, 187-88). Kierkegaard even goes so far as to identify the erotic love embodied by
Socrates as an ironic love, with the result that, just as Socratic
irony is distinguished from Platonic irony in the text, so too

---

[3]Whether such a method would constitute a feminist hermeneutics, however,
is highly debateable, inasmuch as feminists more often than not tend to view the
traditional concept of the feminine itself as a patriarchal construct. See, e.g.,
Simone de Beauvoir's classic analysis in *The Second Sex*, trans. H. M. Parshley
(New York: Vintage Books, 1989). Moreover, feminist assessments of Kierkegaard's use of gender categories and his attitude toward women and the feminine
vary considerably. For a range of feminist approaches to his writings, see *Feminist
Interpretations of Søren Kierkegaard*, ed. Céline Léon and Sylvia Walsh (University
Park: Pennsylvania State University Press, 1997). My own assessment is both
critical and commendatory, as I find him quite ambivalent on the topic of woman
and gender, reflecting in many ways the prejudices and presuppositions of his
time while also pointing the way to the possibility of true selfhood for both
women and men. See my essays in the volume cited above and "Issues That
Divide: Interpreting Kierkegaard on Woman and Gender" in *Kierkegaard Revisited*,
Kierkegaard Studies Monograph Series 1 (Berlin and New York: Walter de
Gruyter, 1997) 191-205. One may note a range of conflicting feminist assessments
of Plato's use of feminine imagery as well in *Feminist Interpretations of Plato*, ed.
Nancy Tuana (University Park: Pennsylvania State University Press, 1994). While
some interpreters in this volume view the image of Socratic midwifery negatively
as an attempt of male philosophers to appropriate female reproductive powers
to themselves (duBois, Tuana), others read Plato's dialogues more positively as
using such imagery (the personification of truth and philosophy as female, for
example) to mount a Socratic critique and/or subversion of masculinist features
of Greek culture (Brown, Hampton) and Platonic philosophy (Nye).

Socratic eros is revealed to be significantly different from Platonic eros in it.[4]

To substantiate these claims it will be necessary to attend the development of Kierkegaard's textual analysis rather closely, adopting, as it were, the manner of an amorist interpreter myself in order to allow the concept of erotic love to emerge in its essential connection with Socratic irony. I shall begin with an examination of Kierkegaard's attempt as an amorist interpreter himself to construct a "reliable and authentic view" of the "historical-actual, phenomenological existence" of Socrates from ancient accounts of the philosopher by Xenophon, Plato, and Aristophanes (CI, 9, 13).

Lacking a sense of the importance of situation for Socrates and an ear for the irony, or "reverse echoing," of his rejoinders, Xenophon's account, as Kierkegaard understands it, portrays him erotically as an ordinary, repulsive pederast who brags about the love potions with which he lures young men to himself (CI, 16, 18-19). The general reaction to such pedestrian behavior, Kierkegaard observes, is that "we are just as disgusted with him as with an aged coquette who still believes herself capable of captivating—indeed, we are even more disgusted, because we cannot perceive the possibility of Socrates' ever having been capable of it" (CI, 24; cf. *Memorabilia* III, 11).[5]

In conparison to Xenophon, Plato, for whom Kierkegaard confesses to harbor a "somewhat youthful infatuation" himself, presents a much more complex, duplex picture of Socrates (CI, 27). In Plato's account Socrates is portrayed as an original or primitive personality whose impact upon the race and individuals was "not

---

[4]On the difference between Socratic eros and Platonic eros, see also Gregory Vlastos, *Socrates: Ironist and Moral Philosopher* (Ithaca NY: Cornell University Press, 1991) 38-39. Noting that the two are often conflated by interpreters, Vlastos identifies four major differences between them.

[5]Contra Kierkegaard, Vlastos finds both "simple" (what is said is not what is meant) and "complex" (what is said both is and is not meant, in that it is meant to be true in one sense, false in another) irony in Xenophon's account (Ibid., 31). Thus, where Kierkegaard interprets Socrates' remarks in the *Memorabilia* as an indication that he engages in carnal pederasty, Vlastos reads him ironically on this score. In line with Vlastos, K. J. Dover, in *Greek Homosexuality* (Cambridge: Harvard University Press, 1978), contends that both Xenophon's Socrates and the Platonic Socrates "condemn homosexual copulation" (160).

merely inciting but epoch-making," in both positive and negative ways (CI, 28-29). Like Christ, Socrates communicates life and spirit to individuals as well as indirectly aids them, in the manner of a midwife, "to come to" or to give birth to themselves as individuals (CI, 29). The latter activity, Kierkegaard points out, is the one most often accentuated with respect to Socrates. In Plato's dialogues Socratic midwifery is characterized as a relation of love in the form of a spiritual pederasty (as opposed to Xenophon's carnal pederasty) in which young men are awakened to spiritual development through their relationships with Socrates (CI, 29n.).

As for Plato's own love relation to Socrates, Kierkegaard finds it to be so symbiotic that one has difficulty distinguishing the actual Socrates from the poetic Socrates who is a product of Plato's spiritual unity with him (CI, 30). Nevertheless, Kierkegaard believes it is possible to differentiate between them and to detect the genuine or "unalloyed" Socratic elements in Plato's dialogues (CI, 40). This may be done by paying close attention, first of all, to the method of dialectic, the art of asking questions or conversing, in the dialogues. As Kierkegaard analyzes it, this questioning may be either *speculative* (Platonic) or *ironic* (Socratic) in intent, seeking a fullness or plenitude in the answer or interested only in sucking out its apparent content so as to leave an emptiness behind (CI, 36). This distinction "appears in a more definite form," he claims, "as the relation between the abstract and the mythical in Plato's dialogues" (CI, 40). The former terminates in (Socratic) irony, while the latter heralds "a more copious [Platonic] speculation" (CI, 40-41).

Kierkegaard engages in a close analysis of these elements in five of Plato's early dialogues: *Symposium, Protagoras, Phaedo, Apology,* and *Republic,* Book I (CI, 53). He begins with the *Symposium,* a dialogue especially important for our purposes since it focuses on the concept of love. Only a cursory review of the speeches leading up to Socrates' oration in the dialogue is given, since in Kierkegaard's opinion none of them stands "in any necessary relation to the final one" and together they constitute merely a collection of "heterogeneous viewpoints found in life"

(CI, 42).[6] More importantly, in Kierkegaard's opinion they reveal nothing about the nature of love, which remains invisible in them. Kierkegaard thus moves on quickly to the speech of Socrates, which takes up and further develops the theme of love as desire and longing for union in the speech of Aristophanes.

Noting the reputation of Socrates as an ironist, which in Kierkegaard's estimation is based on far more than a knack for the use of rhetorical irony, our amorist interpreter focuses his analysis of Socrates' speech on the way in which the dialectical method functions in it (CI, 45). Unlike the method of Hegel, which moves from an abstract universal constituting everything to its unfolding in the concrete, the Socratic method, he contends, moves in the opposite direction, from the concrete to the abstract, "simplifying life's multifarious complexities by leading them back to an ever more abstract abbreviation" (CI, 32, 41, 46; cf. 267). In this instance the Socratic method yields a negative, abstract definition of love as "the want of and desire for what one does not have" (CI, 32, 41, 45). But this is a definition of love which, in Kierkegaard's estimation, is really no definition, since it lacks substance or content, denoting "a relation to a something that is not given" rather than the fullness of divine or infinite love (CI, 45-46). It thus constitutes an ironic definition of love, or to state it more precisely, erotic love is defined here as ironic love, the opposite of what love is in its fullness or positive definition.

This dialectical, negative, ironic, purely abstract view of love is complemented by another development in the *Symposium* which in Kierkegaard's view establishes a point of conjunction between Socrates and Plato, or between the ironical (the dialectical) and the speculative (the idea in its fullness), by having the idea of love exemplified in the person of Socrates (CI, 46-47). This development may be observed in the speech of Alcibiades, which Kierkegaard

---

[6]Briefly, Kierkegaard notes the eternal, victorious character of Eros, the god of love, in the speech of Phaedrus. In the oration of Pausanias he finds a concentration on the god's dual (heavenly/vulgar) nature. In Eryximachus's speech the unity of dichotomous factors in love is emphasized. In Aristophanes' mythological account it is the negative element in love's yearning for union that stands out. And in Agathon's speech the perpetually youthful, delicate, and lovely demeanor of the god is eulogized (CI, 42-44).

proceeds to examine next, bypassing for the moment the speech of Diotima as reported by Socrates. The reason for overleaping Diotima's speech at this point is because it introduces the element of the mythical and thus is deferred until consideration of that factor in the dialogue.

In the speech of Alcibiades, Kierkegaard notes that, unlike the previous speakers, who groped for the idea of love like blind men, Alcibiades is able to grasp it "with immediate certainty" because he is in a heightened state of immediacy due to alcoholic intoxication (CI, 47). Although Alcibiades becomes attached to Socrates with "vehement passion" in an ambiguous love relation that is at once enslaving and painful to him, their relation is characterized as an *intellectual* one by Kierkegaard (CI, 48). But it is not a normal intellectual relationship involving a mutual exchange of ideas or a process of give and take between teacher and student in which the idea is present as a third term binding them together. Rather, it is one in which the idea remains hidden, masked by irony, as "it is essential for the ironist never to articulate the idea as such but only casually to suggest it, to give with one hand and take away with the other, to hold the idea as personal property," Kierkegaard maintains (CI, 48-49). He thus concludes that "even in Alcibiades' view of Socrates irony is his essential aspect," with the result that nothing can be learned about the nature of love from their relation (CI, 49). Even in moments of Socrates' transfiguration, when Alcibiades is able to behold the divine images, or a divine fullness, in his soul, this fullness is hidden in such a way as not to function as a positive source of inspiration for his pupil. What attracts Alcibiades and incites his love is Socrates' personality, which stands ironically in a "negative self-relation to the idea," that is, turned in upon himself in a kind of "omphalopsychic staring" at himself, Kierkegaard observes (CI, 50). Thus, even in the exemplification of love in his own person Socrates provides only a negative or ironic manifestation of an intellectual love equivalent to "what lovers' games and quarrels are in the realm of baser love" for the incitement of love (CI, 51). While our amorist interpreter is willing to admit that the ironist possesses an *Urgrund* [primordial ground] or intrinsic value in himself, this fullness is a determination of nature or vitality of being that never discloses itself in the ironist's dealings with the world (CI, 51-52).

This view of Socrates will reappear and receive further treatment in Kierkegaard's analysis of Aristophanes' portrayal of the ironic philosopher. Before moving on to that account, however, we must attend to the second factor by which Kierkegaard thinks Plato's thought may be differentiated from that of Socrates in the early dialogues, namely, the mythical. Whereas the dialectical prevails in Plato's earliest dialogues, which end either indeterminately without a conclusion or else ironically with a negative conclusion, the mythical element is more prominent in the *Symposium* and *Phaedo*, Kierkegaard observes (CI, 54-55, 62). Moreover, these two dialogues bear a certain kinship with one another inasmuch as longing constitutes the substance of both (CI, 62, 72n). In the *Symposium* this longing takes the form of a desire to possess, while in the *Phaedo* it is manifested as a desire to lose, as in the philosopher's apathetic wish for death, which Kierkegaard regards as a "snobbish sickness found only in the highest social circles" (CI, 72n, 75-77). In his judgment, however, both forms of longing are negative inasmuch as they signify an ignorance of "the what" into which the subjects would either hurl or volatilize themselves (CI, 72n).

However, the thoroughgoing negativity of Socratic dialectic in these and other early dialogues of Plato is complemented by the contrasting presence of the mythical, or the imaginative representation of ideality in the form of actuality. As Kierkegaard sees it, the mythical belongs to Plato rather than to Socrates, for whom the dialectical is characteristic. If the dialectical may be understood erotically as a desire or craving for the idea, the mythical corresponds to an erotic "embrace" of the idea (CI, 103). It appears in the early dialogues as an unconscious, poetic reaction on Plato's part to Socrates' negative dialectic, and in the later dialogues as a conscious mirroring of the idea in the form of metaphor. In the *Symposium*, which is the dialogue of primary interest to us here, the mythical makes its appearance, Kierkegaard observes, in Diotima's speech, which contains two mythical components. The first emerges in Diotima's attempt to let the negative element in thought, that is, its eternal restlessness, be *seen* under the qualifications of time and space in the figure of Eros, who is characterized by the Mantinean priestess as an intermediate being neither divine nor human, immortal nor mortal, rich nor poor, wise nor ignorant

(*Symposium*, 203C-204B; cf. CI, 106). In Kierkegaard's opinion, however, the mythical element in Diotima's speech does not consist in its reference to the myth of Eros as such but rather to the way in which the speech seeks "to maintain something that actually is not" in the form of an ideal reality concocted by the imagination that gives positive content to the idea of love (CI, 106).

The second mythical component of Diotima's speech may be discerned in its advancement of the beautiful as the object of Eros. First, the concept of beauty is stripped of all physical and psychic qualifications by an increasingly abstract dialectical movement from beautiful bodies to beautiful souls, beautiful observations, beautiful knowledge, and finally to the beautiful in itself. A mythical dimension is then added to this abstract dialectical movement by Diotima's suggestion that the essence of beauty, or "'beauty itself, sheer, pure, unalloyed, not clad in human flesh and hues or other mortal vanity,'" may be "*beheld*," that is, grasped in determinate form (CI, 107). As with the figure of Eros, Kierkegaard emphasizes that the mythical presentation does not consist in its being put into the mouth of Diotima, who is believed by most Plato scholars to be a fictional figure.[7] Rather, it consists in the object—in this instance the beautiful—being placed outside of thought only to be brought back again under the aegis of the imagination—a feature that is intrinsic to the mythical, Kierkegaard claims (CI, 108).

In focusing on the mythical elements in Diotima's speech and in associating them with Plato rather than Socrates, Kierkegaard considerably downplays the importance of Diotima's philosophic characterization of Eros as a lover of wisdom (*philosophon*) in the dialogue. But a passion for wisdom is everywhere assumed as the basis of Socratic eros in his account, as in, for example, the use of a passage from the *Phaedrus*—"passion for a loved one joined with the love of wisdom"—to explain what is meant by calling Socrates an amorist in an intellectual sense (CI, 191).

---

[7]For a discussion of whether Diotima is a mythical figure or an actual historical person, see David M. Halperin, "Why Diotima Is a Woman," in *One Hundred Years of Homosexuality and Other Essays on Greek Love* (New York: Routledge, 1990) 119-24. See also K. J. Dover, *Greek Homosexuality*, 161n.11.

On the whole, however, it is not Plato's view of Socrates that most informs Kierkegaard's phenomenological interpretation of him, but rather that of Aristophanes, who is credited by our amorist interpreter with opening up "the possibility of a new approach" to the Greek philosopher by depicting him dramatically in *The Clouds* as a comic figure (CI, 128). As Kierkegaard sees it (following Rötscher), the essence of comedy consists in "viewing actuality ideally," that is, in construing a personality or character as the representative of an idea or principle (CI, 129).[8] The principle Socrates represents for Aristophanes is the principle of subjectivity—but only in its barest, most abstract, negative or ironic form. Thus, as the representative of subjectivity Socrates provides merely a glimpse of the idea, not a representation of it in its positive fullness (CI, 132).

In his analysis of Aristophanes' dramatic presentation of Socrates, Kierkegaard pays close attention to three items considered to be "of primary importance" in the play: the understanding of Socrates as a personality, the priority of the dialectical in his teaching, and his position vis à vis the principle of subjectivity (CI, 145, 147). Concerning the first of these, Socrates is understood as a *personality* or individual because he is an ironist, who falls under the rubric of personality by virtue of the fact that he is "always singular" and takes everything back into himself (CI, 147). The latter characteristic, in Kierkegaard's estimation, constitutes the primary qualification of personality, although an ironist qualifies as only an "abbreviation" or "outline" of a complete personality since his life lacks any positive content (CI, 147, 149, 220n). In consonance with Plato's characterization of Socrates as omphalopsychically staring at himself, therefore, Aristophanes portrays Socrates as an ironic personality who is totally immersed in himself (CI, 141, 145-46). His *dialectic* is described in like manner as a purely negative one that "continually remains in itself" and is self-sufficient, desiring nothing, never going out "into the qualifications of life or of the idea" and thus entirely without content (CI,

---

[8]It should be noted that Kierkegaard views both Aristophanes and Plato as providing an ideal, as opposed to an empirical, interpretation of Socrates, but the former portrays him ideally as a comic figure, while the latter presents him as a tragic ideality.

135-36, 145, 149-51, 154). As for his *position*, Socrates is graphically portrayed by the Greek dramatist as suspended in a basket, hovering between ideality and actuality, in a position of "complete isolation" (CI, 146, 152). Socrates has pupils but is not attached to them or involved in any real relationship with them. Rather, like the clouds symbolizing his ethereal position, he "continually hovers freely above them, enigmatically attracting and repelling" young men while remaining detached and seemingly indifferent to them (CI, 137, 146).

In spite of the fact that Kierkegaard thinks Aristophanes' portrayal of Socrates' ironic position is "entirely correct," as an amorist interpreter he understands himself to play the role of a neutral "third party" whose hermeneutical task is to mediate between opposing views or interpretations, reconciling their differences through an explanation of the phenomenon that can account for the discrepancies between them (CI, 146, 155). In this way there comes into existence the possibility of a "final view" that offers not merely a view or interpretation (*Opfattelse*) of the phenomenon, as in the accounts of Xenophon, Plato, and Aristophanes, but in a stricter sense of the word a reproduction or reconstruction of the phenomenon, which is the goal of Kierkegaard's hermeneutics and dissertation (CI, 155; SV XIII, 239-40). Ironically contrasting his approach to "the now widespread and in so many ways meritorious scholarly method" of the time, which in his estimation begins with, rather than arrives at, a final view, Kierkegaard criticizes the scholarly approach for its loss of the element of contemplation in relation to previous views, which are merely assigned a place in the final view (CI, 156). Contemplation is always important to interpretation, he maintains, but in this instance it is doubly important because that is the only way the phenomenon, not being present for immediate observation, may be regained (CI, 156).

Kierkegaard proceeds to construct or "actualize" a final— presumably his own—view of Socrates by taking into account certain historical phenomena which may be explained, he suggests, by keeping them, in an amorist fashion, "in their inviolate innocence" (CI, 156). These phenomena consist of two facts: 1) that Socrates assumed he possessed a daimon; and 2) that he was condemned to death for not accepting the gods of the state and for seducing the youth (CI, 157, 168, 183).

With regard to the daimon of Socrates, Kierkegaard notes that it is something abstract, divine, beyond definition, indescribable, and wholly negative, having the effect of making him relate polemically to actuality or the state (CI, 158-60). In agreement with Hegel, who views the daimon as separate from Socrates yet as something inward that confirms his position as subjectivity, Kierkegaard also regards the daimon as a qualification of subjectivity. But in opposition to Hegel he maintains that in Socrates subjectivity did not disclose itself in its fullness via a positive relation to the idea (CI, 163-65). Rather, the idea was a "boundary from which Socrates turned back into himself in ironic satisfaction," egotistically closing himself off from the established order as well as from close relationships with others (CI, 165-66, 168-69).

As Kierkegaard interprets it, therefore, the Socratic maxim "know thyself" did not signify the attainment of any positive content on the part of Socrates but only meant "separate yourself from the other" (CI, 177). Although Socrates lived in "lively contact" with others and entered into personal relations with them, these relations were always loose and momentary, never developing into anything deeper or permanent (CI, 180-82). Thus he is aptly described by Kierkegaard as "a virtuoso in casual contacts" (CI, 181). "[N]o relationship was strong enough to bind him," Kierkegaard contends, nor did he exhibit the earnestness and pathos required of a teacher toward his pupils (CI, 182, 187). Standing aristocratically above every relationship, sufficient unto himself in ironic contentment, Socrates freed others from their substantial ties to family and state but gave them nothing to put in the place of these relations (CI, 176, 182). As Kierkegaard expresses it:

> One could not think of Socrates as someone who under the celestial vault of ideas elevated his pupils through the intuition of their eternal essence, as someone who impregnated youths with the rich fullness of a vision, as someone who ethically laid an enormous responsibiliity upon his own shoulders and watched them with fatherly concern, reluctantly let them go but never lost sight of them, as someone who, to recall a previous expression, loved them in the idea. (CI, 187)

Although Socrates possessed "an extraordinary enthusiasm for knowledge," in Kierkegaard's opinion he harbored "no deeper speculative craving" as a result of the negative freedom he attained (CI, 176, 188). His pupils, however, were unable to enjoy their emancipation with the same ironic satisfaction as he. A longing was thus awakened in them that was not satisfied by him, precipitating the charge of Alcibiades—with which Kierkegaard here concurs—that Socrates was a seducer who attracted youths and deceived them into believing that he loved them when it was really they who loved him (CI, 176, 188). An ironic reversal of roles thus took place, with Socrates becoming the beloved rather than the lover in relation to his pupils (CI, 188, 191). In his role as the beloved, however, Socrates remained detached and seemingly indifferent to his lovers, as may be witnessed in his relation to Alcibiades, whose sexual advances were continually spurned by him (CI, 189-90, 47).

Kierkegaard's characterization of Socrates as the beloved thus corresponds closely to the *eromenos* (beloved) of Greek homosexual tradition who, according to Kenneth Dover and Martha Nussbaum, was also self-absorbed and self-sufficient, in need of nothing beyond himself.[9] But whereas the Greek *eromenos* engaged in carnal pederasty with his admirers, allowing them to touch and hug him physically without his being sexually aroused, Socrates' pederasty is understood metaphorically by Kierkegaard as the symbol of an intellectual love of possibility (CI, 191-92). As in Greek pederasty, Socrates' relations to his lovers never went beyond the category of possibility inasmuch as they were only the beginning of relationships that never achieved any deeper meaning (CI, 189, 192). The same or worse may be said of Socrates' relation to his (supposedly) shrewish wife Xanthippe, whose main significance for Socrates, according to Xenophon, consisted in serving as "an exercise in controlling mankind"—which "does not indicate much conjugal love" on his part, Kierkegaard notes (CI, 192n).

---

[9]See Martha C. Nussbaum, *The Fragility of Goodness: Luck and Ethics in Greek Tragedy and Philosophy* (Cambridge: Cambridge University Press, 1986) 188; K. J. Dover, *Greek Homosexuality* II, chap. 5.

Kierkegaard thus concludes that Socrates was "far too personally isolated" and his relations "too loosely joined" to result in anything more than casual contacts with others (CI, 182). However, this does not signify a depreciation of Socrates on the part of Kierkegaard. On the contrary, Socrates is hailed by him as a hero in the (Hegelian) sense that he knew what was required for his time—that is, the next, necessary step for progress—and dedicated himself to promoting it (CI, 211, n. 497).[10] Thus, in Kierkegaard's judgment, Socratic irony was world-historically justified inasmuch as Socrates served as a turning point in world history: He did not bring the new principle of subjectivity in its fullness but was the obstetrician (*accoucheur*) who delivered it in others (CI, 199-200, 211).

In like manner, we may conclude that just as irony is only the beginning or possibility of subjectivity, so too Socrates' ironic love represents only the beginning or possibility of love, not love in its fullness. As reconstructed in Kierkegaard's final view, Socratic eros hardly qualifies as the model of erotic love in either its Platonic or modern understanding, since these require a sustained, positive relation to the idea and through that to others which is altogether lacking in its Socratic manifestation. It is not surprising, therefore, that in the conclusion of *The Concept of Irony* Kierkegaard calls for the mastering of irony so as to make it a "controlled element" and "serving spirit" in one's personal life—something Socrates, having been overwhelmed by irony, was not able to do (CI, 264, 325). Along with controlled irony, Kierkegaard also looks forward to the emergence of an erotic longing for a higher actuality that will constitute "a sound and healthy love," one which embraces actuality rather than rejects it, thereby making "life's content ...a genuine and meaningful element in the higher actuality whose fullness the soul craves" (CI, 328-29). Far from embracing Socratic irony and eros, then, as some interpreters would have it, the concluding irony of *The Concept of Irony* is the negation of both in

---

[10]In Kierkegaard's opinion, however, Socrates is not a tragic hero, who stands in contrast to the ironist by virtue of the fact that he advances the new, whereas an ironist does not possess the new (CI, 260-61; 271).

their unmitigated negativity toward actuality and complete self-isolation from others.[11]

In light of Kierkegaard's later writings, it can be seen too that the "final view" of Socrates set forth in this text turns out not to be his final view after all. For he later criticizes his own earlier interpretation of Socrates and views him in a substantially different light, as not simply an ironist but an ethicist who uses irony as an incognito of his inner relation to the ethical requirement (see CUP, 503-504).[12] Kierkegaard thus comes to view Socratic irony more like Plato and Hegel, as a controlled element in service to the idea rather than as absolute infinite negativity, although he continues to assert that "Socrates lacked the positive" (PF, 23). This modification is already anticipated in *The Concept of Irony*, inasmuch as in irony which is world-historically justified, such as that of Socrates, the emancipation of subjectivity is carried out, Kierkegaard claims, "in the service of the idea, even if the ironic subject is not clearly conscious of this" (CI, 263). By the time of *Concluding Unscientific Postscript*, however, he has come to see more clearly that Socratic or "essential irony" signifies "the cultivation of the spirit" or the infinite within the subjectively existing individual (CUP, 504). The form of the subjective thinker, like that of its paradigm, Socrates, is continually negative in the cognizance of the illusiveness of the

---

[11]For some perspectives that offer an ironic, as opposed to an amorist, interpretation of *The Concept of Irony*, see Sylviane Agacinski, *Aparté: Conceptions and Deaths of Søren Kierkegaard*, trans. Kevin Newmark (Tallahassee: Florida State University Press, 1988) 33-78; Louis Mackey, "Starting from Scratch: Kierkegaard Unfair to Hegel," in *Points of View: Readings of Kierkegaard* (Tallahassee: Florida State University Press, 1986), 1-22; and John Vignaux Smyth, *A Question of Eros: Irony in Sterne, Kierkegaard, and Barthes* (Tallahassee: Florida State University Press, 1986) 101-222.

[12]See also *Philosophical Fragments*, 23-24 and 30, where the relation between Socrates and his pupils is viewed as constituting the highest in human relations, and the charge that Socrates is a seducer is explicitly denied; rather, it is Socrates' pupils who are regarded as unsuccessfully employing the arts of seduction to entice Socrates into seducing them. Moreover, Socrates' ironic love is characterized in this text as an "assisting love" that is sympathetic as well as autopathic in nature, providing an occasion for both the teacher and the learner to acquire self-understanding. For a fuller discussion of Kierkegaard's revised view of Socrates, see my book, *Living Poetically: Kierkegaard's Existential Aesthetics* (University Park: Pennsylvania State University Press, 1994) 211-12.

infinite in existence, but at the same time the subjective thinker, again like Socrates, is passionately, positively related to the infinite as his or her ethical telos (CUP, 84).[13]

The problem with an ironic interpretation of *The Concept of Irony*—and with Kierkegaard's own "final view" or ironic interpretation of the phenomenon Socrates—is that it is not ironic enough, inasmuch as the irony of Socrates is taken literally rather than ironically. That is, Socrates' "seeming indifference" to others may be just that, a seeming indifference rather than an actual one, and thus the mask or incognito of a genuine ethical concern for others. In that case, the incongruence of *The Concept of Irony* with the later authorship's interpretation of Socrates would not be as great as it at first seems. Furthermore, what appears to be an ambivalence or inconsistency in Kierkegaard's view of Socrates in *The Concept of Irony* itself would be resolved. For if Socrates is truly indifferent toward others, he must be interpreted as narcissistic and malevolent, not as an amorist at all.[14]

In one important respect, however, Kierkegaard's view of Socrates never changes, namely, as continually turning into himself. In *The Concept of Anxiety*, for example, Vigilius Haufniensis specifically identifies Socratic irony as inclosing reserve (*Indesluttethed*) or the attempt of a person to close him- or herself off from others so as to become shut up within him- or herself (CA, 134). Ordinarily this phenomenon is understood as being demonic in nature, expressing an anxiety about the good or a state of unfreedom with respect to communication or disclosure of oneself to others (CA, 118-36).[15] In contrast to this demonic form of shutupness, however, Vigilius also speaks of a "lofty inclosing reserve" which should be encouraged and developed in persons. This can

---

[13]On the relation between the positive and the negative in *Concluding Unscientific Postscript* and in Kierkegaard's later religious writings, see my article, "Kierkegaard's Inverse Dialectic," *Kierkegaardiana* 11 (1980): 34-54.

[14]In one passage of the text Kierkegaard actually admits that "by bringing others into the same situation [of a negative relation to the state] he [Socrates] actually did do evil" (CI, 183; cf. also 185n.), and Socrates' self-immersion is characterized as "egotistical" several places in the text, although it is not as egotistic (and sickly) as that of the later romantic ironists (CI, 166, 213n.).

[15]See also *The Sickness unto Death*, 61-66, where this phenomenon is identified with despair in weakness in its most intense (suicidal) form.

be done, he thinks, by leaving others to themselves "in the very highest degree and on the greatest possible scale," letting them learn, like a child, to walk alone (CA, 126; cf. CUP, 74, 80). From Vigilius's perspective this kind of inclosing reserve, like that of Socrates, is not negative or abstract but rather signifies a certitude or inwardness that is synonymous with a concrete subjectivity, earnestness, or religious self-consciousness, and thus with an actual personality, in whom anxiety, like irony, becomes "a serving spirit" (CA, 134, 138-54, 159).

Similarly, in *Works of Love* Kierkegaard asserts that the greatest or highest beneficence one individual can do for another is to help that person stand alone and become independent without being aware of being helped, and he specifically alludes to "that noble rogue," Socrates, as being "a master in this wisdom" (WL, 276; cf. also PF, 24 and CUP, 80). "In this understanding of what it is to help another human being, the one who truly loves and that noble rogue agree," Kierkegaard contends (WL, 276). But there is one crucial difference between them: "however noble and magnanimous and unselfish that rogue was, he still did not in the sense of concern love the one he wanted to help" (WL, 277). For one who truly loves understands that it is only through God's help, not by one's own assistance, that others are enabled to become wholly free. Thus, in helping the other the true lover is "God's co-worker" who works invisibly and without reward, annihilating him- or herself in self-sacrifice so as to become "completely and wholly transformed into simply being an active power in the hands of God" (WL, 279; cf. 405-406).

While Socrates may not qualify as a true lover from Kierkegaard's later, more specifically Christian perspective, or even from the standpoint of his ironic interpretation of Socratic eros in *The Concept of Irony*, an amorist interpretation of the phenomenon may yet conclude that ironic love is to be commended. For it opens up the possibility of subjectivity or inwardness for both the lover and the beloved, enabling each to stand alone as an independent personality. Does such independence compromise a relational, and thus traditionally feminine, understanding of subjectivity and love as envisioned in Kierkegaard's erotic hermeneutics? I think not, since one of the distinguishing characteristics of irony, as Kierkegaard understands it, is that phenomenon and essence are not the same (CI, 247). Thus, what appears to be egotism and indifference toward others may not, in essence, be the case. To become true lovers we must become freestanding individuals ourselves as well as encourage that in others. Just as "one must warn against irony as against a seducer," therefore, one may also commend "diving into the sea of irony, not in order to stay there, of course, but in order to come out healthy, happy, and buoyant" (CI, 327).

4

The Upbuilding in the Irony of Kierkegaard's The Concept of Irony

Andrew J. Burgess

Dissertations are seldom edifying or upbuilding, either for the writer or reader. While the Danish word for "edifying," *opbyggelig*, means literally a "building up," the common testimony of dissertation writers is that the experience tore them apart instead. Their readers, on the other hand, were likely to fare better than the writers, escaping with nothing worse than a near terminal case of boredom.

If Kierkegaard's dissertation is an exception to the general rule in this respect, it can only be because it breaks other rules as well, in particular the cardinal principle that a dissertation should avoid ambiguity and say what it means. In fact, a widespread interpretation holds that Kierkegaard's dissertation, *The Concept of Irony, with Continual Reference to Socrates,* is itself ironical throughout. That is to say, while the dissertation goes to great pains to stress the dependence of its interpretation of irony upon Hegel, that apparent adherence to Hegel may itself be ironical and the whole dissertation a comic way to undermine Hegel's philosophy.

In looking for the upbuilding in the irony of Kierkegaard's dissertation, this essay makes a triple reading of the text. The first reading yields an apparently Hegelian treatment of Socratic irony, the second an ethical factor in the ironical twist, and the third, something that is not irony but, strangely, related to it: the edifying or, as the standard English translation calls it, following the Danish, "the upbuilding." Finding a possibility for upbuilding in a philosophy dissertation may be a bit disconcerting, but in this particular dissertation surprises are the order of the day.

What Is Irony?

Part of the difficulty of this dissertation is that it is hard to find a firm place on which to stand and get a clear perspective on it. Technical terms sometimes seem to change their meaning from one context to the next, especially the key term, "irony." Happily, soon after the start of Part II of his dissertation, Kierkegaard offers a short section he calls "Observations for Orientation" (CI, 246-58). The pages are welcome, because they orient the reader both to what is to come and also to the preceding two thirds of the dissertation. The "Orientation" section does this by defining the concept of irony in its ordinary, nonphilosophical sense and then going on to relate that sense of the term to the kind of Socratic irony that forms the main theme of the book.

Kierkegaard begins by identifying four features characteristic of irony in all its forms, drawing on examples from oratory: saying the opposite of what is meant, keeping the subject "negatively free," self-canceling, and maintaining a certain attitude of superiority toward those who are not in on the ironic secret:

(1) The basic characteristic of irony is "saying the opposite of what is meant." Kierkegaard also puts this into technical Hegelian terminology, defining irony as where "the phenomenon is not the essence but the opposite of the essence" (CI, 247), the "outer" aspect of things not the same as the "inner." In speech, the word is the "phenomenon" and its meaning the "essence." By using the Hegelian terms Kierkegaard leaves open the possibility for speaking of irony in more general ways than simply in speech situations. This generalizing of what is meant by the term "irony" is part of what makes possible the extended uses of the term in other parts of the dissertation.

(2) The second characteristic, that "the subject is negatively free," is much harder to explicate than the first. "When I am aware as I speak that what I am saying is what I mean and that what I have said adequately expresses my meaning, and I assume that the person to whom I am talking grasps my meaning completely, then I am bound in what has been said–that is, I am positively free therein," he writes (CI, 247). "If, however, what I said is not my meaning or the opposite of my meaning, then I am free in relation

to others and to myself" (CI, 247-48). The distinction between positive and negative freedom seems to work this way: when I say what I mean, I am bound (by what I say), but that is still freedom, because I am the one who binds myself; this is what he means by "positive freedom." On the other hand, when what I say is *not* what I mean or the opposite of what I mean, then I am *not* bound by what I say, either by myself or in how I am understood by my listeners. This latter case, too, shows a kind of freedom, a "negative freedom," in that I am *not* bound by what I said but am leaving open the truth or falsity of what I say.

Here again, as with the first characteristic of irony, Kierkegaard seems to be making a simple matter complex, but his purpose is to lay a foundation for uses of the term "irony" beyond the customary ones. What he describes here as "positive" and "negative" freedom are concepts that bring out the ethical aspects of the communication situation that are critical to what Kierkegaard elsewhere calls "Socratic irony."

(3) After describing negative freedom in this way, Kierkegaard quickly goes on to qualify his description with a correlative feature: "self-canceling." He points out that in irony the speaker, although negatively free, is also in another sense bound by what is said. The reason for this is that "The ironic figure of speech cancels itself . . . inasmuch as the one who is speaking assumes that his hearers understand him, and thus, through a negation of the immediate phenomenon, the essence becomes identical with the phenomenon" (CI, 248). Someone who spoke regardless of the truth or falsity of what was said would not be speaking ironically, only babbling. Irony, too, has its rules that bind the speaker and the listener, because for the irony to be effective "the hearer in the know shares the secret lying behind it . . . it is like a riddle to which one at the same time has the solution" (CI, 248).

Unlike the other three characteristics of irony he lists, Kierkegaard does not say of self-canceling that the irony always cancels itself. Sometimes, he says, the ironic figure of speech is misunderstood, not through the fault of the speaker but because of the incapacity of some of the listeners. Yet the irony cannot always be misunderstood by the target audience; sometimes it must succeed. Otherwise there will be not only no self-canceling of the irony but also no negative freedom.

(4) The description of irony's negative freedom leads naturally to the fourth general characteristic of irony, its attitude of "superiority" (CI, 248), or, as an earlier translator put it, "a certain exclusiveness."[1] Irony does not free all listeners equally, only those "in the know." Irony is inherently elitist. Sometimes this elitism is carried so far that intellectuals "speak ironically so that lay people will not be able to understand them, and to that extent irony is in the process of isolating itself; it does not wish to be generally understood"; but in that case "irony does not cancel itself" (CI, 249).

Irony essentially isolates, not just intellectuals from lay people, but also every individual from every other. When members of a group speak in a code language that others cannot follow, that is not true irony. Kierkegaard's metaphor here is right to the point: "This is why there is just as little social unity in a coterie of ironists as there is real honesty in a band of thieves" (CI, 249).

No doubt irony's capacity to isolate one person from another is part of irony's attraction for Kierkegaard. For him, being ironical is an ethical task, one of life's highest ethical tasks, and in ethics no one can push off the responsibility for decisions on someone else.

Although the list of irony's defining characteristics Kierkegaard gives here is incomplete, he elsewhere supplements it. For example, while discussing Plato's *Apology* Kierkegaard mentions the feature of surprise. Irony, he says, "requires strong contrast and would utterly vanish in such boring company as argumentation" (CI, 90). Later in the "Orientation" section he mentions several other features of irony as well, in order to distinguish irony from dissimulation, hypocrisy, mockery, doubt, and the upbuilding (CI, 256-58). I shall discuss the last of these, the upbuilding, in a later section.

First Reading: Literary Irony vs. Socratic Irony

The topic of the dissertation, however, is not irony as a figure of speech or literary irony, but Socratic irony, and Socratic irony is identified as Socrates' position in life. This is the specialized con-

---

[1]Søren Kierkegaard, *The Concept of Irony with Constant Reference to Socrates*, trans. and intro. by Lee M. Capel (New York: Harper & Row, 1965) 265.

cept of irony that he calls in the "Orientation" section "pure irony" or "irony as a position" (CI, 253), the kind of irony that Hegel describes as "infinite absolute negativity" (CI, 254).

Socratic irony differs radically from the usual, literary kind of irony. Literary irony is "momentary," he says (CI, 253), whereas pure irony is not. The ironical person, as usually understood, is not purely ironical; even for the world view of a diplomat who looks at the world ironically "there is much it earnestly wants to affirm" (CI, 254). In the usual sense of the term, irony may be part of one's life—a large part, perhaps, in some lives, such as the diplomat, but still only a part. On the other hand, Kierkegaard maintains that the "pure ironist," such as Socrates, is not just ironical; such a person *is* irony.

But what can this possibly mean? How could anyone, or anyone's position, *be* irony, as opposed to being ironical? Irony is a mode of discourse, not a person or position. Some insight into Kierkegaard's approach here may be found by looking at other similar places in *The Concept of Irony* where he uses the technical terms of language study as metaphors for ways of living.[2] At one point, for example, he pictures the ironist as living in a "totally hypothetical and subjunctive way" (CI, 284). Sometimes these metaphors personifying features of grammar and language use can get highly involved, such as when he describes a human relationship that "empties itself in mere reciprocity . . . like a *pronomen reciprocum* [reciprocally retroactive pronoun] it does not have the nominative but only *casus obliqui* [dependent cases] and only in the dual and plural forms" (CI, 36). Socrates himself is described in another passage in the dissertation as like a punctuation mark, a "dash" [*Tankestreg*], in world history (CI, 198). Or again: "It would indeed be comic to see Socrates try to conjugate his life according to the paradigm of the state, inasmuch as his life was entirely irregular" (CI, 194).

Calling Socrates himself "irony" in the dissertation is a metaphor somewhat of this sort. It draws on Kierkegaard's classical lan-

---

[2]If the account in *Johannes Climacus* can be taken autobiographically on this point, Kierkegaard may have acquired this tendency to treat grammar "philosophically" in preparatory school from his Greek teacher Frederick O. Lange (JC, 121, 321n.7).

guage training, and especially upon his study of the Roman satirists immediately preceding his work on the dissertation (JP, 5:5262). The whole dissertation, then, might be described as a book-length elaboration of this metaphor, in order to make explicit the analogies between Socratic irony and literary irony. Here saying something different from what one means, negative freedom, self-canceling, and superiority get different senses from what they had in literary irony–different, though related, sometimes in roundabout ways.

(1) *Not meaning what one says.* Socrates was doubly ironic. He spoke ironically, in the usual sense of the term; he "could only be misunderstood through his words" (CI, 14n). But not only did Socrates say something different from what he meant, he also really was something different from the way he appeared. In Hegelian terminology, Socrates's essence was completely different from his manifestation. "The outer was not at all in harmony with the inner but was rather its opposite" (CI, 12). People of Socrates' time called Socrates the ugliest and nastiest [*stygeste*] man in Athens (JP, 4:4246; CI, 447), but they also had to acknowledge that his outer person masked a completely different inner being. The way he appeared was not at all what he was.

Accordingly, Socrates' ignorance also has two sides. When Socrates claimed to be ignorant, people could see that he was merely speaking ironically because he spoke wisely. Yet, in a deeper sense, what Socrates said about his ignorance was not ironical but true. He really was ignorant. He was not ignorant empirically; on the contrary, he was unusually well informed. "In the philosophical sense, however, he was ignorant. He was ignorant of the ground of all being, the eternal, the divine–that is, he knew that it was, but he did not know what it was" (CI, 169). He was cut off from the cultural roots of his time and place. "For him, the whole given actuality had entirely lost its validity; he had become alien to the actuality of the whole substantial world" (CI, 264). He was not ignorant of this piece of information or that, but of the whole a priori of his society, the point from which everything could begin to make sense. There is, Kierkegaard writes, "an intrinsic apriority" in pure irony, such that "it is not by successively destroying one portion of actuality after another that it arrives at its total view, but it is by virtue of this that it destroys in the particular instance" (CI, 254). The detachment between a pure ironist, such as Socrates, and the world is altogether complete.

For this reason, says Kierkegaard, scholars who have said Socrates was ironical have missed the point. Socrates not only sounded ironical, he *was* irony, in the deeper, metaphorical sense. Socrates was irony personified, the incongruence of inner and outer, and he was this completely. His position was what Hegel calls "infinite absolute negativity."

(2) Socrates was also *negatively free*. That "the whole given actuality had entirely lost its validity" made him negatively free. He was free not just from this word or expression or that, as any ironist would be, but also free from the whole Greek world view, and thus a "pure ironist" as well. Through his infinite absolute irony Socrates "stood ironically above every relationship . . . His connection with the single individual was only momentary, and he himself was suspended high above all this in ironic contentment" (CI, 182).

(3) That same sort of negative freedom in pure irony can also be described as a kind of *self-cancellation*, though not at all the self-cancellation that brings the speaker of literary irony back to a mutual understanding with the listener. Here irony is "a position that continually cancels itself; it is a nothing that devours everything, and a something one can never grab hold of, something that is and is not at the same time, but something that at rock bottom is comic" (CI, 131). In another passage Kierkegaard describes this power of irony still more graphically in the image of an old witch, who "continually makes the very tantalizing attempt to eat everything first of all and thereupon to eat up itself" (CI, 56). The negating process feeds on itself and never stops, because it is, in Hegel's terminology, "infinite absolute negativity."

(4) The *superiority* felt by Socrates as pure ironist was part of his negative freedom. "The ironic freedom he enjoyed because no relationship was strong enough to bind him and he continually felt himself free above it, the enjoyment of being sufficient unto himself, to which he abandoned himself–all this suggests something aristocratic" (CI, 182). This feeling of superiority isolates him from his pupils, and the way he teaches isolates the pupils from each other, compelling each of them as individuals to deal with the cultural alienation to which his relentless questioning drives them.

His dialectic leaves them with nothing, because his irony annihilates everything through its infinite absolute negativity.

Even where it is not used explicitly, the phrase "infinite absolute negativity" echoes throughout the dissertation, from its first appearance (CI, 26) to the end. The phrase has a distinctly Hegelian ring to it, and the "Orientation" section makes that source explicit: "It is not this or that phenomenon but the totality of existence that it contemplates *sub specie ironiae* [under the aspect of irony]. To this extent we see the correctness of Hegel's view of irony as infinite absolute negativity" (CI, 254).

Identifying this key phrase with Hegel, however, creates overwhelming problems. For in his texts on irony Hegel used the phrase "infinite absolute negativity" only once,[3] in his introduction to the *Lectures on Fine Art*.[4] There the reference is not to Hegel's own views, nor to Socrates, but to those of one of the German romantic philosophers, Karl Wilhelm Ferdinand Solger, and the phrase identifies "the manifestation of absolute evil"![5] Clearly the above presentation of Kierkegaard's Socrates is incomplete in relation to Hegel, if not flatly wrong. It is time to read the dissertation again.

Second reading: Socrates and "The Truth of Irony"

Kierkegaard's dissertation reads differently the second time through than the first. This time the reader notices how susceptible the whole book is to an ironical interpretation, how important Solger is throughout the book, and how the book gets a surprising ethical twist from its concluding section.

Two of Kierkegaard's qualifications to his general thesis are particularly significant. The first qualifies Kierkegaard's overall positive evaluation of Socrates, while the second qualifies Kierkegaard's linkage between Hegel and Socrates. First, Kierkegaard

---

[3]Ernst Behler, "Kierkegaard's *The Concept of Irony* with Constant Reference to Romanticism," *Kierkegaard Revisited*, ed. Niels Jørgen Cappelørn and Jon Stewart (Berlin: Walter de Gruyter, 1997) 20.

[4]G. W. F. Hegel, *Aesthetics: Lectures on Fine Art*, trans. T. M. Knox (Oxford: Clarendon Press, 1975) 1:68.

[5]Behler, "Constant Reference to Romanticism" 21.

himself does not fully identify with Socrates' position, so that it is hardly surprising Hegel does not do so. On the contrary, Kierkegaard asserts that Socrates has only reached a limited stage in human development, "the negative qualification that subjectivity intrinsically determines itself, but he lacked the objectivity in which subjectivity in its intrinsic freedom is free . . . " (CI, 211). Negative freedom Socrates had, but not positive freedom. Second, Kierkegaard acknowledges that Hegel "declares himself against viewing Socrates' position as irony" (CI, 264-65). This is an important admission, since if Hegel does not view Socrates' position as irony (in the sense of infinite absolute negativity) then, even though Hegel too admires Socrates greatly, Hegel would no longer be committed by that attitude also to admire pure irony.

However, neither of these turns out to make much difference in the argument of the dissertation. Thus, although Kierkegaard has reservations about Socrates at one point, he usually praises Socrates to the skies, and even insists that Socrates is a "hero" (CI, 211) and a "divine missionary" (CI, 236). Similarly, although Kierkegaard admits that Hegel explicitly rejects the view that Socrates' position is irony, he still brings forward a group of reasons (though none of them very convincing) to argue that Hegel's philosophy does not entail such a rejection; so that Kierkegaard concludes "I believe, therefore, that everyone will agree with me that there is nothing in these Hegelian observations to preclude the assumption that Socrates' position was irony" (CI, 270).

So elusive is Kierkegaard's position regarding Hegel that commentators have been driven to desperate measures, with the result that today the dominant scholarly view is that Kierkegaard's dissertation on irony is itself ironical and that its sometimes extravagant praise of Hegel is merely a part of this ironical pose. This viewpoint, advanced earlier in this century by Pierre Mesnard[6] and refined by Lee Capel,[7] reaches its definitive statement in

---

[6]*Le Vrai Visage de Kierkegaard* (Paris: Beauchesne, 1948).

[7]Capel, "Introduction," esp. pp. 34-36. More recently the view has been elaborated by Sanne Elisa Grunnet, *Ironi og subjektivitet: En studie over S. Kierkegaards disputats "Om Begrebet Ironi"* (Copenhagen: Reitzels, 1987) and Michael Strawser, *Both/And: Reading Kierkegaard from Irony to Edification* (New York: Fordham University Press, 1997).

Niels Thulstrup's exhaustive study *Kierkegaard's Relation to Hegel*.[8] Thulstrup corroborates the earlier research of Emanuel Hirsch, who showed that Kierkegaard was not an Hegelian before writing his dissertation,[9] and then Thulstrup goes on to show in detail that even by the time of the dissertation Kierkegaard had not read any of the major systematic works Hegel himself published.[10] Moreover, Kierkegaard's dissertation also puts forward some theses that are totally at odds with Hegel's viewpoint; for example, the first thesis Kierkegaard advances for his dissertation defense (CI, 6).[11] From all of this Thulstrup concludes that the Hegelian features of the dissertation are only to be understood as a kind of "mask,"[12] and that the book is an experiment in which Kierkegaard tried on the role of Hegelian philosopher.[13]

Answering the question whether the dissertation on irony is a thoroughly ironical work depends on resolving the basic question: what is irony? That question may be answered in many ways. If, however, one follows Kierkegaard's own delineation of literary irony, then some of the criteria are clear: saying the opposite of what is meant, negative freedom, self-canceling, and superiority, and one can make a start at answering the question of the basis of those criteria.

The basic feature that defines irony is clearly saying the opposite of what is meant. Recently Jon Stewart has challenged Thulstrup's claim, on what is essentially this basis, in a pair of articles. Stewart shows that in section after section of the dissertation Kierkegaard is conducting far too serious a critique of Hegel's positions for his arguments to be merely an ironical gesture.[14]

---

[8]Niels Thulstrup, *Kierkegaard's Relation to Hegel*, trans. George L. Stengren (Princeton NJ: Princeton University Press, 1980); Danish original (Copenhagen: Gyldendal, 1967).

[9]Emanuel Hirsch, *Kierkegaard Studien* (Gütersloh: Bertelsmann, 1933; repr. Vaduz/Liechtenstein, 1978) 2:84 [530].

[10]Thulstrup, *Relation to Hegel*, 245.

[11]Thulstrup, *Relation to Hegel*, 258-59.

[12]Thulstrup, *Relation to Hegel*, 257.

[13]Thulstrup, *Relation to Hegel*, 261.

[14]Jon Stewart, "Hegel's Presence in *The Concept of Irony*," *Kierkegaard Studies Yearbook 1999*, ed. Niels Jørgen Cappelørn and Hermann Deuser (Berlin: Walter de Gruyter, 1999) 253-75.

Judging from the text itself, one has to conclude that Kierkegaard was saying what Kierkegaard meant. Moreover, years later Kierkegaard in his journal criticizes some of the views he held in the dissertation, and there seems no sense for Kierkegaard to abandon positions he never maintained.[15]

The criterion of self-canceling also applies. Where are the hearers "in the know" who see through the irony here? Not everyone will see through the irony, but the best informed listeners at the dissertation defense should. Such a listener as F. C. Sibbern is in some respects an ideal person to detect the irony in such a dissertation. As dissertation director and as the author of a recent book severely criticizing Hegel he had the insight and motivation to know that philosopher's weaknesses, yet Sibbern remained convinced all his life that Kierkegaard was a disciple of Hegel during the dissertation period.[16]

Classifying the dissertation as a whole, either as ironical or not ironical, is difficult. In part, the dissertation represents a sustained appreciation and also critique of one aspect of Hegel's thought. Kierkegaard takes Hegel seriously. That much is acknowledged by all sides. As Capel writes, "Compelled to study Hegel in order to maintain himself, he came to the conclusion that there was much more to it than his contemporaries perceived, and for this he chided them."[17] In part, too, the dissertation exhibits Kierkegaard's irrepressible tendency toward irony, satire, and parody, which would not be stifled even in the most critical academic context. Irony is surely there, even though at this distance one cannot always tell where it is. But there is also a third aspect of the dissertation that easily gets overlooked, the extreme pressure from time and personal crisis under which it was written. During the eleven months when Kierkegaard did much of the research and wrote about two thirds of the dissertation he also had all the duties of the required "Pastoral Seminar" and, still more pressing, he had

---

[15]Jon Stewart, "Hegel und die Ironiethese. Zu Kierkegaards Über den Begriff der Ironie," Jahrbuch für Hegelforschung 3 (1997): 171-75.

[16]Capel, "Translator's Notes," 355.

[17]Capel, "Introduction," 36-37.

the crisis of his relationship with Regine to worry about.[18] Thus some puzzling passages may have survived into the printed form of the dissertation not because they signal some subtle ironic twist but simply because Kierkegaard had no time to edit them out.

Despite the difficulty of deciding whether the dissertation as a whole is ironic, some parts can be clearly singled out that are, according to Kierkegaard's definition of literary irony. One such part is the key phrase attributed to Hegel, irony as "infinite absolute negativity." At least when the dissertation first introduces the phrase it would have some ironical bite, since readers such as F. C. Sibbern, H. L. Martensen, and especially J. L. Heiberg could not fail to notice how Hegelian the phrase sounds and yet how much Kierkegaard's overall thesis diverges from Hegel, and they also might well remember that Hegel identifies the phrase with Solger rather than Socrates. Of course, as the dissertation progresses, the irony of the phrase becomes more and more obvious, until its punch is lost; but at the beginning of the dissertation, putting the phrase into an Hegelian context makes it mean something different from what it says, and the irony is self-canceled because the knowing listener catches on.

One consequence of taking the phrase ironically is that Solger becomes more important than before in the argument of the dissertation. To all appearances, the dissertation consists of three parts, the first of which pursues an Hegelian thesis about Socrates, the second which uses Hegel to destroy the romantic ironists, and the third which takes up the "truth of irony." If Solger rather than Hegel were the person who fit the thesis that irony is infinite absolute negativity, however, then Solger would also get some of the credit for the kind of Socrates Kierkegaard describes. The whole book could then be read from the standpoint of Solger. The dissertation would take off from the eighth thesis, "Irony as infinite and absolute negativity is the lightest and weakest indication of subjectivity" (CI, 6), and develop the implications of this thesis. Solger's role would be important, though behind the

---

[18]Emanuel Hirsch, introduction to *Über den Begriff der Ironie* (Düsseldorf/Köln: Eugen Diederichs, 1961) vii-viii.

scenes, since "infinite and absolute negativity" is the characterization of irony Hegel attributes to Solger.

Not all goes well for the Solger reading of the book, however.
By the middle of the dissertation, the implications of that definition
of irony have ended up in a position that is "infinitely ambiguous"
(CI, 218). This result is very much like Solger's view in general, as
Kierkegaard represents it when he gets around to describing
Solger's viewpoint near the end of the dissertation. Solger argues
that "the negative . . . infinitizes the finite and it finitizes the
infinite" (CI, 310), and this is the way Solger sets out "to bring
about the absolute identity of the finite and the infinite" (CI, 311).
Describing such a position intelligibly is not easy, but Kierkegaard's phrase "infinitely ambiguous" does the trick very well.
Solger's ideas remind one of some of Schelling's more extravagant
speculations, and it is true that Schelling is the main tradition from
which Solger comes.[19]

Kierkegaard tries valiantly to make sense out of Solger, but the
more he clarifies Solger's claims the more dubious they appear.
When all the implications of Solger's scheme are cashed out,
"moral qualifications have no validity" (CI, 312), moral responsibility and repentance fade away (CI, 313), and nothing is left but
Solger's peculiar brand of pantheism (CI, 314). Also Solger's
aesthetics proves disappointing; for example, tragedy does not
provide a catharsis that points to a higher actuality but instead
merely brings home to the spectator at the tragedy the desolate
emptiness of human affairs (CI, 322).

Still, Kierkegaard does manage to salvage from Solger one
fragment that he can use to show "the truth of irony." Just a few
pages from the end of the discussion of Solger, Kierkegaard
suddenly starts to treat part of Solger's aesthetics as belonging to
a "completely different position" (CI, 319). As Capel notes, this is
a "wholly arbitrary decision," but it has the result that Kierkegaard
is able to rescue from the Hegelian dialectic "a substantial area of
agreement between Kierkegaard and Solger."[20] Kierkegaard
discovers an idea he shares with Solger in a review of August

---

[19]Behler, "Constant Reference to Romanticism," 26.
[20]Capel, "Introduction," 332 and 442.

Schlegel's lectures, where Solger writes: "Any thought we might entertain of going beyond finite ends is foolish and empty conceit" (CI, 320). Kierkegaard immediately commends Solger's remark as a "profound truth" and then follows this up with still higher praise by saying "I am sure everyone will agree that one would think that Goethe rather than Solger is speaking here" (CI, 320). Kierkegaard takes Solger's remark and makes of it all he can, interpreting it to mean that "man can fulfill his destiny precisely by limiting himself" (CI, 320).

The reference to Goethe, together with the theme of self-limitation, provides a bridge from the treatment of Solger to the third main part of the dissertation, the short, six page conclusion called "The Truth of Irony." Goethe is one of the three paradigm figures used in this conclusion. What attracts Kierkegaard to Solger's remark about self-limitation is evidently the way it anticipates his own position in the conclusion of the dissertation: "Irony limits, finitizes, and circumscribes and thereby yields truth, actuality, content; it disciplines and punishes and thereby yields balance and consistency" (CI, 326).

The short conclusion on "The Truth of Irony" envisions a supreme kind of irony, called "controlled irony," that may even serve as a guide for the moral life. Kierkegaard begins by considering controlled irony within the practice of three great poets, Shakespeare, Goethe, and Kierkegaard's contemporary, J. L. Heiberg. Controlled irony is that aspect of their craft through which great artists set limits within their writing and thereby maintain their artistic poise. Similarly, all people, whether or not they are poets, can "live poetically," putting the same discipline into their lives that great writers achieve in their poetry (CI, 326).[21]

Despite its brevity, the short conclusion on "The Truth of Irony" exerts a powerful leverage on the book as a whole. After pondering this conclusion, the reader looks back at the dissertation and sees it in a different light from before. No longer is it just an historical and philosophical treatise. Instead, it reads like a summons to a particular kind of moral life. Yes, one might say, the

---

[21]Sylvia Walsh, "Living Poetically in a Religious Manner," in *Living Poetically: Kierkegaard's Existential Aesthetics* (University Park: Pennsylvania State University Press, 1994) 56-62.

book is ironical, but it is "controlled irony," calling upon the reader to keep life within limits. Like a classical tragedy, which is when properly understood "uplifting," and even "upbuilding" (CI, 322), this dissertation aims at helping a "higher actuality" to emerge for the reader.

The effect of this second reading of the dissertation is to show that the book presents two, incompatible interpretations of irony. The first is "pure irony," marked by "infinite absolute negativity." The pure ironist is radically alienated from contemporary culture, gazing down on human life with amused condescension. The second kind of irony, on the other hand, "the truth of irony," is called "controlled irony" because it sets limits for one's life and thereby keeps irony from running rampant. The pure ironist stays remote from human relationships, but the controlled ironist seeks out ethical engagement. Socrates is the hero for pure irony, but his name is pointedly omitted from the chapter on "the truth of irony," where the standard bearers are Shakespeare, Goethe, and Heiberg.

Yet how can this be the overall message of the dissertation? Whatever else irony is, it is not the upbuilding. That much Kierkegaard's distinction between irony and the upbuilding seems to make clear right from the start (CI, 257-58). Or is controlled irony itself the upbuilding? What an irony that would be, if *The Concept of Irony* turned out to be an upbuilding discourse!

Third Reading: From Irony to the Upbuilding

The third reading focuses on the part of the dissertation where Kierkegaard draws the distinction between the ironic and the upbuilding. Although this is only an isolated piece of the book, it has implications not only for the dissertation but also for his later writings.

This crucial text comes in a paragraph at the end of the "Orientation" section, where Kierkegaard distinguishes Socratic irony from the kind of attitude promoted in the deeper "devotional literature" (or, literally, "upbuilding writings" [*Opbyggelsesskrifter*]):

insofar as irony, when it realizes that existence has no reality [*Realitet*], pronounces the same thesis as the pious mentality, irony might seem to be a kind of religious devotion. If I may put it this way, in religious devotion the lower actuality [*Virkelighed*], that is, the relationships with the world, loses its validity, but this occurs only insofar as the relationships with God simultaneously affirm their absolute reality. The devout mind also declares that all is vanity, but this is only insofar as through this negation all disturbing factors are set aside and the eternally existing order comes into view. (CI, 257-58)

The similarity here is that both Socratic irony and the upbuilding literature deny that relationships with the world have "reality." A "pure ironist," such as Socrates, who is completely alienated from his culture, would find a partial ally in anyone who reads devotional literature and accepts that "all is vanity." For Socrates, and also for the "devout mind" that exemplifies the upbuilding, the things of the world are not as they seem. In the Hegelian terminology Kierkegaard used to set out the first characteristic of irony, one might say that for both Socrates and the devout mind the "phenomenon" is not the same as the "essence."

There the similarity between pure irony and the upbuilding ends, however, since the other characteristics of irony do not fit the upbuilding. For example, the devout mind does not find itself to be superior to others, as the pure ironist does. Unlike the pure ironist, "if the devout mind finds everything to be vanity, it makes no exception of its own person" (CI, 258). For this reason the devout mind also does not have negative freedom in the same sense as the pure ironist. With irony "since everything [else[22]] is shown to be vanity, the subject becomes free" (CI, 258). The freedom of the pure ironist Kierkegaard had earlier portrayed by using the image of Socrates suspended over the world in "ironic contentment" (CI, 182). That kind of freedom is unlikely to characterize the devout mind that sees itself as "the most wretched of all" (CI, 258).

Although the distinction Kierkegaard draws here is between the upbuilding and pure irony, not controlled irony, a comparison between the upbuilding and controlled irony would lead to the same result. On the one hand, controlled irony is more like the upbuilding than pure irony because it does not insist on pure

---

[22]Capel inserts the word "else" here, which is needed to make clear that the self is excepted. Capel, trans. of *The Concept of Irony*, 275.

irony's negative freedom and thereby also avoids its condescending attitude. On the other hand, controlled irony does not accept the judgment that all is vanity, and that is just the point that made Kierkegaard draw the parallel between irony and the upbuilding in the first place.

In any case, both pure and controlled irony differ from the upbuilding on one of the upbuilding's most distinctive features, "that if the devout mind finds everything to the vanity, it makes no exception of its own person . . . on the contrary, it also must be set aside" (CI, 258). The Socrates in the dissertation was not the only one who might have had trouble with such extreme self-deprecation. Shakespeare, Goethe, and Heiberg might have swallowed hard, too, before admitting that they were "the most wretched of all."

Why does the concept of the upbuilding come up in this dissertation at all? Nothing in the account either of pure or controlled irony seems to require it. The answer seems to be that the period when Kierkegaard wrote his dissertation was a time when his extraordinary creative powers were temporarily forced into a narrow channel and that his mind was bursting with ideas that did not fit. At the same time as he was drafting the dissertation he was also sketching out ideas for the second part of his massive volumes of *Either/Or*, where some of the differences between pure and controlled irony are fleshed out through the characters of Mr. A and Judge William. Other important themes surface just for a moment, and one of these is the upbuilding.

External evidence that Kierkegaard was reflecting on the nature of the upbuilding during the months while he was finishing the dissertation shows up in one of the sermon notebooks he kept for the compulsory Pastoral Seminar. There he jotted down ideas for a possible sermon on the topic "The Upbuilding that Lies in the Thought that in Relation to God We are Always in the Wrong" (JP, 5:5486; EO, 2:386).

Two years later those notes grew into the powerful sermon on that topic that stands as the "Ultimatum" at the end of the second volume of *Either/Or*. The sermon implicitly raises the question about the question of the relation of irony and the upbuilding, but without answering it. On the one hand, the thought that "in relation to God we are always in the wrong" teases the listener like a riddle, and this feature is not unlike irony. On the other hand, the sermon is clearly not only *about* the concept of the upbuilding but also meant to *be* upbuilding for the listener. The sermon contains elements of both irony and the upbuilding, but how the two are related it does not explain.

Later writings continue to struggle with the distinction between irony and the upbuilding. In *Concluding Unscientific Postscript* (1846) the author, Johannes Climacus, comments on Kierkegaard's upbuilding discourses and notes that there is a distinct change in the last four upbuilding discourses from those that preceded them, in that these discourses have "a carefully shaded touch of the humorous" (CUP, 1:270), and the humorous is here "not essentially different from irony" (CUP, 1:271). These four discourses set the standard for religious faith higher than the earlier discourses, with the result that the listener finds the concepts discussed stranger than before, so high, in fact, that the listener may refuse to accept them at all. For this reason, these discourses do use a kind of irony or humor more frequently than the earlier discourses, to summon the readers to change their ways of thinking and behavior. Some of the last of these discourses in particular bring out the consciousness of guilt, and the irony bites sharply, since that consciousness comes from an awareness of the gap between what one is and what one should be.

In some ways the sermon on the thought "that over against God we are always in the wrong" fits better with the last four upbuilding discourses of 1844 than where it is usually classified, along with the very first two discourses of 1843. Not only does it use irony, or something like it, but it also stresses guilt consciousness, in fact, consciousness of total guilt. Such consciousness is what *Concluding Unscientific Postscript* identifies as the last and "decisive expression" of the kind of religiosity that is preparatory to Christianity (CUP, 525-37). Thus if the sermon from the end of *Either/Or* were moved over to stand along with one of the last upbuilding discourses instead of the first, it would fit right in, both in its use of irony or humor and in the themes it expresses. Placed alongside the last 1844 discourse, "One Who Prays Aright Struggles in Prayer and is Victorious–in That God Is Victorious," the sermon from *Either/Or* would find its soul mate. In addition, in that position among the 1843–1844 upbuilding discourses the sermon would help to bracket all of the discourses into one cohesive group.

Kierkegaard's clearest presentation of the relation of irony to the upbuilding comes still later, after *Concluding Unscientific Post-script*. In 1847 he wrote an entry in his journal in which he reflected upon the difference between an upbuilding discourse and what he called a "deliberation," a form of discourse that needed to include irony in order to be effective. Deliberations, he wrote, differ from upbuilding discourses in what they assume in the listener, and because of this difference they also differ in purpose and mood. "A deliberation [*Overveielse*] does not presuppose the definitions as given and understood; therefore, it must not so much move, mollify, reassure, persuade, as *awaken* and provoke people and sharpen thought. . . . Irony is necessary here and the even more significant ingredient of the comic" (WL, 469; cf. JP, 1:641). An upbuilding discourse about love would assume that the listeners knew what that kind of love was, while a deliberation would not assume this but would set out to "turn their comfort-able way of thinking topsy-turvy with the dialectic of truth" (WL, 469-70; JP, 1:641). For an upbuilding discourse, then, irony would not be needed, while for a deliberation it would. On the basis of this definition, the sermon that concludes *Either/Or* and the last four discourses in 1844 would not be upbuilding discourses, properly speaking, but rather something akin to deliberations.

One reason why the concepts of irony and the upbuilding some-times come up together is that they both fall under the general category of negativity. In a recent essay Søren Bruun shows that the negative is a defining category for the upbuilding in all its forms.[23] Negativity is part of what Kierkegaard during the period of writing *Christian Discourses* (1847) called his "inverted dialectic" (JP, 1:760).[24] To begin through "negativity" typically means for him to start from human limitations and weaknesses when presenting religious concepts. *Concluding Unscientific Postscript* brings out this approach especially well, with its remark: "the sign of the religious

---

[23]Søren Bruun, "The Concept of 'The Edifying' in Søren Kierkegaard's Author-ship," *Kierkegaard Studies Yearbook 1997* (Berlin: Walter de Gruyter, 1997) 228-52.

[24]Sylvia Walsh Utterbach, "Kierkegaard's Inverse Dialectic," *Kierkegaardiana* 11 (1980): 34-54.

sphere is . . . that the positive is distinguished by the negative."
The explanatory footnote for this sentence reads: "The reader will
recall that revelation is marked by mystery, eternal happiness
[Salighed] by suffering, the certitude of faith by uncertainty,
easiness by difficulty, truth by absurdity . . . " (CUP, 1:432).

Although Kierkegaard shares much with Hegel, Kierkegaard
tends to give such themes his own interpretation. Thus despite
some indebtedness by Kierkegaard to Hegel's negation theory, for
example, "Kierkegaard appropriates the theory and transforms it
at the same time."[25] By the time Kierkegaard's use of the concept
of negativity has been incorporated into the "inverted dialectic" in
the religious discourses, the Hegelian sources have become so remote as to be barely recognizable. The dissertation's account of the
relationship between irony and the upbuilding also remains distinctively Kierkegaardian. Kierkegaard and Hegel share a common
opposition to obscurantism and preachiness in philosophy,[26] but in
other respects Hegel differs with Kierkegaard concerning both
irony and the upbuilding. Hegel flatly rejects the philosophy of the
romantic ironists (CI, 265), while Kierkegaard finds some value in
them, and Hegel is much more likely than Kierkegaard to oppose
the use of the upbuilding in philosophy.[27] That Hegel does not
make the same kind of connection between these two concepts as
Kierkegaard does is therefore only to be expected.

With the concepts of irony and negativity for guidance, like
signposts, the roads of the upbuilding can be traced through every
one of Kierkegaard's works, from the beginning to the end. In this
way the third reading of Kierkegaard's dissertation leads not so
much through the dissertation as out from it into all the rest of his
authorship. The ideas from his dissertation reappear again and
again in the later works, even though they are often barely
recognizable in their new dress.

---

[25]Michael Theunissen, "Kierkegaard's Negativistic Method," *Kierkegaard's
Truth: The Disclosure of the Self*, ed. Joseph H. Smith (New Haven CT: Yale
University Press, 1981) 399.

[26]Joachim Ringleben, *Aneigung: Die Spekulative Theologie Søren Kierkegaards*
(Berlin: Walter de Gruyter, 1983) 467-68.

[27]For example, G. W. F. Hegel, *Phenomenology of Spirit*, trans. A. V. Miller
(Oxford: Oxford University Press, 1977) 6.

5

Clouds of Irony

Martin Andic

"Aristophanes has come very close to the truth in his depiction of Socrates."

This is Kierkegaard's seventh thesis in his dissertation, *The Concept of Irony, with Continual Reference to Socrates*. It is meant to draw our attention, and it certainly does. For it collides with the received opinion, going back to antiquity, that Plato's view is correct and that his and Aristophanes' portraits of Socrates are in fundamental opposition. This opinion has always seemed to rest on solid reasons. After all, Socrates tells his judges in Plato's *Apology* that they are liable to be unfairly prejudiced against him by Aristophanes' mocking caricature of him in the *Clouds* as a natural scientist and paid teacher of argumentation. He declares that his most dangerous accusers are those who who have repeated this malicious slander, on which Meletus and the rest relied in charging him with corrupting the youth and ignoring the city's gods in favor of new ones of his own For his part, Aristophanes seems to show him as an atheist, not even believing in the Clouds that he publicly presents as divinities while privately debunking them to his initiates in favor of nature and necessity, and as a sophist teaching the Worse Logic that outtalks all comers. On the face of it, Socrates is portrayed in the comedy as a knave and fool who does not know what harm he does to his pupils and the city and himself, fully deserving the punishment he receives, the destruction of his school at the incitement of the gods he denies. Aristophanes presents a different person to us than the one Plato shows us, so it is said, and we rightly trust the depiction of the philosopher by the *philosopher* who loves him and not by the poet who sneers at him and cannot even tell him from the sophists with whom he constantly battles. The poet shows the philosopher from the viewpoint of Strepsiades, a silly rogue whose view of his teacher cannot rightly be held decisive. And of course we ought to prefer the *thoughtful* man's portrait of the thoughtful man to the *thoughtless* man's.

We have generally dismissed Xenophon's defense and recollections of Socrates as only superficially philosophical, in comparison with Plato's (as Kierkegaard does: CI, 13, 27); but we have used them to support Plato's version of Socrates as not a sophist but a philosopher in polemical opposition to sophists. Yet how do we prove that Plato and Xenophon are right, and Plato more than Xenophon? Our uneasy conscience shows in our attempts to contrast Plato's Socrates with the historical one, and to appeal to content, style, vocabulary, and syntax to make out differences between early Socratic dialogues that are supposed to be historically faithful, and middle dialogues that make "Socrates" the spokesman for Plato's own theories, and both from later dialogues in which these theories are criticized by "Socrates" and others. Yet the appeal to content rests on decisions about what Plato and his characters meant and whether it is true, and these remain disputable to this day. As for appeal to style, an ancient tradition has it that Plato carefully revised his dialogues in his old age; and besides it is impossible with any great confidence to make comparative datings within each of the three groups respectively. Have we good reason to say that Plato wrote *Apology* and *Crito* first of all, or *Timaeus* last?[1] Apart from that, the question remains, can we

---

[1]Charles Young, "Plato and Computer Dating," in *Oxford Studies in Ancient Philosophy* 12 (1994): 227-50, a discussion of Gerald Ledger's *Re-Counting Plato: A Computer Analysis of Plato's Style* (Oxford and New York: Oxford University Press, 1989), and Leonard Brandwood, *The Chronology of Plato's Dialogues* (Cambridge: Cambridge University Press, 1990). Ledger, for example, accepts as genuinely Platonic *First Alcibiades, Greater Hippias, Epinomis, Letters* 3, 7-8, but rejects *Lesser Hippias*; he suspends judgment on *Second Alcibiades* despite stylistic conformity, and accepts *Menexenus* and *Parmenides* despite many anomalies. Young notes the ancient tradition preserved by Dionysius of Halicarnassus (first century BCE), *On Literary Composition* 25.210, that Plato went on into his old age "combing and curling and in every way braiding his dialogues," namely, like a barber or hairdresser. (Did he, e.g., fold late work into the *Republic* at 5.474b-80 to complete the trilogy implied in *Sophist* 217ab?) If the story is true, or could be, then even if Plato's editing touched style but not substance and content, our trust in

show that the philosopher's account of the philosopher is more true than the comic poet's? Can they be objective, and can we?

And now comes Kierkegaard to say that Aristophanes is very near the truth, and at the same time to contrast Socrates with Plato (his third thesis is that Plato "raised him too high").

This seems wrong, wilful, arbitrary; nevertheless, it is right. Kierkegaard got Aristophanes right, because he got Socrates right, and saw how Aristophanes did too; but in order to grasp in what sense this is so we will have to spell out Kierkegaard's conception of irony. For he is not only a careful reader but a cunning writer, who models *what* he presents in *how* he presents it, and accordingly makes us work for our own understanding of the truth. I will begin with Aristophanes' comedy and argue first that he is presenting the *same* person that we find in the Platonic dialogues, and next that if we may rely on them, we can see a way in which his portrait is *not* a malicious slander of Socrates. Many have thought that it was hostile mockery, just as others have thought it the plain truth; neither group has grasped the irony of the play, in which Aristophanes brilliantly reflects the irony of Socrates. To explain this I will pursue the question, what are the Clouds and what does Socrates think of them and they of him? It will become clear not only that Kierkegaard has read the play accurately, but also why he emphasizes the *negativity* in Socratic irony and contrasts Socrates with Plato so sharply, and why he thinks that Aristophanes comes closest to the actuality of Socrates. In closing I will show briefly that Kierkegaard's treatment of irony here substantially anticipates his later discussion of the subjective, existential thinker, though the meaning of subjectivity has moved back closer to the notion of irony.

Does Aristophanes Contradict Plato?

Aristophanes shows Socrates operating a school of science and rhetoric. Strepsiades goes there, and sends his son, especially for the instruction in clever speaking and arguing, and he expects to pay for the lessons. Plato, on the other hand, makes Socrates tell his judges emphatically that he knows nothing of science and that

---

stylometry must be qualified. But how are we to know?

they have never heard him discussing it, nor does he teach how to be a good human being and citizen to anyone who will pay his fee. People who repeat these things are liable to think that someone who studies the cosmos does not believe in the gods, inasmuch as to seek a natural explanation of things is to reject the religious one; and to make the worse argument better than the better argument is certainly to subvert justice, which he, however, for his part puts above everything else, as heaven does.

Plato's Socrates, nevertheless, tells his friends in the *Phaedo* that as a young man he was passionately interested in physiology and cosmology; and he goes on to spend his last hour speculating with them about how the cosmos is organized to support philosophy and its pursuit of moral goodness. But it is this moral goodness that was the theme of his public discussions: what makes us good and our lives good. Moreover, he speaks with favor of the art of logic as rescuing us from misology, the despair of reasoning; and in other dialogues he is constantly raising moral questions with sophists and examining closely their definitions and arguments and examples, seeking out every opportunity to discuss why right is better than wrong. He criticizes the theology of Homer and Hesiod and Pindar and the tragic poets for saying that the gods often do wrong and harm to one another and human beings, and for their accounts of the virtues and vices and their respective rewards and punishments; if he believes in the god before whom his judges try him, it is not in the way his accusers do. Both *what* he believes, and *how* he believes it, are not the same as for them. To him, a god is made divine by the ideal goodness that it knows and embodies; it is simply and unambiguously good, the cause of all other good, and only of good; evils—and the only real evils are moral evils, our own wrong actions—come from us, not heaven. Moreover, he will die rather than disobey the god. This is not atheism except as a purification; it is a deeper earnestness that rebukes what men call piety.[2]

---

[2]Cosmology and rhetoric: *Apology* 18-20c, 28b-29b. *Phaedo* 96-99d, 107c-15a; 89c-90, esp. 90b "the art of logic," *tes peri tous logous technes*. Piety: *Euthyphro* 6ac, *Republic* 2.377e-3.392c, *Apology* 35d, cf. *Euthydemus* 302c, *Philebus* 12c, *Cratylus* 400d, 425c. *Phaedrus* 249c, 247cd, *Republic* 2.379bc, cf. *Euthyphro* 15a. Obedience unto death: *Apology* 29c-30c.

The question of a *fee* matters to Plato's Socrates because he does not profess to teach what he does not claim to know, and he has learned from the god himself that it is wise for a man not to think that he is wise; nevertheless, we must do everything we can do to acquire wisdom from heaven, for whatever good we have is received from there. Socrates can only search for the truth and for fellow searchers. He does not teach but he can help others to learn, as everyone must, by oneself from within oneself. Thus he cannot charge a fee for imparting knowledge, for he has only his ignorance (the wise acknowledgment of it) to impart, and his questions and his earnest love of truth; and he can only awaken these in another, who must acquire knowledge for oneself from the divinity beyond and within. Knowledge is the property of the god, and *is* the god; and taking part in it is transformation into likeness. What belongs to the god alone to give or withhold, and has to be received and appropriated by each for oneself, cannot be *sold*, much less to just anyone willing to pay. It is especially this that Socrates considers to be a slander against him in calling him a sophist.[3]

Aristophanes, however, never shows Socrates asking for payment, and when Strepsiades gives him something Socrates ignores it, though he probably approves the sentiment of gratitude.[4] Science is studied in his school, but we do not see Socrates himself teaching it. In fact he seems to forbid students from being much out of doors, as if to discourage their pursuing astronomy and geometry by observation, though he may mean to keep them from earthbound thoughts, or to preserve them in their deathlike pallor and the discipline it emblemizes.[5] We first see him swinging high in a basket,[6] declaring that he walks on air to look down on

---

[3] *Apology* 19-24b, esp. 22d-23b; 33ab. *Meno* 80d-86c, esp. 85d; 94e-95a.

[4] *Clouds* 1146, cf. 98, 245, 668, and *Lesser Hippias* 372c, *Gorgias* 470c, *Theaetetus* 155d. Socrates never says that he taught Hyperbolus or anyone else, whether for a fee or free: see *Clouds* 876.

[5] Higher things: *Clouds* 227-33, cf. 171-73, and *Republic* 7.529-30, *Timaeus* 47, 90ad, 91d, 92c, cf. *Symposium* 174d, 175bc, 220c. Indoor: *Clouds* 227-33; 103, 119, 1112, 1171).

[6] He comes before us like a tragic *deus ex machina*, which might seem to be hubris, or worse still like Ixion on his wheel of fire punished for *his* hubris: see 218-34, 250-53, 1502-1509, with Pindar, *Pythian* 2.33-89. Ixion lay with a cloud that he thought was divine Hera; scholiasts say it was Hermes who carried out the

the sun, to lift his mind into the purer air in order to form exact notions of higher things. But these may be things higher even than the sun and moon and stars that we see; and in any case he descends at once to talk with his visitor. Socrates asked Chaerophon how many of its own feet a flea could leap, and how gnats hum, but it is not said that Socrates asked for his own benefit rather than Chaerophon's, as a problem of method; besides he might have been pointing to the relativity of magnitude and due measure, or perhaps how little we should think of little things, and to the difference between making music and making sound.[7] Likewise Socrates' interest in chickens and roosters seems to be to teach a lesson in grammar or logic, that sex belongs to the definition of these names, as gratitude and respect belong to the definition of a son and learner. Socrates has a theory of clouds as the cause of thunder and rain, but as we shall see his notion of clouds is more theology and moral psychology than physics. When he says that there is no Zeus he may mean that there is no Zeus as Strepsiades conceives him, who makes rain where he will and punishes misdoers with thunderbolts. Socrates need not believe the theory with which he tempts the taste of Strepsiades, any more than Plato's Socrates need believe the phenomenalism that he draws out of Theaetetus. Plato's Socrates emphasizes the inward moral reward and punishment of right and wrong action respectively in the benefit and harm they respectively do to the agent. If the historic Socrates held this view then there is nothing in the comedy to exclude it there.[8]

As for sophistry, this is the one thing Strepsiades is bent on learning. He has twisted and turned all night until hitting on "a divinely direct and supernatural way" (*atrapon daimonios huperphua*) to escape his creditors, which is to send his son to the school of Socrates. "That is a thinkery of wise souls, and the men who live there can argue that the heaven is a cook pot covering us all and we are the hot coals inside it, and they make us believe it. They

---

penalty of Zeus.

[7]Cf. *Statesman* 284b, *Apology* 29e-30a; and *Phaedo* 99b.

[8]*Clouds* 250ff, esp. 367, 381. *Theaetetus* 157cd, 161ab, and 176d-177a, *Crito* 47de, *Republic* 1.335de, 9.589c-90c, cf. 2.366d-67a.

teach you, if you pay them, how to win any case, right or wrong."[9] He wants Pheidippides to learn how to talk his way out of debts, but Pheidippides refuses because of the unwholesome and unhappy look of the inmates. Strepsiades visits the school himself and is sure that he wants instruction from the moment he hears how Socrates provided for dinner by stealing a cloak from the wrestling school next door: this is the very man for him. From the start he repeats to Socrates that knowing how to make worse seem better and wrong appear right is the *only* thing he wishes to learn. Socrates introduces him to the Clouds who are the divinities honored there, as if to test his aptitude for study, and with some reservations takes him in. But soon Socrates comes out complaining of the stupidity and unretentiveness of his new pupil; he calls him out into the light to lay a foundation in measures, rhythm, and diction, and then makes him lie down to think out some brainy schemes for himself; but these are so foolish that Socrates dismisses him. When Strepsiades persuades his son to go learn the two logics, but especially the worse that argues wrong to beat the better one, Socrates despite even greater reservations about the son's youth agrees to undertake it; but, he says (886-87), "He will learn them himself from the two logics themselves; I will not be there." The two logics come out and display themselves, and Strepsiades sends Pheidippides in with them to be taught the worse, with blows if needed; he must have a razor tongue, one edge for petty lawsuits, the other for greater ones.[10] Socrates brings

---

[9]Divine way: *Clouds* 76. (Unless indicated otherwise, I am responsible for all translations from Greek writers presented here.) Thinkery: 95-99; see further 110-18, 129-30, 175-83, 239-46. The word *phrontisterion* (98, 128, 142, 181) can be rendered as thinkery, think shop, think tank, house of thought, reflectory, or more broadly as school, academy, college, institute. *Phrontis*, thought or mind, is related to our words "phrenology," "frenetic," and "frenzy," which are now eyebrow raising expressions as "mental" often is. Strepsiades' name means "Twister," and the poet plays on this throughout the comedy: 36, 88, 434, 450, 776, 792, 1455. Let us notice that Mister Twister means to corrupt his own son, and that his son disobeys him, even before they have met Socrates.

[10]Socrates assures him that he will get his son back as a shrewd sophist, just as he wanted (882, 1111); and the Clouds declare that "this sophist" Strepsiades will be punished for his knavery (1309). Socrates himself seemed to criticize sophists at 331-34, as among or like the airy quacks sustained and nourished by

him out, telling the father that his son has mastered what he wished him to learn. Strepsiades is delighted with Pheidippides' pale Athenian "Who me?" look of someone who knows how to challenge everything and to seem wronged when doing wrong. The father is seen trying out some of these tricks on his creditors whose ignorance deprives them (like slaves) of any right to anything; but when his son has struck him in a dispute over some immoral verses of Euripides about incest, Strepsiades is outraged. His son exclaims "How sweet it is to be hip and cool and to look down on any old rule!"[11] It is right, he says, to punish one's father and return blow for blow: for the one who first *said* that it is wrong was only a man, and I am a man too who is free to *say* it is not wrong; if it is natural to chickens and other beasts to defend themselves against their fathers, then so it is for us.[12] Strepsiades sees sense in this; but when his son takes a step further and proposes to beat his mother too and prove it right to do it, the father is outraged and, blaming in turn the Clouds, himself, and then Socrates, he goes on to torch the school.

As the Clouds tell him, he has brought this trouble on himself by his own dishonest purpose (1454), and this is the salient point. It was Strepsiades who came to learn sophistry. Socrates never offered to teach it and did not do so; his work was only to assist him and his son to learn what *he* wished, and Strepsiades has had to discover the hard way that wrong rebounds on the doer of

---

the Clouds. But the Clouds call Socrates the only one of the sophists-of-things-above (*meteorosophiston*) whom they hear along with Prodicus: we listen to him for his wisdom and judgment, they say, and to you for your pride in serving us and enduring hardships for us (cf. 415-17), barefoot and swaggering and rolling your eyes or peering sideways from under your brows (360-63, cf. *Phaedo* 117b, 86d, and *Symposium* 221ab). Whatever they mean by calling him a meteorosophist, they are not blaming him.

[11]1399-1400.

[12]At 1433, Strepsiades seems to say, if *you* are right, then your son will be right to punish *you*, but if *I* am right, and since I am, you will be right to punish *him* and not the other way; Pheidippides retorts, but if I follow you but have no son, then I will have suffered when you punished me and will not have repaid it to anyone, and so you will have had the last laugh on me. Plato's Socrates sides with Strepsiades, e.g., in *Euthyphro* 4e, 15de, *Crito* 50e-51a, *Republic* 5.465a, 8.562e, cf. 1. 329a, and *Letter* 7.331ad.

wrong. Aristophanes is not saying that Socrates is a sophist claiming to make others to be like himself, for a fee.

So far from contradicting Plato by presenting Socrates as a sophist, Aristophanes positively supports Plato in showing Socrates as a *philosopher*. His Socrates, like Plato's, is poor and unworldly, as the sophists generally were not. He and his school live like Pythagoreans, known among nonphilosophers for their asceticism, their cultivation of purity and detachment from self and the body, and of self-examination and memory; their study of geometry and natural science, music and ethics, their practice of philosophy as a mystery with silence towards noninitiates; their selectivity and elitism, their common meals, their rejection of suicide, their reverence for the authority of their founder. Moreover, the thinkers share the fate of the Pythagoreans incinerated at Croton and elsewhere.[13]

Pheidippides refuses at first to enter the phrontistery, calling the inmates "Those wretches! I know who you mean, those pasty phonies who go around barefoot, like that miserable Socrates and Chaerophon." His father wants him to go there to learn how to argue; and though the Clouds promise Strepsiades that if he works hard with Socrates he will win political influence or, since he wants only financial security, at least a name for being good at business and litigation, Strepsiades never objects that Socrates has none of these—neither power nor wealth nor prestige—and never asks, "If he's so smart, then why isn't *he* rich and powerful?," as if taking it for granted that Socrates has no such worldly ambitions. Socrates and his generally well born associates are willing to be cold and hungry for the sake of their studies, dirty and fleasy, tired and pleasureless as if dying to the world and half-dead

---

[13]Poverty: *Apology* 20ac, 23b, *Meno* 91de. Pythagoreans: see A. E. Taylor, "The *Phrontisterion*," *Varia Socratica*, First Series, St. Andrews University Publications 9 (Oxford: James Parker, 1911) 129-77. Ovid says that Pythagoras explained "what Nature is, and what the gods, whence come the snows, the lightning flash, whether it is Jupiter who thunders, or the winds splitting the clouds apart"; see further 15.148 " 'I joy to journey among the stars, high above, to leave the earth and this dull abode, to ride on the clouds and stand on stout Atlas' shoulders, looking down from afar on men as they wander aimlessly. . . . ' " *Metamorphoses* 15.69, trans. Mary Innes (New York: Viking Penguin, 1955) 337, 338-39.

already. Socrates tells Strepsiades to examine himself and his thoughts and is disgusted not only at their imbecility but also at the man's inability to remember anything. His students investigate science and music, perhaps as purification. Their work is to them a *mystery* to be spoken aloud only to initiates after due induction with ritual crowning and dedication in self-sacrifice and stripping of worldly garments. Socrates will not accept just anyone into his school and, after preliminary screening to see whether he can learn and how he learns it, he sends Strepsiades away. One reason is the rustic's desperate proposal that he could avoid losing a suit for nonpayment by commiting suicide, because a dead man cannot be sued. When there is no food for the students' dinner, Socrates provides it by geometry. His students refer to him as "himself," and Pheidippides learns to clinch arguments and end them by invoking his name. Socrates and his companions barely escape destruction in their school and sharing the fate of the Pythagoreans in Italy.[14]

More than this, Aristophanes portrays the *Socratic* philosopher much as Plato depicts him, not merely in his precision and arguments from analogy and concrete lowly examples, as well as his neglect of his own affairs, but also in his talking with everyone he meets; in his avoidance of teaching and claims to know in favor of questioning people about their own beliefs and drawing knowledge out of them, or as it will more often be, admissions of ignorance; and above all in the expression of this as *midwifery*, assisting delivery in childbirth.

Socrates demands that things be called by their right names, and he argues from humble instances like watercress and flatulence, and talks of making slippers and rigging; he seems to

---

[14]Aristocratic: 101 *kaloi te kagathoi*, cf. *Apology* 23c. Wretched: 103-104, cf . 503-504. Unworldly: see 429-75. Ascetic and fleasy: 103-104, 146, 198, 363, 414-17, 440-42, 503-504, 634, 699, 710, 836-37; cf. *Phaedo* 64-65a; at 721 Strepsiades complains that he is reduced to nothing, "singing at my post" (*phrouras adon*), cf. *Phaedo* 62b, 81e, 82b, and 60c-61b, 77d-78a, 84d-85d, 88c-91c, 114d-115a. Self-examination and memory: 700, 728, 740, 482-83, 628-31, 785, 854-55. Science and music: 187-235, 368-424, 636-55. Mystery: 143, 254-66, 497-508, cf. 822-24, and *Phaedo* 69d, cf. *Symposium* 210a, *Euthydemus* 277de, *Phaedrus* 250bc. Stripping: 497-500. Exclusion: 482-96, 627-790. Suicide: 775-83, cf. *Phaedo* 61b-62c, Dinner: 175-80. Authority: 195, 1432. Destruction by fire: 1483-1509, 1508 "After them!"

include himself among the otherwise idle devotees of the Clouds who are kept safe and nourished by them. He leaves his basket and climbs down to Strepsiades to converse with him, and goes on speaking with him even after—and perhaps because—his visitor has shown his immoral purpose, and until his visitor has fully demonstrated his ineptitude for study. Socrates teaches Strepsiades by *questioning* him about himself and showing him the implications of his own beliefs ("I'll teach you from your own case"); and he tries to get him to do this for himself, to think out one of his problems. Socrates *sends him to bed* to do this, as if to childbed to see what brainchildren of his own he can bring forth; Strespsiades wishes that he could learn fleecing from the fleeces thrown over him, but Socrates' way is indirect, singing encouragement to Strepsiades and asking him about what thoughts he has to show for his labor; unfortunately they are in effect only wind eggs. The biting bedbugs or fleas of which Strepsiades complains here may represent the stinging questions of Socrates. His whole school thinks that it is wise not to *think* that one is wise, and so when Pheidippides asks him what useful thing could one ever learn from *them*, his father answers "What are you asking? All human wisdom! You'll know yourself, how ignorant and dense you are!"[15]

In this ignorance and maieutic Aristophanes has surely found features deeply characteristic of the Platonic Socrates. And in bringing out the Worse and Better Logics *themselves* for Strepsiades *himself* to learn, we see not only *that* Socrates' characteristic idiom and his keen interest in the choice of lives, but also his *nondirection* of his partners in making that choice; we might also call it his

---

[15]Precision: 658-94, cf. 847-53, 1178-1200, 1247-52, cf. *Phaedo* 115e. Humble examples: 234, 385-94, 144-52, 868-69; cf. *Gorgias* 491a, *Symposium* 221e. Idleness: 316, 334, cf *Apology* 36d, *Theaetetus* 172ce. Questioning: 385. Thinking out: 694-706, 727-29, 735-45. Midwifery: 694-745 & ff, cf. *Theaetetus* 149-51; Aristotle explains in *History of Animals* 6.2 that a wind egg is an unfertilized egg that produces no chicken, so that it represents here a figment unbegotten by divine truth and not living knowledge. Fleece: 729-30, cf. *Symposium* 175cd, but also 196a, 203e, with *Theages* 130de and Aeschines, fr. 11 (is there for Socrates a flowing wisdom of love?). Bites: cf. *Apology* 30e. Wise ignorance: 840-42; cf. 135, 242, 329, 331, and *Apology* 23ab.

indirection in offering reasons and objections but leaving them free to make it for themselves.[16]

It is true that in the dialogues where this choice is most explicitly discussed, *Gorgias* and *Republic*, he is rather less non-direct and indirect; and we will consider this below. It is true also that Aristophanes does not show the *erotic* side of Socrates, who claims that love is the one thing he knows, unless it counts that his special divinities are goddesses and appear as women. Nor on the face of it does his Socrates show any irony, apart from the eye rolling or peering sideways from under his brows mentioned by the Clouds. He is sarcastic and dismissive to Strepsiades, but that is not the same thing; Strepsiades for his part longs to be known as an ironist: that is to say, as a clever *liar*, a *wily* citizen not to be trifled with. If anyone or anything in the play has any irony like that of the Platonic Socrates, it is, on the face of it, the Clouds.[17]

This comic Socrates has not yet heard what the god has said about him through his *oracle* at Delphi, and gone public to test

---

[16]886-87; *Gorgias* 472c, 487e, 500c, *Republic* 1.343d-44c, 347e-49a, 2.357-68c, 10.618bc.

[17]Love: *Symposium* 177d, 198d; *Phaedrus* 257a, Lysis 204bc, *Theages* 128b; *Clouds*, 265, 329, 365, cf. *Symposium* 217bc, 219bd, 222ab. Rolling eye: 362. Sarcasm: 492, 726, 757, 773, 781, 783, 789. Strepsiades: 439. As we shall see, Socrates has irony too, though it is not apparent to Stepsiades. Likewise, the students *may* be speaking ironically to him about the flea and gnat and lizard and the rest (143-74), deliberately mystifying the new student, having fun with the late learning country gentleman.

We should distinguish conscious irony from unconscious. *Conscious* irony really means something different and more than what it seemingly means to its targeted hearers, and it intends so to be understood by its true hearers (thus CI, 247-49). As irony is opposed to openness, so conscious irony speaks *slyly* to those addressed, not freely and simply and transparently (as it seems to them); yet those who use their ears will hear. To hear it and suspect its good faith, e.g., to think that this ironic simplicity and humility are only a crafty opportunistic pose, could be a misunderstanding (cf. *Republic* 1.337a and *Symposium* 218d). *Unconscious* irony is not intended, as when someone says what one's own actions contradict or fulfil, so that it does not mean exactly what one means by it. Events and their outcomes too may have irony when they prove to be something different and more than what they seemed to be to onlookers and even to the people to whom they occurred when they did. Thus there may be unconscious irony in what Strepsiades says, e.g., at 75-77 and 127; and conscious irony in Socrates' words at 225 and 242 even if it is unheard by Strepsiades.

what the god can mean and why it is true, to prove it to (and on)
the Athenians and indeed to mankind as the god's spokesman to
them. He stays at home with his associates and his divinities, and
does not yet go out into the streets of Athens to accost and
challenge everyone he meets, encouraging all to join him in his
search and scolding them for neglecting it in favor of any other
pursuit.[18]

All the same, Aristophanes gives us a Socrates we can recognize from the dialogues of Plato. That would be a reason to think
that Plato has told the truth, if *even* the hostile critic of his Socrates
supports him, or at least the man who has incited the hostile critics
in the nameless crowd, nameless for who they are they do not
know themselves. But *is* Aristophanes himself hostile, and is his
comedy a malicious slander?

Is Clouds *a Malicious Slander?*

If Aristophanes were hostile then it would not be easy to
understand the forbearance not only of Socrates but of Plato who
might be expected to show anger toward the poet, at the first
opportunity, if not to pay him back in good measure. In fact,
however, there are several reports from antiquity that Socrates
himself took it well. Aelian says that Socrates had a front seat at
Clouds and when people asked who the Socrates on stage was, he
stood up and remained standing through the play. If Socrates
meant to show that he was not like his caricature and to rebuke it,
and meant it in cold anger, he seems to have got over it and
resolved to bear it with patience and even good humor. Lucian is
surely thinking of him when he causes Philosophy to say "You
mean you're angry because somebody called you names? Yet you
know the sort of things I have to listen to from Comedy at the
Festivals of Dionysus, and you know that, in spite of it, I've
always considered her a friend and never once took her to court
or held it against her. It was the usual playing around you expect
at the festivals, so I overlooked it. You see, I know that jokes never
do any harm." For a little further Lucian makes Diogenes the

---

[18]Thus his mission statement at *Apology* 23b. I owe this point to David
Konstan.

Cynic explain that Socrates is the only one that Aristophanes and Eupolis dared to mock and it was only during the Festival. Similarly Diogenes Laertius gives as Socrates' own words "We should not mind being the butt of the comic poets, for if they mock our faults they do us good and if not they do us no harm." And Plutarch relates that "When Aristophanes poured all kinds of abuse on Socrates in *Clouds*, someone there asked Socrates 'Aren't you angry at his mocking you this way?' 'Not I, by Zeus,' said Socrates, 'I take his goofing on me in the theater as if it were a big party of friends [*symposion*].'"[19] These are relatively late writers, all from the second and third centuries CE, but their agreement is a reason to think that they are reporting an authentic tradition.

Plato for his part does not show the bitterness towards Aristophanes that we might expect him to feel for an enemy of Socrates and his philosophy. Plato unites poet and philosopher in the *Symposium*, giving the poet some of the best and most memorable words in the conversation; there Alcibiades quotes without resentment the description of Socrates in *Clouds* 362, and the supposed enemies talk the night away about the art of poetry.[20] Even in the *Apology* where the comedy is mentioned, Plato does not make Socrates blame the poet but the public who judged Socrates by his caricature alone; perhaps they misjudged both.[21]

---

[19]Aelian, *Varia Historia* 2.13, cf. CI, 449; Lucian, *The Dead Come to Life, or, The Fisherman* 14, 25-26, in *Selected Satires of Lucian*, trans. Lionel Casson (Chicago: Aldine, 1962) 341, 347-48; Diogenes Laertius, *Life of Socrates* 2.36; Plutarch, *The Education of Children* 10c.

[20]Some scholars detect allusions to Pericles, Alcibiades, and Anaxagoras, in the words and deeds of Strepsiades, Pheidippides, and Socrates. Thus Michael Vickers, "Alcibiades in Cloudedoverland," in *Nomodeiktes, Greek Studies in Honor of Martin Ostwald*, ed. Ralph Mark Rosen and Joseph Farrell (Ann Arbor: University of Michigan Press, 1993) 603-18. He is renewing the argument of the German scholar J. V. Suvern (1826), who is cited with favor in CI, 131, 143*. By making Alcibiades quote the comedy in the *Symposium*, Plato might be acknowledging these allusions and noting their harmlessness.

[21]*Clouds* was first performed in 423 BCE, when Socrates was 46; the inner dialogue of *Symposium* seems to be set seven years later in 416, when Socrates is 53. His trial in 399 is 24 years after the play. But we cannot be sure when Plato wrote the two dialogues. The comedy placed third (last) in 423, and was not performed again in the poet's lifetime so far as we know; lines 518-62 (cf. *Wasps* 1045-50) indicate that he began to revise it but there is scholarly consensus that

We ought to assume that on such a topic Plato faithfully reports what Socrates himself actually thought. And there is reason to believe that he agrees with his mentor. The Alexandrian *Life of Aristophanes* says that Plato sent the poetry of Aristophanes to Dionysius of Syracuse to show him what Athenian goverment was. The sixth century Neoplatonist Olympiodorus, introducing his commentary on the *Alcibiades*, says that when Plato died the writings of Aristophanes and Sophron were found in his bed. He goes on to ascribe to Plato the epigram "The Graces, looking for a temple for themselves that would never fall, found it in the soul of Aristophanes."[22] If these stories are true, then either Plato like his Socrates was remarkably patient and forbearing,[23] or else he did not consider that there was much to forbear.

---

he abandoned the project and did not offer the play again; only this partial revision survives.

[22]*Symposium* 221ab, also 189b-93d, 205d-206a, 223cd. *Apology* 18ad, 19ac. *Life of Aristophanes* 42, trans. Mary Lefkowitz in *The Lives of the Greek Poets* (Baltimore: Johns Hopkins University Press, 1981) 169-72; Kierkegaard refers to this story in CI, 154. Olympiodorus, *Commentary on the First Alcibiades of Plato* 2.65-75, trans. L. G. Westerinck (Amsterdam: North Holland, 1956) 3.

Nietzsche mentions the report of Plato's reading in *Beyond Good and Evil* 2.28, trans. Marianne Cowen (Chicago: Henry Regnery, 1955) 34-35:

And as for Aristophanes, that transfiguring and complementary spirit, for whose sake one *forgives* everything Greek for having existed (assuming one fully understands *what* at all needed forgiveness and required transfiguration), I know of nothing which has made me daydream more about Plato's concealed and sphinx-like nature than that happily preserved little fact that under his pillow on his deathbed there was no "bible," no Egyptian, Pythagorean, or Platonic writings, but only a copy of Aristophanes. Of course! How could Plato have endured life (Greek life to which he said "no") without an Aristophanes!

Greek life is to Plato mostly a cave, but he does not reject it. He rejects worldly life, materialism and opportunism and jingoism, just as Nietzsche did. Yet for Plato the philosopher's *home* and *work* is in the cave: *Republic* 7.519b-21b; cf. the prison work in *Phaedo* 62ac, and the allegory in *Phaedrus* 247a, e.

[23]*Apology* 41de, cf. *Lesser Hippias* 372a, 373b, *Republic* 2.366cd, 4.426de. The musician Aristoxenos, whose father knew Socrates, reports (fr. 54a, 54b, 56) that the philosopher had a hot temper, possibly reflected in *Republic* 7.536ab referring back to 6.495b-96a, 497e-98c. The story of Zopyros, in Cicero's *Tusculan Disputations* 4.80 (CI, 212*.) indicates that Socrates cultivated restraint and patience.

If Plato does admire Aristophanes and bears no grudge against him for the comedy, then we could expect him to make some appropriate response to it in writing. This he does, in the *Euthydemus*. Socrates becomes the ignorant man asking to be taught by the elderly sophists, who will instruct anyone who pays them to refute anything anyone says, be it false or true. Like Strepsiades, he and Ctesippus say that they are ready to be destroyed, boiled, flayed, so long as they turn out good and wise; but the teaching proves to be only quibbling over words. The sophists call him what in the comedy he calls Strepsiades, a Cronos and old fool; he says that he himself is what in the play he says that Strepsiades is, ignorant and dull, and he asks pardon as Strepsiades did. Crito reports that someone who heard these sophists said that they were driveling and making a worthless fuss about worthless things, as we should say about the head of the reflectory. With other verbal similarities, the dialogue follows the comedy so closely as to amount to tribute and praise, at the same time that it shows Socrates more explicitly as a *critic* of the sophists, not one of their number.[24]

Certainly there is teasing in the comedy. Socrates first appears to us swung in a basket saying that he is walking on air to look on the sun below, clearing his mind to aid precision about higher things; but this could be making playful fun of his aspiration, reported by Plato, to purify his soul and wing it with love of beautiful excellence and so to unite it to the cosmic soul crossing and overseeing the whole in its astronomy and geometry and

---

[24]Elderly: *Euthydemus* 272b, cf. *Sophist* 251bc, *Clouds* 263, 358, 512-17, 746, 790, 794. Teaching refutation for pay: *Euthydemus* 272ab, 304c, cf. *Clouds* 98-99. Flaying: 285ac, cf. *Clouds* 439-56. Quibbling: 288a, cf. *Clouds* 658-91. Cronus: 287b, 295d, cf. *Clouds* 915, 929. Ignorant: 295d, cf. *Clouds* 492, 629, 655, 790. Pardon: 296a, cf. *Clouds* 138. Drivel: 304e, cf. *Clouds* 1480, 1484. See further 271c, 283e, cf. *Clouds* 332 "Thurians"; 283e, *Clouds* 660 "if I'm not mad"; 303d, *Clouds* 205 "a democratic teaching"; 298d, *Clouds* 1203 "you stones." For the comparison and details, see Benjamin Bickley Rogers, *The Comedies of Aristophanes*, 6 vols. (London: George Bell, 1916) 2:xxvii-xxviii: "the *Euthydemus* of Plato is in reality nothing more than a revised edition of the *Clouds*." The dialogue is set in 411, when Socrates is 58, twelve years after the play. Kierkegaard does not cite the *Euthydemus* in this connection; but the question is whether Plato was bitter toward Aristophanes.

justice.[25] Strepsiades is delighted to hear how Socrates provided dinner for the school by an act of geometry with a meat spit bent into tongs for lifting a cloak from the palaestra adjacent; but the rustic is alarmed when he is asked to give up his cloak, imagining it is for a beating or to show he is not smuggling anything in, and apparently his shoes are taken as well; the Clouds go on to tell Socrates to clean the panicked and bewildered man of all he can while he can. Strepsiades and his son go on to act as though they have learned that everything belongs to the wise. So we may think that Socrates is running a school of thieving. But the stripping at the door is clearly intended as a symbolic parting from the worldly life, and the Clouds are probably urging Socrates not to fleece him of his belongings but to free him from from his errors. Socrates, moreover, is accustomed in Plato to urging people to strip and show themselves, meaning that they should speak and reveal their real mind. And if Strepsiades and his son have learned to disregard the property rights of others, they have learned from Worse Logic only to dare to do what Strepsiades has always wanted to do. (Socrates may have said that everything belongs to the wise, but it was likely to have been in the context that only the wise truly own what they own because only they know how to use it and share it rightly and well, to make themselves and others and their lives good.)[26] If comedy relied on three actors, and if the same actor in the same mask portrayed both Socrates and Worse Logic,

[25]*Phaedo* cf. 70bc; *Phaedrus* 246bc, *Theaetetus* 173e, 175bd, *Phaedo* 109b-10a, *Republic* 6.500cd, cf. 486a, 10.604c, 608c; at 6.488e Socrates seems to refer to this passage in *Clouds*.

[26]Stealing and stripping: 177-79, 497-500 (cf. Plato, *Laws* 12.954a); 719, 804-13, 856-59, 1498. Helping oneself: 1202, 1249-52, 1283-85. Kierkegaard is fond of quoting *loquere ut videam te*, "Speak so I can see you" (thus CI, 14, 244; cf. EO, 2: 275; SLW, 398; LD, 52, 153; JP, 1:1058, 2:2115), which seem to originate in Plato's *Protagoras* 352ab, *Theaetetus* 169ab, *Charmides* 154e, 1 *Alcibiades* 132a; but these words occur first in Apuleius, *Florida* 2. Socrates wants others to say what they really believe, so that the truth may be clarified and so that their actions and lives and their very souls can be examined as well as their words, thus, e.g., *Crito* 49d, *Gorgias* 495a, *Republic* 1.345b, 346a; but he himself speaks with irony that many will think is *only* irony, namely, *pretending*, lying, thus *Republic* 1.337a. Ownership: *Lysis* 207d-10d, *Meno* 88, *Euthydemus* 278e-82d, 288d-89b, *Republic* 4.423e-24a.

then this would help to explain why Socrates had a bad name for the rest of his life in Athens.[27]

But is this malicious slander, or even mockery? To be malicious it would have to be moved by hatred for Socrates and his philosophy, and we need not assume this. To be slander it would have to misrepresent him in a way opposed to his deepest convictions and highest ideals, showing him imagining himself to be a wise man who can make anyone else wise who is able and willing to pay his fee; but *Clouds* does not do this. Socrates is the victim of calumny, and so is anyone who works for justice and wisdom.[28] But to call *Clouds* a work of calumny, spiteful lying, is too much. To say that it mocks Socrates would mean that it laughs at him, ridicules him, as self-ignorant and self-deluded.[29] But Plato's Aristophanes knows the difference between being amusing and being ridiculous, and that the laugh may be on oneself. Socrates in his basket, taking Strepsiades' cloak and shoes and sprinkling him with flour, calling forth the singing and dancing chorus of Clouds, perhaps all with

---

[27]Better Logic says to Worse (926) "Oh, the madness in you and the city that feeds you who corrupt the youth!" That Right Logic deserts to Wrong (1102-104), if we may put it this way, seems to show that in Socrates' school Right is *right for no one*, not even for Right itself, as in "the really exquisite conclusion" in Plato's *Theaetetus* 171ac that Protagoras' Truth is *true* for no one. But whereas Right Logic runs *to* Wrong, "Protagoras" runs *from* Theodorus and Socrates and their criticism, so that whereas Right Logic itself abandons right, the sophist "Protagoras" abandons philosophy.

[28]*Apology* 24a, 28a, 31e, 39b it is *necessary* and *right* that the good are wronged by the bad, who suffer more harm than they do, *Republic* 2.360e-62a, 6.500cd the philosopher consorting with the divine and orderly becomes as divine and orderly as a man can, "despite calumny everywhere." Cf. Shakespeare, *Hamlet* 1.3.38 "Virtue itself scapes not calumnious strokes," 3.1.140-41 "be thou chaste as ice, / as pure as snow, thou shalt not escape calumny"; *Measure for Measure* 3.2.196-98 "No might nor greatness in mortality / Can censure scape; backwounding calumny / The whitest virtue strikes," 5.5.525, 530. As Zossima says in Dostoevsky's *Karamazovs* 6.2, "men like to see the fall of a righteous man and to witness his disgrace," namely, to see it and to imagine it. We are all too liable to do this when our rival thinks himself just, and when we think this of ourselves. Even a hypocrite will generally not return like for like, a just man never will.

[29]Cf. Plato's *Philebus* 48c-50b. Henri Bergson, *Laughter* 2.1.5 a comic person is self-ignorant and "As though wearing the ring of Gyges, with severe effect, he becomes invisible to himself, while remaining visible to all the world."

snub noses like his, is at most goofy, not derisible.[30] The real target of Aristophanes' laughter is not Socrates but *Strepsiades*. This becomes clear if we consider the meaning of the Clouds.

Who or What Are the Clouds?

The Clouds are on the face of it a projection and caricature of Socrates' own words and thoughts and studies, the art of words and argument that Strepsiades hopes to acquire himself, or for his son, at least that part of it that will allow him to outtalk others and free him from his debts.[31] The Clouds are to him goddesses of obscurity and imprecision and mystification, the very skill Strepsiades wishes to master, for he imagines it would be a godsend to him in his difficulties. If there is more to Socrates' work in the thinkery, this is all that Strepsiades can see, and it is what he wants. When Socrates introduces the Clouds, he seems to emphasize their patronage of every kind of idle eloquence and circumlocution, doubletalk and dazzle, smokeblowing and bullshit. But when Strepsiades asks why they have the form of women, Socrates explains that they appear to a person not as they are but as the person himself is, revealing and mocking him by reflecting him back to himself and to others, presumably by what they inspire him to say and do;[32] just now they appear like women because they have seen Cleisthenes, a womanish character often ridiculed

---

[30]Laughter: *Symposium* 189b; cf. *Republic* 5.452de, 457ab. Noses: *Clouds* 344, *Theaetetus* 143e, 209c.

[31]Cf. the nebulous claim by Plato's Gorgias that *his* rhetoric is an art of words concerning and producing "the greatest good for mankind, . . . freedom to mankind and power to the speaker over others in one's own city." *Gorgias* 452d. Socrates has to work for pages to pin him down to something precise enough to discuss critically.

[32]This is how in later writings Kierkegaard characterizes the subjectivity of subjective texts and authors, but as I will explain, it is how he characterizes irony here. See, e.g., CUP, 1: 52: "Like is understood only by like, and the old sentence, whatever is known is known in the mode of the knower, must indeed be amplified in such a way that there is also a mode in which the knower knows nothing whatever or that his knowing amounts to a delusion." Irony, and in its later meaning for Kierkegaard, subjectivity, both mean to be understood but expect that by some they will not be, in wilful ignorance, and both smile at such incomprehension and the rash reactions it provokes.

by the poet. The "ever-flowing" Clouds praise Strepsiades for his earnestness and Socrates for his devotion, and they promise Strepsiades that he will learn what he wishes if only he works hard for it. When he fails every test, they suggest that he send his grown son instead, and tell Socrates to take from him what he can. They hear the display of the two Logics and declare that everything is at stake for their friends; they speak to Better Logic with respect and encouragement, and tell Worse that he will need clever tricks to avoid being ridiculous. When Better deserts and Pheidippides is sent to learn Worse, the Clouds tell Strepsiades he will regret it, and go on to say what they will do to enforce justice, more particularly the award of first prize for their play. Now Strepsiades receives the graduate and takes him home to celebrate; visited by creditors, he practices the new tricks on them himself, and the Clouds exclaim, "What a thing it is to love baseness!" He wants to cheat on his debts, they say, but this sophist will have to pay for his knavery; he wanted his son to learn to defeat everyone however bad his cause; maybe, *maybe* now he will wish his son loses his tongue. The evil falls; Strepsiades comes out beaten and outraged by reasons why *he* is in the wrong. He blames the Clouds but they tell him that he brought it on himself by twisting himself into evil. Yes, we led you on, they say; but "We always do this when we find someone loves wrongdoing; we drive him into destruction to learn to fear the gods."[33] Strepsiades takes the point but, blaming Socrates and imagining he hears the divine voice of Hermes telling him not to bother with a lawsuit but to set fire to the school, he proceeds to do that, so he claims, as an act of piety towards the gods dishonored by the thinkers.

Is Socrates punished for his impiety and sophistry, and by the very gods of his own invention? He did not teach Strepsiades to use Worse Logic, but let him study what he wished; he denied the Zeus that makes rain and punishes with thunderbolts (what is *our* view of these?), but there are gods for him who know him for their own. These gods, the Clouds, are not imaginary, for we have seen

---

[33]Baseness: 1303. Destruction: 1458-61. Cf. Sophocles' *Antigone* 616-23 "Roving Hope comforts many and deludes many who know nothing until they step into fire. He was wise who said that when the gods ruin a man they make evil seem good to him, so that he does it blindly."

and heard them throughout the play. They are not patrons of fools and rogues, for they speak for justice and enforce it, and they themselves call on Zeus and the other gods.[34] They do not move against Socrates, but against Strepsiades who finds his own way into wrong doing. They do not betray Socrates who serves them faithfully, though he loses his school, for that is nothing to him if he has his philosophy and his associates and his moral integrity; to him it is simply another test and occasion to practice his ideal, doing whatever right thing there is to do and taking his chances as heaven sends. He is not self-ignorant and irresponsible in dealing with men such as Strepsiades and his son, for it is his work to deal with everyone he can. He does not teach the worse logic but lets Strepsiades study what he wishes; he denies the Zeus that makes rain and punishes with bolts of light, but divinity is real to him. *He* is not the silly knave who is the butt of the comedy and its mockery and ridicule; it is Strepsiades.[35] For all that we see, Socrates could be the same here as he is for Plato, but as perceived by foolish rogues like Strepsiades and nonphilosophers generally.

---

[34]They serve the justice of "Zeus who gathers the clouds" (as Homer says in *Iliad* 1.511, 560.) They invoke Zeus and Poseidon as well as Helios and their father Ocean (563-74, 275-87), Apollo and Artemis, Athena and Dionysos (595-606), and Selene the Moon (607-26). It is a familar tradition that from within the clouds Zeus enacts justice and mercy, and confirms truth: cf. Shakespeare, *Romeo & Juliet* 3.5.198-99 "Is there no pity sitting in the clouds / That sees into the bottom of my grief?"; *Coriolanus* 4.5.109-12 "If Jupiter / Should from yond cloud speak divine things, / And say ''Tis true,' I'd not believe them more / Than thee, noble Marcius."

[35]John Newell, "Aristophanes on Socrates," *Ancient Philosophy* 19 (1999): 109-19. Socrates tells him (296) "Don't act in our schools like those Comedy-fools with their scurrilous scandalous ways" (trans. Rogers). Ian Storey compares Strepsiades to the cartoon character Homer Simpson, in his introduction to Aristophanes, *Clouds*, translated by Peter Meineck (Indianapolis: Hackett, 2000) xxxviin.48. Both Strepsiades and Simpson could repeat as their motto, "I'm down, but I won't stay down" (126). Storey thinks that in the end Strepsiades "repents of what he has done," but surely he is just once again wriggling out of blame; in his extremity he calls on Hermes (1478-85), whom he probably honors as a god of thieves. For Plato, on the other hand, Hermes is a god of language and speech, and a messenger like Iris and divine love: *Cratylus* 407e-408d, 411b, *Theaetetus* 155d, *Symposium* 202d-203a.

Aristophanes does not mock him the way he does Strepsiades; he lets us laugh at Socrates, and if we do then the joke is on us.

The Clouds are a comic image of Socrates' philosophy, with its strange seemingly idle and questions and explanations and arguments. You see them not as they are in themselves, but as you are in yourself; you see yourself reflected in them. If you are a silly knave, then you see a silly knave, in the Clouds and in Socrates too. They lead you on to be judged by the way in which you judge them. The Clouds' different appearances to the son of Xenophantus and Simon and Cleonymus and Cleisthenes (340-55) are comparable to Socrates' different appearances to Meno and Theaetetus, Critias and Cebes, Thrasymachus and Glaucon, Callicles and Alcibiades.

Kierkegaard speaks of this when he writes that

> it is therefore with profound irony that Aristophanes, in the scene where Strepsiades is supposed to be initiated into this wisdom, has Socrates invoke the clouds, the aeriform reflection of his own hollow interior. (CI, 133)

Here Kierkegaard intends the interior of Socrates, but it is also and all the more true of the interior of Strepsiades. He characterizes this irony further when he goes on to speak of the reciprocity of

> the subject, who in wanting the objective obtains only his own likeness, and . . . the clouds, which merely catch the likeness of the subject but reproduce it only as long as they see it. (CI, 135)

At this point Kierkegaard is emphasizing the poet's seeming mockery of the philosopher, but he revealingly goes on at once to say that

> This is is a superb description of *the purely negative dialectic* that continually remains in itself, never goes out into the qualifications of life or of the idea, and therefore does indeed rejoice in a freedom that scorns the chains that continuity lays on, the dialectic that is a power only in the most abstract sense, a king without a country who delights in the sheer possibility of renouncing everything in the moment of specious possession of everything, although the possession as well as the renunciation is illusory, a dialectic that is not embarassed by the past, is not inclosed by its ironbound consequences, is not uneasy about the future because it so quickly forgets that even the future is practically forgotten before it is experienced, a dialectic that

regrets nothing, desires nothing, is unto itself enough, and leaps
over everything as recklessly and casually as a straying child. . . .
(CI, 135-36, emphasis added)

He is speaking of "the purely negative dialectic" of *irony* as he has
been explaining it, precisely as this appears from an external point
of view like that of Strepsiades and the nonphilosophers in the
audience and now among his readers, or of Meno and Critias,
Thrasymachus and Callicles in Plato's written conversations, where
the possession and renunciation, the consequences and continuity
are assessed by their worldly criteria, the standards of materialism
and opportunism relied on by nonphilosophers. Socrates has his
own criteria and standards and point of view, but of these he will
not speak, or not directly; his whole and only speaking, and
earnestness, is his irony.

It follows that, if the Clouds of Aristophanes' comedy are
clouds of Socrates' philosophy, his dialectic and questions and ideas
as they appear to nonphilosophers, then they are *clouds of irony*.
For Socrates' irony is the soul of his philosophy, and has all the
elusive ambiguity and all the streaming inexhaustibility of the
clouds.

Strepsiades does not perceive it, or it is to him only exaspera-
tion and mockery. Eyerolling is generally turned away from its
target, and a penetrating sidewise look from under the brows can
be missed or ignored or misunderstood even, and especially, when
one's words and acts invite and deserve it.

A difficulty makes itself felt at this point. Has Socrates, he of
the famous paradoxes, *nothing* positive to say? Is his irony, and is
he himself, always so *negative*?

Is Irony Essentially Negative?

For Kierkegaard, Socrates is a philosopher of irony: at least he
makes it a personal principle even if he does not, like Kierkegaard,
philosophize about it explicitly. Socrates raises moral questions,
but if he has anything to communicate, he cannot say it; he can
only point, by criticizing all answers and refuting every claim to
adequate knowledge. If he seems to agree, beware, for he may be
leading one into a contradiction to find one's own way out. He
cannot be any one's authority; no one can rely on him for one's

reasons, or one has not learned. He repels everyone who is drawn to him for guidance. We listen carefully, so it has been said, hoping to learn much that is wise; but all we learn is how to listen.[36] Socrates has only his moral earnestness to offer, but irony is the form that it takes, reducing every definitive result to nothing.

This fits much of what Plato's Socrates says about himself in calling himself only a midwife to the childbirth of others.[37] He knows who is really thinking, *laboring* with some perplexity, and not repeating thoughts at second hand; he knows how to *ease* this labor with telling questions that can lead to insight or abort it by showing it to be a blind alley; and he can tell who is able to learn what and from whom, so that he can *match* people with good teachers for what they have it in them to learn; but unlike a midwife of the usual kind, he can also *test* the newborn and tell real brainchildren from imposters, words of living knowledge from words of delusion not based on good reasons. Generally he delivers others *from* delusion, but occasionally he delivers them *of* knowledge. Nevertheless he has never given birth to any knowledge of his own. And yet he has just said that a midwife must have had experience of birth herself.

We wonder at this, because of course Plato's Socrates *has* a conception of the ethical, and he is generally arguing from or to some detail of it: namely, that the only happiness is moral excellence, and that this is wisdom, and self-knowledge; but since only the *god* has and knows these fully and adequately, and does what he knows is right and best, *our* best human happiness and excellence, wisdom and self-knowledge, is to recognize and admit our lack of them, and to work to learn and acquire them as best we may from the god as *the god's*. Thus his paradoxes, for example that to know

---

[36]I am applying to Socrates what Philip Merlan says about Plato in his myths, in "Form and Content in Plato's Philosophy," *Journal of the History of Ideas* 8 (1947): 406-30. Merlan argues that these myths are "aimed at the hearer and relate him to himself rather than offer him direct instruction," like refutation and dialectic (411). The myths relate him to himself as he knows he should be, and as he should work to become in earnest subjectivity; they incite his active aspiration to it.

[37]*Theaetetus* 149-51.

goodness is to possess it and do it, while to be good and practice it one must know it, and that only a good person is truly happy, and whatever befalls him he can never be unhappy.[38] Occasionally he develops these into detailed theories of the soul and the state and their virtues, as in the *Republic* and *Phaedo*. Yet he never affirms anything as definitive and settled for good.

Does he mean that he has never given birth to any knowledge so long as he is working as a midwife? For he may sometimes be leading a hunt, or planting a garden and tending it, or simply working out his own thoughts in solitude. On the other hand, he will want to confirm his conclusions, and activate and encourage others to draw their own.[39]

This is the decisive point: that Plato's Socrates is always in search as one of several searchers, and it is as if his goal were the search itself, to be taking part in it with others. To him this is human wisdom and excellence, the goodness that makes us and our lives good. Thus he always disavows knowledge, raises new difficulties, invites objections, tells others not to rely on him, so much so that we must suppose that the true rhetoric that he describes in the *Phaedrus* will be an art of the *indirect* communication that is *irony*.[40]

---

[38] As Alcibiades says, Socrates has characteristic *logoi* that are unlike anyone else's in their meaning and images of excellence and their helpfulness to anyone who aspires to be a truly good human being, *logoi* wrapped up in words that transport and possess anyone who hears him say them or another repeat them (*Symposium* 221d-22a, 215ce). He means, anyone who feels the aspiration of Socrates, and his earnestness, that is to say his irony.

[39] *Republic* 4.427ce, 432be, 5.450-51b; *Phaedrus* 276b-77a; *Symposium* 174d, 175b, 220c. *Protagoras* 348cd "When two team up, one catches on more quickly" (*Iliad* 10.224, trans. Robert Fitzgerald [Garden City: Anchor Books, 1975]). This is the *suzetesis*, shared inquiry, mentioned in *Meno* 80d, 90b, *Cratylus* 384c, *Greater Hippias* 295b. It means seeking truth and fellow seekers, as Gregory Vlastos has said. See "The Paradox of Socrates," in *Studies in Greek Philosophy II, Socrates, Plato, and Their Tradition*, ed. Daniel Graham (Princeton: Princeton University Press, 1995) 3-18, at 12. See also "Socrates' Disavowal of Knowledge" in *Socratic Studies* (Cambridge: Cambridge University Press, 1994) 39-66; and "Socratic Irony" in *Socrates, Ironist and Moral Philosopher* (Cambridge: Cambridge University Press, 1991) 21-44.

[40] *Apology* 20d, 23ab, 38a; *Phaedrus* 261a, 270b-72b, 277bc, cf. *Gorgias* 502d-503a, 504de, 513e, 517ac, 521d. This art includes Socrates' *music*, as in *Phaedo* 60c-61b, *Symposium* 215ce, 221d-22a, *Republic* 3.412a: see nn. 14, 37, above.

Kierkegaard takes this view too. Like Hegel he emphasizes relentlessly the *negativity* of Socrates:

> Indeed, the whole *Apology* in its totality is an ironic work, inasmuch as most of the accusations boil down to a nothing . . . that Socrates simply passes off as the content of his life, which again is irony. . . .
>
> Here, then [*Apology* 41b], we see irony in all its divine infinitude, which allows nothing whatever to endure. Like Samson, Socrates grasps the pillars that support knowledge and tumbles everything down into the nothingness of ignorance.
>
> What kept Socrates from a speculative absorption in the remotely intimated positivity behind this ignorance was, of course, the divine call that he had to convince every individual of the same thing. He had come not to save the world but to judge it. His life was dedicated to that, and it was this activity that also kept him from taking part in the affairs of the state . . . he addressed himself to each one individually, wrested everything from him, and sent him away empty-handed.[41]

In the third passage, Kierkegaard means by "the world" the worldliness of everyday life, the materialism and selfseeking that the ninth thesis calls substantiality and actuality by contrast with ideality, things as they humanly-all-too-humanly are and not as they should be. He mentions the abstention from ordinary politics that further on (CI, 231-34) and following Hegel he calls a deficiency in Socrates. In later years he berates himself for taking such a view:

> Influenced as I was by Hegel and whatever was modern, without the maturity really to comprehend greatness, I could not resist pointing out somewhere in my dissertation that it was a defect on the part of Socrates to disregard the whole and only consider numerically the individuals.
>
> What a Hegelian fool I was! It is precisely this that powerfully demonstrates what a great ethicist Socrates was.
>
> Such an ethicist uses irony as his incognito. In this sense Socrates was an ethicist, but, please note, bordering on the religious. . . .

---

[41]CI, 37n, 40, 173. Socrates understood the god's oracle as addressed to all mankind with himself simply as example and spokesman. *Apology* 23b: "When the god says this man Socrates, he is using my name as an example, as if he said [to mankind], 'This man among you, mortals, is wisest who, like Socrates, understands that his wisdom is worthless.' "

What, then, is irony, if one wants to call Socrates an ironist and does not, like Magister Kierkegaard, consciously or unconsciously want to bring out only the one side?[42]

He and Climacus are a little unfair to himself here because in the dissertation he is already presenting the other side: the *ethical greatness* of Socrates and, more particularly, his constantly starting all over again and going right up to the Idea, continually pointing to the ethical that all profess to think so much of but few know even enough to acknowledge their own ignorance, so as to be even at the beginning. Socrates takes people all the way to the Idea as "the boundary from which he turned back into himself in ironic satisfaction," that is to say, not just in enjoyment in getting free of materialism but contentment in having done his task; for "he had no deeper speculative craving," no craving for any definitive result in which to rest. Kierkegaard repeatedly cites with favor the remark of Hegel that "with Socrates it is not so much a matter of speculation as of individual life," so that the task is not merely to think and talk about justice and excellence but to appropriate and fulfil them in living actuality. His irony can "never unmask itself" or "advance a thesis," and it repels those whom it draws so that they have to think for themselves without relying on him.

> And yet underneath this indifference to them they felt, more than they saw, the piercing sidelong glance that instantly pierced their souls like a dagger. It seemed as if he had secretly listened to the most intimate conversations of their souls, as if he constrained them to speak aloud about [their secret thoughts] in his presence.[43]

Socrates does not declare any definitive and adequate knowledge of the ideal even to himself, and even if it shows in him and his words, he does not *know* it, or it is only true opinion to him; or we

---

[42]JP, 4: 4281. CUP, 1: 503. For Socrates on the numerical, see Plato, *Gorgias* 471e-72c, 474ab, 475e-76a.

[43]CI, 149 "Socrates had acquired a prescriptive title to being the most honest man in Greece"; 198 "He is the nothing from which the beginning must nevertheless begin," 216 he "could begin anywhere," 253, cf. LD, 262-63; CI, 154, 165, 197, 176. Hegel: CI, 166-67, 221, 223-24, 227, cf. 327-28. Unmasking: 48; 169; 182, 187-88. Glance: 190 and above at n. 10.

could say with the poet Yeats that so to embody it is his whole and only knowledge of it.[44]

Kierkegaard has thus identified a decisive mark of Socratic philosophy. On the one hand, it gives him a welcome reason to say that witty Aristophanes complements Plato in a way that dull Xenophon does not. For we want Plato's Socrates in our lives, and if he did not exist then philosophy would have to invent him, and in truth we would have to invent philosophy. We cannot be fully human without it; and it everywhere presupposes him and is inconceivable without him. If we ask ourselves whether we can be objective and just in preferring the philosopher's account to the nonphilosopher's, the sophist's and the poet's where they differ, then we can only appeal like Plato to the philosopher's experience and analysis and language to discuss and discover the truth, and ask, What does the nonphilosopher have?

On the other hand, irony gives Kierkegaard a way to contrast Socrates himself, the actual one of history, with Plato's Socrates. Emerson says that "Socrates and Plato are the double star which the most powerful instruments cannot entirely separate." Kierkegaard offers a way to do it: wherever our philosopher positively asserts or strongly implies anything, it is Plato speaking in his voice, "raising him too high"; Socrates himself had the *courage* to be negative to the end.[45]

---

[44]CI, 262n "Like water in relation to what it reflects, the negative has the quality of showing as high above itself that which it supports as it shows beneath itself that which it is battling; but the negative, like the water, does not know this." Cf. Plato, *Charmides* 164ac, *Meno* 99-100, and *Sophist* 267c, 268a. *The Letters of W. B. Yeats*, ed. Allan Wade (MacMillan 1955) 922.

[45]*Republic* 9.580d-83a. Ralph Waldo Emerson, *Representative Men* (1850), "Plato; or, The Philosopher" in *Essays and Lectures* (New York: The Library of America, 1983) 649. In "Shakespeare; or, The Poet," 721, Emerson argues that "So far from Shakespeare's being the least known, he is the one person known to us"; this might be said of Socrates too and for comparable reasons, though its truth is evident only to the ears and eyes of irony. Courage: JP, 5:5796 the draft of an ironic criticism of Magister Kierkegaard by Climacus that really supports him.

Irony, Subjectivity, and the Existential

In irony as he has explained it in his dissertation, Kierkegaard has enfolded many of the themes he is going to unfold in his authorship over the next fourteen years. Socrates wrote nothing so far as we know but shapes in the sand, like Jesus;[46] but an ironist like Kierkegaard who does become an author will be earnest to communicate not words but what he himself is, not a teaching so much as an authenticity of *existence*, and thus an attitude not of mere scientific objectivity towards the truth but earnest *subjectivity* towards it, so that it is seen not as a final result so much as an infinite *way* with the result steadily deferred. To read a subjective, existential author is constantly to face ethical reality, not the author's but always only one's own, so that the author is someone whom in his or her ethical reality we do not and cannot *know* and should not try to know. In the *dialectical reduplication* that is irony, the author will repel our understanding and turn us ceaselessly back to ourselves. His or her own life will be hidden. Thus we are not surprised to find Kierkegaard's pseudonym Climacus writing that

> when Socrates . . . isolated himself from any and every relation
> and . . . presumed that everyone had to do it in that way, such
> a lifeview would essentially become a secret, because it could not
> be communicated directly; at most he was capable of artistically,
> maieutically helping another person negatively to the same view.
> Everything subjective, which on account of its dialectical inward-
> ness evades the direct form of expression, is an essential secret.[47]

---

[46]*Meno* 82b-85b. Cf. *John* 8.6; in JP, 1: 345, 360, 369; 4:4858 Kierkegaard emphasizes not the conscious irony of Jesus, as he might have done, but the unconscious irony of the words of the crowd and Pilate and the high priest, as if to illustrate *John* 12.47-48; Paul Duke, *Irony in the Fourth Gospel* (Atlanta: John Knox Press, 1985).

[47]CUP, 1:80; see generally 72-80, 247-49, 320-26, 357-58, and CI, 327-28; but also JP, 4: 4313: we should ask who is talking and how someone lives, to see if he deserves our attention or is merely a sophist; JP, 2:1957-58, 1962 indirect communication, midwifery, cannot and should not be the final form and maintained to the end, but must give way to witnessing to the ideal and acknowledgment that one is only its useless servant, for otherwise one risks proving only that it is true for no one, and taking "demonic" delight in laying

Climacus goes on, however, to contrast *irony* with *humor*, and to associate irony with the boundary between the aesthetic and ethical spheres, and humor with that between the ethical and religious, so that he can connect Socrates with irony and Hamann with humor. However, we have noted well his remark that "Socrates was an ethicist bordering on the religious."[48]

The meaning of subjectivity has changed, however, and been pulled back closer to that of irony. In the dissertation, irony is the first appearance of subjectivity, which in turn is inwardness aiming at *self-knowledge* and so is reflexive, reflective, *speculative*, that is to say, mirror gazing. Subjectivity tends to theory; but Kierkegaard maintains that Socratic irony always retreats from impersonal theory back into personal practice.[49] The more Kierkegaard contrasts irony and subjectivity here in the dissertation, in order to separate Socrates from Plato, the more subjectivity looks like the objectivity criticized by Climacus in the *Postscript*. But we should expect that when we recall the Hegelian origins of the notion.

Conclusion

The Concept of Irony is itself an ironic work, as has been said, not just because it involves mockery and wit, but because it means something different and more than what it seems to mean. There is in it an urgent concern for the ethical and a particular conception of it and of the irony that expresses it in word and action. This irony seems entirely *negative* but that is an appearance to a viewpoint outside it. Irony is meant to be understood, and from within it is seen to be positive in its orientation to the ethical. However, it expects misunderstanding and invites it and confronts it. Yet even to those in on the secret it will not speak nor yet will it be silent, but it will only point. An ironist as such is turned out

---

burdens on others that one has not yet taken up oneself; and JP, 6:6394 self-deprecation may be false humility and really "defrauding God and the truth," not trusting God who has given what one has; cf. the upbuilding discourse "Against Cowardliness," EUD, 347-75, especially 359, 368, 369-75.

[48]CUP, 1:291-92, 500-508, 531-32n; 503.

[49]Irony and subjectivity: CI, 123, 242, 263, and the eighth thesis. Inwardness: CI, 152, 163. Reflection: 177, cf. 272. Theory: 166-67, 175-76.

toward others in such a way that he understands himself as having nothing to *say* to others directly to build them up. He is there not to tell them what to think or say or do, but to awaken, to strip, to turn from falsehood towards truth. He declares to himself what he declares to others, that he has no knowledge to speak of, except of his ignorance; he has only the questions, and the direction to take them. Later in his authorship Kierkegaard will redescribe the ironist as a *subjective, existential* thinker who earnestly communicates indirectly what he himself is; he presents not a content so much as a *way*.

Kierkegaard came to understand this through Socrates, and in studying the ancient accounts of Socrates he saw that not only were Plato's dialogues works of irony, but so and in the same sense was Aristophanes' *Clouds*. He considered Xenophon to be missing the irony of Socrates, and thereby what is deepest in him. As for Plato and Aristophanes, there is no fundamental opposition between them. They have both the same philosopher in sight and in good focus, but from different viewpoints. We cannot even say that they offer different assessments of him. For as Kierkegaard explains them, both authors see the irony of Socrates and both appropriate it and rely on it in formulating their portraits of him. In some ways Aristophanes has taken it up even *more* fully than Plato has, precisely in showing Socrates from the outside.[50] If irony is saying what is different and more than what it seems, Aristophanes presents what *seems* while hinting that there is more to it. *Clouds* was not written simply to mock Socrates from the viewpoint of nonphilosophers—the general public, the many—to provoke laughter, and criticism of philosophers who are ready to criticize everyone and everything; he wrote it to mock this *public*, these thoughtless nonphilosophers, for their knavery and foolishness; and with delicious ever-flowing irony[51] he shows them in Strep-

---

[50]Of course Plato's Socrates too deprecates himself, repeating against himself what people will say about him. Thus, e.g., *Theaetetus* 195c. Cf. 149ab, *Meno* 71ab, 80c, *Charmides* 175-76a, *Euthydemus* 286e, *Lesser Hippias* 372ad, *Greater Hippias* 304be, *Phaedo* 70bc; Aristotle, *Nicomachean Ethics* 4.7 1127b23-26.

[51]Everflowing like *truth*, in the comparison of Confucius and Mencius, Heraclitus, and Hermes who calls it "a violent torrent" in that it cannot be held in simple unqualified formulations that express it fully and adequately, and once

siades reducing philosophy to their measure as if to prove in practice the truth of the Clouds and Socrates who honors and serves them.

For Kierkegaard, Socrates succumbed to irony,[52] but that is to say, he had the *strength* to be ironical always; so that if Plato ever shows him speaking out positively, it is Plato speaking through him: irony is the criterion to discern the two, if it is ever to be done. This is a coherent and attractive view, and it may well be right.

---

and for all, because in any *different* moment and situation what is true is *different* as a whole. Confucius, *Analects* 9.16; Mencius IV B 18; Heraclitus B 12, 49, 91, cf. 67; Hermes, *Asclepius* 3.

[52]CI, 131, 261, 264 "his fervor in this service consumed him, and in the end irony overwhelmed him," 271 "He became a sacrifice."

6

From Clouds *to* Corsair:
Kierkegaard, Aristophanes, and the Problem of Socrates

Eric Ziolkowski

Aristophanes' comedy *Clouds*, the earliest surviving document to mention Socrates,[1] is generally seen to attack him as "the arch-sophist, atheist, and corrupter of the young."[2] The play presents him as a quack pedagogue who holes up in his *phrontistērion* or "thinkery" amidst pale, nerdish pupils; devotes himself to astronomy, at times while suspended aloft in a basket, and to the study of subterranean phenomena; denies the traditional deities in favor of revering clouds and air; allows students to be trained to win an argument whether it is right or wrong;[3] and charges a fee for his instruction—or so it seems to some.[4] *Clouds* failed upon its first and only attested performance in 423 BCE, despite Aristoph-

---

[1]As noted by Karl Jaspers, *The Great Philosophers*, 2 vols., ed. Hannah Arendt, trans. Ralph Manheim (New York NY: Harcourt, Brace, & World, 1962) 1:15. Cf. Richard Levin, ed., *The Question of Socrates* (New York NY: Harcourt, Brace & World, 1961) 1; John Newell, "Aristophanes on Socrates," *Ancient Philosophy* 19 (1999): 109-19; see 109.

[2]Jeffrey Henderson, "Introductory Note," *Aristophanes. Clouds. Wasps. Peace*, new ed., ed. and trans. Jeffrey Henderson, Loeb Classical Library (Cambridge MA: Harvard University Press, 1998) 5.

[3]As Gregory Vlastos puts it, Socrates "does not himself inculcate crooked argument," but "he panders to the demand for it" (*Socrates, Ironist, and Moral Philosopher* [Ithaca NY: Cornell University Press, 1991] 29).

[4]The conventional claim that Aristophanes portrays Socrates as charging fees reflects a loose reading of *Clouds*, lines 245-46, 876, 1146. That the text does not present Socrates as charging or even mentioning fees of his own is noted by A. E. Taylor, "The *Phrontisterion*," in his *Varia Socratica: First Series* (Oxford: James Parker, 1911) 176-77; and Gilbert Murray, *Aristophanes: A Study* (Oxford: Clarendon, 1933) 89, 94.

anes' opinion of it as his most sophisticated comedy.[5] The play apparently "was too subtle for the public," and "treated Socrates and his school too sympathetically and with too much friendly humour instead of rough satire."[6] So Aristophanes revised the script, abandoning it unfinished sometime between 419 and 416.[7] In that incomplete form, which was subsequently circulated and is the only version of *Clouds* we know today, Aristophanes toughened up the play's satire by inserting the parabasis (lines 518-52), the debate between Better Argument and Worse Argument, and the torching of Socrates' domicile at the end.

Augmenting the allusions to him in three of Aristophanes' other extant comedies (*Wasps*, *Birds*, and *Frogs*), the caricature of Socrates in *Clouds* strikes most readers as discrepant with the only other surviving portrayals by contemporaries, Plato and Xenophon—both of whom had known Socrates personally but wrote after his death. Thus George Grote opined in the mid-nineteenth century that the teachings of the Aristophanic Socrates seem "utterly different" from those of the real Socrates, against whom *Clouds* levels "calumnies."[8] After Grote, classicists and historians of philosophy tended to regard Aristophanes' depiction of Socrates as "astonishingly false,"[9] "unfair,"[10] and "very unfortunate for the fame of Aristophanes."[11] Such opinions, accompanied by a sense of the play's satire as "hostile," "malicious," or "ill-natured,"[12] are

---

[5]See *Wasps*, lines 1037-47; *Clouds*, line 522.

[6]Murray, *Aristophanes*, 87-88. Cf. Aristophanes, *Wasps*, lines 1043-45.

[7]See Henderson, "Introductory Note," *Aristophanes*, 3. Cf. K. J. Dover, ed., introduction to Aristophanes, *Clouds* (Oxford: Clarendon, 1968) lxxx-lxxxi.

[8]George Grote, *A History of Greece; from the Earliest Period to the Close of the Generation Contemporary with Alexander the Great*, 10 vols. (London: John Murray, 1888) 7:89, 147.

[9]Jaspers, *Great Philosophers*, 1:21.

[10]W. W. Merry, ed., introduction to Aristophanes, *The Clouds*, new ed. (Oxford: Clarendon, 1899) vii; and C. E. Graves, ed., introduction to Aristophanes, *Clouds* (Cambridge: Cambridge University Press, 1911) ix.

[11]C. C. Felton, ed., preface to Aristophanes, *The Clouds* (Boston MA: John Allyn, 1877) xi.

[12]Quotes drawn successively from Grote, *History of Greece*, 1:359n.2; *The Oxford Companion to Classical Literature*, 2nd ed., ed. M. C. Howatson (Oxford: Oxford University Press, 1989) 529 s.v. "Socrates"; and Albert W. Levi, "The Idea of Socrates: The Philosophic Hero in the Nineteenth Century," *Journal of the History*

thought to have "removed the *Clouds* from serious consideration as a possible source of information about Socrates' philosophy and intellectual biography."[13]

Given the notoreity of *Clouds*, the seventh of the fifteen theses heading Kierkegaard's M.A. dissertation *On the Concept of Irony with Continual Reference to Socrates* (1841) gives pause for thought: "Aristophanes has come very close to the truth in his depiction of Socrates" (CI, 6; expounded 128-54). The consensus today that the Aristophanic Socrates lacks historicity is not all that might cause eyebrows to rise regarding this thesis. To the annoyance of his professors,[14] Kierkegaard's tone in the dissertation is illustrative of the "concept" under consideration. Thus, with earlier commentators, Lee Capel views *The Concept of Irony* as "a consciously ironic work,"[15] and, regarding Thesis VII, "wonders whether Kierkegaard, being aware of Hegel's recent rehabilitation of the Aristophanic Socrates" in his *Lectures on the History of Philosophy* (delivered 1805–1831; published posthumously), "is not here writing with tongue in cheek" and "follow[ing] Hegel with a serious bent on parody."[16]

---

of Ideas 17 (1956): 89-107; here 93.

[13]Paul Vander Waerdt, *The Socratic Movement* (Ithaca NY: Cornell University Press, 1991) 54-55; quoted by Newell, "Aristophanes on Socrates," 109. However, Niels Thulstrup identifies certain German scholars who found in *Clouds* many "reliable historical traits for a description of Socrates in youth and middle age, his attitude toward philosophy of nature, toward the Sophists, and his maieutic as well as his irony" (*Kierkegaard's Relation to Hegel*, trans. George L. Stengren [Princeton NJ: Princeton University Press, 1980] 233n.12). Cf. Newell's interpretation, which we will later consider.

[14]On their complaints regarding the form and style of the dissertation, see Lee M. Capel, "Historical Introduction" to Søren Kierkegaard, *The Concept of Irony, with Constant Reference to Socrates*, trans. Lee M. Capel (New York NY: Harper & Row, 1965; 1st Midland edition: Bloomington IN: Indiana University Press, 1968) 10-12; and the Hongs' "Historical Introduction," CI, xii.

[15]Capel (n. 14 above) 14; see also 8. This view can be traced back to the review of the dissertation in *The Corsair* 51 (22 October 1841): cols. 7-8: "Thank you, beloved Kierkegaard, for your irony!" (COR, 92-93). The same view, as documented in Capel's survey of the interpretation of the dissertation (Capel, n. 14 above, 351n.2-357), persists among certain later scholars. Cf. Thulstrup, who regularly detects irony in the allusions to Hegel in the dissertation (*Kierkegaard's Relation to Hegel*, 213-61).

[16]Capel (n. 14 above) 385n2. *Clouds* is treated in G.W.F. Hegel, *Lectures on the History of Philosophy*, 3 vols., trans. E. S. Haldane (London: Kegan Paul, Trench,

As with the rest of the dissertation's first part, entitled "The Position of Socrates Viewed as Irony" (CI, 7), it would be difficult to consider Thesis VII without remembering that Socrates always occupied the highest spot in Kierkegaard's estimation of human beings (excepting, of course, Christ). Having felt and conveyed "an inexplicable rapport from a very early age" with Socrates,[17] whom Johannes de Silentio would call "the most interesting man who ever lived" (FT, 83), Kierkegaard is seen as the "Danish Socrates" or "modern Socrates,"[18] "the Christianizer of the Greek sage,"[19] and hence "Christianity's Socrates."[20] To be sure, some scholars demur, submitting that Kierkegaard as a Christian "could not limit his pedagogic efforts to potential philosophers, as did the *Republic*'s Socrates,"[21] or that "His attempt to resurrect Socratic dialectic was shipwrecked, ironically, upon modern objective thinking."[22] Nonetheless, others insist that "Kierkegaard's unconcern for the opinion of the many and his intense inwardness would surely appeal to a returned Socrates,"[23] and that "Socrates attained no objective knowledge of the divine, but in spite of this clung to the passion which arises from the negativity and inwardness of dialectical conclusions. Now this is precisely the way by which Kierkegaard comes to the absolute."[24]

Trübner, 1896) 1:426-30.

[17]25 March 1853, JP, 6:6839. See also 4:4243-4304 passim, s.v. "Socrates."

[18]Both epithets are used by David Swenson, "Søren Kierkegaard—A Danish Socrates" (written prior to 1930), in his *Something About Kierkegaard*, rev. and enl. ed., ed. Lillian Marvin Swenson (Minneapolis MN: Augsburg Publishing House, 1945; repr. with additions: Macon GA: Mercer University Press, 1983) 34-69; see 36. See also M. Whitcomb Hess, "Kierkegaard and Socrates," *The Christian Century* 82/1 (1965): 736-38, on 737.

[19]Hess, "Kierkegaard and Socrates," 738.

[20]Gregor Malantschuk, JP, 4, p. 677, s.v. "Socrates."

[21]Harry Neumann, "Kierkegaard and Socrates on the Dignity of Man," *The Personalist* 48 (1967): 453-60; here 456.

[22]Raymond L. Weiss, "Kierkegaard's 'Return' to Socrates," *The New Scholasticism* 45 (1971): 573-83; here 583.

[23]"Socrates and Kierkegaard," in Geddes MacGregor, *The Hemlock and the Cross: Humanism, Socrates and Christ* (Philadelphia PA: J. B. Lippincott, 1963) 185-95; here 195.

[24]Hermann Diem, "The Socratic Paradox," in his *Kierkegaard's Dialectic of Existence*, trans. Harold Knight and F. H. Simson (Edinburgh: Oliver and Boyd,

Aware of Kierkegaard's special relation to Socrates, readers considering his seventh thesis naturally tend to regard Aristophanes simply as one of the three lenses through which Kierkegaard attempts to fathom the Athenian sage. Yet this tendency entails a neglect of whatever significance Aristophanes may have held in his own right for Kierkegaard. Oddly, despite this pivotal thesis on Aristophanes in the dissertation, despite the crucialness of the comic as an aesthetic and existential category throughout all of Kierkegaard's writings, and despite his amply documented "lifelong enthusiasm for the theatre," and the fact that "the world of the theatre pervades his authorship, providing him with a constant supply of illustrative material" and "a paradigm of the aesthetic consciousness, a paradigm which relates equally to aesthetics (as the sphere of artistic practices) and 'the aesthetic' (as an existential category)"[25]—despite all these factors, Kierkegaard's view of the preeminent comic dramatist of ancient Greece remains unappreciated.

This essay will take account of those views, primarily as they emerge from Kierkegaard's exposition of Thesis VII, but also as they develop further in his writings beyond the dissertation. Because Kierkegaard is unusual in the approach he takes to the Aristophanic portrait of Socrates, and in the weight he grants that portrait in relation to the Platonic and the Xenophontic, I will first provide a context for our examination by sketching the history of the interpretation of Socrates from antiquity on. Next I will consider the pertinence of *Clouds* to Socrates' trial. Kierkegaard refrains from discussing that issue because, as Thesis VII will reveal, his image of Aristophanes seems to converge with that of Socrates in the categories of irony and the comic. In my closing account of the allusions to Aristophanes in Kierkegaard's writings beyond the dissertation, the question will arise as to whether this Christian Socrates might have viewed himself also as a Christian Aristophanes.

1959) 46-50; here 48.
    [25]See George Pattison, *Kierkegaard: The Aesthetic and the Religious: From the Magic Theatre to the Crucifixion of the Image* (Houndmills, Basingstoke, Hampshire: Macmillan, 1992) esp. 95-111; quotes on 95.

The Problem of Socrates

It is often observed that only two things about Socrates can be known with certainty: that he was publicly visible enough in Athens by his middle age to be burlesqued on stage,[26] and that he was later executed in the archonship of Laches (400/399 BCE).[27] Because he wrote nothing down, our only access to him and his teaching is through the surviving accounts by his three contemporaries, Aristophanes, Plato, and Xenophon. Hence emerges the so-called problem of Socrates: the historical-philosophical problem of ascertaining who the "historical" Socrates really was, and what he actually taught. To this problem, around which has accrued a scholarly literature of oceanic proportions,[28] it is usually conceded there can be no definite solution, and that the person today "looking for the historical truth about Socrates, finds himself in a swamp of myth, archaic interpretation, and emotional need."[29]

The Socratic problem stems from the clash of attitudes and perspectives in which not only does Aristophanes' "antagonism" toward Socrates differ from the "reverence" of Plato and Xenophon for him (as disciples), but Xenophon's "common sense, stolid Socrates" differs from Plato's "spiritual, even mystic Socrates."[30] Construed otherwise, the Xenophontic Socrates may seem "an eminently worthy but dull, prosy and sententious moralist ('the patron saint of moral twaddle', said Hegel)," in contrast to the

---

[26]E.g., Grote, *History of Greece* 7:140; Taylor, *"Phrontisterion,"* 142, 142n.2; A. E. Taylor, *Socrates* (Boston: Beacon, 1951) 94; Olof Gigon, *Sokrates: Sein Bild in Dichtung und Geschichte* (Bern: A. Francke, 1947) 21; Dover, introduction to *Clouds,* liii.

[27]E.g., John Burnet, "Socrates," in *The Encyclopaedia of Religion and Ethics,* ed. James Hastings (New York: Charles Scribner, 1908–1926) 11:665; A. E. Taylor, *Socrates* (Boston: Beacon, 1951) 9.

[28]The most exhaustive treatment remains V. de Magalhães-Vilhena's *Le Problème de Socrate: le Socrate historique et le Socrate de Platon* (Paris: Presses Universitaires de France, 1952).

[29]Levi, "Idea," 94.

[30]Ibid., 91.

Platonic Socrates, who appears "witty and humorous, and a great metaphysical thinker as well."[31]

As if the differences between the Aristophanic, Platonic, and Xenophontic portraits were not enough to ensure that posterity could never recognize with certainty the character and teachings of Socrates, the mystery of his true identity was heightened by other factors after his life. First, Aristotle, who was born fifteen years after Socrates' death but spent twenty as a student in Plato's Academy at Athens, left his own testimony on Socrates that contradicts Plato's in denying that Socrates ascribed independent existence to the universals, or that he separated them from the particulars as Ideas or Forms.[32] Another complicating factor was the emergence of the various Minor Socratic Schools (the Megarians, the Elean-Eretrian School, the Cynics, and the Cyrenaic School), each of which stressed one or another particular aspect of Socrates' teachings, whether in connection with logic, eristics, dialectic, or ethics, often synthesizing it with doctrines from other thinkers or traditions.

As in the case of the historical Jesus, the historical Socrates and whatever he actually taught became obscured beneath the proliferating myths and images of his character and the interpretations of his teachings. Just as the ancient Judaic tradition yielded claims that Socrates had been a disciple of the biblical Jewish sage Ahithophel,[33] or that his philosophical teachings had been based upon pre-Septuagintal Greek renderings of the Pentateuch,[34] the Church fathers respected Socrates as the wisest of pagans, and some esteemed him as a heroic paragon, an anticipator of the Christian martyrs, even a type and adumbration of Christ.[35] Like

---

[31]John Ferguson, comp. and trans., *Socrates: A Source Book* (London: The Open University, Macmillan, 1970) 1. Cf. Jaspers, *Great Philosophers* 1:26.

[32]Aristotle, *Metaphysics* 13.4.1078b.17-32, 13.9.1086b.2-3.

[33]According to an ancient source quoted by Moses Isserles, *Torat ha-Olat*, 1.11; cited in *The Encyclopaedia Judaica*, 16 vols. (New York: Macmillan, 1971–1972) 2:466, s.v. "Ahithophel the Gilonite."

[34]Aristobolus (2nd cent. BCE), as cited in *Encyclopaedia Judaica* 3:444, s.v. "Aristobulus of Paneas."

[35]The seminal study was Adolf Harnack's *Sokrates und die alte Kirche* (Giessen: J. Ricker [Alfred Töpelmann], 1901), which is challenged on specific points by Wilhelm Walther, "Sokrates und die alte Kirche.I," *Allgemeine Evangelisch-Luther-*

Christ and the martyrs, he had been accused of blasphemy and executed for his beliefs. For Justin Martyr (d. 165), the first Christian apologist to discuss Socrates, Christ, and the Christians in the same breath, Socrates made manifest the same divine Logos Christ would later embody: "those who lived reasonably [μετὰ λόγου] are Christians, even though they have been thought atheists; as, among the Greeks, Socrates and Heraclitus, and men like them." Like Christ, "who was partially known even by Socrates," Socrates opposed Greek religion.[36] Following Justin, as generalized by Pelikan, "A comparison between the suffering of Christ and that of Socrates seems to have become a common idea in Christian apologetics."[37]

---

ische Kirchenzeitung, no. 8 (1902) cols. 170-76; idem, "Sokrates und die alte Kirche.II," Allgemeine Evangelisch-Lutherische Kirchenzeitung, no. 9 (1902) cols. 197-202; idem, "Nachtrag zu 'Sokrates und die alte Kirche,'" Allgemeine Evangelisch-Lutherische Kirchenzeitung, no. 20 (1902) col. 480; and by Johannes Geffcken, Sokrates und das alte Christentum (Heidelberg: Carl Winter's Universitätsbuchhandlung, 1908). See also Adolf Harnack, History of Dogma, 7 vols., trans. from the 3rd German ed. by Neil Buchanan (Boston: Little, Brown, 1897–1900) 2:180-81, 191; Etienne Gilson, History of Christian Philosophy in the Middle Ages (New York: Random House, 1955) 13; Jaspers, Great Philosophers, 1:28; MacGregor, The Hemlock and the Cross, 77-78; Jaroslav Pelikan, The Christian Tradition: A History of the Development of Doctrine, 5 vols. (Chicago: University of Chicago Press, 1971–1989) 1:31-32, 58; idem, Jesus Through the Centuries: His Place in the History of Culture (New Haven CT: Yale University Press, 1985) 44.

[36]Quotes from I Apology 46 and II Apology 10, in Patrologia cursus completus, Series graeca, 161 vols., dir. J.-P. Migne (Paris: Migne, 1857–1866) 6:397C, 461A; ET: The Ante-Nicene Fathers, 10 vols., ed. Alexander Roberts and James Donaldson, American reprint of the Edinburgh edition, rev. by A. Cleveland Coxe (Buffalo: Christian Literature Publishing, 1885–1897) 1:178, 191. Cf. I Apology 5. Harnack's claim that Justin was "der Erste, . . . der Christus und Sokrates einander am nächsten gerückt hat" (Sokrates und die alte Kirche, 9), a claim echoed by Thomas Deman, Socrate et Jésus, 5th ed. (Paris: L'Artisan du livre, 1944) 9, 39-40, is denied by Walther, "Sokrates und die alte Kirche. I," cols. 172-73.

[37]Pelikan, Christian Tradition 1:58. However, certain patristics after Justin, especially in the Latin Church, betray toward Socrates an ambivalence, or even a distinct negativism which modern scholars often overlook. For example, it is misleading to suggest, as does James C. O'Flaherty, that the notion of Socrates as Christ's forerunner "had been held by" Lactantius and Minucius Felix (Hamann's "Socratic Memorabilia": A Translation and Commentary [Baltimore: Johns Hopkins University Press, 1967] 6). Minucius's Octavius 13 quotes the anti-Christian pagan Caecilius as urging any would-be Christian philosopher to "imitate" Socrates

According to Karl Jaspers, "In the Middle Ages [Socrates']
name lost its radiance."[38] However, it might be more accurate to
say that that "radiance" was rekindled in the Middle Ages after
having already diminished among Christian apologists by late
antiquity (see note 37 above). For within the medieval Islamic
world, Socrates was venerated by the Faylasüfs (philosophers)
from Ya'qūb al-Kindî (d. after 870) and Muhammad b. Zakariyyā
al-Rāzî (d. 925 or 934) on. In the *Epistles of the Pure Brethren*
(Ikhawān al-Safā'), a popular compendium of Hellenic lore and
science composed during the 'Abbāsid caliphate, Socrates as
martyr for truth represents the typical case of those who resign
themselves to the will of destiny, and his death is compared with
the deaths of Jesus, the mystic martyr al-Hallāj, and the soldiers of
Husayn (grandson of the Prophet) who were martyred by Umay-
yad forces at Karbalā' in 680.[39] Moreover, Socrates did have an
important impact upon medieval European thought, through the
fusion of his Delphic precept "Know thyself"[40] with the biblical
notion of the human being's divine image (Gen. 1:26-27). That
fusion gave rise to what Etienne Gilson calls Christian Socratism,
a tendency in medieval philosophy defined by the conviction that
it is through self-knowledge that one comes to know the nature
God gave humans and the place God marked out for humans in
the cosmic order.[41] As Jaspers acknowledges, Socrates also was still
evoked by name from by Jewish and Christian thinkers in
medieval Europe. Judah Halevi (before 1075–1141) points to him
as epitomizing the highest human wisdom, which nonetheless is
insufficient for comphrehending the divine.[42] Albert the Great (ca.

---

through abiding by the latter's proverb that "What is above us is nothing to us."
Lactantius's *Divine Institutes* 3.20.11-12 and *Epitome of the Divine Institutes* 37 (cited
in some editions as 32.4) condemn Socrates as a rejector and derider of religion.

[38]Jaspers, *Great Philosophers* 1:28.

[39]As documented by Paul Kraus, "Rasiana I.," *Orientalia* 4, n.s. (1935): 300-34,
on 304; and Marshall G. S. Hodgson, *The Venture of Islam*, 3 vols. (Chicago:
University of Chicago Press, 1974) 1:429, 431.

[40]See Xenophon, *Memorabilia* 4.2.24.

[41]Etienne Gilson, *The Spirit of Mediaeval Philosophy (Gifford Lectures 1931–1932)*,
trans. A. H. C. Downes (London: Sheed and Ward, 1936) 209-28.

[42]See Judah Halevi, *The Kuzari (Kitab al Khazari): An Argument for the Faith of
Israel*, trans. Hartwig Hirschfeld (New York: Schocken, 1964) pt. 1, sec. 1 (p. 38);

1200–1280) views Socrates' executioners as exemples of those who sin against the light of reason.[43] The Catalan mystic poet Ramon Llull (ca. 1235–1316) constructs a dialogue with Socrates in which he himself gradually wins the ancient sage over to the principles of his own *Ars magna*.[44]

From the Renaissance on, as reflected in Erasmus's oft-quoted entreaty *Sancte Socrates, ora pro nobis*, a rejuvenated esteem for Socrates as champion of independent philosophy and ethical freedom is expressed by such representative thinkers as Montaigne, for whom his thinking bespeaks skepticism and naturalism; and Moses Mendelssohn, for whom he is a moral paragon who proffered proofs of God's existence and of immortality. Anticipated by the twelve discourses that constitute Jean-Louis Guez de Balzac's *Socrate chrétien* (1652),[45] and culminating a century and a half later in Joseph Priestley's *Socrates and Jesus Compared*,[46] interest was renewed in the parallels and differences between Socratic and Christian thinking, and between Socrates and Jesus as outstanding ethical teachers executed for treason against the faiths of their communities.[47] The Socrates-Christ affinity is also asserted in Johann Georg Hamann's *Socratic Memorabilia* (1759), although the text never mentions Christ by name. Dedicated to Immanuel Kant and Johann Christoph Berens, this tactful religious response to Enlightenment philosophy aims at revealing that the resemblance between Socrates and Christ is much closer than the Enlighteners allowed—so close, indeed, that Hamann presents Socrates as one of Christ's prototypes.[48]

---

pt. 3, sec. 1 (p. 136); pt. 4, sec. 13; pt. 5, sec. 14 (p. 272).

[43]*Politicorum* 3.6, in *B. Alberti Magni Ratisbonensis episcopi, ordinis Praedicatorum, Opera omnia*, 9 vols., ed. Auguste Borgnet (Paris: Apud Ludovicum Vivès, 1890–1899) 8:803-804; cited by Gilson, *History of Christian Philosophy*, 279.

[44]Otto Keicher, *Raymundus Lullus und seine Stellung zur arabischen Philosophie. Mit einem Anhang, enthaltend die zum ersten male veröffentlichte "Declaratio Raymundi per modum dialogi edita"* (München: Aschendorff, 1909) 95-221; cited by Gilson, *History of Christian Philosophy*, 352; see also 701nn.59-60.

[45]In *Oeuvres de J.-L. de Guez sieur de Balzac*, 2 vols., ed. P. Moreau (Paris: Jacques Lecoffre, 1854) 2:9-131.

[46]Joseph Priestley, *Socrates and Jesus Compared* (London: For J. Johnson, 1803).

[47]As discussed by Pelikan, *Jesus*, 188-89. Cf. Pelikan, *Christian Tradition* 5:110.

[48]O'Flaherty, Hamann's "*Socratic Memorabilia*," esp. 58, 70-71, 81-82, 107.

Throughout the eighteenth century, Socrates was the most beloved philosopher,[49] and, beginning with J. Brucker (1741), the Xenophontic Socrates was favored over the Platonic Socrates, presumably because the Xenophontic more closely approximated the current ideal of what a philosopher should be.[50] During this time, the philosophical rationalism and scholarly historicism that engendered the quest of the historical Jesus led to a quest of the historical Socrates. The occasional dovetailing of these two enterprises is exemplified by the analogy drawn in Strauss's *Das Leben Jesu* (1835) between the closing scene of Plato's *Symposium* and Christ's transfiguration,[51] an analogy cited two years later by F.C. Baur in his "philosophical-religious" monograph comparing Socrates and Christ,[52] and, again, disapprovingly, by Kierkegaard in his dissertation (CI, 52).

Schleiermacher gave the Socratic problem its initial, oft-cited formulation: "What *can* Socrates have been, in addition to what Xenophon reports of him, without however contradicting the distinguishing features and principles of life which Xenophon assuredly puts forward as Socratic; and what *must* he have been to have given Plato motive and justification to present him as he does in his dialogues?"[53] A century later the classicist John Burnet would lament that this rule of thumb had been eclipsed by Hegel's dictum that "in regard to the personality and method, the externals of his teaching, we may certainly receive from Plato a satisfactory, and perhaps a more complete representation of what Socrates was.

---

[49]Benno Böhm, *Sokrates im achtzehnten Jahrhundert. Studien zum Werdegange des modernen Persönlichkeitsbewusstseins* (Leipzig: Quelle und Meyer, 1929).

[50]As observed by John Burnet, *Greek Philosophy. Thales to Plato* (London: Macmillan, 1928) 127, referring to J. Brucker, *Historia critica philosophiae a mundi incunabulis ad nostram aetatem perducta* (Lipsiae, 1742–1744).

[51]David Friedrich Strauss, *Das Leben Jesu*, 2 vols. (Tübingen: C. F. Osiander, 1835) 2:276.

[52]Ferdinand Christian Baur, *Das Christliche des Platonismus, oder Socrates und Christus: Eine religionsphilosophische Untersuchung* (Tübingen: Ludwig Friedrich Fues, 1837) 107n.-108.

[53]Friedrich Schleiermacher, "Ueber den Werth des Sokrates als Philosophen" (1815), *Abhandlungen der Königlichen Akademie der Wissenschaften in Berlin. Aus den Jahren 1814–1815* (Berlin: Der Realschul-Buchhandlung, 1818) 50-68; here 59; my translation.

But in regard to the content of [Socrates'] teaching and the point reached by him in the development of thought, we have in the main to look to Xenophon."[54]

However, by Burnet's time, the debate over the Socratic problem had become even more complex and contentious. Differing views on Socrates had been presented by three of the most important nineteenth-century philosophers after Hegel: Kierkegaard, Nietzsche, and John Stuart Mill, the first two of whom are credited with having put forward "the two most influential conceptions of Socrates in the modern world,"[55] but the third of whom, as influenced by Grote, was the only one to have a practical bearing upon Burnet's views.[56] Moreover, as late as the 1890s, certain scholars still deemed either the Xenophontic or the Aristotelian portrait of Socrates as the most historically accurate.[57] Burnet himself preferred the Platonic Socrates, reasoning: "while it is quite impossible to regard the Sokrates of Aristophanes and the Sokrates of Xenophon as the same person, there is no difficulty in regarding both as distorted images of the Sokrates we know from Plato."[58]

Although other scholars dealt with the Socratic problem by trying to reconcile the Platonic, Xenophontic, and Aristotelian portraits of Socrates with each other so that "no unjustified violence . . . is done to any of the sources,"[59] Burnet's favoritism for the Platonic portrait carried the most sway as one of two extreme views held by twentieth-century classicists and historians of philosophy, especially as his position was supported and elaborated by his contemporary A.E. Taylor.[60] Adherents to the other extreme

[54]Hegel, *Lectures* 1:414. See Burnet, "Socrates" 11:672; Burnet, ed., introduction to *Plato's Phaedo* (Oxford: Clarendon, 1911) xiii.

[55]O'Flaherty, *Hamann's "Socratic Memorabilia,"* 108.

[56]See Levi, "Idea," 91n.8.

[57]See, e.g., August Döring, *Die Lehre des Sokrates als sociales Reformsystem. Neuer Versuch zur Lösung des Problems der sokratischen Philosophie* (Munich: Beck, 1895), who favored Xenophon; and Karl Joël, *Der echte und der xenophontische Sokrates,* 2 vols. (Berlin: R. Gaertner, 1893–1901), who favored Aristotle.

[58]Burnet, *Greek Philosophy,* 149.

[59]See, e.g., Copleston, *History of Philosophy,* 1:99-100, 102-104; quote on 100.

[60]See, e.g., any of the writings by Burnet and Taylor cited in this essay. See also I. G. Kidd, "Socrates," in *The Encyclopedia of Philosophy,* 8 vols., ed. Paul Edwards (New York: Macmillan and The Free Press, 1967) 8:481; Robert E.

view, characterized as "nihilist" or "agnostic," hold that we cannot know anything for sure about the historical Socrates, and that therefore the Aristophanic, Platonic, Xenophontic, and Aristotelian portraits of him must each be viewed as fiction or poetry.[61]

Of these portraits, nonetheless, the Aristophanic is the only one that, by virtue of its belonging to the comic-dramatic genre, *self-evidently* constitutes a poetic fiction,[62] even if "In the opinion of the plain man, the 'Socrates' whom Aristophanes libelled and caricatured in the *Clouds* will continue to be the historical Socrates."[63] *Clouds* is also the only source to ascribe to him an informed interest in astronomy and geology, to deny that he was a pious man, and to suggest that he taught his pupils how to succeed in the world through exploitation of such worldly arts as rhetoric and the law. According to K. J. Dover, there are three possible explanations of this basic conflict between Aristophanes on the one hand and Plato and Xenophon on the other:

(i)   Aristophanes portrays, through caricature, the truth; Plato and Xenophon are writing fiction, putting their own ideas into [Socrates'] mouth. . . .

(ii) Aristophanes caricatures Socrates as he was in 424/3; Plato and Xenophon portray him as he became in the last twenty years of this life. . . .

(iii) Plato and Xenophon tell the truth; Aristophanes attaches to Socrates the characteristics which belonged to the sophists in general but did not belong to Socrates.[64]

Cushman, "Socrates," in *The Encyclopedia of Religion*, 16 vols., ed. Mircea Eliade (New York: Macmillan, 1987) 3:401-403; here 402.

[61]See Alfred Gercke, "Geschichte der Philosophie," in *Einleitung in die Altertumswissenschaft*, 3 vols., 3rd ed., ed. Alfred Gercke and Eduard Norden (Berlin: B. G. Teubner, 1914–1927) 2:463-69, 468-69; Eugène Dupréel, *La Légende socratique et les sources de Platon* (Brussels: R. Sand, 1922); Gigon, *Sokrates*. For discussion, see Burnet, *Greek Philosophy*, 149-50; Jaspers, *Great Philosophers* 1:29; Levi, "Idea," 92-93; Kidd, "Socrates," 480-81.

[62]Cf. Leo Strauss, *Socrates and Aristophanes* (New York: Basic Books, 1966) 314.

[63]W. J. M. Starkie, introduction to *The Clouds of Aristophanes* (London: Macmillan, 1911) 1.

[64]Dover, introduction to *Clouds*, xlvi, xlix. The first of these views approximates what Newell calls the "tight" interpretation of *Clouds*, while the third view and, to a certain extent, the second as well, approximate what he calls the "loose" interpretation (see his "Aristophanes on Socrates," 109-10).

Of these explanations, the third, to which Dover subscribes, is the one most widely accepted, despite the arguments of Burnet and Taylor favoring the second. However, the idea that Aristophanes depicted the truth through caricature has not gone without its own espousers.[65] And John Newell has proposed yet another interpretation, suggesting that the irony for which the real Socrates was known allowed Aristophanes in *Clouds* "to present any philosophical view he pleased (or any combination of views) *without sacrificing realism*, because Socrates' irony made him a kind of mimetic actor who could believably present a variety of intellectual views, however much he might personally disagree with them."[66]

In ascribing irony to the Aristophanic Socrates, this last interpretation resembles Kierkegaard's, even though Newell, unlike Kierkegaard, whom he never cites, approaches *Clouds* philologically rather than philosophically. But before we consider Kierkegaard's own championing of the Aristophanic Socrates in the context of the interpretive history we have just sketched, let us take into account the question of the relationship of that portrayal to Socrates' actual condemnation and death—a question Kierkegaard will all but entirely ignore.

The Implication of Clouds in Socrates' Condemnation

One vexing problem raised by Thesis VII in Kierkegaard's dissertation has to do not with anything he says in promoting *Clouds* as the truest portrayal of Socrates, but with his avoidance of acknowledging the play's pertinence to Socrates' indictment, trial, condemnation, and execution (399 BCE). Throughout the discussion of *Clouds* (CI, 128-54), Socrates' condemnation goes unmentioned, and throughout the subsequent discussion of Socrates' condemnation (CI, 167-97), *Clouds* goes unmentioned. These silences seem remarkable today. For despite Hegel's surprising assertion that

---

[65]See, e.g., M. Montuori, *Socrates: An Approach*, trans. M. de la Pae Beresford (Amsterdam: J. C. Gieben), which Newell cites as an example of the "tight" interpretation of the Aristophanic Socrates ("Aristophanes on Socrates," 109n9). For other examples, consult Thulstrup, as referenced in n. 13 above.

[66]Newell, "Aristophanes on Socrates," 114.

Clouds "had no influence on the condemnation of Socrates,"[67] classicists and historians of philosophy since Grote have generally not been content simply to see Aristophanes as having "exactly forecast[ed] the charges . . . against Socrates,"[68] or to accept its parodying of Socrates simply as a passive "expression" or "reflection" of the attitudes and prejudices of contemporary Athens.[69] Rather, the tendency has been to hold *Clouds* responsible for fostering the public antagonism that led to the philosopher's doom.[70]

The perception of a causal connection between *Clouds* and Socrates's condemnation finds its loci classici in Plato, Xenophon, and several later Greek sources. According to Aelian and Diogenes Laertius, it was Anytus, one of the three men who eventually brought Socrates to trial on the charge of impiety and corrupting the youth, that incited Aristophanes to compose a play lampooning Socrates.[71] In Plato, the indicted Socrates himself cites *Clouds* as a specimen of the sort of slander with which anonymous people have long targeted him. Noting the impossibility of summoning an unseen adversary for cross-examination, he reminds the jury that it was nothing new for him to be accused of such acts of "criminal meddling" as inquiring into things beneath the earth and in the heavens, making the weaker argument defeat the stronger, and instructing others to emulate him: "You have seen it for yourselves in the play by Aristophanes, where Socrates goes whirling round proclaiming that he is walking on air, and uttering a great deal of

---

[67]Hegel, *Lectures* 1:427.

[68]Newell, "Aristophanes on Socrates," 110.

[69]Henderson, "Introductory Note," *Aristophanes*, 5; *Oxford Companion*, 529. Cf. Starkie, "Introduction," *Clouds of Aristophanes*, liv.

[70]See Grote, *History of Greece* 7:147; cf. 154; Felton, preface to Aristophanes, *The Clouds*, ix; Burnet, "Socrates," 11:671; Murray, *Aristophanes*, 88; Taylor, *Socrates*, 92-93; Jaspers, *Great Philosophers*, 1:21; Kidd, "Socrates," 480; Cushman, "Socrates," 3:401.

[71]*Variae historiae* 2.13, in *Aelian: Historical Miscellany*, ed. and trans. N. G. Wilson, Loeb Classical Library (Cambridge MA: Harvard University Press, 1997) 79-81; *Socrates*, 38, in Diogenes Laertius, *Lives of Eminent Philosophers*, 2 vols., trans. R. D. Hicks, Loeb Classical Library (London: William Heinemann, 1925) 1:169.

other nonsense about things of which I know nothing whatsoever."[72]

The fodder *Clouds* provided for Socrates' detractors long before
his trial is exemplified by the unnamed Syracusan who interrupts
the conversation of Socrates in Xenophon's *Symposium* (c. 380),
which is set at a banquet purportedly held in Athens in 421, two
years after the production of Aristophanes' play at Dionysia.
Alluding to Socrates as "a thinker on celestial subjects" (μετεώρων
φροντιστής), an expression of reproach that was used parodically
against Socrates in *Clouds* and would later carry grave implications
at his trial,[73] the Syracusan evokes another passage from the play
to ridicule him: "But tell me the distance between us in flea's feet;
for people say that your geometry includes such measurements as
that."[74]

Despite these classical linkages of *Clouds* with Socrates' condemnation, together with the long lineage of Christian, Islamic,
and Enlightenment comparisons of Socrates and Christ as martyrs,
it seems curious that Aristophanes is seldom censured for having
pilloried "the first philosopher who was tried and put to death"
(πρῶτος φιλοσόφων καταδικασθεὶς ἐτελεύτα)."[75] As he is thought
probably to have been in Athens during the trial, we cannot help
wondering what he was doing then, and how he regarded this
event.[76] After Socrates' death, as Socrates had prophesied (according to Plato), and as Diogenes reports, the Athenians promptly
repented, executed one of his accusers, and banished the rest.[77] Yet
Aristophanes evidently suffered no repercussion other than to be
much later branded "a vulgar and ridiculous humorist."[78] Al-

---

[72]Plato, *Apology* 18b-c; quote from 19c. Hereafter all quotations of Plato are
from *The Collected Dialogues of Plato, Including the Letters*, ed. Edith Hamilton and
Huntington Cairns (Princeton NJ: Princeton University Press, 1961).

[73]As noted by E. C. Marchant and O. J. Todd, trans., *The Banquet* [i.e.,
Symposium], in *Xenophon*, 7 vols., Loeb Classical Library (Cambridge MA: Harvard
University Press, 1979–1986) 4:606n.1. Hereafter all translations of Xenophon are
from this edition.

[74]Xenophon, *Symposium* 6.8. Cf. *Clouds*, lines 144-52; 830-31.

[75]*Socrates*, 20, in Diogenes, *Lives* 1:151.

[76]Cf. Murray, *Aristophanes*, 102; Levi, "Idea," 94n.20.

[77]Plato, *Apology* 39c; and *Socrates*, 43, in Diogenes, *Lives* 1:173.

[78]*Variae historiae* 2.13, in Aelian 79.

though the rumors Aelian repeated about Aristophanes may have "tarnished [Aristophanes'] name, until the learning and sagacity of modern critics should redeem it from the bitter reproach of having caused the death of the noblest man of his age,"[79] some critics assure us that no offence was taken by Socrates when *Clouds* was performed, and that Aristophanes and Plato later remained good friends.[80]

Whatever effect Socrates' death may or may not have had upon the Athenians' attitude toward Aristophanes, the fact that his burlesquing of Socrates has received relatively little criticism since being "rehabilitated" by Hegel might be attributable as much to the sway of Hegel's argument as to modern assumptions about poetic license and artistic freedom. Hegel initially turns to *Clouds* while arguing that the condemnation of Socrates was right and just, on the grounds that Socrates had subverted the Athenian "spirit" by replacing external religion with the judgment of inward consciousness as the sole criterion of truth. Anticipating the objection that Socrates in this play "was treated quite unjustly," Hegel responds

> but then we must recognize the merit of Aristophanes, who in his "Clouds" was perfectly right. This poet, who exposed Socrates to scorn in the most laughable and bitter way, was thus no ordinary joker and shallow wag who mocked what is highest and best, and sacrificed all to wit with a view to making the Athenians laugh. For everything has to him a much deeper basis, and in all his jokes there lies a depth of seriousness. He did not wish merely to mock; and moreover to mock what was worthy of honour would be perfectly bald and flat. It is a pitiful wit which has no substance, and does not rest on contradictions lying in the matter itself. But Aristophanes was no bad jester.[81]

Hegel was not the only defender of *Clouds* against possible censure. To the insinuation that Aristophanes ridiculed Socrates simply to elicit cheap laughs, the response is offered in Robert Browning's poem of 1875, *Aristophanes' Apology* (lines 3257-58):

[79]Felton, preface to Aristophanes, *The Clouds*, ix.
[80]See, e.g, Burnet, *Greek Philosophy*, 143; Murray, *Aristophanes*, 102; Taylor, *Socrates*, 92; *Oxford Companion*, 529; cf. Strauss, *Socrates and Aristophanes*, 5.
[81]Hegel, *Lectures* 1:427.

"Our poet means no mischief! All should know— / Ribaldry here implies a compliment!"[82]

Written within a decade after Hegel's death, and four decades before Browning's poem, *The Concept of Irony* will only once, obliquely but revealingly, hint at the bearing of *Clouds* on Socrates' condemnation.

"Very Close to the Truth"

Thesis VII, in leading to a pivotal "point of rest" (CI, 155) in Kierkegaard's dissertation, caps off his treatment of the Socratic problem, a problem he broached in introducing his first, paradoxical thesis (to which one of his professors will object because of its "delicate subject matter"[83]): "The similarity between Christ and Socrates consists in their dissimilarity" (CI, 6; expounded 13-15; cf. 220fn.-221). The immediate stimulus behind this thesis was Baur's book-length comparison (see JP, 4:4243, 1 November 1837). What has caught Kierkegaard's attention, and what he now challenges, is Baur's likening of the relation between Xenophon and Plato to the relation between the Synoptic Gospels and the Gospel of John (see CI, 13-14)—a comparison that represents another overlapping of the interests in the historical Jesus and the historical Socrates.

Another possible stimulus behind Thesis I, albeit one Kierkegaard does not acknowledge, may be the typological linkages drawn between Socrates and Christ in Johann Georg Hamann's *Socratic Memorabilia*.[84] Whereas Baur's discussion of Socrates is based almost exclusively upon Plato and Xenophon, Hamann makes several key allusions to *Clouds* near the close of his own book. Of these, one is to the Aristophanic Socrates' attestation that he and his followers believe only in "this Void, and the Clouds,

---

[82]In *Robert Browning: The Poems*, 2 vols., ed. John Pettigrew, suppl. Thomas J. Collins (New Haven CT: Yale University Press, 1981) 2:268.

[83]P. O. Brønsted, quoted by Capel, in "Historical Introduction" to Kierkegaard, *The Concept of Irony* (n. 14 above) 13.

[84]On Kierkegaard's possible acquaintance with Hamann's work on Socrates, see Emanuel Hirsch, "Geschichtliche Einleitung" to *Über den Begriff der Ironie*, trans. Hirsch, in Søren Kierkegaard, *Gesammelte Werke*, 31 vols. (Düsseldorf: E. Diederich, 1951–1966) 1:ix; O'Flaherty, *Hamann's "Socratic Memorabilia,"* 107.

and the Tongue, and only these three" (*Clouds*, line 424).[85] Interestingly, Kierkegaard will discuss this very line in expounding Thesis VII. But whereas Hamann cites it to illustrate the Athenians' actual charge that Socrates did not honor the gods, and that he desired to introduce new ones,[86] Kierkegaard will quote it in conjunction with the Aristophanic Socrates' oath, "By Respiration, by Void, by Air" (*Clouds*, line 627), to exemplify how the titular image of *Clouds* is "set forth as a creed, which like any creed contains both the subjective and the objective side" (CI, 137n)—the subjective being represented by "respiration" or "tongue" (γλῶττα), and the objective, by "clouds" (νεφέλαι) and "chaos" or "void" (χάος).

These different uses Hamann and Kierkegaard make of the same line from *Clouds* help illuminate what in my view is the most intriguing aspect of Thesis VII's championing of Aristophanes' caricature of Socrates: Kierkegaard's almost complete silence about the pertinence of that caricature to the allegations and legal proceedings that led to Socrates' death. In contrast to that silence, Hamann weaves into his *Socratic Memorabilia*'s penultimate paragraph yet another ironic allusion to the fateful slandering of Socrates in Aristophanes' play,[87] and then, associating the deaths of Socrates and Christ with each other, closes by remarking: "if it

---

[85]All quotations hereafter are of Henderson's edition (n. 2 above).

[86]*Hamann's "Socratic Memorabilia,"* 180-81.

[87]Hamann suggests that whoever "does not know how to live on crumbs and alms not on prey, or to renounce everything for a sword [*und für ein Schwert alles zu entbehren*], is not fit for the service of truth" (*Hamann's "Socratic Memorabilia,"* 184-85). Of Hamann's two footnotes to this passage, one quotes verses from *Clouds*, lines 1064-66: "A knife? What a civilized reward the poor sucker got! Now Hyperbolus, the man from the lamp market, has made a vast amount of money by being a rascal, but never a knife, no indeed!" These are the words by which Worse Argument mocks Achilles' father Peleus for having been given by the gods a knife with which to defend himself against wild beasts. Although, in the myth, that gift was meant by the gods as a reward for Peleus's having refused a proposition by Acastus's wife, Worse Argument offers the counteranecdote about Hyperbolus to suggest that a rascal is likely to garner more wealth than is someone decent like Peleus. The irony of Hamann's allusion to this passage is that, whereas Worse Argument would have been taken by Socrates' critics as representing his own morally corruptive mode of teaching, Hamann appropriates Worse Argument's own words to associate "renounc[ing] everything for a sword" with "service of truth."

is true, I say, that God himself became a man, and came into the world to bear witness to the truth, no omniscience would be necessary to foresee that he would not escape from the world as well as Socrates."[88] By following up his allusions to *Clouds* with this thought, Hamann seems to come close to implying that if Socrates and Christ are to be juxtaposed, then Aristophanes' satire of Socrates, which contributed to the slander that led to the philosopher's trial and death, might be considered at least to some extent analogous to the vilification of Jesus that led to the Crucifixion. Kierkegaard, who we know considered blasphemous any comparison of Socrates' and Christ's deaths (see EPW, 99), let alone other aspects of their lives (see CD, 241), never pursues such an implication.

In finding the Aristophanic depiction of Socrates "very close to the truth," Kierkegaard's Thesis VII seems somewhat peculiar in the light of the two extreme views on the Socratic problem summarized earlier. The thesis not only contradicts the Burnet-Taylor perception of that depiction as a "distorted" image of the "truer" Platonic portrait of Socrates, but defies the opposed nihilist or agnostic view by ascribing a "truth" value to the one surviving portrait that is, generically speaking, fictional or poetic rather than philosophical, historical, or biographical.

Thesis VII also confirms Kierkegaard's separation from both Hegel and his own anti-Hegelian professor of ancient philosophy, Paul Martin Møller, in his stance toward the Socratic problem. Capel, as cited earlier, senses that this thesis *parodies* Hegel's "rehabilitation of the Aristophanic Socrates," a matter about which we will later say more. Suffice it here to remind ourselves that Hegel himself favored the Platonic Socrates and, even more so, the Xenophontic Socrates. Kierkegaard disregards this point, noting only that "there is nothing at all in [Hegel's] presentation of Socrates . . . to illuminate the relations of the three different contemporay views of Socrates" (CI, 221). To be sure, Kierkegaard himself could later express remorse over having written the dissertation as "a Hegelian fool" (entry of 1850, JP, 4:4281 [repr. CI,

---

[88]Hamann, *Sokratische Denkwürdigkeiten*, 82, lines 9-13; in O'Flaherty, *Hamann's "Socratic Memorabilia,"* 184-85.

453]). Yet his disregard toward Hegel's preference for the Xeno-phontic and the Platonic Socrates is already shown by his arguing in Thesis II that the Xenophontic Socrates never passes beyond the useful or the empirical to arrive at the idea (CI, 6; expounded 15-27); and in Thesis III that when Xenophon and Plato are compared, Xenophon will be seen to take too much from Socrates, and Plato, to raise him too high, and neither of them discovers the truth (CI, 6; expounded 27-34).[89]

Having concluded from his consideration of the Xenophontic and Platonic views of Socrates in Theses II-VI that Xenophon, "like a huckster, has deflated his Socrates," whereas Plato, "like an artist, has created his Socrates in supranatural dimensions" (CI, 127), Kierkegaard submits that Aristophanes' view "will provide just the necessary contrast to Plato's and precisely by means of this contrast open the possibility of a new approach for our evaluation" (CI, 128). It is especially on this point that Kierkegaard parts from Møller, who had proposed that Aristotle's testimony on Socrates be employed to mediate (et Tredie) between Xenophon and Plato, as the latter two "must in some way correct each other, and what is common to them both must belong to the historical Socrates."[90] For Kierkegaard, what makes the Aristophanic appraisal of Socrates so valuable is that "just as every process usually ends with a parodying itself, and such a parody is an assurance that this process has outlived its day, so the comic view is an element, in many ways a perpetually corrective element, in making a personal-ity or an enterprise completely intelligible" (CI, 128; cf. JP, 4:4066, 4067, 4775). This "corrective element" in "the comic view" helps justify the anachronism of Kierkegaard's approach; as he will later acknowledge, he has classified these three interpretations of Socrates "more according to their relation to the idea (the purely historical [Xenophon]—the ideal [Plato]—the comic [Aristophanes]) than according to time," even though it is not his desire "to deprive the Aristophanic view of the weight it does have because it is closest to Socrates in time" (CI, 154*).

---

[89]Cf. the opening paragraph of the dissertation, where Kierkegaard already disagrees with Baur for "think[ing] that, along with Plato, Xenophon should be most highly regarded" (CI, 13).

[90]As translated by Capel (n. 14 above) 365n.25.

That Kierkegaard will ignore the question of the bearing of *Clouds* upon Socrates' trial seems ensured by a maneuver he now makes that resembles something Hegel did in his own discussion of the Aristophanic Socrates. Hegel resolved "not here to consider the real nature of the Comedy of Aristophanes, nor the wanton way in which he was said to have treated Socrates."[91] Similarly, having evidently rejected or missed the point of Socrates' last (unrecorded) speech in Plato's *Symposium* (223d), where the former contends that the poet is capable of composing both comedy and tragedy, Kierkegaard sets in opposition the "tragic" ideality of the Platonic depiction of Socrates and the "comic" ideality of the Aristophanic, and dismisses as "totally irrelevant to this study" (CI, 128-29) the question of what motivated Aristophanes to see Socrates this way. Was Aristophanes bribed by Socrates' accusers or embittered by Socrates' friendship with Euripides? Did he oppose Anaxagorean speculations of nature through Socrates or identify him with the Sophists?

The bracketing of such questions of motivation would render pointless any investigation of the historical consequences of *Clouds*, since the aim of such an investigation would be to determine the degree to which those consequences may have borne out the motivation. So in choosing, unlike Hegel, to focus upon the charge against Socrates as strictly "a historical document," Kierkegaard will later bracket also the question of whether the Athenians were right to execute him (CI, 167-68; quote on 168).

Despite his apparent intent through such bracketings to eschew what might be called in the literary-critical parlance of more recent times the intentionalist and the affectivist fallacies, Kierkegaard does not confine his focus exclusively to the text of *Clouds* in arguing that Aristophanes' depiction of Socrates closely approaches "the truth." For support, he rehearses an anecdote from another classical source, which he significantly modifies, whether wittingly or not, or whether or not for ironic effect. Submitting that it would have been both beneath Aristophanes' dignity simply to portray Socrates empirically "as he walked and stood in life," and, at the same time, outside the interest of Greek comedy "to idealize him

---

[91]Hegel, *Lectures* 1:427.

on a scale whereby he became completely unrecognizable," Kierkegaard finds the latter point "attested by antiquity, which recounts
that the performance of *The Clouds* was honored in this respect by
the presence of its severest critic, Socrates himelf, who to the
public's delight stood up during the performance so that the
theater crowd could see for themselves the fitting likeness" (CI,
129). Citing no source, Kierkegaard seems unaware that this anecdote comes from Aelian's *Variae historiae* (2.13),[92] according to
which Socrates' reason for rising from his seat on that occasion
was not to demonstrate the verisimilitude of Aristophanes' portrayal, as Kierkegaard infers, but to show how great his contempt
was for comedy and the Athenians.[93]

This anecdote is cited by the German Hegelian Heinrich Theodor Rötscher (1803–1871) in his "philological-philosophical" study
Aristophanes und sein Zeitalter, which is undoubtedly where Kierkegaard encountered it.[94] Anticipating a point stressed later by
Taylor, Burnet, and others about the Aristophanic Socrates and the
nature of caricature as an art,[95] Kierkegaard avers in his next
breath that a Greek audience would not have accepted a portrayal
of Socrates that was utterly discrepant with the character of the
actual Socrates.

> We must certainly agree with the perspicacious Rötscher that
> such a purely eccentric ideal view would not lie within the
> interest of Greek comedy, either. He has so excellently explained
> how the essence of comedy consisted expressly in viewing
> actuality ideally, in bringing an actual personality on stage, yet

---

[92]As attested in entry of 1842–1843, JP, 4:4251, Kierkegaard did not learn until
after he wrote his dissertation that Aelian was the source of this anecdote. By his
own admission in an entry of 1852, he had not read Aelian when he wrote his
dissertation (JP, 4:4289).

[93]Likewise, during a performance of a Euripedean drama, Socrates is said to
have gotten up and exited the theater in protest against the script. See Diogenes,
Lives 2.33.

[94]H. Theodor Rötscher, *Aristophanes und sein Zeitalter. Eine philologisch-
philosophische Abhandlung zur Alterthumsforschung* (Berlin: Voss, 1827) 18. Cf. JP,
4:4246.

[95]Taylor, "*Phrontisterion*," 131: "To succeed at all with any public . . . caricature
must be, or must be believed by the public to be, like its original." Cf. Burnet,
Greek Philosophy, 145; Copleston, *History of Philosophy* 1:113n.3.

in such a way that this one is indeed seen as a representative of the idea, which is why we find also in Aristophanes the three great comic paradigms: Cleon, Euripedes, and Socrates, whose roles comically represent the aspiration of the age in its three trends. (CI, 129)

As shown by Kierkegaard's constant further references to it, Rötscher's study is, of the several scholarly sources he cites on *Clouds* (excepting Hegel), the one he most favors, and with which he most deeply and fruitfully engages.[96] While focusing successively upon the play's titular symbol (CI, 132-39), its plot (CI, 139-43), its comic and ironic elements (CI, 143-46), and its portrayal of Socrates' personality, teaching, and existential "position" (CI, 146-52), Kierkegaard refers favorably to Rötscher's interpretation on the following points: the notion that Socrates became a comic figure for Aristophanes only insofar as Aristophanes saw in him "the representative of a new principle,"[97] the perceived unity of the Aristophanic Socrates and "the actual Socrates,"[98] and the representation of the play's chorus as clouds,[99] in which Kierkegaard in turn finds "Socrates' thoughts objectively envisioned" (CI, 137). Kierkegaard's analysis of *Clouds* is based so extensively on Rötscher's that in one instance he reproduces Rötscher's language without acknowledgment.[100]

Aside from quibbling over Rötscher's interpretation of a specific passage in *Clouds*,[101] Kierkegaard questions only one major aspect of Rötscher's approach, namely, "whether the earnestness he so definitely claims for this play does not make [Rötscher] somewhat at odds with the irony he otherwise attributes to

---

[96]Cf. Thulstrup, *Kierkegaard's Relation to Hegel*, 233n.12. For Kierkegaard's other sources see CI, 129n.-130, 131, 143n.-144.

[97]CI, 130; see Rötscher, *Aristophanes und sein Zeitalter*, 319-30.

[98]See CI, 131-32; cf. 146; see Rötscher, *Aristophanes und sein Zeitalter*, 276-88, 312-19.

[99]See CI, 132, 136; see Rötscher, *Aristophanes und sein Zeitalter*, 50-59, 325.

[100]As Rötscher conjectures about the Aristophanic Socrates that "unter seiner Maske die Sophisten gemeint wären" (*Aristophanes und sein Zeitalter*, 288), so Kierkegaard speaks of "whether Aristophanes, behind the mask of Socrates, wanted to mock the Sophists" (CI, 138).

[101]CI, 144*, citing Rötscher, *Aristophanes und sein Zeitalter*, 284-88 on *Clouds*, lines 852-61.

Aristophanes" (CI, 130).[102] This question, and Kierkegaard's dealing with it, warrant scrutiny. The very phrasing of the question, with its reference to Rötscher's ascription of irony to Aristophanes, introduces what becomes an element of confusion in Kierkegaard's discussion of *Clouds*. If an overriding assumption in his dissertation is that "irony was constitutive in Socrates' life" (CI, 131; cf. 6, 12, 37, 40, etc.), Kierkegaard now also speaks of "Aristophanic irony" (CI, 135) and "irony worthy of an Aristophanes" (CI, 139). Because he never differentiates between his conceptions of Aristophanic irony and of Socratic irony, the two conceptions seem ultimately indistinguishable.

Even more influential upon Kierkegaard is Rötscher's characterization of Aristophanes' attitude in *Clouds* as "total earnestness of attitude" ("ganze Ernst der Gesinnung"),[103] a characterization undoubtedly based upon Hegel's perception of "a deep political earnestness"[104] in the merriment Aristophanes makes over the Athenian democracy. This notion furnishes Kierkegaard with a foil against which to develop his own defense of the play's comic dimension, and, later, to elaborate his own defense of Aristophanes against the charge of having slandered Socrates. If it is assumed that Socrates' life consisted of irony, says Kierkegaard,

> one will certainly admit that this affords a much more comic side than would be the case if the principle of subjectivity, the principle of inwardness, along with the whole train of ensuing ideas, were taken to be the Socratic principle, and if the authorization of Aristophanes were to be sought in the earnestness with which [according to Rötscher] he as an advocate of early Greek culture had to try to destroy this modern monstrosity. This earnestness bears down too heavily, just as it restricts the comic infinity, which as such recognizes no limits. Irony, on the other hand, is simultaneously a new position and as such is absolutely polemical toward early Greek culture. (CI, 131)

Confusingly, again, the mention of "irony" in the last sentence could refer not only to Socratic irony but to Aristophanic irony, since "irony" is precisely what Kierkegaard wants substituted for

---

[102]See, e.g., ibid., 325.
[103]See Rötscher, *Aristophanes und sein Zeitalter*, 319-30; quote on 319.
[104]Hegel, *Lectures* 1:428.

"earnestness" as the proper designation of Aristophanes' attitude toward Socrates. This confusion is now exacerbated by Kierkegaard's calling irony "something that at rock bottom is comic" (CI, 131). "Comic" in the sense that Kierkegaard has called Socrates "comic" (CI, 129; cf. 145, 152)? Or "comic" in the sense that he will later call Aristophanes "comic" (CI, 153-54)? Kierkegaard offers no clarification. Nor, in classifying the Aristophanic portrait of Socrates anachronistically in its relation to the Platonic and Xenophontic, does he seem aware that, as Burnet notes, "the 'irony' of Sokrates comes entirely from Plato."[105] Kierkegaard is well familiar with Hegel's view of the irony of the Platonic Socrates as "a controlled element, a way of associating with people" (CI, 237).[106] And he will adopt Hegel's notion of irony as "infinite absolute negativity" (CI, 254, 259), which has been viewed as a "dazzling mystification" by which Kierkegaard's own treatment of Socratic irony "is hopelessly perplexed."[107] Nonetheless, just as his presentation of Socrates as totally negative represents a break from Hegel, who, in keeping with his own comprehensive perspective, "necessarily had to find a positive element in Socrates, as he had to find it in every philosopher,"[108] so Kierkegaard's attribution of irony to the *Aristophanic* Socrates is entirely original.[109]

Later, in discussing the delineation of the Socratic dialectic in *Clouds*, Kierkegaard will again comment upon Rötscher's ascription of earnestness to the poet, and in this context hints for the first and

---

[105]Burnet, *Greek Philosophy*, 127n.2; cf. Taylor, *Socrates*, 21-22. Burnet elaborates: "it is only the opponents of Sokrates that charge him with 'irony' (εἰρωνεία), a word which undoubtedly suggested the idea of humbug; but Plato shows us over and over again the real trait in his character which this uncomplimentary description was aimed at, with the result that the word 'irony' has changed its meaning for us" (*Greek Philosophy*, 132). The development of the word's meaning is traced by Vlastos, *Socrates, Ironist*, 23-44. Cf. Newell, "Aristophanes on Socrates," 112.

[106]See Hegel, *Lectures* 1:398-402.

[107]Vlastos, *Socrates, Ironist*, 43n.81. See G. W. F. Hegel, *Aesthetics: Lectures on Fine Art*, 2 vols., trans. T. M. Knox (Oxford: Clarendon Press, 1975) 1:68-69; cf. 160.

[108]Thulstrup, *Kierkegaard's Relation to Hegel*, 232.

[109]Vlastos, *Socrates, Ironist*, 29: "The antihero of the *Clouds* is many things to many men, but an ironist to none." Vlastos, who here has forgotten Kierkegaard's interpretation, would today have to qualify this pronouncement also in the light of Newell's interpretation in "Aristophanes on Socrates."

only time at the play's pertinence to Socrates' condemnation. The Socratic dialectic, he claims, can be discussed "only insofar as it can be construed purely intellectually; whereas we have nothing at all to do with the altogether immoral conduct in which such a dialectic can become an active collaborator in the service of a corrupted will" (CI, 149)—as when the dim-witted farmer Strepsiades hoodwinks his creditors and his own prodigal son then beats him, after they both have been corrupted through witnessing a dialogue between Better Argument and Worse Argument in Socrates' *phrontistērion*.

> Aristophanes himself must have been aware of this; if not, I really do not see how Aristophanes can be saved from the old accusation of having slandered Socrates. Even though Aristophanes with ever so much justification depicted Socrates as a representative of a principle that threatened early Greek culture with destruction, it nevertheless would always be an injustice to charge Socrates with corrupting the morals of the youth, with introducing a dissoluteness and superficiality that both the old and the new Greek culture must necessarily abominate. It would be an injustice not merely because Socrates had acquired a prescriptive title to being the most honest man in Greece, but mainly because without a doubt Socrates' position was so abstractly intellectual (something already sufficiently manifest in the well-known definition of sin as ignorance) that with regard to a view of him I think it would be more correct if one eliminated some of the bombast about his virtue and his noble heart but at the same time considered his life immune to all the charges of corrupting the morals. (CI, 149)

This passage, which defends *both* Aristophanes (against the charge of slander) *and* the Aristophanic Socrates (against the charges of corrupting the morals), brings to a head the convergence of Kierkegaard's views on the two figures. This convergence, dependent as it is upon the conviction that Aristophanes' portrayal of Socrates was done "with . . . justification," presupposes the stimulus of Hegel. For it is from Hegel's own justification of Aristophanes that Kierkegaard has drawn that conviction, together with the recognition of Socrates' dialectic as negative (a recognition which Hegel credited Aristophanes as having been the first to reach).[110] Likewise, it is in apparent emulation of Hegel that Kierkegaard above dismissed "the bombast about [Socrates'] virtue," and will later ridicule "the scholarly professional mourners and the crowd of shallow but lachrymose humanitarians whose blubbering and sighing" over Socrates' death "still echo through the centuries" (CI, 167-68).[111] Yet, when Kierkegaard invokes Rötscher once more as a foil, this time to his own defense of Aristophanes, he implicitly makes Hegel a foil as well: "Let Rötscher inflate as much as he wishes the earnestness with which Aristophanes laid hold of his task in *The Clouds*—Aristophanes is not exonerated thereby" (CI, 149).

Just as he later will recall Hegel's analysis of Socrates' irony (see CI, 237), so must Kierkegaard presumably now recollect Hegel's perception of a deep "earnestness" in Aristophanes. Given Kierkegaard's acceptance of "the qualification of irony, which Hegel so frequently stresses, that for irony nothing is a matter of earnestness" (CI, 235),[112] it seems consistent with his own ascription of irony to Aristophanes that Kierkegaard should now want to dismiss Rötscher's Hegelian "inflation" of a perceived anti-ironic earnestness in Aristophanes. This dismissal helps prepare for Kierkegaard's summary point on Thesis VII, where he invokes once more "Rötscher's designation of Socrates' position as that of subjectivity" (CI, 152; cf. 131)[113]—a designation that accords with Hegel's interpretation of Socrates.[114] If one agrees with this designation, writes Kierkegaard, then "Aristophanes' view of Socrates will be found to be more true in terms of the comic and consequently more just" (here he includes a note on Hegel's observation that "it is Aristophanes who has understood Socrates' philosophy merely from its negative side"),

> and likewise one will also see a way to remove some of the difficulties that otherwise would remain in this Aristophanic play if

---

[110]See CI, 152*., citing Hegel, *Lectures* 1:426; and CI, 226-27, quoting Hegel, *Lectures* 1:430. See also Kierkegaard's Thesis IV (CI, 6; expounded 34-37).

[111]Cf. Hegel's mockery of Tennemann's pitying statements (*History of Philosophy* 1:430).

[112]Cf. Hegel, *Lectures* 2:401.

[113]See Rötscher, *Aristophanes und sein Zeitalter*, 247-58.

[114]See Hegel, *Lectures*, esp. 1:407-14.

one defines this position more specifically as an ironic position—that is, allows the subjectivity to pour out in its profusion, but prior to this lets it egotistically terminate in irony. (CI, 152-53)

Here, in confirming his own movement beyond Hegel and Rötscher by associating the Aristophanic Socrates with not merely subjectivity but irony as well, Kierkegaard follows through on his own insight that "irony is beyond subjective thinking" (CI, 124), an insight whose origins the Hongs trace to Martensen and Heiberg (see CI, 510n302). Kierkegaard rounds out his exposition of Thesis VII by concluding that "there are elements of the views of both [Xenophon and Plato] in Aristophanes" (CI, 153): if "Plato tried to fill up the cryptic nothing that actually constitutes the point in Socrates' life by giving him the idea," and "Xenophon tried to do it with the prolixities of the useful" (CI, 153), then "with respect to Plato Aristophanes has subtracted, and with respect to Xenophon has added" (CI, 154).

For Kierkegaard, the Aristophanic Socrates thus represents the mean between the Platonic and the Xenophontic Socrates, and, as such, very closely approximates "the truth." In arguing this thesis, as we have seen, Kierkegaard has done some "subtracting" and "adding" of his own. From Aristophanes he has subtracted the earnestness ascribed by Hegel and Rötscher, and to the Aristophanic Socrates he has added the irony he himself perceives in him. As a result, the images of Aristophanes and Socrates, the satirist and the satirized, seem to converge in the categories of irony and the comic.

How does Aristophanes figure in Kierkegaard's writings beyond the dissertation?

A Christian Aristophanes?

Kierkegaard's special fondness for Aristophanes is evident in his writings both before and after his dissertation. In an outline on the development of comedy derived by Kierkegaard in a Journal entry of 16 January 1837 (JP, 5:5192) from a piece by J.L. Heiberg in *Kjøbenhavns flyvende Post*,[115] Aristophanes is designated as repre-

---

[115]No. 13, 1828, p. 3.

sentative of the "immediate" type of "universal" comedy. Sometime during the next several years, Kierkegaard drafted "The Battle between the Old and the New Soap-Cellars" (EPW, 105-24), a philosophical drama he never finished or published.[116]

Aptly described by Capel as "a satirical, quasi-Aristophanic comedy,"[117] "Soap-Cellars" lampoons Hegelians and Hegelianism in a manner comparable to the satire of Socrates and the Sophists in *Clouds*.[118] In both plays, the troubled protagonist—the financially strapped Strepsiades, and Willibald, a doubter and relativist (see EPW, 116)—seeks remedies to his problems from philosophers: the sophistical Socrates and his pupils, who lodge in the *phrontistērion*, and the Hegelians Mr. von Jumping-Jack and Mr. Phrase and their associates, who lodge in "the prytaneum" (EPW, 106, 113, etc.), the same type of Greek public building which Plato's Socrates told his judges he deserved to be maintained in after they had pronounced him guilty.[119] In a scene Kierkegaard will comment upon in his dissertation (CI, 146†), Strepsiades is surprised to be told by Socrates that thunder and rain are produced not by Zeus but by Clouds (*Clouds*, lines 368-424). Likewise Willibald is mystified by a celestial phenomenon, "namely, why it was that the sun in the prytaneum never changed its position at all, as a result of which the light was always the same" (EPW, 120; see also 123). And just as Phidippides, after Strepsiades has failed to learn from Socrates, is himself delivered by Socrates to Better Argument and Worse Argument to be instructed through hearing them debate (*Clouds*,

---

[116]This play has been dated variously between spring 1838 and spring 1840. See Thulstrup, *Kierkegaard's Relation to Hegel*, 180-200; JP, 4:viii; Julia Watkin's comment, EPW, 259-60; and the studies by Cain and Law cited below.

[117]Capel, "Historical Introduction" to Kierkegaard, *The Concept of Irony* (n. 14 above) 27.

[118]On the satire of Hegelianism in "Soap-Cellars," see Watkin, "Historical Introduction" to EPW, xxxii-xxxvi. As far as I am aware, the relation of "Soap-Cellars" to *Clouds* has yet to be explored. Aristophanes goes unmentioned in the excellent analyses of this play by David Cain, "Kierkegaard's Anticipation of Authorship: 'Where Shall I Find a Foothold?' " and David R. Law, "The Literary Sources of Kierkegaard's *The Battle between the Old and the New Soap-Cellars*," in *IKC: Early Polemical Writings*, ed. Robert L. Perkins (Macon GA: Mercer University Press, 1999) 131-57 and 160-94 respectively.

[119]Plato, *Apology* 36d-37a; cf. CI, 195.

lines 884-1111), so Willibald, "who had not found himself much edified or satisfied by Jumping-Jack's philosophical lectures" (EPW, 119), is referred to the "World-Historical College," where he hears pompous and convoluted lectures by the Hegelians (EPW, 119-23).

In summer 1840, sometime not long after he wrote "Soap-Cellars," Kierkegaard found *himself* parodied on the stage of Copenhagen's Royal Theater as a Hegelian (*sic!*) hairdresser in a comic play by Hans Christian Andersen.[120] However, although he expressed irritation at having been depicted as "a prating Hegelian,"[121] and although he already esteemed Socrates "a remarkable personality" (entry of 1 November 1837, JP, 4:4243), Kierkegaard never acknowledged the affinity he now shared with Socrates as the victim of a theatrical burlesque.[122]

The year after this experience, Kierkegaard's dissertation was accepted and defended (16 July and 29 September 1841). For us, the question remains: if Brandes and others after him have been right in deeming *The Concept of Irony* "the true point of departure for Kierkegaard's authorship,"[123] what specific legacies might Thesis VII be shown to have in his writings? As noted by the Hongs (CI, 515), Rötscher's view of Socrates' position as subjectivity, a view first taken up by Kierkegaard in expounding of Thesis VII, proves pertinent to the conception of subjectivity that runs

---

[120]This play, entitled *A Comedy in the Open Air* (*En Comedie i det Grønne*), premiered 13 May. A translation of the pertinent scene is provided in EPW, 202-204.

[121]In an unpublished retort to Andersen, "Just a Moment, Mr. Andersen!," *Pap.* III B 1; EPW, 218-22; quote on 220.

[122]Of course, any such comparison of Kierkegaard and Socrates can be taken only so far. Unlike Socrates in *Clouds*, the character representing Kierkegaard in Andersen's play goes by a different name. Whereas Socrates evidently did nothing personal to provoke Aristophanes, Kierkegaard had provoked Andersen with the scathing review, "Andersen as a Novelist, with Continual Reference to His Latest Work: *Only a Fiddler*" (1838; in EPW, 61-102). And whereas it was because Socrates was a well-known and controversial figure in Athens that he proved such an easy target for Aristophanes and other contemporary comic playwrights, Kierkegaard was, as he himself acknowledged, an "insignificant personage" at the time Andersen's play was performed ("Just a Moment . . . !," EPW, 218).

[123]Georg Brandes, *Søren Kierkegaard. En kritisk Fremstilling i Grundrids* (Copenhagen, 1877) 187; quoted by Capel, "Historical Introduction" to Kierkegaard, *The Concept of Irony*, 7-8. Cf. the Hongs, "Historical Introduction," CI, xvii; and the view of Vilhelm Andersen as summarized by Capel, 352.

through the pseudonymous corpus (see esp. EO, 2, PF, CUP, and SUD passim). (Kierkegaard, indeed, would continue consulting, admiring, and citing Rötscher's scholarship long after the dissertation.[124]) But what about Kierkegaard's consideration of Aristophanes in connection with Thesis VII? How did Aristophanes and his comedies bear upon Kierkegaard's development as a thinker and writer beyond the dissertation?

In his writings from the first five years following the dissertation, Kierkegaard hardly ever alludes to Aristophanes' Clouds. Aside from recording his belated discovery that it was Aelian who purported to place the historical Socrates at the play's performance (see note 92, above), Kierkegaard has Quidam refer without acknowledgment to the pre-Socratic principle of existence ascribed to Socrates in Clouds (see SLW, 224, 710n66). And from both the draft and the final copy of Concluding Unscientific Postcript (1846), he deletes two iterations of a jocular reference by Climacus to Strepsiades' notion of rain as Zeus urinating through a sieve (see CUP, 2:37; Clouds, 375). Despite all the dissertation says about the symbolic linkage drawn in Aristophanes' play between the image of clouds and Socrates' thoughts (see CI, 133-39), both playwright and play go unmentioned in the draft of the unpublished "Writing Sampler," whose narrator claims to "take a fancy to the clouds" (entry of 1844–1845, JP, 5:5764; rpt. WS, 140), and in the unpub-

---

[124]From H. T. Rötscher's Die Kunst der dramatischen Darstellung, 3 vols. (Berlin: Wilhelm Thome, 1841–1846) 1:20, Kierkegaard notes a quotation of the Sophist Gorgias on tragedy (entry of 1844, JP, 4:4840), later used by the ethicist in SLW, 119. Kierkegaard also applies something found in Rötscher's Kunst, 1:394-97 about "the accent on the ethical" to his own recollections on his break with Regine (entry of 1844, JP, 5:5748; rpt. SLW, 514), and notes that Rötscher in Kunst, 2:105, "uses the category: qualitativer Sprung [qualitative leap]—although he is a Hegelian" (JP, 3:2350). Johannes Climacus notes that Rötscher "in his book on Aristophanes does indeed understand the necessity of the transition in the world-historical development" (CUP, 1:116; see Rötscher, Aristophanes, 31-37). But the most significant allusions to Rötscher in the pseudonymous oeuvre are those Taciturnus and Climacus make to his view of Hamlet as "morbidly reflective"; both pseudonyms approve that Rötscher, despite being a systematician, is "forced to use existence-categories" (quotes from SLW, 453; cf. JP, 3:2344; rpt. SLW, 635-36; JP, 2:1561; CUP, 1:116; see Rötscher, Kunst, 2:99-132). Climacus also cites Rötscher's Seydelmanns Leben und Wirken (Berlin, 1845); see CUP, 1:446n. Kierkegaard again cites Rötscher on Plato as late as 1852; see JP, 1:1088.

lished draft of "Writings of a Young Man," which contains ruminations on clouds and thoughts as perfect "symbols" of each other (entry of 1846, JP, 3:2842; rpt. WS, 157-58).

Nonetheless, certain jottings of 1842–1843 on the endsheet of a copy of *The Concept of Irony* reveal that Kierkegaard, in those first two years after the dissertation, continued filling in gaps in his knowledge about the relationship of *Clouds* to Socrates, and now went on to read (in Danish translation) other plays by Aristophanes. These jottings note that Socrates was also depicted by comic poets other than Aristophanes (JP, 4:4258; rpt. CI, 450); that Aristophanes' *Frogs* closes with a reference to Socrates by name as an idle gossip and denigrator of tragedy (JP, 4:4256; rpt. CI, 450); and that Aristophanes, through the chorus leader in *Wasps*,[125] "names the evil of which he [i.e., Aristophanes] wanted to cleanse the state with *The Clouds*: idleness and legal trickery" (JP, 4:4257; rpt. CI, 450). Kierkegaard must have recognized the reference in *Frogs* as a denigration of Socrates. Yet, true to his refusal in his dissertation to see *Clouds* as slandering Socrates, and consistent with the fact that *Wasps* does not mention Socrates by name, he may not assume, as scholars typically do,[126] that the allusion to *Clouds* in *Wasps* implicitly associates Socrates with the "evil" Aristophanes "wanted" to purge. Evidently Kierkegaard, like Hegel and Rötscher, still regards the poet of *Clouds* as a conservative reformer or "cleanser" of the state; yet unlike them, he still refuses to associate Socrates with what he thinks Aristophanes meant to attack.

This refusal is crucial, because it protects Kierkegaard's esteem for Aristophanes as reformer from coming into conflict with his ever-growing reverence for Socrates as ironist. Indeed, mirroring the convergence already observed in Kierkegaard's images of the two men in the categories of irony and the comic, Kierkegaard's newly honed perception of Aristophanes as someone who wanted with *Clouds* "to cleanse the state" of "idleness and legal trickery" (e.g., Sophistry) practically matches his perception of Socrates as someone who was out "to destroy [the Sophists] . . . radically" (CI, 201).

---

[125]See lines 1036–42 of the Loeb edition.
[126]See, e.g., Ferguson, *Socrates: A Source Book*, 172.

Together with this ongoing convergence the images of Socrates and Aristophanes, there becomes manifest in his writings a pessimistic perception of a similarity between the age of Socrates and Aristophanes, and his own modern age. Referring to Hegel and Rötscher for discussion, Kierkegaard in his dissertation spoke of "the decline of the Athenian state" brought about by "the principle of decay" (CI, 200) that became more and more evident after Pericles: "There was a restlessness in Athenian life; there was a palpitation of the heart intimating that the hour of disintegration was at hand" (CI, 201). Accordingly, in reference to "Greece . . . at the time when the state was in the process of disintegration," the aesthete of *Either/Or* (1843) asks: "And does not our age have a striking likeness to that age, which not even Aristophanes could make more ludicrous than it actually was?" (EO, 1:141). Sensing his own age to be one of political and religious dissolution, one "more depressed and therefore deeper in despair" than Aristophanes' age, and one that "excels" that age in the unwillingness of anyone "to have responsibility," "A" exclaims: "Would not this inverted story of responsibility be an appropriate subject for Aristophanes!" (EO, 1:142). In this same cynical spirit, and anticipating Climacus's dismissal of rational theistic proofs (see PF, 39-44), "A" quotes from Aristophanes' *Knights* a passage he says yields "yet another demonstration of the existence of God" (EO, 1:36): Nicias's amusing claim that he "knows" the gods exist through his sense of himself as "such a wretched god-detested chap" (*Knights*, lines 32-35; quoted in EO, 1:36-37). "A" is so fond of Aristophanes that he prefaces "Rotation of Crops" with a quotation from Aristophanes' *Plutus* which suggests that, of all things other than Zeus, humans have too much (EO, 1:282-83).

Clearly Aristophanes is for Kierkegaard now the prototypical satirist and comic poet. His pertinence as such to the aesthetic stage of existence seems punctuated by a declaration made in a satirical article, later ascribed dubiously to Kierkegaard, that appeared in *Ny Portefeuille* two weeks before the publication of *Either/Or*: "Life parodies itself and does it with an esthetic thoroughness that puts every Aristophanes to shame."[127] This idea, regardless of whether Kierkegaard wrote that article, finds expression later in his Journal.[128] Thus two different speakers at the aesthetical banquet of *Stages on Life's Way* (1845) appeal to Aristophanes as a comic touchstone on the subject of love. Having summarized the theory of erotic attraction ascribed to Aristophanes in Plato's *Symposium*, 189d-93b, according to which the gods divided primeval man into two parts, which now seek each other (see SLW, 35), the Young Man takes up this thought again. Noting that whenever two persons "in union and in love form one self," they end up subordinated to serving the species, the Young Man "find[s] this more ludicrous than what Aristophanes found so ludicrous. For the ludicrousness in that bisection lies in the contradiction, which Aristophanes did not adequately emphasize": the contradiction of a "complete" human being "running around after his other half" (SLW, 43).

Perhaps inspired by the Young Man, Constantin too appeals to Aristophanes, but in a different connection: to make a point about the incompatability of jealousy with intellect. In contrast to Othello, who, in Constantin's racist view, as "a colored man . . . cannot be assumed to represent intellect," a person of intellect "either does not become jealous or in becoming that becomes comic, and most of all if he comes running with a dagger" (SLW, 50). One can hardly even imagine Socrates surprising Xanthippe "in the act," as "it would already be un-Socratic to imagine Socrates essentially concerned about or even spying on Xanthippe's faithfulness" (SLW, 50). On the other hand, continues Constantin,

---

[127]"Literary Quicksilver, or A Venture in the Higher Lunacy with *Lucida Intervalla*," in *Ny Portefeuille* 1/7 (7 February 1843); as translated in COR, 73-86; quote on 80. On the question of authorship see the Hongs, "Historical Introduction," COR, xxxvn.134. On the basis of a comparative statistical analysis of the punctuation profile of "Literary Quicksilver" and nine newspaper articles by Kierkegaard, Alastair McKinnon denies that the former could have been written by Kierkegaard ("Could Kierkegaard Have Written 'Literary Quicksilver'?" *IKC: The Corsair Affair*, ed. Robert L. Perkins [Macon GA: Mercer University Press, 1990] 163-78).

[128]Entry of 1849, JP, 6:6392: "How witty actual life is! I do not believe that it would occur even to the wittiest poet to use a hackney cabman à la Aristophanes."

since Aristophanes at times wanted to portray Socrates as ludicrous, it is inconceivable that it never occurred to him to have
Socrates come running onstage shouting: Where is she, where is
she, so that I can murder her, that is, the unfaithful Xanthippe.
Whether Socrates was made a cuckold or not really makes no
difference. . . . Socrates, even with horns on his forehead, remains
the same intellectual hero; but that he could become jealous, that
he could want to murder Xanthippe—ah, then Xanthippe would
have had a power over him that the whole Greek state and the
death penalty did not have: to make him ridiculous. (SLW, 50)

This passage is significant in two respects. First, reflecting the
cynicism of Constantin's aesthetic disposition, it breaks from Kierkegaard's own refusal to acknowledge that Aristophanes "wanted
to portray Socrates as ludicrous." And second, in drawing that
desire of Aristophanes vis-à-vis Socrates into a more-than-sublimi-
nal association with the state's failure "to make him ridiculous,"
it ipso facto associates *Clouds* with Socrates' execution. This, we
will see, is not the last time this association will be hinted at in
Kierkegaard's writings; but it is perhaps the closest the association
comes to explicitness.

Aside from the depiction of Socrates, the one Aristophanic
theme by which Kierkegaard proves most deeply captivated is that
of the Athenian sausage peddler who, as predicted through a
series of oracles, becomes the deliverer and reformer of the state.
For the religious thinker Frater Taciturnus, as for Kierkegaard
himself, this theme of *Knights* epitomizes the principle of contradiction that underlies anything "comic in the Aristophanic sense"
("Letter to the Reader," SLW, 409; cf. TA, 82). Having remarked
how "completely unusable for poetry" the modern hero is who
works for a finite goal, Taciturnus quips that "possibly he could be
used as the sausage peddler in Aristophanes" (SLW, 410; cf. 412).
In several other instances between 1845 and 1849, Kierkegaard
again refers to the sausage-peddler theme in *Knights*, each time for
the purpose of paralleling his contemporary age with Aristophanes' age (TA, 133; cf. 82-83; COR, 193; JP, 6:6392). Likewise he
speaks of both the modern concern with the natural sciences, and
modern Christian scholarship, as furnishing motifs superbly
suitable to an Aristophanic comedy—especially, in the former case,

if the poet "has Socrates present and has him peer into a micro-scope" (entry of 1846, JP, 3:2814; see also BA, 45).

Given his own experience as the butt of public satire during the *Corsair* affair of 1846, it is not surprising that Kierkegaard that year should strive emphatically to distinguish the *Corsair*'s mean, destructive brand of satire and irony from the sort of satire exemplified by Aristophanes. "Anyone who understands the comic," he reflects, "readily sees that the comic does not consist at all in what the present age imagines it does and that satire in our day, if it is to be at all beneficial and not cause irreparble harm, must have the resource of a consistent and well-grounded ethical view, a sacrificial unselfishness, and a highborn nobility that renounce the moment; otherwise the medicine becomes infinitely and incomparably worse than the sickness" (TA, 74; rpt. in COR, xvii)—as illustrated by the *Corsair*'s attacks on him. In contrast, he observes, in antiquity, the attacker had to appear personally in the square so that one got to see who it was; the attack was open; and when the attack was over, it was forgotten (see COR, 177-78; cf. TA, 91). And "the public," an abstraction created by the modern press, "simply could not have appeared in antiquity" (TA, 91). He concludes:

> The concept of literary contemptibility may be characterized as follows: even if it has talent of a sort, it does not have the justification of an idea, has no view of life, is cowardly, servile, avaricious—therefore, to be anonymous comes naturally. To see the distinction properly, think in contrast of the disintegration of Greece and Aristophanes' comedies. Aristophanes has the authority of an idea; he is distinguished by genius and elevated by personal courage. . . . But just as antiquity could not arrive at the abstraction of modern disintegration, so also . . . it had nothing really analogous to the kind of cowardly moral turpitude which anonymity encourages. Admittedly Socrates says in the *Apology* [18d] that his real accusers . . . were like shadows no one can grasp, but if town talk and talking between man and man are like shadows, they are still formed in a way by actual human beings, but with anonymity one single person can conjure up a legion of shadows. (JP, 1:154).

Here, Kierkegaard manages in one breath to contrast Aristo-phanic comedy favorably with modern, anonymous "literary con-temptibility," and to recall Socrates' allusion to his accusers. Yet unlike the aesthete Constantin, he once again avoids acknowledging that Aristophanes wanted to satirize Socrates with *Clouds*. Why? Let us venture an explanation.

As augured, ironically, by the *Corsair*'s derisive reference to Taciturnus as "Socrates' successor,"[129] Kierkegaard is keenly aware that his own predicament in relation to the Copenhagen public *actually is* now comparable to Socrates' in relation to the Athenians. In a Journal entry of 1846 he writes: "It is the press that actually destroys all personality, that a cowardly wretch can sit in hiding and write and print for the thousands. All personal conduct and all personal power must run aground on this. It would be most interesting to talk with Socrates about the matter" (JP, 5:5899). In another entry from that year, this one labeled "The Dialectic of Contemptibleness," he brings to bear upon his own experience as an abused, innocent man, the reply Socrates reportedly made to his wife when asked how an innocent man could be sentenced to death: "Would you rather have me guilty?" (COR, 161; quoting Diogenes, *Lives*, 2.35). Because his long-standing kinship with Socrates as a practitioner of maieutic dialectic is now augmented by a growing sense of affinity with him as a victim of slander (even if the modern press deploying the slander differs from the ancient media of slander), Kierkegaard could not stress Aristophanes' satirizing of Socrates without subverting his own almost equally long-standing if not quite so obvious sense of affinity with Aristophanes as an employer of the proper form of the comic.

These converging senses of affinity with both Socrates and Aristophanes are nowhere clearer than in Kierkegaard's unpublished essay of 1846, "A Personal Statement in Costume" (COR, 178-94). Here, in an attempt to conceptualize the comic as antithetical and antidotal to the *Corsair*, Kierkegaard aims "to deal with the comic in fear and trembling, to maintain the conception of responsibility rooted in ethical and religious earnestness together with the delight of the jest" (COR, 178-79). Feeling himself to be "rather alone in my thinking and perhaps the only one who herewith renounces any reputation for having a sense of the comic," he

---

[129]"The New Planet," *The Corsair* 277 (9 January 1846): col. 7; quoted in COR, 117.

is reminded of "the question Socrates asked in a similar situation," that is, at the trial: does everybody but one know how to ride horses, or do only a few riding masters know this art, while others know nothing about it? (COR, 179; see Plato, *Apology* 25a-b). Claiming that "in a small country like Denmark a disproportionate and immoral phenomenon such as *The Corsair* does great harm and is of no benefit whatsoever . . . because it counterfeits and taints the comic and thereby silences the authentic comic," Kierkegaard knows that "the proof" of this claim "is valid only on the basis of my understanding of the comic and thus only for the individuals who Socratically assume that the comic is like riding, that only a few know how but the majority do not" (COR, 179, 180).

To whom, then, might Kierkegaard appeal as a sharer of this assumption about of the comic? Although he arrived at this assumption "Socratically," it is not to Socrates, but to Aristophanes that he appeals at the essay's end. After recounting how notorious the *Corsair* has made him in Copenhagen for wearing trousers with legs of uneven length, he distinguishes as follows between Aristophanic comedy and the *Corsair*'s sort of crude cartooning.

> You see, the poet does, after all, exaggerate a little so that the pathos and the comic may stand out. For example, to depict the topsy-turvy situation in Athens, Aristophanes had a sausage dealer become the supreme power in the country. So it was in the play; in actuality it was not that bad. But in Copenhagen a pair of trousers has actually attained the position of highest standing and importance. I wonder what Aristophanes would think of that? Certainly he would be envious of this comedy I am writing herewith, but that contemptible paper and the curious are so muddled that they do not grasp the comedy of this, which is comic only according to my view of the comic. (COR, 193)

If the question here about "what Aristophanes might think" seems consonant with his earlier-quoted comment that "It would be most interesting to talk with Socrates about" the destructive power of the modern press, the consonance may not be merely coincidental. The *Corsair*'s mocking of Kierkegaard's physical appearance undoubtedly strengthened all the more his sense of affinity with Socrates, whose own reputation as "the ugliest of men" he discussed years before in his Journal and dissertation (quote in JP, 4:4244; rpt. in CI, 442; cf. JP, 4:4246; rpt. CI, 447-48;

see also CI, 148, 212*). Yet, at the same time, it is surely his sense of affinity with Aristophanes as an exemplar of the "good" form of the comic that explains the special indignation Kierkegaard expresses in 1848 at the thought of the *Corsair*'s "attempt at being a sort of moral enterprise in which ethical satire would be beneficial to the good (à la Aristophanes). I regard it as very important to have gotten this lie exposed" (JP, 6:6282). This sense of affinity becomes one of virtual identication in a Journal entry of 1850, where Kierkegaard lambasts the suggestion by M. A. Goldschmidt, the *Corsair*'s editor, that the *Corsair* and the comic embody "the first stage" in the development of a life. "As a rule," Kierkegaard responds, "the comic is at the end—comedy quite properly concludes Hegel's *Esthetics*, and an Aristophanes certainly would feel strange if he were advised to make his life as comic poet the first part—and then become 'earnest'" (JP, 6:6602). Consistent with his dissertation's dismissal years earlier of the Hegelian ascription of "earnestness" to Aristophanes, Kierkegaard now attests: "As a writer, I have never banned the comic; it was utilized in an auxiliary way by the pseudonymns," in whom "the comic is, if anything, too high a stage, since it is something demonic" (JP, 6:6602).

Is Kierkegaard, the so-called Christian Socrates, also a Christian Aristophanes? To say yes would be to stretch my point, which has been to suggest that he was able to preserve the balance of his dual esteem for both Socrates and Aristophanes, especially during the *Corsair* affair, only by not confronting fully the pertinence of *Clouds* to Socrates' condemnation. Such a confrontation would have forced him into an either/or position of having to choose a side. Having accepted "the clinical task assigned to me: Copenhagen in moral disintegration" (JP, 6:6602; cf. 6:6282; PV, 119, 276-79), he would have been forced to side *either* with the poet whose comedies represented an effort to reform and preserve Athens in its own "age of disintegraton," *or* with the philosopher whose dialectic was seen, perhaps by Aristophanes himself, as contributing to that disintegration.

Kierkegaard never made that choice—except, perhaps implicitly, at the opening of *For Self-Examination* (1851). There he once more alludes, but only as obliquely as ever, to the implication of Aristophanes in Socrates' doom. Having noted that Socrates "lived in circumstances that in my opinion quite correspond to our situation today," Kierkegaard adopts as his own the voice of Socrates from Plato's *Apology*, who he imagines to have suggested: "The thoughts, ideas, and concepts that I, known by everyone, ridiculed by your comic poets, regarded as an eccentric, daily attacked by 'the anonymous' (it is his word), . . . have developed in conversation with the first person to come along in the marketplace—these thoughts are my life" (FSE, 9).

The distance from *Clouds* to the *Corsair* is far indeed, and not just temporally. Yet, even from amid all else that Kierkegaard had written to distinguish proper from improper employment of the comic,[130] the words above stand out: "ridiculed by your comic poets." By 1854, contemplating the "life and death" stakes that Socrates faces in the *Apology*, and recognizing that "On a small scale something like this is apparent in my life," Kierkegaard reaches a conclusion which would seem to negate the whole seventh thesis of his dissertation thirteen years after the fact. Without mentioning Aristophanes, he blurts out: "How ridiculous for a poet to want to seize hold of Socrates" (JP, 4:4301)!

---

[130]For further references and discussion see Andrew J. Burgess, "A Word-Experiment on the Category of the Comic," and Lee Barrett, "The Uses and Misuses of the Comic: Reflections on the *Corsair* Affair," In *IKC: The Corsair Affair*, ed. Robert L. Perkins (Macon GA: Mercer University Press, 1990) 85-121 and 123-39 respectively.

7

Was the Death of Socrates a Tragedy? Kierkegaard versus Hegel on the Possibility of the Mediation of the Tragic in Ethics[1]

Adriaan van Heerden

"The fate of Socrates is hence really tragic. . . . "
(Hegel, *Lectures on the History of Philosophy*)

" . . . but nevertheless Socrates' death is not basically tragic."
(Kierkegaard, *The Concept of Irony*)

Introduction

Was the death of Socrates a tragedy? Hegel and Kierkegaard are both ambivalent on this question: *on the one hand* it was, *on the other hand* it wasn't. But ultimately Hegel comes down in favour of designating the event as *essentially* tragic, whereas for Kierkegaard it is essentially *not* tragic. Indeed, for Kierkegaard the event only acquires a tragic sheen by *accident*, and the force of his counter-argument implies that if one thinks of the death of Socrates as a tragedy it shows that one has completely *misunderstood* his character and the essence of his moral philosophy.

I will argue that the difference between Hegel and Kierkegaard on this point will tell us something important about their opposing views regarding the status of subjectivity in moral existence (within the context of modernity), as well as about their respective moral ideals and imperatives. It also has wider implications for (1) our reading of Kierkegaard in general—I want to propose that we

---

[1] I am indebted to Paul Cruysberghs, Martin Kusch, and George Pattison for valuable comments and criticisms on previous drafts of this paper.

read him as a "Christian-Socratic" moral philosopher—and (2) for our understanding of the role of the concept of the tragic in Kierkegaard's later moral philosophy.

What I mean by the first point is that Kierkegaard takes the Socratic project of self-examination and maieutics (helping the interlocutor to give intellectual birth to him/herself[2]) as the main point of departure for his moral philosophy, and infuses this project with the energy of the Christian ethical imperative to "love thy neighbour as thyself." We can see Kierkegaard's project, at least from one perspective, as the attempt to bring these two understandings or frequencies into some kind of harmony, not by collapsing them into an amorphous, mediated or sublimated product, but by training the ear (spirit) to hear (respond to) both frequencies at the same time. We can see the development of this idea signposted in such works as *The Concept of Irony*, *Philosophical Fragments* and *Works of Love*. *The Concept of Irony* is significant not least because in many ways it lays the foundation for the subsequent development of this important idea. Kierkegaard's moral project is thus the *continuation* (appropriation, repetition) of the Socratic moral project in the light of the additional qualifications of Christian ethics. The infusion of Socratic irony into Christianity, on the other hand, means that Kierkegaard's project consists partly in the problematization of Christianity and "Christendom" (i.e. the "synthesis" of state, culture and Christianity), e.g. by asking what it would really be like to be a Christian, and how to distinguish between true religion and superstition.[3]

On the second point it is interesting to note that Hegel's placement and description of Socrates' death in the context of world history marks (for Hegel) the inevitable death of tragedy in

---

[2]Cf. e.g. JP, 1:13, 18-34, 626, 651; 2:1611, etc. Of special note in terms of the present discussion are JP, 1:13, where Kierkegaard joins his understanding of Christianity to the maieutic method, and JP, 2:1611, where Kierkegaard contrasts the maieutic method (which he approves in Socrates and aspires to in his own philosophy) to the Hegelian method, describing the latter as a misunderstanding of what it is to live.

[3]This line of enquiry is the development of a hermeneutic line already identified by A. B. Drachmann, "Hedenskab og Christendom hos S. K.," *Udvalgte Afhandlinger* (Copenhagen, 1911) 124-40. Cf. Lee M. Capel's notes to the 1966 translation of *The Concept of Irony* (London: Collins, 1966) 351-52.

the classical sense, together with the mediation of the tragic (which is here manifested in the reconciliation of subjectivity and substantiality) in the *Sittlichkeit* (ethical life) of Objective Spirit. Furthermore, in an important sense the Hegelian system may be viewed by its main architect and many contributors as the *completion* of the Socratic project. A similar movement takes place in Kierkegaard but in the opposite direction: tragedy (in the classical sense) *does* die with Socrates, but this death heralds the possibility, or even the necessity, of the rebirth (repetition) of the tragic in a new form, notably in the religious sphere of existence. These movements are (in the case of Hegel) in the direction of the objective, and (in the case of Kierkegaard) in the direction of the subjective. Kierkegaard identifies these directions of movement as *resignation* (towards the objective) and *irony* (towards the subjective): they are "two opposite poles" (JP, 2:1676; CI, 428).[4] For Kierkegaard, as we shall see, the supposed "mediation" of subjectivity, irony and the tragic constitutes not so much a *completion* of Socratic moral philosophy as a *betrayal* of the Socratic project, of Christianity, and of the human spirit itself.

I will proceed directly to the main body of the argument, with section 1 looking at the Hegelian picture and section 2 at the Kierkegaardian one. I will conclude by indicating some implications of the argument within the broader context of Kierkegaard's authorship.

Hegel on Socrates, Substance, Subjectivity, and Tragedy

I mentioned above that both Hegel and Kierkegaard are ambivalent on the question of whether the death of Socrates was a tragedy. The reason for Hegel's duplexity in this matter stems from his theory of tragedy. In *The Philosophy of History*, Hegel writes that

---

[4]In the given passage Kierkegaard does not identify the difference between irony and resignation in terms of subjectivity and objectivity, but I think we may deduce as much from the context. Resignation is described as consciousness of limitation and conforming to "a structure of world-order," whereas irony is "infinite and unlimited" (JP, 2:1676; CI, 428; cf. CI, 125-26, 262).

when on account of the giving utterance to that principle which
was advancing to recognition [i.e. the principle of subjectivity, of
"the absolute inherent independence of Thought"], Socrates is
condemned to death, the sentence bears on the one hand the
aspect of unimpeachable rectitude—inasmuch as the Athenian
people condemns its deadliest foe—but on the other hand, that
of a *deeply tragical* character, inasmuch as the Athenians had to
make the discovery, that what they reprobated in Socrates [i.e.
the aforementioned principle of subjectivity] had already struck
firm root among themselves, and that they must be pronounced
guilty or innocent with him.[5]

In Hegel's theory, "tragedy" refers to the *dramatization of the
intrinsic conflict between two substantial moral powers that are equally
justified*, the archetypal example being (for Hegel) the conflict
between Antigone and Creon in Sophocles' tragedy *Antigone*, with
Antigone representing duties towards one's immediate family, and
Creon those towards the state.[6] This is the essence of ancient Greek
tragedy, and of tragedy per se, according to Hegel.[7] If the conflict
is simply between a good ethical power and an evil (pathological)
one, as we sometimes find in modern drama (e.g. in Shakespeare's
Othello and in Sartre's *The Flies*), we have moved some way away

---

[5]Hegel, *The Philosophy of History*, trans. J. Sibree (New York, 1899) 270, quoted
in Anne Paolucci and Henry Paolucci, eds., *Hegel on Tragedy* (Westport CT:
Greenwood Press, 1962) 346; my emphasis.
[6]Cf. Hegel, *The Philosophy of Fine Art*, vol. 4, trans. F. P. B. Osmaston (London,
1920), quoted in Paolucci, eds., *Hegel on Tragedy*, 73-74.
[7]This was also the view—correct, in my opinion—of A. C. Bradley in his essay
on "Hegel's Theory of Tragedy," in Paolucci, eds., *Hegel on Tragedy*, 367-88: "The
essentially tragic fact is the self-division and intestinal warfare of the ethical substance, not so much a war of good with evil as the war of good with good" (369).
The contrary view is presented by Clyde Charles Holler III, in his discussion of
Hegel's theory of tragedy and its influence on Kierkegaard, "Kierkegaard's Concept of Tragedy in the Context of his Pseudonymous Works" (Ph.D. diss., Boston
University Graduate School, 1981) 71. He writes that "The essence of ancient
tragedy . . . is not the essence of tragedy. For Hegel, later developments of the
concept are not accretions to the essence; the essence is in fact what the later
development of the concept reveals it to be." Holler is simply wrong in this interpretation: he misses the point of certain crucial passages in Hegel's *Aesthetics* (the
detailed discussion of which lies outside the scope of the present essay).

from the essence of tragedy. In *The Philosophy of Right* Hegel explains that

> (The *just* destruction of utter scoundrels and criminals who flaunt their villainy—the hero of a modern tragedy, *Die Schuld*, is one—has an interest for criminal law, but none at all for [tragic] art proper . . .) The *tragic* destruction of figures whose ethical life is on the highest plane can interest and elevate us and reconcile us to its occurrence only in so far as they come on the scene in opposition to one another together with equally justified but different ethical powers which have come into collision through misfortune, because the result is that then these figures acquire guilt through their opposition to an ethical law.[8]

We can now see why Hegel might be ambivalent on the question of whether Socrates' death was a tragedy. From one perspective Socrates appears as a criminal, and he is indeed charged with criminal offences (corrupting the youth and introducing new spiritual things to the detriment of the old gods[9]) at the occasion of his trial: he is an enemy of the state, its "deadliest foe," and the state is fully justified in demanding that he reform his ways, and when he refuses it is within its rights to exact the death penalty. But from another perspective Socrates appears morally justified: not only did he have a reputation for being the most honest man (not to mention the wisest[10] and one of the bravest[11]) in the polis (cf. CI, 149), but with the guarantee of this honesty (of which he offers his poverty as proof) he described himself as a "divine gift" to the *polis*.[12] In *The Philosophy of Right* Hegel interprets this "divine" aspect of Socrates' philosophy as follows:

> In the "divine sign" of Socrates . . . we see the will which formerly had simply transferred itself beyond itself now beginning to apply itself to itself and so to recognize its own inward nature. This is the beginning of a self-knowing and so of a genuine freedom.[13]

---

[8]Hegel, *The Philosophy of Right*, trans. T. M. Knox (rept.: Oxford: Clarendon Press, 1945 = 1942) 102 (footnote to ¶140 [f]).

[9]Plato, *Apology* 26b.

[10]Plato, *Apology* 21a, 23b.

[11]Cf. Plato, *Symposium* 219e-221b.

[12]Plato, *Apology* 30e-31b.

[13]Hegel, *The Philosophy of Right*, 184 (¶279).

Socrates, then, is the "divine" bearer of true freedom. In this regard he appears akin to such tragic predecessors as Prometheus and Dionysus who, after having delivered their divine gifts, are subsequently (for whatever reason) destroyed and/or subjected to excruciating suffering. Socrates is destroyed by the beneficiaries of his "divine gift" (if we consider the whole polis as the beneficiary of the gift), but what makes the whole situation tragic is that those who thus condemn him to death have some intimation of the power and sublime beauty of the gift: to some extent they have tasted the fruit of the tree of knowledge of good and evil[14] and they could never go back to seeing things the way they did before. The tragic conflict between these two equally justified moral powers results in the destruction of both, one by the other.

In Hegel's view the death of Socrates marks a turning point in the development of world intellectual history, because it is with Socrates that subjectivity comes to full awareness of itself and its own possibilities—possibilities which seem in the first instance to be set in opposition to the substantiality of the state with its complex nexus of taboos, laws, duties, privileges and conscious or unconscious ideologies. But it is precisely such a complex nexus of substantial relations on which ancient tragedy relies for a living. If Vernant and Vidal-Naquet are correct in stating that "[tragedy] confronts heroic values and ancient religious representations with the new modes of thought that characterize the advent of law within the city-state,"[15] then Socrates surveys the whole realm of heroic myth, tragedy and (moral, legal, and cultural) substantiality from the perspective of an ironically detached *individual*, on whom these traditionally powerful forms of expression and practice apparently have no binding power. The state, of course, finds such detachment intolerable and a threat to its very survival, and it cannot really do otherwise than condemn Socrates to death.

An important question arises here concerning the evaluative import of Socrates' perspective, whether he viewed the state as

---

[14]Cf. Hegel, *Lectures on the History of Philosophy*, vol. 1, trans. E. S. Haldane and F. H. Simson (rept.: London: Routledge and Kegan Paul, 1974 = 1892) 446-47.

[15]Jean-Pierre Vernant and Pierre Vidal-Naquet, *Myth and Tragedy in Ancient Greece*, trans. Janet Lloyd (New York: Zone Books, 1988) 26.

essentially a positive or negative thing, a good thing or bad, and what he conceived to be his own relation to it. According to Hegel, Socrates' apparent negativity was only a way of arriving at the abstract universal (i.e., *the good*) in which a positive role for the state is affirmed; Socrates' irony was only "a manner of speech."[16] Although Hegel maintains that this abstract attitude failed to manifest itself in concrete qualifications, he nevertheless detects a fundamentally positive orientation in Socrates, and he quotes from Xenophon's *Memorabilia*, where Socrates says that "the best and happiest State is that in which the citizens are of one mind and obedient to law,"[17] to substantiate this claim. In the place of the immediately evident and accepted laws that his irony had rendered shaky, Socrates once again sets the (universal) principle: obey the laws. Hegel remarks on this that "Here we see the universal determined and realized: a general announcement of laws. But inasmuch as these laws are vanishing elements, we see in truth the indeterminate universal, and *the deficiency* of its indeterminateness *as yet* incomplete" (CI, 234). The mode in which the actualisation of the universal appeared to Socrates is the individual subject itself: it is itself the deciding factor, as that which arbitrarily determines itself within itself (CI, 234). It is thus possible for the universal to be limited, to be manifested in concrete qualifications, but only if the subject itself constantly and consistently posits the curtailment of the universal, and only if the universal is acknowledged in its determinateness in a total system of actuality.[18] Hegel believes that Socrates did both these things but failed to complete the project of reintegrating subjectivity in the state, and it is this latter task that Hegel sees himself as having accomplished with the concept of Objective Spirit. We can now see

---

[16]Cf. Hegel, *Lectures on the History of Philosophy* 1:402: "Socrates' premeditated irony may be called a manner of speech, a pleasant rallying; there is in it no satirical laughter or pretence, as though the idea were nothing but a joke. But his tragic irony is his opposition of subjective reflection to morality as it exists [or, translating more correctly, with the dominant/accepted ethical life (what Hegel calls *schöne Sittlichkeit*) of the time], not a consciousness of the fact that he stands above it, but the natural aim of leading men, through thought, to the true good and to the universal Idea."

[17]Hegel, *Lectures on the History of Philosophy* 1:416 (cf. CI, 232).

[18]Hegel, *Lectures on the History of Philosophy* 1:419 (cf. CI, 234).

how Hegel might have conceived of his own philosophy as the completion of the Socratic project.

The implications of this situation are therefore two-fold: on the one hand the death of Socrates in the context of world history marks the death of tragedy in the classical sense (subjectivity defeats substantiality), and on the other hand this is combined with the mediation of the tragic in the ethical life (*Sittlichkeit*) of Objective Spirit, which takes place with the reconciliation of subjectivity and substantiality in the ideal Hegelian state. With these broad outlines in mind we now need to consider the definitions in question ("substantiality," "subjectivity," "irony") in somewhat more detail, and consider how Hegel weaves them into the argument which forms the object of Kierkegaard's critique.

Let us first focus on the concept of a "substantial power" as this appears in Hegel's philosophy. In this regard I find the definitions in the *Encyclopaedia somewhat* more enlightening than the comments on substance and subject at the beginning of the *Phenomenology of Spirit*,[19] and I think the comments in the latter text are best read with the definitions of the former in mind. In the *Encyclopaedia*[20] (¶¶97-101) Hegel defines *substance* as the "absolute identity of actuality and necessity," as "the absolute power and fullness of *value* in all its contents," and as "the unity of necessity and free creativity." Substance is the "*sufficient Cause*" that "posits actual existences" and which "ties all actualities back to its own power"; it is thus "the universal connection of all things."[21] Cause and effect (where "effect" is here understood as finite actualities,

---

[19]Hegel, *Phenomenology of Spirit*, trans. A. V. Miller (Oxford: Oxford University Press, 1977) 9-10.

[20]Hegel, *Encyclopaedia of Philosophy*, trans. G. E. Mueller (New York: Philosophical Library, 1959).

[21]We can now see why T. M. Knox (translator of *The Philosophy of Right*, 347) made use of a quote from Hobbes to explain the meaning of "substance," viz., "a thing which has subsistence in itself, a thing that upholdeth that which else would fall." Cf. also Hegel, *Logic* (part one of the *Encyclopaedia* of 1830), trans. William Wallace (rept.: Oxford: Clarendon Press, 1975 = 1873) 213 (¶151): "*Substance* is accordingly the totality of the *Accidents*, revealing itself in them as their absolute negativity (that is to say, as absolute power) and at the same time as the wealth of all content."

accidents, existents and individuals) are related in "a circular movement of reciprocal action."[22]

Cause (or substance) is related to effect as object is related to subject. Or rather, cause *starts out* as pure objectivity, but by means of this "circular movement of reciprocal action" it becomes conscious of itself (in its infinite differentiations and modalities) and thereby assumes the aspect of a subject, and concomitantly it has made itself its own object. But having posited this infinity of actualities, substance (as "One," or "the whole")—once again by means of the aforementioned "circular movement of reciprocal action"—sublates and mediates (*aufheben*) them into itself, thereby restoring itself in a higher unity.[23] Thus it becomes more appropriate to speak of this higher unity as "subject-object": "As conscious of itself it is the subject which makes itself its own object. It reveals itself as subject-object which is the *Concept*."[24] As T. M. Knox describes it, "the subjective and the objective have undergone modification by each other, so that subjective and objective elements are distinguishable within each of them; i.e. each of them is a synthesis of object and subject and so is the 'totality' of the Idea."[25] Or, as Hegel explains in ¶¶102-106 of the *Encyclopaedia*: "*Substance is subject*: Subject is substantial when it dedicates itself to the fullness and objective necessity of actuality; substance is subjective when it affirms its necessity as its own will and freedom."

This higher unity (synthesis, totality) is also the unity of positivity and negativity, and here we turn to the *Phenomenology of Spirit*. Hegel's comments on the relation between substance and subject in the Preface to the *Phenomenology of Spirit* lead us to believe that substance is related to subject as positivity is to negativity: "This Substance is, *as Subject* [my emphasis], pure, *simple negativity* [sic]; it is the doubling which sets up opposition,

[22]Hegel, *Encyclopaedia*, ¶102.
[23]Cf. Hegel, *Encyclopaedia*, ¶97-98: "[Substance] maintains itself as One in the interplay of its actualities. Substance posits, cancels, and preserves them in all their real modalities. Any momentary actuality in its immediacy or in abstraction from substance is *accidental*."
[24]Hegel, *Encyclopaedia*, ¶102.
[25]In Hegel, *The Philosophy of Right*, 346 (commentary on ¶143).

and then again the negation of this indifferent diversity and of its antithesis [the immediate simplicity]."[26]

We are now in a position to put some of the pieces of the puzzle together into what is beginning to look like a coherent picture.[27] On the one hand we have substance, cause, objectivity, the positive (positivity); on the other hand we have subject, effect (actualities, accidents, existents, individuals), subjectivity, the negative (negativity). These two hands are clasped in friendship in Objective Spirit when substance and subject recognize their mutuality, interpenetration and interdependence. However, ultimately all value resides in one of these hands: in substantiality (remember Hegel's definition of substance as "the absolute power and fullness of *value* in all its contents"). Individuals—as bearers of subjective consciousness—are related to the ethical substance (of which the state is the ultimate incarnation) as accidents to substance,[28] and pure subjectivity is essentially negative and contains an inherent propensity towards evil.[29] Subjectivity is (or becomes) good only insofar as it recognizes the claims of the ethical substance on itself, and endeavours to actualize these claims in its accidental, finite existence.[30] A subjectivity which considers itself isolated from objective ethical life (*Sittlichkeit*) and which considers

---

[26]Hegel, *Phenomenology of Spirit*, 10.

[27]At this point it is worth mentioning that the matter can be construed very differently. What I am offering here is merely *one* interpretation and probably not the one that does the most justice to Hegel. It is still an open question, and I think an important one, whether Kierkegaard *misreads* Hegel, and if so to what extent; but even more importantly we need an account of what recalcitrant disagreements remain after the initial misunderstandings have been cleared away. In short, what I am presenting here is one way in which Hegel's various texts may be construed, a reading that in some ways (hopefully) approximates Kierkegaard's reading of them, thereby casting some light on the background of Kierkegaard's critique.

[28]Cf. Hegel, *Philosophy of Right*, ¶145: "the ethical order is freedom or the absolute will as what is objective, a circle of necessity whose moments are the ethical powers which regulate the life of individuals. *To these powers individuals are related as accidents to substance*, and it is in individuals that these powers are represented, have the shape of appearance, and become actualized" (my emphasis).

[29]Cf. Hegel, *Encyclopaedia*, ¶390.

[30]Cf. Hegel, *Philosophy of Right*, ¶¶129-132: "For the subjective will, the good and the good alone is the essential, and the subjective will has value and dignity only insofar as its insight and intention accord with the good" (¶131).

itself "the final court of appeal" in ethical matters is "evil, in fact evil through and through and universally."[31]

The pinnacle of this kind of evil subjective consciousness ("subjectivism"), according to Hegel, is *irony*. This creates a prima facie problem for Hegel's interpretation of Socrates: if Socrates represents the ironic consciousness—and consequently qualifies as *evil* on Hegel's analysis—then he cannot be a tragic figure in the way that Hegel has sketched him (Socrates cannot be both evil *and* morally justified in the sense required by Hegel's definition of tragedy). Let us briefly consider the question of *why* irony achieves this special status in the *Philosophy of Right* and why Hegel believes that Socrates' position is *not* irony.

Hegel's damning indictment of irony in the *Philosophy of Right* comes at the end of the section on "Good and Conscience" (in the second part of the book, dealing with "Morality"). Let us trace the steps as they lead to this conclusion in this section. In ¶129 Hegel defines "the good" as "the Idea as the unity of the concept of the will with the particular will." In this unity, he says,

> abstract right, welfare, the subjectivity of knowing and the contingency of external fact, have their independent self-subsistence superseded, though at the same time they are still contained and retained within it in their essence.

In this Idea (of the good), "welfare has no independent validity as the embodiment of a single particular will but only as universal welfare and essentially as universal in principle" (¶130). True conscience, says Hegel, "is the disposition to will what is absolutely good." As such, it has "fixed principles and it is aware of these as explicitly *objective* determinants and duties" (my emphasis). However, Hegel argues that this *objective content* (or truth) should be distinguished from *conscience* itself, which "is only the formal side of the activity of the will, which as *this* will has no special content of its own," and he says that these two elements (i.e., "the objective system of these principles and duties, and the union of subjective knowing with this system") are not united "until we come to the standpoint of ethical life [i.e., *Sittlichkeit*]." Consequently it is not true (according to Hegel) to say that conscience is good

---

[31]Hegel, *Philosophy of Right*, ¶140.

per se: its goodness or lack of it can only be determined with reference to the objective content of the will, and Hegel concludes that when conscience "appeals only to itself for a decision, it is directly at variance with what it wishes to be, namely the rule for a mode of conduct which is rational, absolutely valid, and universal. For this reason, the state cannot give recognition to conscience in its private form as subjective knowing, any more than science can grant validity to subjective opinion, dogmatism, and the appeal to a subjective opinion" (¶137).

Hegel interprets his contemporary situation as having slipped into evil by divorcing conscience (subjective consciousness) from the sphere (system) of objective good. This confusion between good and evil is—interestingly enough—the result of (abstract, purely formal) Kantian "morality" (*Moralität*), since "morality" culminates in the self-consciousness of its own power to effect this perversion of the good and to apotheosize itself into the absolute arbiter of truth and right. In his remark to ¶140 Hegel discusses the most pertinent forms of the contemporary evil subjective consciousness: (a and b) hypocrisy, (c) Probabilism (the belief that any action is permissible as long as one can find a single good reason for doing it), (d) the view that the goodness of the will consists in its willing the good (i.e. the Kantian view of morality), (e) the view that subjective opinion is the measuring rod of right and duty, and, finally, (f) irony. Irony, according to Hegel, is the final culmination of the development of evil subjectivism: "the supreme form in which this subjectivism is completely comprised and expressed is the phenomenon which has been called by a name borrowed from Plato—'Irony'." However, Hegel denies that either Plato or Socrates employed irony in the manner in which some of his own contemporaries (notably Friedrich Schlegel and Friedrich Ast[32]) did:

---

[32]Hegel, *Lectures on the History of Philosophy* 1:418. Kierkegaard's discussion and critique of "romantic irony" may be found at CI, 275-323. We may single out a few important ideas regarding romantic irony in Kierkegaard's understanding of it (and on which points he agrees with Hegel): (1) it functions as that (the "I") for which nothing (no actuality) is established, which is finished with everything, and which has absolute power to do anything (CI, 275); (2) the romantic ironist has placed him/herself outside morality and ethics (*Sittlichkeit*)—since these are

The name alone, however, is taken from Plato; he used it to describe a way of speaking which Socrates employed in conversation when defending the Idea of truth and justice against the conceit of the Sophists and the uneducated. What he treated ironically, however, was only their type of mind, not the Idea itself. Irony is only a manner of talking against *people*. Except as directed against persons, the essential movement of thought is dialectic, and Plato was so far from regarding the dialectical in itself, still less irony, as the last word in thought and a substitute for the Idea, that he terminated the flux and reflux of thinking, let alone of a subjective opinion, and submerged it in the substantiality of the Idea.[33]

According to Hegel, then, Socrates' position is not truly ironical because Socrates' relation to the (Idea of the) good is positive. Understood in this way we can see how Socrates can be the representative of true freedom and the highest good. Indeed, for Hegel these are ultimately one and the same thing when they are reconciled in Objective Spirit: "The good is thus freedom realized, the absolute end and aim of the world."[34]

Hegel can thus consistently claim that the death of Socrates was a tragedy, since the mutual destruction of Socrates and the ancient (organic) Greek state represents the conflict of two equally justified (positive, good) moral powers; and however unfortunate the outcome of this conflict, we can be retrospectively reconciled to its occurrence when we realize that it was a necessary event in the progression towards the realisation of Objective Spirit in the modern (organic) state.

In the *Philosophy of Right*, ¶279, Hegel gives further content to the concept of Objective Spirit when he writes that "This realized freedom of the Idea consists precisely in giving to each of the moments of rationality its own self-conscious actuality here and now. Hence it is this freedom which makes the ultimate self-deter-

---

also only expressions of an inadequate actuality—in an attempt to live "poetical-ly" (CI, 283); (3) in the disjunction and war between flesh and spirit posited by Christianity, romantic irony places itself in direct and conscious opposition to Christianity by wanting to vanquish spirit by means of the flesh, whereas Christianity seeks to negate the flesh by means of the spirit (CI, 289).

[33]Hegel, *Philosophy of Right*, ¶140.
[34]Hegel, *Philosophy of Right*, ¶129.

mining certitude—the culmination of the concept of the will—the function of a single consciousness"; i.e. everyone in the state has to will the same thing, which implies mutual recognition and respect between individuals and the state, and between the individuals themselves.[35] In this process the individual is firmly reintegrated in the state, which is his or her only true and proper spiritual home: "The rational end of man is life in the state . . . The great advance of the state in modern times is that nowadays all the citizens have one and the same end, an absolute and permanent end; it is no longer open to individuals, as it was in the Middle Ages, to make private stipulations in connection with it."[36] The Idea of the good is made actual within the parameters of the division of labour in civil society;[37] this division of labour becomes crystallized in class divisions and the different stations of life that attend them,[38] and ethical life (*Sittlichkeit*) requires that one restrict oneself to, and actualize oneself within, one of these particular spheres (classes) of production and consumption. By so doing one mediates oneself with the universal and gains "recognition both in one's own eyes and in the eyes of others."[39]

In this "ethical" disposition of resigning oneself to "one's station and its duties" and actualising oneself within one of the spheres of civil society, we find that tragedy has been replaced by what I will call "bourgeois heroism." Hegel describes bourgeois

---

[35]Cf. also Hegel, *Philosophy of Right*, 287 (addition to ¶275): "The state, then, as something mental, is the exhibition of all its moments, but individuality is at the same time the bearer of its soul and its life-giving principle, i.e., the sovereignty which contains all differences in itself." And *Philosophy of Right*, 287 (addition to ¶276): "Much the same thing as this ideality of the moments of the state occurs with life in the physical organism. Life is present in every cell. There is only one life in all the cells and nothing withstands it. Separated from that life, every cell dies. This is the same as the ideality of every single class, power, and Corporation as soon as they have the impulse to subsist and be independent. It is with them as it is with the belly in the organism. It, too, asserts its independence, but at the same time its independence is set aside and it is sacrificed and absorbed into the whole."

[36]Hegel, *Philosophy of Right*, 242 (addition to ¶75).

[37]Hegel, *Philosophy of Right*, ¶199.

[38]Hegel, *Philosophy of Right*, ¶200.

[39]Hegel, *Philosophy of Right*, ¶207.

existence as being permeated by pain, suffering, evil, anxiety, disappointment, disillusionment and futility in all its value-dimensions;[40] nevertheless, "the ethical Idea is actual and present in the world of social institutions without the misfortune of tragic clashes and the destruction of individuals overcome by this misfortune."[41] The "good bourgeois" throws him/herself passionately and wholeheartedly into causes and projects which do not merit such devotion but, in spite of this knowledge, consciously affirms existence in its totality, carries on with the task at hand and never complains about his or her fate: "he suffers misfortune without being overwhelmed by sorrow."[42] Apparently Hegel believes that this is in line with the ethical core of the Christian religion.[43]

The argument from the perspective of Hegel's system may thus be summarized as follows. (1) Tragedy dramatizes the intrinsic conflict between two substantial moral powers; (2) Socrates' death also dramatizes such a collision since it involves the conflict between traditional, familial Greek morality and what we may call Socrates' own "higher morality" of self-reflection and self-examination; (3) however, in the case of the conflict between Socrates and the state the very principles on which classical tragedy is based—i.e., the *objectivity* and *substantiality* of the powers at stake—are shaken to the foundations, because in Socrates the "individual consciousness made itself independent of the universal spirit and became for itself";[44] (4) fortunately these conflicting powers of the subjective and objective are reconciled in Objective Spirit, in which the state recognizes the demands of free individuals and free individuals recognize that they need the state in order to actualize their highest form of existence, with the result that the death of Socrates acquires its significance as merely another (unfortunate but necessary) event in the progression towards this state of affairs (i.e. the triumph of Objective Spirit); tragedy is replaced by "bourgeois heroism."

---

[40]Hegel, *Encyclopaedia*, ¶¶391-98.
[41]Hegel, *Philosophy of Right*, 102 (footnote to ¶140).
[42]Hegel, *Encyclopaedia*, ¶391.
[43]Cf. the translator's notes to Hegel, *Encyclopaedia*, ¶398.
[44]Hegel, *Lectures on the History of Philosophy* 1:447.

Of course, this conclusion follows only if Socrates did indeed have a positive relation to the Idea of the good, as Hegel claims. And this is what Kierkegaard denies. According to Kierkegaard, Hegel errs on a number of points: (1) he confuses (conflates) Socrates with Plato, and (2) he fails to appreciate the radical nature of Socrates' irony (cf. CI, 267, on both these points). It is now time to turn to a closer investigation of Kierkegaard's debate with Hegel.

Kierkegaard on Socrates, Hegel, Irony, and the Tragic

Let us begin with a thought experiment. If Hegel is right about Socrates, we would expect Socrates to fit into the ideal Hegelian state (where subjectivity and objectivity are mediated in Objective Spirit), to accept the demands of objective ethical life (*Sittlichkeit*), and to reconcile himself to his "station and its duties." But can we really resign ourselves to the idea of Socrates being "tamed" in this manner? Are we not more inclined to think that, since Socrates himself vowed to continue his quintessential questioning activity even in Hades,[45] he would go around the ideal Hegelian state in much the same way as he had always done in the ancient Greek state: questioning anyone who had pretensions to (positive) wisdom and knowledge? If we are inclined to answer Yes to the latter question, then Socrates would present a difficult problem for Hegel, with the result that Hegel would have to class Socrates with the likes of Schlegel as being "evil through and through and universally," and the death of Socrates couldn't be tragic in terms of Hegel's theory of tragedy.

One reason for answering Yes to the question above may be based on the intuitions that Socrates' focus is on the individual rather than the state, and that his relation to the Idea is essentially negative, not positive as Hegel would have us believe.[46] It is these

---

[45]Cf. Plato, *Apology* 41a-c.

[46]There is some disagreement in the scholarly literature about whether Socrates did actually have (or arrive at) the positive. In his monumental study of Socrates, Gregory Vlastos, *Socrates: Ironist and Moral Philosopher* (Cambridge: Cambridge University Press, 1991) 31-32, claims a positive teaching for Socrates by distinguishing between "simple" and "complex" irony, thereby assuming

intuitions that Kierkegaard develops into a counter-argument and critique of Hegel. According to Kierkegaard, Hegel's confusion in this regard is due to the fact that he fails to distinguish properly between Socrates and Plato, between Socratic irony and Platonic irony. Let us consider these distinctions in somewhat more detail.

Kierkegaard identifies two kinds of irony (with two corresponding forms of dialectic) in Plato's writings:

> That irony and dialectic are the two great forces in Plato everyone will surely admit, but that there is a double kind of irony and a double kind of dialectic cannot be denied, either. [1] There is an irony that is only a *stimulus* for thought, that quickens it when it becomes drowsy, disciplines it when it becomes dissolute. [2] There is an irony that is itself the activator and in turn is itself the terminus striven for. [1] There is a dialectic that in perpetual movement continually sees to it that the question does not become entrapped in an incidental understanding, that is never weary and is always prepared to set the issue afloat if it runs aground—in short, that always knows how to keep the issue in suspension and precisely therein and thereby wants to resolve it. [2] There is a dialectic that, in proceeding from the most abstract ideas, wants to let these display themselves in more concrete qualifications, a dialectic that wants to construct actuality with the idea. (CI, 121)

---

something of a Hegelian position on this point (although he is otherwise critical of Hegel's definition of irony). He explains the difference as follows: "In 'simple' irony what is said just isn't what is meant: taken in its ordinary, commonly understood sense the statement is simply false. In 'complex' irony what is said both is and isn't what is meant: its surface content is meant to be true in one sense, false in another." Vlastos repudiates (amongst other things) Kierkegaard's treatment of Socrates' irony, accusing it of being "hopelessly perplexed" because of his (Kierkegaard's) acceptance of Hegel's definition of irony as "infinite absolute negativity," which he (Vlastos) calls a "dazzling mystification" (*Socrates: Ironist and Moral Philosopher*, 43). Vlastos has himself in turn recently been criticized on this point by Alexander Nehamas. Nehamas, *Virtues of Authenticity* (Princeton: Princeton University Press, 1999) 101, prefers Kierkegaard's picture of Socrates to Vlastos's, arguing that we cannot accept Vlastos's claim that "there are truths that Socrates knows and that he knows that he knows." He argues that we should "leave Socratic irony intact," and that Socrates' sincere irony supplied him "with a much more profound ironical mask . . . —a mask that it is difficult, if not impossible, to remove" (*Virtues of Authenticity*, 102-103).

Now, Kierkegaard says that the first [1] of these kinds (both irony and dialectic) is Socratic while the second [2] is Platonic. The first kind, he says, "must be designated as scepticism, as a kind of introduction that nevertheless does not lead into the subject, as a running start that nevertheless does not reach the goal" (CI, 122). In his endeavour to replicate Socratic irony Plato couldn't resist adding a positive content, with the result that Platonic irony is "a negative power in the service of a positive idea" (CI, 122-23). In Plato, irony is transformed into subjective thinking (reasoning): both irony and subjective thinking are subjectively liberating, but the position of irony is essentially negative while that of subjective thinking is positive (CI, 123). Kierkegaard explains this last point with reference to the dialogue form:

> As for form, dialogue is equally necessary for both positions. It expressly indicates the *I* and its relation to the world; but in the one case it is the *I* that continually devours the world, and in the other it is the *I* that wants to take up the world; in the one case the *I* is continually talking itself out of the world, and in the other it is continually talking itself into the world; in the one position it is a questioning that consumes the answer, and in the other a questioning that develops the answer. As for method, this is the dialectical method, in both positions the abstractly dialectical. Of course, as such it does not exhaust the idea. What is left over is, in the one position, nothing; that is, in the other position the negative consciousness into which the abstract dialectic is taken is a beyond, an abstract qualification, but one that is maintained positively. If irony is beyond subjective thinking, it is beyond it to the extent that it is a fulfilled position that turns back into itself; whereas subjective thinking has a frailty, a weakness, through which a higher position must work itself forward. In another sense, irony is a lower position insofar as it lacks this possibility, insofar as it remains inaccessible to every challenge, refuses to become involved any more with the world, but is itself enough. (CI, 124)

Summarizing the difference between these two positions, Kierkegaard writes that, "if Plato's view of Socrates were to be expressed in a few words, it could be said that he [Plato] provides him [Socrates] with the idea [i.e. the idea (ideality) of *infinity*]" (CI, 126).

We turn now to Hegel's ascription of a positive element to Socrates' philosophy. Although Hegel seems to be quite careful on this topic—e.g. he indicates the negative thrust in Socrates' thought at various points[47]—he nevertheless wants to claim the idea of the good for Socrates (as we have already noted above), and this, says Kierkegaard, is wrong. Kierkegaard quotes the following passage from Hegel's *Lectures on the History of Philosophy*:[48]

> Socrates expresses essence [real existence] as the universal I, as the good, the consciousness resting in itself; the good as such, free from existent reality, free towards the relation of consciousness to existent reality. (CI, 226)

Hegel, then, recognizes a positive and a negative aspect to Socrates' "universality" (CI, 227, 231). On the negative side, Socrates annulled truth and communal laws as these exist in natural consciousness; on the positive side, his moralising took the form of prompting everyone to think about their duties, in the process directing their thinking away from the specific, concrete incident to the universal, to the "in-and-for-itself truth and beauty" (CI, 227). As Kierkegaard puts it, "Socrates destroyed the immediate, substantial political consciousness and did not arrive at the idea of the state, and as a result virtue can be defined only in this abstract way and has reality neither in the state nor in the full personality yielded only by the state" (CI, 229).

Hegel thus follows the tradition of antiquity which identifies Socrates as the founder of morality, but, as we have seen already (and as Kierkegaard notes in this context), morality (*Moralität*) is

---

[47]Some of the relevant passages are quoted and discussed by Kierkegaard in CI, 219-30. Cf., e.g.: "That Socrates' teaching, in Hegel's opinion, was negative, was intended to be negative, was designed to shake up and not to firm up, that in Socrates the negative is not immanental in a positivity, but is self-oriented, is already apparent in the several scattered quotations I have given and from a multitude of observations found in the section treating particularly of Socrates, but it comes out ever more clearly in the way in which Hegel discusses Aristophanes' view of Socrates" (CI, 226).

[48]Hegel, *Lectures on the History of Philosophy* 1:385. I use the Hongs' given translation of the passage and give Haldane and Simson's translation in brackets where this differs from the Hongs'.

only a precursor to ethics (*Sittlichkeit*) in Hegel's system.[49] Socrates is thus a pivotal figure in the sense of being a hinge between two historical epochs (cf. CI, 264): although not perfect in itself, morality is spiritually preferable to unreflected substantiality and a necessary precursor to ethics (*Sittlichkeit*). On this understanding we can see how Socrates' "teaching" can be positive and negative at the same time.

There are two sides to Kierkegaard's disagreement with Hegel on Socrates' "positivity": (1) given that Hegel acknowledges the negative thrust of Socrates' moral dialectic, Kierkegaard has to show—in the terms in which he (Kierkegaard) himself constructs the argument—that Hegel believed that Socrates not merely *arrived* at the good but *proceeded* from it, and (2) the more fundamental issue concerns the question of the nature of "the good" in Socrates' own thinking, and whether he *possessed* (or claimed to possess) it.

With regards to the first part of this disagreement, Kierkegaard quotes from Hegel's discussion of Socrates in his *Lectures on the History of Philosophy*, where Hegel tries to demonstrate a positive side to Socrates' universality by appealing to Socrates' conversation with the Sophist Hippias (from Xenophon's *Memorabilia*): "[Socrates] showed them [the young men] the good and true in what is determined, going back into it because he did not wish to remain in mere abstraction" (CI, 232).[50] The positive element here is that Socrates did not want to "remain in mere abstraction" but was somehow working his way towards re-relating himself to the state (albeit presumably a *higher form* of the state). In the Xenophon passage, Socrates "affirms the thesis that it is the just who obey the laws" and that in general "the best and the happiest state is the one in which the citizens are of one mind and obey the laws" (CI, 232[51]). Hegel sees in this a positive content to Socrates' moral reasoning and teaching, but Kierkegaard argues that the only reason this appears positive in that context is because Socrates has

---

[49]Paul Cruysberghs kindly pointed out that this is the case in the *Encyclopaedia* but not in the *Phenomenology of Spirit* or the *Philosophy of History*.

[50]Cf. Hegel, *Lectures on the History of Philosophy* 1:415.

[51]Cf. Hegel, *Lectures on the History of Philosophy* 1:416: "Now this is the one side in which Socrates looks away from the contradiction and makes laws and justice, as they are accepted by each individually, to be the affirmative content."

not (yet) carried through his essential position, so that the positivity at stake here is one that *precedes* the "in-and-for-itself good," and not one that *follows* from it (CI, 233). Kierkegaard points out that although Hegel had an intimation of this truth he had failed to take it seriously enough and to follow it to its logical conclusion.

With regards to the second part of the disagreement, Hegel claims that Socrates *did indeed possess* the idea of the good (the universal), but that he only *pretended* not to know in order to deflate the pseudo-wisdom of the Sophists and others who claimed to possess (substantive) knowledge (CI, 235, 266). Consequently Hegel spends a lot of time trying "to show how Socrates interpreted the good" (CI, 235). Kierkegaard argues that Hegel is misguided in this regard because he fails to comprehend the true direction of Socrates' philosophy:

> The movement in Socrates is towards arriving at the good. His significance in the world development is to arrive there (not to have arrived there at some time). . . . Now, this does not mean that he arrived there almost towards the end of his life, but that his life was a continual arriving at the good and having others arrive at this. (CI, 235)

Socrates took everyone *out* of the state: he did not come back to the state in a higher form (CI, 234, 236). He repeated his characteristic movement—from the concrete to the abstract (i.e. the good in-and-for-itself)—with each individual:

> He began anywhere and quickly was in full swing clearing each one. But as soon as he had taken one person across, he immediately came back. No actuality could resist him, but what became visible was ideality in the most evanescent intimation of the slightest limitation—that is, ideality as infinitely abstract. (CI, 236)

Does this then leave us with the conclusion that Socrates was *evil* (given that Kierkegaard—at this stage, at any rate—seems to agree with Hegel that the infinite, positive good can only be actualized in the state/system[52])? No, because (1) unlike Schlegel,

---

[52]In *The Concept of Irony*, Kierkegaard seems to agree with Hegel that "morality" (*Moralität* in Hegel's terminology) is a truncated movement: it does not fully actualize the good of personality because this is only possible in the nurturing context of mutual recognition and respect which can only occur in the

Socrates is oriented towards the good, but (2) at the same time Socrates' irony is beyond good and evil, beyond the state/system.[53] With regards to the second point we can say that what Socrates puts in place of the positive is not evil (as Hegel accuses Schlegel of doing) but *nothing*. Kierkegaard at this point introduces a third category required for understanding Socrates' position: rather than being "positive" or "negative" (in the sense of being "evil" from the perspective of the Hegelian system), Socrates is "negative"—i.e. he represents "infinite, absolute negativity"—in the sense that he swallows all positivity, substantiality and actuality up into utter nothingness (much as a black hole attracts and traps all matter and energy that comes its way).

Why do people put up with seeing their substantiality evaporate before their eyes? Kierkegaard puts this down to the personality of Socrates and the tantalising nature of irony itself. In discussing the relation between Socrates and Alcibiades, Kierkegaard concludes that the relation between Socrates and his sympathetic interlocutors (lovers) is similar to the relation between vampire and victim,

---

mature Hegelian state/system. It appears that Kierkegaard later distanced himself from his earlier view and came to think of the state rather as a "necessary evil" (JP, 4:4238; CI, 453-54). Cf. also JP, 4:4281 (CI, 453): "*A passage in my dissertation.* Influenced as I was by Hegel and whatever was modern, without the maturity really to comprehend greatness, I could not resist pointing out somewhere in my dissertation that it was a defect on the part of Socrates to disregard the whole and only consider numerically the individuals. What a Hegelian fool I was! It is precisely this that powerfully demonstrates what a great ethicist Socrates was." For an introductory discussion of Hegel's influence on Kierkegaard at the time of *The Concept of Irony*, cf. Lee Capel's translation of *The Concept of Irony*, 351-57 (n. 2).
[53]Cf. CI, 256: "Insofar as it is essential for irony to have an external side that is opposite to the internal, it might seem that it would be identical with hypocrisy. . . . But hypocrisy actually belongs to the sphere of morality. The hypocrite is always trying to appear good, although he is evil. Irony, on the other hand, lies in the metaphysical sphere, and the ironist is always only making himself seem to be other than he actually is; thus, just as the ironist hides his jest in earnestness, his earnestness in jest . . . , so it may also occur to him to pretend to be evil, although he is good. *Only remember that the moral categories are actually too concrete for irony*" (my emphasis). Cf. in this context also Hegel's discussion of hypocrisy in *Philosophy of Right*, 94-95 (¶140).

> Since . . . it is essential for the ironist never to articulate the idea as such but only casually to suggest it, to give with one hand and take away with the other, to hold the idea as personal property, the relation naturally becomes even more exciting. In this manner there quietly develops in the individual the disease that is just as ironic as any other wasting disease and allows the individual to feel best when he is closest to disintegration. The ironist is the vampire who has sucked the blood of the lover and while doing so has fanned him cool, lulled him to sleep, and tormented him with troubled dreams. (CI, 49)

Are vampires evil? The answer to this question will depend on where one stands and what one stands to lose. From the vampire's perspective his activity is neither good nor evil: it is simply in the nature of a vampire to be parasitic. (Of course, Socrates' situation is a bit more complex because he acts as he does under the compulsion of his "daimon." But since this daimon is a purely personal and subjective force, incomprehensible to all others, we may for simplification treat it as part of the "nature" of Socrates.[54]) From the perspective of the victim's concerned family, however, the activity of the vampire must be considered evil.[55] The victim's own perspective is more complex, being something of a love-hate relationship (if we can use Alcibiades' speech in Plato's *Symposium* as anything to go by).

It is because Hegel doesn't use this third category of *nothingness* in relation to Socrates that he is compelled to classify Socrates' arrival at the good as a positive thing, rather than as a nothing, seeing as he doesn't want to group Socrates together with Schlegel as being evil.[56] Kierkegaard commends Hegel for reprimanding romantic irony (cf. CI, 265-66, 279), but he argues that this differs from what Hegel calls Socratic irony (but which is actually Platonic irony), and insists that Socrates' position was nevertheless irony (in

---

[54]Cf. CI, 165-66.

[55]The state also considers the vampire's activity an offence (cf. CI, 178).

[56]Hegel probably wouldn't have been happy to concede that Socrates' Idea was, at the end of the day, *nothing*. In the *Logic*, 130 (¶88), he writes that "Substantial truth is something far above these abstractions [i.e. Being and Nothing] and their oppositions." According to Hegel "Being" and "Nothing" are "barren abstractions," whereas the Idea of the Good at which Socrates (supposedly) arrives is presumably a "substantial truth."

a sense which Hegel misses). Socrates is genuinely ignorant about whether there is life after death, but in either case refutes the idea that death is the greatest evil that can befall a human being (CI, 270); and if one is a good human being, then one has all the more reason to be of good hope as regards death, because "a good man cannot be harmed either in life or in death."[57] But just as death had lost its reality for Socrates, so had "the whole substantial life of Greek culture" lost its validity for him "in its totality" (CI, 270-71):

> with regard to this invalid actuality he [Socrates] let the estab-
> lished order of things appear to remain established and thereby
> brought about its downfall. . . . (CI, 271)

As he systematically sucked the blood out of the Greek state, however, Socrates himself "became lighter and lighter, more and more negatively free" (CI, 271), and in the end he himself was consumed by his own irony, just as his irony had earlier consumed the entirety of Greek substantiality (CI, 264, 271). But in the course of this gradual destruction a powerful new idea had been placed on the agenda of moral philosophy and intellectual history: "what [Socrates'] irony was demanding was the *actuality* of *subjectivity*, of ideality" (CI, 271; my emphasis).

In this manner Socrates became a "sacrifice": he was himself destroyed by the gift of freedom he brought. It would be tempting to apply tragic categories at this point, but Kierkegaard argues that this would be a mistake:

> On this issue [i.e., demanding the actuality of subjectivity],
> history has judged Socrates to be world-historically justified. He
> became a sacrifice. This is basically a tragic fate, but nevertheless
> Socrates' death is not basically tragic; and the Greek state really
> comes too late with its death sentence. On the other hand, the
> execution of the death sentence has little upbuilding effect,
> because death has no reality for Socrates. For the tragic hero,
> death has validity; for him, death is truly the final battle and the
> final suffering. Therefore the age he wanted to destroy can in
> that way satisfy its fury for revenge. But obviously the Greek
> state could not find this satisfaction in Socrates' death, since by
> his ignorance Socrates had frustrated any more meaningful

---

[57]Plato, *Apology*, 41d, trans. G. M. A. Grube, in John M. Cooper, *Plato: Complete Works* (Indianapolis: Hackett Publishing Co., 1997).

connection with the thought of death. Admittedly the tragic hero does not fear death, but still he knows it as a pain, as a hard and harsh course, and to that extent it has validity if he is condemned to die; but Socrates knows nothing at all, and thus it is an irony over the state that it condemns him to death and believes that it has inflicted punishment upon him. (CI, 271)

The death of Socrates thus cannot be a tragedy because (1) death means nothing to him, and because (2) he has dissolved any hold the state might have had over him by virtue of its nexus of substantial relations.

So how, then, are we to evaluate the phenomenon of the ironic itself? In his concluding chapter in *The Concept of Irony*, entitled "Irony as a Controlled Element, the Truth of Irony," Kierkegaard vindicates mastered irony (of which Platonic irony rather than Socratic irony is the quintessential example) as the gateway to authentic subjectivity, as the *via negationis* which leads to a "genuinely human life" (CI, 326, 198-99). This conception indicates Kierkegaard's apparently fundamental agreement with Hegel (at the time he wrote *The Concept of Irony*) that an individual must *act positively* in the world (state/system) in order to develop his or her personality to its full potential. Mastered irony can fit reasonably comfortably in the Hegelian state/system because it controls and disciplines the "wild infinity" (CI, 326) which "uncontrolled" irony essentially is (and against which Hegel had aimed his polemic). With the concept of mastered irony Kierkegaard may perhaps have wanted to show the Hegelians (which in this context basically means J. L. Heiberg and H. L. Martensen[58]) a way in which they could (or should) improve their ideal state/system. Although he seems to agree with Hegel's philosophy of world history (cf. CI, 260, 262-63), he is sounding something of a warning cry, arguing that something has been forgotten in the idealization of Objective Spirit:

> As a rule, irony is understood ideally, is assigned its place as a vanishing element in the system, and is therefore treated very briefly. For this reason it is not easy to comprehend how a whole

---

[58]Kierkegaard had attended Martensen's lectures on "speculative dogmatics" at the University of Copenhagen during the winter semester of 1837-1838 (cf. JP, 5:5277), a few years before defending his dissertation (on 29 September 1841).

life can be taken up with it, since, after all, the content of this life
must be regarded as nothing. But we forget that a position is
never as ideal in life as it is in the system; we forget that irony,
just as any other position in life, has its spiritual trials, its battles,
its retreats, its victories. . . . This is the purely personal life with
which science and scholarship admittedly are not involved, even
though a somewhat more intimate acquaintance with it would
free them from the tautological *idem per idem* [the same with the
same] from which such views often suffer. Whatever the case
may be, grant that science and scholarship are right in ignoring
such things; nevertheless, one who wants to understand the
individual life cannot do so. (CI, 166)

According to this argument one cannot understand subjective
existence without understanding irony. Hegel did not understand
irony, and therefore we have reason to doubt that he had a
profound understanding of subjective existence and, by implication, of the Socratic imperative which demands of every individual
that he or she exist in an "eminent" sense. It is because Hegel
misunderstands the radical nature of irony (by reducing it to a
manner of speech) and of the Socratic project (by failing to note the
possibility of *legitimate* perennial conflict between substance and
subjectivity) that he falls into the trap of designating the death of
Socrates as a tragic event. (It is difficult, for instance, to see how
Hegel could have avoided classifying Socrates as "evil" if Kierkegaard's analogy of the "vampire" is on target.) According to Kierkegaard the conflict between Socrates and the state was not that
between two substantial moral powers; rather, the Greek state was
shadowboxing in its conflict with Socrates: what it was fighting
against was "nothing."

Hegel thought that he had killed ("mediated") both irony and
tragedy with the concept of Objective Spirit. *The Concept of Irony*
heralds the rebirth of irony, albeit in the special form of *mastered*
irony. Interestingly, the rebirth of irony also paves the way for the
rebirth of tragedy (if we recall that irony is the unity of the tragic
and the comic; cf. CI, 52). Mastered irony effectively transforms the
individual into a substantial moral power which relates itself to the
complex nexus of ordinary (received, unreflective) morality from
the perspective of "higher morality." It is therefore always possible
(and perhaps even inevitable) that substantial subjectivity will

conflict with the state,[59] which may result in a tragic state of affairs. The manner in which the substantial individual relates to other individuals and to the state is (in Kierkegaard's philosophy) informed by Christian ethics, which stipulates that the individual may not be blissfully disengaged from others in ironic self-sufficiency.[60] The true Christian suffers not only in his or her God-relationship (which suffering results from the process of giving birth to oneself and the attempt to relate oneself to something that is wholly "unknown" and "other"), but also because he or she endeavours to love "the neighbour" in a fitting and meaningful manner (which is an extraordinary difficult and lifelong task and which also creates the problem of how to communicate the "gospel of suffering"). In a significant Journal entry of 1850, Kierkegaard gives us some idea of what a "Christian-Socratic" moral philosophy might look like:

> Socrates—Christianity. This Socratic thesis is of utmost importance for Christianity: Virtue cannot be taught; that is, it is not a doctrine, it is a being-able, an exercising, an existing [Existeren], an existential [existentiel] transformation, and therefore it is so slow to learn, not at all as simple and easy as the rote-learning of one more language or one more system. No, in respect to virtue there is always particular emphasis on the internal, the inward, "the single individual." Here I come again to my thesis— Christianity is not a doctrine but an existence-communication [Existents-Meddelelse]. (JP, 1:1060)[61]

Conclusion

We see, then, that the difference between Hegel and Kierkegaard on the question of whether the death of Socrates was a tragedy tells us something important about their opposing views

---

[59]It is interesting to note that Kierkegaard's fight is later also with the "demonic" nothingness (vacuity) of civil society (as this is represented e.g. in the "chatter" of the gutter press). Cf. *Two Ages: A Literary Review*.

[60]Cf. WL, 48, where Kierkegaard writes that it is "beneficial and necessary that the single individual carefully and consciously pay attention to himself and, if possible, help others (in such a way as one person can help another, since God is the true helper) to become Christians in an even deeper sense."

[61]Cf. also JP, 1:627.

regarding the status of subjectivity in ethical existence and their respective moral ideals and imperatives. Hegel sees his own philosophy as the completion of the Socratic project: the individual (subjective consciousness) is reintegrated in the state (objective consciousness) and made subservient to it. For Kierkegaard, on the other hand, this supposed *completion* of the Socratic project is rather a *betrayal* of it (or at least a misunderstanding). Hegel's happy reconciliation of subjectivity and objectivity is in fact too easy (cf. CI, 327), because it is always possible (and perhaps inevitable) that an individual who endeavours to "repeat" the Socratic project of "higher morality" will collide with the state and/or be subject to misunderstanding by other people, thereby moving into the realm of the tragic. In Kierkegaard's moral philosophy it is never the case that the tragic can be mediated once and for all; rather, it resurfaces in later works as the gateway to authentic religiousness and selfhood (cf. SLW, 422). The tragic is always a real possibility when substantial powers collide, and it is precisely Kierkegaard's insistence that subjectivity *can* be such a substantial power (and legitimately, not pathologically, so) that distinguishes him from Hegel.

Two things need to be stated at this juncture. First, the process of re-relation of the substantial individual to others does not mean that the project of "higher morality" plays into the hands of the Hegelian system/state, since substantial subjectivity most collides with the state when the latter becomes *pathological*, a possibility that Hegel seems to want to rule out from the start.[62]

Second, the use of the word "substantial" here should not blind us to the fact that the locus and nature of the conflict has shifted from what it was in ancient tragedy. The stage is no longer merely external; rather, the bulk of the action takes place internally (in "subjectivity"), which implies that the concept of the tragic needs to be reconceived to accommodate this shift, and we can also

---

[62]Hegel might have wanted to claim this special status only for the ideal state (i.e., a kind of regulative ideal), to which Kierkegaard would then reply that this is good as far as it goes, but that this should not deflect attention from the *existential* situation of individuals. A good (just) state may to some extent be a necessary condition for substantial subjectivity, but it cannot by itself create authentic subjectivity.

expect a change in the manner in which this conflict is represented. We can trace the process of this reconception and its representation in the authorship through such works as *Either/Or, Fear and Trembling, The Concept of Anxiety, Stages on Life's Way, Philosophical Fragments*, and *Concluding Unscientific Postscript*.[63]

It is also important to note how Kierkegaard's notion of "substantial subjectivity" differs from Hegel's. For Hegel, as we have seen, a subject is substantial "when it dedicates itself to the fullness and objective necessity of actuality."[64] For Kierkegaard, on the contrary, a subject is substantial when it is "religiously, infinitely concerned about itself" (SLW, 486).

Of course, it is a moot point to what extent Kierkegaard was still under the spell of Hegel's philosophy at the time that he wrote The Concept of Irony, but I think we can detect traces of a minimal agreement with Hegel's philosophy of world history and his insistence on the supremacy of the state over the individual, and of the Objective Spirit over the subjective spirit. Nevertheless, in Kierkegaard's insistence (*pace* Hegel) that there is a good kind of irony—where irony is defined as "subjectivity's being-for-itself" (CI, 257)—and that "no genuinely human life is possible without irony" (thesis XV; CI, 6, 326), we can already detect the thin end of the wedge that would drive Kierkegaard farther and farther apart from Hegel as the authorship evolves. Reading the authorship as a project of "Christian-Socratic" moral philosophy, we can see that the more redemption is sought in subjectivity rather than in the state, the more we can expect Kierkegaard's repetition of the project of "higher morality" to move in the direction of Socrates and away from Hegel.

---

[63]For an introduction to these issues, cf. Holler, *Kierkegaard's Concept of Tragedy in the Context of his Pseudonymous Works*; Larry Edward Carden, "Tragic Sensibility and a Christian Understanding of Human Being: Self and the Eternal in the Theological Anthropology of Søren Kierkegaard" (Ph.D. diss., Vanderbilt University Graduate School, 1980); and Karsten Friis Johansen, "Kierkegaard on 'The Tragic'," *Danish Yearbook of Philosophy* 13 (1976) 105-46.

[64]Hegel, *Encyclopaedia*, ¶¶102-106.

8

Ethics and Irony

Pia Søltoft

In the following I will argue that a close and special link exists between irony and ethics. I also claim that the critique which Kierkegaard presents in his *magister* dissertation—not simply of romantic irony, but also of Socratic irony—is an ethical critique, which is based upon his own very rich understanding of what ethics is. This understanding, which is polemically related to Hegel's view of ethics, presages the meaning of ethics as found later in the authorship.

What Is Ethics?

In the ethical tradition going back to Kant it has become usual to distinguish between two kinds of duty: Duty toward oneself and duty toward another. Simply put, duty toward oneself forms the background for a personal ethic which is decisive for subjectivity. Duty toward another lays the basis for a social ethic which regulates the way in which we treat each other, and for this reason is significant for any theory of intersubjectivity.

It is often said that Kierkegaard is primarily interested in personal ethics;[1] for him, ethics has to do with a responsible self-

---

[1]As George J. Stack says: "[T]he conception of the ethical development that Kierkegaard propounds is neither an ethics of consequences nor an ethics of duty (except in the sence that one has a 'duty' to become a self); it is an ethics of self-realization." *Kierkegaard's Existential Ethics* (University AL: University of Alabama Press, 1977) 149. This interpretation is continued by Louise Carroll Keeley when she states: "For Kierkegaard, the ethical is the event of self-development, for its

relationship, while the relationship to the other, the social ethics aspect is almost completely omitted. According to this interpretation, Kierkegaard is an acosmic thinker, something of which Louis Mackey among others has attempted to convince us.[2] Everything is centered around one's own self whose continuous struggle lies in its attempts to become, choose, conquer, and repeat itself. Thus, relationships with other human beings have no significance for the particular individual's subjectivity.

Over and against this acosmic critique, I will present an interpretation of *The Concept of Irony* which advocates that Kierkegaard even from the authorhsip's infancy had an understanding of ethics which linked together personal ethics and social ethics and thus connected subjectivity with intersubjectivity. I hope to make apparent that Kierkegaard actually places the significance of the self's self-relationship on its relation with other human beings, something which reveals itself through the critical position he takes concerning both Socratic and romantic irony. Both forms of irony are criticized precisely for releasing the self-relationship from its relationships to other human beings.

Nonetheless, Kierkegaard still has a high regard for Socratic irony—even in an ethical sense. For it is possible to criticize Socratic irony ethically, if the irony is only the product of a decisive *standpoint*. But irony is particularly useful as an *instrument* employed in the service of another cause, namely that of Christianity. Kierkegaard's critique of irony is thus delivered using *an ethicoreligious control of irony*.

---

study, one's assignment is to oneself." "Subjectivity and World in 'Works of Love' " in *Foundations of Kierkegaard's Vision of Community,* ed. George B. Connell and C. Steven Evans (Atlantic Highlands NJ: Humanities Press, 1992) 96.

[2]Louis Mackey, "The Loss of the World in Kierkegaard's Ethics" in *Points of View: Readings of Kierkegaard* (Tallahassee: Florida State University Press, 1986). Thus Mackey's critique has recently been disputed by Marilyn Piety in "The Reality of the World in Kierkegaard's Postscript," *International Kierkegaard Commentary: Concluding Unscientific Postscript to "Philosophical Fragments"* ed. Robert L. Perkins (Macon GA: Mercer University Press, 1997) 169-86.

What Is Irony?

As a type of speech, irony means to give expression to the opposite of what one really means. Kierkegaard is here playing with the common meaning of irony, because when "what is said is not my meaning or the opposite of my meaning, then I am free in relation to others and to myself" (CI, 247-48). Ironic distance sets the individual free—both in relation to itself and in relation to others.

Philosophically, irony describes a form of spirit which views the finite against the backdrop of the infinite. It is used in this way by Socrates. Kierkegaard criticizes this when it results in the finite's losing its significance. But he responds positively to the thought that irony can result in the finite being seen anew in the light of the infinite. Finitude, concrete actuality, and one's relationship to other human beings must not lose their significance. Instead, they should regain their original significance through the differentiation of irony.

Finally, the romantics employed irony as an expression for the liberty and arbitrariness of the imagination. Kierkegaard keeps his distance from irony of this form. This type of irony avoids all responsibility and is thus unethical. But it is important to remember that the ethical critique to which Kierkegaard subjects the romantics arises from the *same ethical* viewpoint as the critique of Socratic irony. Both forms of irony are criticized for denying the relationships to the surrounding world and to other human beings.

Through irony one not only becomes another human being to another human being, one also becomes another to oneself. Irony is thus self-separating, and this self-separation is, according to Kierkegaard, necessary for achieving consciousness: whether self-consciousness or consciousness of the other(s). Because of this differentiating function, irony has significance for subjectivity, but this significance is exclusively negative. By means of irony, a human being discovers *freedom*, but only a *negative* freedom: a freedom from self, circumstances, and others. Thus, it is said about Socratic irony that "it actually contained nothing more than the separating, the singling out, of what later became the object of knowledge. The phrase 'know yourself' means: separate yourself from the other" (CI, 177).

It is the mere negativity of irony which particularly causes problems, both for subjectivity and intersubjectivity. Subjectivity loses its concreteness when emancipated from other subjects. And intersubjectivity is made impossible by the permanent separation which prevents an ethical regulation of relationships between human beings. These two points form the background for Kierkegaard's ethical critique of irony. So, let us first turn to the critique of Socrates.

Abstract Subjectivity

Irony is the first and most abstract definition of subjectivity. Although Socrates was in real-life contact with other people through his dialogical method, these connections were, in fact, *deficient*. Hence, his contact with other people was actually a *casual* contact, because these relationships were merely *occasions* for the development and employment of irony. For these reasons, Kierkegaard's first point of criticism is that none of the relationships in which Socrates participated had any significance for *his own self-understanding*. Socrates was the occasion for the self-development of the other persons, but this did not lead to his understanding himself in a new way. Personally, he remained isolated, holding himself ironically *above* each and every relationship of which he was a part, for "he himself was suspended high above all this in ironic contentment" (CI, 182). Nor does Socrates develop himself through these relationships, because irony undermines the intersubjective aspect of subjectivity. And so Socrates' self-relationship is untouched; "throughout all this, they [his students] were completely changed, he remained unbudgingly the same" (CI, 190). The problem is that when intersubjectivity is deprived of meaning, then subjectivity ends as a mere abstraction. When relationships to other human beings have no significance to the self's self-relationship, the self's own concreteness is weakened. Subjectivity then becomes itself by "self-pollination" and ends up with a self-appointed and abstract, self-determination: "we may speak of Socrates' moral strength, but the point he reached in this respect was the rather negative qualification that subjectivity intrinsically determines itself" (CI, 210-11).

Given that Socrates keeps his own subjectivity out of his relationship to the other, he can readily act as a midwife for others, while his own self-relationship stagnates. Therefore, Kierkegaard says that, for Socrates, subjectivity has not gotten any further than its first and most abstract stage. Through irony one becomes another to oneself, but there is no possibility to come back to one's original self. And that Socrates remains uninfluenced, that he stays the same, does not mean that he remains himself in a positive sense, but rather that he remains stuck in continual self-alienation.

Ironic Irresponsibility

In relation to other human beings, irony's absolute negativity also has significance for the untruth of the relationship and thus for Kierkegaard's ethical critique. Socrates was a midwife, but because his irony was exclusively negative, he could not offer his students the prospect of a new positivity. Negative freedom then became freedom for whatever one wished, and thus relationships towards other human beings began to go astray in abstraction. Socrates could neither fulfil nor enrich his students, and for this reason he is characterized as a *seducer*, one who awakens longings which he is unable to satisfy (see CI, 188). His relationship to his disciples was one of *awakening*, but it was in no way personal. Socrates was only the impetus for a motion, the provacateur of a movement, whose final goal was known neither by him nor by his students: "He helped the individual to an intellectual delivery; he cut the umbilical cord of substantiality. As an *accoucheur* [obstetrician], he was unrivaled, but more than that he was not. Nor did he assume any real responsibility for the later lives of his students" (CI, 191).

Here a question of social ethics can be found lurking under the surface: Just what is Socrates' duty toward these others, his students? Is he *permitted* to be indifferent concerning the future life of the other? Since *emancipation* from the other, which is the whole point of Socratic irony, is only freedom in the negative sense— freedom *from*—Socrates abdicates from any further responsibility and avoids imposing any positivity, any freedom *for*. The ethical problem results because irony, for Socrates, is not merely to be understood as an *instrument* which should prepare the way for something new but also as a *standpoint* having its own inherent validity: "But his irony was not the instrument he used in the service of the idea; irony was his position [*Standpoint*]—more he did not have" (CI, 214). Thus, concerning Socrates' relationships to other human beings and the missing ethical regulation of said relationships, Kierkegaard writes:

> One could not think of Socrates as someone who under the celestial vault of ideas elevated his pupils through the intuition of their eternal essence, as someone who impregnated the youths with the rich fullness of a vision, as someone who ethically laid an enorous responsibility upon his own shoulders and watched over them with fatherly concern, reluctantly let them go but never lost sight of them, as someone who, to recall a previous expression, loved them in the idea. In relation to others, Socrates' character was too negatively rounded off for such things to take place. (CI, 187-88)

As a *standpoint*, a position, irony destroys both self-relationships and relationships to others and therefore has destructive consequences for both personal and social ethics. But was this the reason Socrates was sentenced to death?

Hegel and Kierkegaard: Was Socrates "Ethically" Guilty?

As we all know, Socrates was arrested by the Athenian state for ignoring its gods and for corrupting its youth. Thus, the first question is, does Kierkegaard view this arrest as an expression of his own ethical criticism and, second, is Kierkegaard in agreement with Hegel's judgement of Socrates?

In connection with the discussion of the case against Socrates, Kierkegaard says that Socrates was really convicted for his indifference. Hegel, given his conception of ethics, perceives this indifference as a valid reason for the death sentence. The basis for the Hegelian conception of ethics is in three parts—right, morality, and ethical life [die Sittlichkeit]—as found and developed in *Grund-*

linien der Philosophie des Rechts,[3] to which Kierkegaard frequently refers. This Hegelian tripartition makes up an organic whole in which the three different areas are worked together. Morality is the domain of self-conscious subjectivity wherein abstract right gives permission to a person, and that person is conceived as an independent subjectivity with its own will in the domain of morality.[4] In this way, through morality, there obtains the most complete agreement between abstract objective right and conscious subjectivity. In the third area, ethical life [*die Sittlichkeit*], subjectivity's relation to right is made *concrete*, and the two previous areas (abstract right and morality) are united. *Die Sittlichkeit* is thus the concrete domain in which free moral subjects can develop in agreement with their family's[5] or the state's[6] interests.

Socratic irony can then be understood as an *infinite absolute negativity* in conflict with the organic unity between the individual and the state. Socrates set subjectivity above family and the state, since through his irony he refused to recognize the validity and legitimacy of the latter. This means that Hegel must declare himself in agreement with Socrates' death sentence. In *Vorlesungen über die Geschichte der Philosophie I*, to which Kierkegaard also makes reference in *The Concept of Irony*, Hegel asks directly whether it could not be supposed that Socrates ought to be found guilty. He then answers himself: Socrates *must* be found guilty.[7]

Kierkegaard is somewhat in agreement with Hegel. The state may have needed to find Socrates guilty, since the state *qua* state cannot allow the individual's interests to be placed above those of the common good. But the question is really whether that indifference which underlies the Socratic standpoint in relation to the state also forms the background for Kierkegaard's own ethical critique of Socrates. For the state's judgment was a juridical one, not an ethical one, and Kierkegaard's ethical critique of Socrates' behavior

---

[3]G. W. F. Hegel, *Grundlinien der Philosophie des Rechts* (Frankfurt am Main: Suhrkamp, 1986) *Werkausgabe* bd. 7.

[4]Hegel, *Grundlinien* §107, s. 205.

[5]Hegel, *Grundlinien* §158, s. 307.

[6]Hegel, *Grundlinien* §187, s. 343.

[7]G. W. F. Hegel, *Vorlesungen über die Geschichte der Philosophie I* (Frankfurt am Main: Suhrkamp, 1993) *Werkausgabe*, 18:508.

does not lie in Socrates' being a spokesperson for an arbitrary subjectivism in relation to the state but rather that Socrates "becomes essentially immoral precisely by [his] *total abstraction.* Here, then is another example of how the celebrated Socratic moral philosophy was constituted. The defect is definitely due to the abstract position [*Erkjendelses-Standpoint*] he took with regard to knowledge" (CI, 185-86, emphasis added). Kierkegaard's ethical charge against Socrates can be specified as follows: "he rejected the established order, inclosed himself within himself, egotistically confined himself within himself" (CI, 168-69). This ethical judgment of Socrates rests upon the assumption that the self-relationship is entangled with one's relationship to the other. Keeping the two relationships apart results in unethical abstraction. But despite this criticism of Socrates from an ethical viewpoint, he is called the founder of morality by both Hegel and Kierkegaard. But are they really saying the same thing?

Hegel and Kierkegaard: How Is Socrates "the Founder of Morality"?

Although Hegel agreed with the judgment of the Athenian state, he also believed that Socrates himself had a positivity which made him the founder of morality. Socrates brought subjectivity to a consciousness of itself,[8] and Hegel posits morality's domain as starting at the point where the individual is not only no longer frightened of punishment but also consciously admits that the common good is also what is good for his own subjectivity.

Hegel perceives Socrates as a *tragic hero.* And the tragic hero is tragic because his fate is decided by the collision of two equally worthy principles. In Socrates' case, we have the collision of objective right personified in the Athenian state and subjective self-determination personified in Socratic irony.[9] The tragic consists in the fact that there is no possible way to mediate or reconcile objective right with subjectivity. In other words: the tragedy of Socrates consists in his lacking a notion of the ethical life [die Sittlichkeit]—the unifying factor between objective right and subjective disposition. Nonetheless, the Socratic standpoint was

[8]Hegel, *Geschichte der Philosophie* 18:441.
[9]Hegel, *Geschichte der Philosophie* 18:514.

considered by Hegel as a further developed subjectivity since Socrates introduces the notion of self-conscious subjectivity. I can, in this regard, thus endorse Ernst Behler's point that Hegel's positive ethical evaluation of Socrates is *not* due to Socratic irony but is exclusively the result of Socratic subjectivity.[10] Furthermore, Hegel separates irony and subjectivity, something which particularly distinguishes his understanding of Socrates from Kierkegaard's.

Kierkegaard, like Hegel, holds that the ancient Greek individual was trapped in substantial but abstract right and hence not free. The Greeks acted from a fear of punishment, rather than from a personal concord with the state. Hence, Kierkegaard emphasizes that Socrates via the separation of irony manages to awaken the Greek individual to self-consciousness. But more he cannot do. In response to Hegel, Kierkegaard stresses that Socrates does remain a negativity, because "the moral individual is the negatively free individual. He is free because he is not bound by another, but he is negatively free precisely because he is not limited in another" (CI, 228). And when Hegel says that the subjectivity Socrates introduced into world history caused a positive transition in the domain of morality, Kierkegaard once again disagrees. He instead focuses on irony as the modus of separation and advances in his eighth thesis that the subjectivity for which Socrates prepared the way was only the most superficial and weakest sense of subjectivity—an empty existence form.

Thus, the divergence between Hegel and Kierkegaard lies in their conceptions of Socrates' positivity. Hegel believes that the subjectivity which Socrates revealed can form the basis of concrete actions. About this, however, Kierkegaard says: "whatever positivity there is here cannot decide anything with regard to the question of the extent to which Socrates maintained a positivity or to which the universal became concrete for him" (CI, 233). For Kierkegaard it is an impossibility that Socratic irony as absolute infinite negativity could provide the foundation for concrete

---

[10]Ernst Behler "Kierkegaard's *The Concept of Irony* with Constant Reference to Romanticism," in *Kierkegaard Revisited: Proceedings from the Conference Kierkegaard and the Meaning of Meaning It: Copenhagen, May 5-9, 1996*, ed. Niels Jørgen Cappelørn and Jon Stewart, Kierkegaard Studies monograph series 1 (Berlin and New York NY: Walter de Gruyeter, 1997) 24.

actions. Kierkegaard further emphasizes that Socrates' lack of positivity is the result of his ignorance that the eternal or the divine was the foundation for everything: "that is, he knew that it was, but he did not know what it was. He was conscious of it, and yet he was not conscious of it, inasmuch as the only thing he could say about it was that he did not know anything about it" (CI, 169). Socrates' positivity was only a possibility, a potential, that never became a reality, an actuality. Therefore Kierkegaard stresses that Socrates did not come to save the world, but rather to judge it, which thus illuminates the difference between the Socratic standpoint and the Christian one. Or, as it says in the first of the dissertation's theses: "The similarity between Christ and Socrates consists essentially in their dissimilarity" (CI, 6).

Kierkegaard is thus able to conclude that Socrates can actually be called the founder of morality in Hegel's sense of the word, but only as the one who introduced subjectivity in its first and hence weakest form. Because, for Kierkegaard, that form is all too abstract to be able to function as a basis for authentic self-determination and hence for moral action. The ideality which Socrates carried within himself as possibility "was *ideality* in the most evanescent intimation of the slightest limitation—that is, ideality as *infinitely* abstract" (CI, 236, emphasis added). The ninth thesis of the dissertation corresponds precisely to this notion: "Socrates drove all his contemporaries out of substantiality as if naked from a shipwreck, undermined actuality, envisioned ideality in the distance, touched it, but did not take possession of it" (CI, 6).

Another Ethics

Even though Kierkegaard cannot completely concur with Hegel's notion of Socrates as the founder of morality (CI, 235), he does concede that Socrates did introduce a new *point of departure* for all subsequent discussion of ethics. This positive evaluation is linked to the fact that Kierkegaard—despite his ethical criticism of Socrates—would in no way deny that irony has a world-historical significance for subjectivity and thus also for ethics, since "irony is the very incitement of subjectivity, and in Socrates irony is truly a *world-historical passion*. In Socrates, one process ends and with him a new one begins" (CI, 211, emphasis added). This contention is supported by the fifteenth and final thesis of the dissertation: "Just as philosophy begins with doubt, so also a life that may be called human begins with irony" (CI, 6).

The significance of Socratic irony for subjectivity is that of self-differentiation through which one becomes another for oneself, thereby achieving the possibility of relating oneself consciously to both oneself and others. Such self-differentiation lays the foundation for an altered self-understanding as well as for an altered understanding of the foundation upon which the established moral codex rests. Thus, in praise of Socrates, he writes: "but it must be added that by its pressure the infinite negativity has made all positivity possible, has been an infinite incitement and stimulation for positivity. . . . Thus as beginning he is positive, but as mere beginning he is negative" (CI, 216-17).

The open space of subjectivity now awaits that content which fled the scene along with those gods whom Socrates was charged with ignoring. This is irony's positive function, its function as an *instrument*: to keep the space of subjectivity open. But because Socrates does not allow himself to be affected by his relationships, avoiding all responsibility for those with whom he enters into relationship, his ironic *standpoint* is open to ethical criticism. What is problematic about Socrates' association with irony is that he has become trapped within the absolute infinite negativity of irony. Irony was his *standpoint*, not merely his instrument, which had the effect that he was unable to allow ideality to make a concrete expression in reality; neither could he positively forge a self-relationship nor a relationship to others. And this is the conclusion found in the sixth thesis of the dissertation: "Socrates not only used irony, but was so dedicated to irony that he himself succumbed to it" (CI, 6).

Romantic Irony Seen in an Ethical Light

In a certain sense, I could halt my survey of irony here and use the evaluation of Socratic irony as the earliest foundation of a new definition of the ethical. Such a move could be justified by employing the oft-advanced viewpoint that the two halves of *The Concept of Irony* are completely unrelated and irreconcilibly so. Even Prof. J. N. Madvig (1804–1886), a member of Kierkegaard's dissertation committee, remarked that the dissertation was flawed "not only is it burdened with a certain free and easy carelessness of composition, but even its exposition of concepts lacks scholarly order, form, and firmness. This is particulary clear in the arrangement of the dissertation's two principal parts and the connection between them."[11] I, by contrast, would argue that a reconciliation between the two halves can be carried out in view of the ethical which runs through both halves of the book and which is contrasted with Hegel's view of ethics. Thus, on the one hand, I am in agreement with Ernst Behler when he points out that Kierkegaard is not interested in romantic irony as a concrete and historical form of thought. But, on the other hand, I take issue with Behler'contention that Kierkegaard for this reason excludes it from ethical critique.[12]

Subjectivity's Higher Power

Fundamentally, Kierkegaard criticizes romantic irony for being *"a qualification* of the *being-for-itself subject"* (CI, 269). And just like Hegel, Kierkegaard emphasizes that the negating activity of romantic irony arises from an arbitrarily placed subject, thus making the self, the "I," into the absolute center. This "I" is not defined or determined by something other than itself; rather, it is an "I" which produces itself by negating everything else. Such romantic irony was advanced within the transcendental philsoophy by J. G. Fichte and finally results in mere *acosmism*, a denial of the world (see CI, 273-74).

According to Kierkegaard, the consequence of this was that subjectivity became contentless. When subjectivity was conceived of as the absolute zero point from which all else was negated, it was deprived of any relationship to itself or to others. That self-differentiating function which laid the foundation for Socratic irony and which Kierkegaard viewed as a positive starting point for the further development of subjectivity is brought to a halt by romantic irony. Essentially, the romantic ironist does not separate

---

[11]Bruce H. Kirmmse, *Encounters with Kierkegaard. A Life as Seen by His Contemporaries* (Princeton NJ: Princeton University Press, 1996) 31.
[12]Behler, "Constant Reference to Romanticism," 28.

himself from his self, but excludes himself from the ethos, the mores, and the customs which control his age: "It was not subjectivity that should forge ahead here, since subjectivity was already given in world situations, but it was an exaggerated subjectivity, a subjectivity raised to the second power" (CI, 275). Subjectivity raised to the second power is that subjectivity which produces or rather constitutes itself and its surroundings by negating everything else: "The *I* became the constituting entity" (CI, 273).

As already mentioned, Kierkegaard defines the freedom which irony establishes as a negative freedom, a freedom *from*. In romantic irony, this negative freedom evolves into a consciously willed negation of everything which is called "living poetically": "because not until one is free in that way does one live poetically, and, as is well known, irony's greatest requirement was to live poetically" (CI, 280). To live poetically means for the ironist to create or produce himself.[13] The "poetic," which here is a synonym for both the ironic and the romantic modes of living,[14] consists in being free of that actuality in which one just happens to exist, thereby freeing the self from taking any responsibility for it. Thus, the ironist does not merely compose himself poetically, he or she also poetically composes him—or herself out of their given actuality: "the whole of existence [Tilværelsen] has become alien to the ironic subject and the ironic subject in turn alien to existence, that as *actuality* [Virkeligheden] has lost its validity for the ironic subject, he himself has to a certain degree become unreal" (CI, 259, translation modified). That both actuality and the individual subject lose their validity forms the background for Kierkegaard's ethical critique.

Living Poetically by Being Poetically Composed

What is exciting about Kierkegaard's view of romantic irony is not so much the critique itself as presented, but rather the

---

[13]See also Sylvia Walsh, *Living Poetically. Kierkegaards Existential Aesthetics* (University Park: Pennsylvania State University Press, 1994) 45-49.

[14]In a footnote Kierkegaard himself says: "Throughout this whole discussion I use the terms irony and ironist. I could just as well say romanticism and romantic. Both terms say essentially *the same thing*" (CI, 275n.1).

standpoint from which it is presented. One could say that Kierkegaard in *The Concept of Irony* introduces the *via negativa*[15] which
would soon come to be the hallmark of the great majority of his
works. Instead of positing his own notions, he proceeds indirectly
by presenting critiques of the opposing notions.

The ethical standpoint from which Kierkegaard attacks
romantic irony is a religious one; indeed, a directly Christian
standpoint. The romantic understanding of living poetically is to
be criticized because it

> did *not* understand it to be what the pious Christian thinks of
> when he becomes aware that life is an upbringing, an education,
> which, please note, is not supposed to make him into someone
> completely different, . . . but is specifically supposed to develop
> the seeds God himself has placed in man, since the Christian
> knows himself as that which has reality for God. Here, in fact,
> the Christian comes to the aid of God, becomes, so to speak, his
> coworker in completing the good work God himself has begun.
> (CI, 280)

In this quotation is to be found the whole foundation for the
notion of subjectivity which colors the entire subsequent authorship. This notion, that a human being is not merely what he or she
immediately and apparently seems to be, but only becomes him—
or herself by relating to that self out of otherness, runs like a silver
thread through all of Kierkegaard's later works. And that such a
development is furthermore ethically defined, that is, connected to
a responsible relationship both to oneself and to others, results
from subjectivity's being normatively determined by something
higher which is neither the common good nor the state, but rather
God:

> In other words, it is indeed one thing to compose oneself
> poetically; it is something else to be composed poetically. The
> Christian lets himself be poetically composed, and in this respect
> a simple Christian lives far more poetically than many a brilliant
> intellectual. But also the person who in the Greek sense poetically

---

[15]Kierkegaard's use of the negative method has been particularly highlighted
by Michael Theunissen, especially as it relates to the work *The Sickness unto Death*.
See, for example, *Das Selbst auf dem Grund der Verzweiflung* (Berlin: Anton Hain,
1991) and *Der Begriff Verzweiflung* (Frankfurt am Main: Suhrkamp, 1993).

composes himself recognizes that he has been given a task. Therefore it is very urgent for him to become conscious of what is original in him, and this originality is the boundary within which he poetically composes, within which he is poetically free. (CI, 280-81)

To *allow* oneself to *be* poetically composed is, on the one hand, to become conscious of oneself as a task for oneself. A task which consists in relating to oneself, so as, precisely through this self-relationship, to become oneself. On the other hand, to *allow* oneself to *be* poetically composed also means that the one's context is one's given circumstances: "An individual who lets himself be poetically composed does have a definite given context into which he has to fit and thus does not become a word without meaning because it is wrenched out of its associations" (CI, 283). In continuation of this quotation, Kierkegaard accuses the romantic ironist of spurning this very context. For the romantic ironist views his circumstances with indifference, and this means that if he feels they do not suit him, he simply recreates them to suit himself: "in other words, he poetically composes not only himself but *he poetically composes his environment also*" (CI, 283, emphasis added).

And it is my point that this self-directed poetic recomposition has not just one, but two, negative consequences. one for *die Sittlichkeit*, which is the only one Hegel emphasized in his critique of romantic irony and with which Kierkegaard agreed and a second for the ethical, which is the most important for Kierkegaard.

"Die Sittlichkeit" and the Ethical

It is important to note that Kierkegaard and Hegel each understood something completely different by the concept of *die Sittlichkeit* even though Kierkegaard uses the Danish word *det Sædelige*, which is a literal translation of the German term *die Sittlichkeit*.

To Hegel the word covers the concrete morality in a given entity, where every single individual willingly and consciously obeys the laws of the society. *Die Sittlichkeit* is understood as "a higher order" wherein the subjectivity of the individual is made concrete in the relation to the civil society, the social roles and the public institutions. *Die Sittlichkeit* is the highest form of morality, that is, the concretion of ethics into the forms and structures of the common life.

Kierkegaard has a totally different understanding. To Kierkegaard the Danish translation of *die Sittlichkeit* as *det Sædelige*, covers the "lowest form" of morality. In fact it is so "low" that it layes *outside* the realm of the ethical. Kierkegaard uses the word *det Sædelige* simply as another definition for social *habit and custom* and thus merely as a definition of the domain in which the conscious decision making and responsibility taking which follows upon self-differentiation, is *not* necessary. Kierkegaard stresses that *det Sædelige* is an unavoidable part of being a member of society, but he argues that this regulation is only founded upon human decisions and therefore relative and changeable. The ethical on the other hand is absolutely determinative for subjectivity and intersubjectivity. To maintain Kierkegaard's distinction between *det Sædelige* and the ethical in the following analysis I will have to abandon the English translation "Ethical life" or "ethics" which is normally used for both the Danish word *det Sædelige* and the German term *die Sittlichkeit*. In stead I will make use of the designation "traditional morality" in the following.[16]

Kierkegaard claims that both in relation to traditional morality—the ordinary social habit and custom—*and* in relation to the ethical, the romantic ironist

> stands proudly inclosed within himself, and just as Adam had the animals pass by, he lets people pass before him and finds no fellowship for himself. In so doing, he continually collides with the actuality to which he belongs. Therefore it becomes important for him *to suspend* what is constitutive in actuality, that which orders and supports it; that is morality [*Moral*] and ethics [*Sædelighed*]. (CI, 283, emphasis added)

Kierkegaard hereby deliveres a *double* point of critique. The ironist's proud self-inclosure brings him into conflict with the actuality to which he belongs, those fortuitous circumstances, the ethical foundation of life, which pertain to the truly human. This, I would claim, is Kierkegaard's most essential point of criticism,

---

[16]I owe this suggestion to Robert L. Perkins, who has been an unremitting and extremely helpful reader of this article.

and it is a point of an ethical nature. But, secondly, it is also claimed that the ironist *as a consequence thereof* suspends traditional morality. This point of criticism coincides with Hegel's moral critique, with which Kierkegaard also agrees. But his agreement is only one part of his lager ethical criticism.

Something more is namely attributed to the romantic ironist: "It cannot really be said that the ironist places himself outside and above morality and ethics [*det Sædelige*], but he lives far too abstractly, far too metaphysically and aesthetically to reach the concretion of the moral and the ethical [*det Sædelige*]" (CI, 283). The concretion of the moral has its expression in precisely such things as customs, mores, social roles and public institutions. These are what the romantic ironist ironically rises above in his refusal to assign absolute validity to anything other than the subject. But the reason why the romantic ironist places himself above all this is that he rejects the more fundamental ethical obligations in life. This is seen most clearly in Kierkegaard's analyses of Friedrich Schlegel and Karl Wilhelm Ferdinand Solger.[17]

Schlegel: Shaking the Ethical Foundation

Kierkegaard characterizes romantic irony as a rebellion against an age which has become "totally *fossilized in finite social forms*" (CI, 303, emphasis added). By *fossilized* is meant that these forms, and their resulting relationships, can only be defined in terms of *traditional morality*. That is to say that habit and custom and social institutions have become the only true ways in which existence can be regulated, for the "glorious principles and maxims of habit and custom were the objects of a pious adultery" (CI, 303).

For this reason, in his analysis of Friedrich Schlegel's novel *Lucinde*, Kierkegaard emphasizes that Schlegel wished to take to task the bourgeois notion of love—a notion which claimed that love was nothing in itself but only became something by its intention of being fit into "the pettiness that creates such a furor in the private theaters of families" (CI, 287). Kierkegaard is quite

---

[17]I will not be discussing Ludwig Tieck, as an analysis of Kierkegaard's critique of his works in this connexion would only be a repitition of the points made in the critique of Schlegel and Solger.

in agreement with Schlegel's rebellion against the "bourgeois" accommodation to love: "There is a moral prudery, a straitjacket, in which no reasonable person can move. In God's name, let it break to pieces" (CI, 288). Or, in other words, Kierkegaard actually agrees with Schlegel in that traditional morality—understood as relative social habits and customs—ought to be denied that absolute significance which has been mistakenly attributed to it. For this reason he is able to relate positively to the notion that "Schlegel's *Lucinde* is an attempt to suspend all ethics [Sæde-lighed]" (CI, 289).

But this positive support of Schlegels breakdown of the moral prudery of the time is followed by a more serious critique. Kierkegaard argues that Schlegel is doing more than simply denying an overly dominant and bourgeois chastity in the present form of the society. Had Schlegel simply stopped at the point of making an ironic critique of the social habits of the time Kierkegaard would have done nothing more than to have laughed right along with him: "if it were merely witty irony over all ethics [*den Sædelighed*] that is identical with custom and habit—who, then, would be so laughable as not to want to laugh at it, who, then, would be such a surly slug that he would not have the time of his life in relishing it?" (CI, 290). However, the quotation then continues: "But this is by no means the case. On the contrary, *Lucinde* has a highly doctrinaire character . . . " (CI, 290). This doctrinaire character is not only built upon Schlegel's irony about the deification of traditional morality, it also directly denies any relation of responsibility between human beings.

Schlegel's "demolition" in *Lucinde* reaches deeper than the bourgeois chastity. It shakes the very foundation of the ethical bulwark: "What *Lucinde* attempts, then is to *annul* all ethics [*Sædelighed*]—not only in the sense of custom and usage, but all the ethics that is the validity of spirit, the mastery of the spirit over the flesh" (CI, 290). Schlegel intends to annul the very thought that there is any Absolute which gives human actuality its *validity* and which lies beyond the subjective inclinations of said actuality. This validity that is not based in relative habits and customs but goes deeper, all the way down into *the substantial depths* where a religious ground for human responsibility is to be found. And this is where Kierkegaard's ethical critique finds its starting point as formulated in the difference between the romantic understanding of living poetically and a religious understanding thereof. Romantic irony misunderstands the poetic as a way of escaping actuality: "On the one side stands *the given actuality* with all its paltry philistinism; on the other, *the ideal actuality* with its dimly emerging shapes" (CI, 305). The ironist thus cannot *reconcile* himself with that actuality in which he is living. He instead exchanges it for a poetic miasma. Thus, the romantic, just like Socrates, remains an alien in the actual world, for "poetry is a kind of reconciliation, but it is not the true reconciliation; for it does not reconcile me with the actuality in which I am living; no transubstantiation of the given actuality takes place by virtue of this reconciliation, but it reconciles me with the given actuality by giving me another, a higher and more perfect actuality" (CI, 297).

This ethical criticism of romantic irony is thus actually a criticism of its acosmism and escapism from actuality. Romantic irony is not capable of bringing about a reconciliation between the subject who has differentiated himself from himself and his circumstances and the subject who despite this differentiation would make actual the connection between himself and his circumstances. Such a reconciliation is only possible, according to Kierkegaard, in the domain of religiosity: "Therefore, only the religious is able to bring about the true reconciliation, because it infinitizes actuality for me" (CI, 297). For Kierkegaard would have it that to live poetically is to become "clear and transparent to oneself, not in finite and egotistical satisfaction but in one's absolute and eternal validity" (CI, 298).

Schlegel rather lacks this religious aspect. He has been mesmerized by the bourgeois glorification of habits and customs and is no longer able either to pull his eyes away or let them rest on a fixed point. After having pronounced his negative critique of the fixed chastity of the time, he let his eyes drift in a subjectivistic idolization of any sensuality. Schlegel has arrived at the infinite, but it is "a negative form of the infinite" that has no significance for the finite, specifically, ethical responsibility in our relations with others.

Solger: Contemplating the Ethical

In his critique of Solger, Kierkegaard again stresses that the finite has lost its significance—and so has the infinite. Whereas Schlegel had absolutely no sense of the religious, Solger is accused of knowing the religious but of denying it any significance in itself and for earthly life with the other. Solger does not even have so much as a concept of creation (see CI, 315). Whereas Schlegel had fallen in love with the finite, despairing over the glorification of forms and customs, Solger instead completely misses both the finite and the infinite by means of his "contemplative irony" (CI, 309). Solger is thus characterized as "the metaphysical knight of the negative" (CI, 309). He does not come into conflict with traditional morality and it's habits and customs like Schlegel, but he fixes his eyes on the undefined, wavering horizon of the blue mountains.

For Solger both the infinite and the finite lose content. Therefore he cannot permit that his relationship to the abstract infinite is expressed in any relationship to the finite: "He cannot achieve concreteness for the infinite. He sees the finite as the *Nichtige*, as the vanishing, as the *nichtige All* [universe]. Therefore moral qualifications have no validity; all finitude together with its moral and immoral striving vanishes in the metaphysical contemplation that sees it as nothing" (CI, 312-13). In other words, Solger fails to take into account the *law of motion* which, according to Kierkegaard, is the very basis of the negative. This is the law of motion which Kierkegaard particularly employed in his interpretation of Socrates and which laid the foundation for his theory of subjectivity. This law of motion is expressed as follows: "The negative has, namely, a double function—it infinitizes the finite and it finitizes the infinite" (CI, 310). The infinitizing of the finite is, in fact, the filling of that emptiness which irony as infinite absolute negativity left standing open as possibility. Infinitizing means that one's self-relationship and one's relationship to one's circumstances move from being relatively determined through traditional morality—the social habits and customs of the time—to being absolutely determined. This is because differentiation calls for renewed and responsible attention to be placed on one's fortuitous circumstances. The finitizing of the infinite consists in seeing this motion as concrete and earthly movement which has significance for actuality as the individual human being experiences it.

In his critique of Solger, Kierkegaard further clarifies what is involved in his own positive starting point. Thus it becomes apparent that the ethical standpoint from which he criticizes both Socratic and romantic irony is that of Christianity. The dismissal of romantic irony as arbitrary subjectivism proceeding to acosmism together with its negation of the pertinent significance of the ethical for subjectivity is based on the rather Christian thought that God is the creator and that humans are his coworkers in this creation.

Controlling Irony Ethicoreligiously

In Kierkegaard's account of the true understanding of what it means *to live poetically*, irony becomes a controlled moment. This controlled irony introduces that self-separation which is absolutely necessary for achieving true subjectivity. To live poetically means that the individual human being "is oriented and thus integrated in the age in which he lives, is positively free in the actuality to which he belongs" (CI, 326). Moreover, that irony is controlled in this way means that it not only provides a freedom *from*, but that it is has also opened up into a freedom *for*. As negative freedom, irony "limits, finitizes, circumscribes," but when it appears as the controlled moment, as an *instrument*, it also opens up positive freedom. As a controlled moment irony thus becomes "the absolute beginning of personal life" (CI, 326). Irony forms the basis for subjectivity's necessary self-differentiation as well as for one's differentiation from one's original fortuitous circumstance: "In every personal life there is so much that must be thrown out, so many wild shoots to be pruned. Here again irony is an excellent surgeon, because, as stated, when irony has been put under control, its function is extremely important in enabling personal life to gain health and truth" (CI, 328).

If irony is, in fact, a controlled moment in that movement which subjectivity must undergo in order to become itself, then this movement cannot stop in negation. One ought therefore to rush into the sea of irony, but "not in order to stay there, of course, but in order to come out healthy, happy, and buoyant and to dress again" (CI, 327). Such necessary "dressing" means that the longing for positivity which arose in the icy seas of infinite absolute negativity must be fulfilled by something other than irony. But it must also be fulfilled *within* the given actuality and not as a longing for something faraway as in romantic irony:

> this longing must not hollow out actuality; on the contrary, life's content must become a genuine and meaningful element in the higher actuality whose fullness the soul craves. Actuality hereby acquires its validity, not as a purgatory—for the soul is not to be purified in such a way that stark naked, so to speak, it runs blank and bare out of life—but as history in which consciousness successively matures, yet in such a way that salvation consists not in forgetting all this but in becoming present in it. (CI, 328-29)

Irony as a controlled moment is one part of subjectivity's movement toward itself, a part of self-consciousness's coming to itself. Therefore Kierkegaard's ethical standpoint in *The Concept of Irony* is concerned partly with focusing upon the original fortuitous circumstances of a human being's self and situation and partly with a separation from those circumstances which irony as an instrument serves to actualize. Thus, ethics is concerned with acquiring conscious responsibility for an already given situation precisely through differentiation from that situation.

This is made even more apparent in Kierkegaard's ethical critique of Socrates where one's self-relationship is connected to one's relationships with other human beings, where subjectivity is part and parcel of intersubjectivity. His critique of Socratic irony as a *standpoint* was, on the one hand, a critique of the tendency of subjectivity to close in on itself and end in abstraction. On the other hand, Socrates is criticized for depriving the relationships which obtain among human beings of any ethical regulation.

In a similar fashion, Kierkegaard's ethical critique of romantic irony is a critique of how the relationship between subjectivity and intersubjectivity has been ruptured, such that subjectivity has here become an arbitrary being-for-itself, denying any connection with another human being. Through these critiques, the outlines of another understanding of ethics in *The Concept of Irony* can be perceived. Thus, I do not follow the rather common perception that

The Concept of Irony should itself be understood as an ironic project on the part of Kierkegaard. Instead, it is my opinion that these outlines form a picture which the rest of the authorship can be seen as further detailing. Even though in the subsequent authorship irony is only treated broadly, sporadically, and rarely as an independent theme, it is nonetheless irony's separating function which has a decisive significance both for Kierkegaard's later theory of subjectivity and for his view of ethics: self-separation together with separation from all others and everything else is the background against which consciousness undertakes the fundamental movement whose structure is repeated again and again throughout the later authorship.

9

"Controlled Irony" and the Emergence of the Self in Kierkegaard's Dissertation

Richard M. Summers

Introduction

One of the most striking things about Kierkegaard's early, "pre-authorship" works is the extent to which they already contain so many of the themes that will figure centrally in his subsequent authorship. Kierkegaard's theory of the self, for example, can already be found in *The Concept of Irony with Continual Reference to Socrates*, where it comes to expression, as I hope to show, in the decisive movement by which irony is brought under "control."

The notion of "controlled irony" is not the least of the challenges with which *The Concept of Irony* confronts its reader.[1] The

---

[1] Only recently has the full complexity of Kierkegaard's handling of irony in his dissertation been properly appreciated, and this has been largely thanks to scholars working with the methods of deconstruction. The following studies in particular contain important discussions of *The Concept of Irony*: John Vignaux Smyth, *A Question of Eros: Irony in Sterne, Kierkegaard, and Barthes* (Tallahassee: Florida State University Press, 1986) 101-222; Sylviane Agacinski, *Aparté: Conceptions and Deaths of Søren Kierkegaard*, trans. and ed. Kevin Newmark (Tallahassee: Florida State University Press, 1988) 33-78; Roger Poole, *Kierkegaard: The Indirect Communication* (Charlottesville: University Press of Virginia, 1993) 36-60; Joakim Garff, *"Den Søvnløse": Kierkegaard læst æstetisk/biografisk* (Copenhagen: C. A. Reitzels Forlag, 1995) 32-59. An earlier study that should also be mentioned is Pierre Mesnard, *Le Vrai Visage de Kierkegaard* (Paris: Beauchesne, 1948) 117-79. It was Mesnard who popularized the idea that the dissertation was itself an ironic text. The degree to which this was a major breakthrough can be seen from the survey of the main interpretations of *The Concept of Irony* (to 1961) given by Lee Capel in the notes to his translation. Søren Kierkegaard, *The Concept of Irony*,

term itself seems almost a contradiction, for if irony really is controlled it ceases in a sense to be irony. And this would seem to apply irrespective of the way the control is exercised, of whether, that is to say, irony is reduced to a concept and assigned a place in a speculative system à la Hegel or incorporated, as a transitional stage, into a personal or religious development. For in both cases it is supplanted by a position which effectively negates it. But if, on the other hand, we wish to retain the free play and open-endedness which are the hallmarks of irony, are we not then forced to abandon any possibility of serious meaning?[2] The question therefore is whether there is any way of holding onto irony, with all that that implies, without thereby having to succumb to a nihilistic relativism.

I will argue that in Kierkegaard's conception of controlled irony, as set out in the final six pages of his dissertation, the power of irony is not lost, but is if anything enhanced. For if irony does lose its absoluteness in one sense, it at the same time gains a new significance from the role assigned to it in the furtherance of personal life. To appreciate the particular status of controlled irony, however, it needs to be seen in relation to Kierkegaard's discussions of Socratic and romantic irony in the *The Concept of Irony*, and these will therefore be examined. As a start, though, it may be helpful to glance briefly at the historical circumstances within which irony first emerged as a problem for Kierkegaard.

The Historical Context

For the young Kierkegaard the encounter with irony was inevitable, as he emerged in the mid-1830s from his home environment and the study of theology into the wider world of the contemporary literary scene. For this was a time of transition and disorientation. Romanticism, which had inspired the previous generation, was everywhere in decline, and as the hopes it had raised collapsed, a tide of nihilism was sweeping through Europe.

---

trans. and ed. Lee M. Capel (London: Collins, 1966) 351-57.

[2]This is the point Sylvia Walsh makes against Agacinski in a vigorous critique of postmodernist appropriations of Kierkegaard: Sylvia Walsh, "Kierkegaard and postmodernism," *International Journal for Philosophy of Religion* 29 (1991): 115.

Ernst Behler sees the clearest indication of this change of climate in the way that in Germany belief in Hegel's notion of history as progress, as a process working towards a goal and governed by reason, was lost during the 1830s (Hegel died in 1831) and replaced by the theme of God's death, which was most dramatically expressed by Heinrich Heine.[3] Heine's *Ideas: The Book of Le Grand* of 1826 contains the image of an intoxicated God who creates the world in a dream.[4] Heine talks of "the irony which God put into the world" and "the world's irony,"[5] and refers to the "irony of the great poet of the world stage up there."[6] *Zerrissenheit*, the tearing asunder of the world, and of the heart of the poet, is another of Heine's themes,[7] and one that was taken up by other poets of this period, such as Grabbe and Lenau, with whom Kierkegaard was familiar, and Georg Büchner.[8]

There was no need, though, for Kierkegaard to look abroad to encounter this attitude, since it was powerfully in evidence in Demmark, where Heine had a significant influence,[9] together with Byron, who was seen as "the poet of despair" and as a challenge to the cosy, idealistic worldview that had become the hallmark of the Danish Golden Age.[10] The movement that was now taking over from Golden Age optimism was characterised by the themes of disappointment, frustration, and despair that were being articulated abroad. Its fruits are seen in Carl Bagger's *Min Broders Levned*

[3]Ernst Behler, "The Theory of Irony in German Romanticism," in Frederick Garber, ed., *Romantic Irony* (Budapest: Akadémiai Kiadó, 1988) 77. One of the first expressions of the death of God theme, of course, was Jean Paul's "Speech of the Dead Christ from the Universe that There Is No God" in his novel *Siebenkäs* of 1796. See Jean Paul, *A Reader*, ed. Timothy J. Casey (Baltimore and London: Johns Hopkins University Press, 1992) 179-83.

[4]Heinrich Heine, *Selected Prose*, trans. and ed. Ritchie Robertson (Harmondsworth: Penguin Books, 1993) 95. For the German text see Heinrich Heine, *Sämtliche Schriften*, ed. Klaus Briegleb (München: Carl Hanser Verlag, 1969) 2:253.

[5]Heine, *Selected Prose* 185-86; *Sämtliche Schriften* 2:522.

[6]Heine, *Sämtliche Schriften* 2:424.

[7]E.g., Heine, *Sämtliche Schriften* 2:405-406.

[8]On similarities between these writers and Kierkegaard, see Steffen Steffensen, "Kierkegaard und Goethe," *Nerthus: Nordische-deutsche Beiträge* 3 (1972) 24-26.

[9]Gustav Albeck, Oluf Friis, and Peter P. Rohde, *Dansk Litteratur Historie* (Copenhagen: Politikens Forlag, 1965) 2:256-57. Friis is the author of this section.

[10]Friis, *Dansk Litteratur Historie* 2:256.

(The Life of My Brother) (1835), Hans Christian Andersen's early novels, and the early work of Paludan-Müller, especially *Dandserin-den* (The Danseuse) (1832), which has been called the major work of Danish Byronism.[11] The dominant mood of this movement, in Denmark as in Europe, was revolt—"revolt," in the words of one critic, "against *all* authorities—literary, philosophical, moral, religious and political."[12]

If this then was the mood of the time, there were factors in Kierkegaard's personal life that could well have predisposed him to find it congenial. It was probably at this point indeed, as Henning Fenger has suggested,[13] and not later, that the important experience of his "aesthetic period" occurred. The recent past had been a miserable time for him, overshadowed as it was by several deaths in the family, including that of his mother, and he was also probably finding the study of theology constricting, so it is hardly surprising if the theme of revolt had a strong appeal.

That Kierkegaard was personally acquainted with irony is revealed by the two very important journal entries of the summer of 1835,[14] the draft letter to Peter Wilhelm Lund in Brazil and the famous "Gilleleie entry" (JP, 5:5092, 5100), which show him trying to come to grips with his situation. In the Gilleleie entry (JP, 5:5100, p. 37) he refers explicitly to "that irony of life which . . . in the waters of morality . . . is especially at home to those who still have not entered the tradewinds of virtue," and goes on to describe its various tricks. It is plain from his description that he is speaking from personal experience here. What is particularly significant, though, is that he is doing so from a new position, for he thinks he now has the remedy which will enable him to avoid these negative effects of irony. That remedy is ethical action, and

---

[11]Friis, *Dansk Litteratur Historie* 2:520.

[12]Hans Hertel, "P. L. Møller and *romantismen* in Danish Literature," *Scandinavica* 8/1 (1969): 40-41.

[13]Henning Fenger, "Kierkegaard, P. E. Lind og *Johan Gordon*," *Kierkegaardiana* 7 (1968): 16.

[14]Whether these entries were actually penned in 1835, when Kierkegaard was on holiday in Gilleleie, or the following year, as he relived the experience in Copenhagen, as Henning Fenger has argued, is not significant in the present context. See Henning Fenger, *Kierkegaard, The Myths and their Origins*, trans. George C. Schoolfield (New Haven and London: Yale University Press, 1980) 96.

specifically the idea of taking up responsibility for the self one will become, which is expressed here for the first time. With this principle, Kierkegaard thinks he has the means of mastering the "irony of life" he describes. The importance of the Gilleleie entry for Kierkegaard's life and work cannot be exaggerated. Among other things it gives him a clear sense of direction, and one of the fruits of that is seen in the work he did in 1836–1837 on irony and the way it is overcome not in speculative understanding but in humor. His guides here were not Hegel, but Jean Paul Richter and E. T. A. Hoffmann, with Hamann also very much in the picture. This is the background to *The Concept of Irony*, and the notion of "controlled irony."

Socrates

It is around the figure of Socrates that Kierkegaard's treatment of irony in his dissertation revolves. Thesis X states that irony first came into the world with Socrates (CI, 6). But Kierkegaard is very aware of the difficulties of trying to gain an adequate conception of Socrates, for not only did he leave no writings for posterity, but his sayings cannot be taken at face value either. Socrates, he declares, "was not like a philosopher delivering his opinions in such a way that just the lecture itself is the presence of the idea, but what Socrates said meant something different. The outer was not at all in harmony with the inner but was rather its opposite" (CI, 12). As well as this there is the distance in time that separates us from Socrates and the fact that even his contemporaries could not grasp his immediacy. If we then add the assumption that the substance of his existence was irony and further postulate that irony is a negative concept then, Kierkegaard says, we get an idea of the difficulty of forming a picture of him, a difficulty which he compares with that of trying to depict an elf with the cap that makes him invisible (CI, 12). The only way to proceed is therefore to piece together the indirect information we have, and so Kierkegaard takes the varying, and in places contradictory, views of Socrates's contemporaries Xenophon, Plato and Aristophanes and by this means tries to form a picture of the figure that gave rise to them.

Xenophon he soon dismisses as having, among other shortcomings, no ear for irony. Plato is for Kierkegaard a much more important source, and it is to Plato that he devotes the longest section of the dissertation. However, it is not Plato but Aristophanes, whom Kierkegaard sees as coming closest to capturing the real Socrates.[15] Aristophanes portrays Socrates in his play, *The Clouds*, and the characteristic that, according to Kierkegaard, he identifies as fundamental is his irony. It is this that is represented by his device of having Socrates suspended from the ceiling in a basket. For, as Kierkegaard puts it, "[t]he ironist, to be sure, is lighter than the world, but on the other hand he still belongs to the world; like Mohammed's coffin, he is suspended between two magnets" (CI, 152).

In Aristophanes, then, Kierkegaard finds his interpretation of Socrates as ironist confirmed. The importance of the qualification of Socrates's position as irony, rather than subjectivity, is that while irony is of course a form of subjectivity, subjectivity always contains a positive element, while irony, for Kierkegaard, is a purely negative position (cf. CI, 145). This is the point where he parts company, quite fundamentally, with Hegel. For while he accepts Hegel's view that Socrates represented the standpoint of subjectivity, he modifies it essentially, declaring that while Socrates's position was "in many ways" that of subjectivity, its specific characteristic was that "the subjectivity did not disclose itself in its full opulence, such that the idea became the boundary from which Socrates turned back into himself in ironic satisfaction" (CI, 165). That "Socrates had the idea as boundary" (CI, 169) was fundamental for Kierkegaard. It meant that Socrates's position was wholly negative. Thus while in principle his famous ignorance could have contained a positive principle, in that to know that one knows nothing implies that one has an idea of what knowledge is,

---

[15]Hegel had seen in Aristophanes an important witness to one aspect of Socrates, and this idea was developed further by the neo-Hegelians, P. W. Forchhammer in his *Die Athener und Sokrates: Die Gesetzlichen und der Revolutionär* (Berlin: Nicolaischen Buchhandlung, 1837) and H. T. Rötscher in his *Aristophanes und sein Zeitalter* (Berlin: Vossischen Buchhandlung, 1827). It is to this latter that Kierkegaard's view of the Aristophanic Socrates owes most, as he acknowledges (CI, 129-30).

Socrates, according to Kierkegaard, never developed this potential positivity. He kept it in a state of potentiality which never developed into actuality (CI, 170). Thus the Socratic motto "know yourself" did not, in Kierkegaard's view, express the fullness of subjectivity but meant only "separate yourself from the other" (CI, 177). It was therefore essentially negative.

Further examples of Socrates's negativity are seen in his attitude to the state and the family and, supremely, in his response to the vote of condemnation. Yet for all his emphasis on Socrates's negativity, Kierkegaard does also acknowledge a respect in which that negativity also contains "a rich and profound positivity" (CI, 170).[16] The point for Kierkegaard is that Socrates never let this become actuality. As Kierkegaard puts it, "[Socrates] is positive to the extent that the infinite negativity contains within itself an infinity; he is negative because for him the infinity is not a disclosure but a boundary" (CI, 209). Thus it is that while he himself never crossed the boundary into the new territory, Socrates can nevertheless represent the beginning of something new.

This new thing, the potential positivity in his position, appears not in Socrates himself but in his effect on other people. This may at first sight seem an odd claim, since Kierkegaard goes to some length to stress the negative aspect of Socrates's relation to his disciples, showing how the great mental gifts he had were indeed seductive, but in no way orientated to permanent relationships, for "communicate, fill up, enrich—this he could not do" (CI, 188). The longings he awakened in the youths he was unable to satisfy, and so at the decisive moment they were abandoned to their own devices. Yet, paradoxically, it was precisely in this way that Socrates was really of service to them. He disappointed those who wished to remain attached to him, but those prepared to take up the challenge of discovering the wealth they had in themselves he set free. His essential role was thus as a midwife. In Kierkegaard's words, "He helped the individual to an intellectual delivery; he cut the umbilical cord of substantiality. As an *accoucheur* [obstetrician],

---

[16]Cf. Emanuel Hirsch, *Kierkegaard-Studien* (Gütersloh: C. Bertelsmann, 1933) 594-95.

he was unrivalled, but more than that he was not" (CI, 191). Yet this in itself was no mean thing.

The full significance of Socrates's position becomes apparent when he is seen in his historical circumstances. Here Kierkegaard explicitly follows Hegel's account (CI, 200), according to which the decline of the Athenian state and the rise of the Sophists provided the context in which Socrates emerged.[17] On this view, the breakdown of a moral order based on tradition, as people began to question established customs and discover contradictions in what before had been straightforward, created a vacuum into which the Sophists stepped. They saw how it was the power of reflection, which makes everything uncertain by revealing contradictions and inconsistencies, that had caused the confusion, but they also saw how reflection could provide the remedy, for it teaches how to give reasons for everything (CI, 204). This remedy was illusory, however, for the answers the Sophists offered were always only for the moment, for the particular case (CI, 208), and they were unable to rise above the concerns of the moment to posit the universal, whence alone the true remedy could come. It is at this point that, for Kierkegaard, the world-historical significance of Socrates's negativity becomes fully apparent, for it was the means by which Greece was to be liberated from the illusory positivity of the Sophists (CI, 209). Had Socrates not been totally negative in his encounter with the Sophists he would have been much less well equipped to attack them. For their wisdom was tolerant and if Socrates had been positive, the battle between them would have simply been between different types of positivity. As it is, in every case Socrates counters the positivity of the Sophists with a negative (CI, 210).[18]

---

[17]G. W. F. Hegel, *Lectures on the History of Philosophy*, trans. E. S. Haldane and Frances H. Simson (London: Routledge and Kegan Paul, 1968) 1:407-11.

[18]There are obvious parallels between the situation described here and Kierkegaard's own time, one of which he points to explicitly (CI, 203-204). Similarly his view of the role of Socrates vis-à-vis the Sophists shows the position Kierkegaard is already taking up towards his age. Here he was undoubtedly influenced by Hamann and his *Socratic Memorabilia*, a parallel to which he refers explicitly: "Hamann's relationship to his contemporaries—Socrates' to the Sophists" (JP, 2:1547).

Thus Socratic irony had an essential role to play in the particular circumstances in which it appeared. Classical Hellenism had outlived itself, and a new principle had to appear. Before this principle could appear in its truth, however, "all the prolific weeds of misunderstanding's pernicious anticipations had to be plowed under, destroyed down to the deepest roots" (CI, 211). World history needed an *accoucheur*, and this was the task that Socrates accomplished. He was not the one who was to bring the new principle in its richness; his task was to make the emergence of this principle possible (CI, 211). And for this his standpoint had to be negativity.

The problem in justifying irony as an historical phenomenon is that as "infinite absolute negativity," it is no longer directed at any particular thing but at the whole of existence as it confronts the ironist (CI, 259). The ironist, that is to say, feels himself alienated from the historical context in which he is placed; for him it has lost its meaning and thus its validity. There are times, however, Kierkegaard suggests, when this negative attitude to the historically given actuality is justified. These times are the turning points of history when one form of historical actuality has outlived itself but the new form, which is to replace it, has not yet emerged. In this situation the attitude of the ironic subject, for whom the given actuality has lost its validity but who does not possess the new one (CI, 261), may be historically justified. This, though, is something that only history can judge (CI, 264). It is Kierkegaard's argument that it was the case with Socrates. For it was not actuality as a whole that Socrates's irony negated but a particular, historical form of actuality, namely that of "substantial morality," as it existed in the Greece of his time. The actuality Socrates's irony demanded, the new principle for which he prepared the way, was subjectivity, ideality, and here, Kierkegaard claims, history has vindicated his stand (CI, 271).

Romantic Irony

If the case of Socrates shows that there can be a right relation between irony and subjectivity, in which irony is a historically justified form of subjectivity, the romantics, for Kierkegaard, illustrate the opposite situation of an irony that is not justified. He sees both forms of irony as related, however, for since irony is a qualification of subjectivity it must necessarily appear in two aspects. The first of these is when subjectivity "asserts its rights in world history for the first time" (CI, 242). This is the position with Socrates. The second form of irony is defined by Kierkegaard as "a subjectivity raised to the second power, a subjectivity's subjectivity" corresponding to the "reflection's reflection" of the idealists, which he finds in the philosophical development which began with Kant and reached its climax in Fichte, who served as the inspiration for the romantics. It was in them that this subjectivity to the second power reached its full expression. The examples Kierkegaard looks at are Friedrich Schlegel, Tieck and Solger.

In finding the origin of romantic irony in the way the romantics took over Fichte's theory about the constitutive role of the ego in the construction of actuality, Kierkegaard follows Hegel.[19] For Fichte, of course, this principle was a strictly metaphysical one: when he spoke of "constructing the world," it was a systematic (philosophical) construction he meant. But what Schlegel and Tieck did, according to Kierkegaard, who is here echoing Hegel, was to take the Fichtean principle, "that subjectivity, the I, has constitutive validity, is the sole omnipotence," and apply it directly to actuality (CI, 275). The result was to make the subject absolute in relation to every form of actuality. Once the subject was thus enthroned in absolute sovereignty, irony had "the absolute power to bind and to unbind" (CI, 276); nothing could survive before it. Irony, that is to say, becomes the principle of an unbridled subjectivism.[20]

---

[19]See G. W. F. Hegel, *Aesthetics: Lectures on Fine Art*, trans. T. M. Knox (Oxford: Clarendon Press, 1975) 1:64, and *History of Philosophy* 3:507. On Kierkegaard and Hegel's respective responses to romantic irony see Robert L. Perkins, "Hegel and Kierkegaard: Two Critics of Romantic Irony," *Review of National Literatures* 1/2 (1970): 232-54.

[20]This view of romantic irony falls seriously short of doing it justice, at least as it was originally intended. Modern scholarship is revealing a richer and more complex picture, as seen, for example, in the major studies by Ingrid Strohschneider-Kohrs, *Die Ironie in Theorie und Gestaltung* (Tübingen: Max Niemeyer Verlag, 1960) and Ernst Behler, *Klassische Ironie, Romantische Ironie, Tragische Ironie: Zum Ursprung dieser Begriffe* (Darmstadt: Wissenschaftliche Buchgesellschaft, 1972). A brief historical survey of the main conceptions of romantic irony is given by Helmut Prang, *Die romantische Ironie* (Darmstadt: Wissenschaftliche Buchgesell-

The result, for Kierkegaard, is seen in the attitude of the Romantics to concrete actuality in its various forms. History, for example, the romantics turned into myth (CI, 277). As to religion, if one or other religion was absolute for a time, the reason for its absoluteness was always that the ironist willed it (CI, 278). In the field of knowledge the attitude of the ironist was always to judge, but never to investigate (CI, 278). The freedom of irony was also manifested in the personal sphere, as freedom from the constraints of the past and of concrete circumstances, which might have been expected to lead to great things in the way of living poetically, but which in practice resulted in the ironist coming to resemble what he most despised, "an altogether commonplace person" (CI, 281). In fact the ironist most frequently ended up as a nonentity. But even then he retained his poetic freedom, and made becoming a nonentity the most noble of all callings. Hence the "Taugenichts" (good-for-nothing) was always the most poetic person in the poetry of the romantic school (CI, 281). The positive side to infinite poetic freedom was that the ironist had normally entertained a great number of possibilities before ending up as nothing at all (CI, 281-82). A wealth of possibilities, however, can make choice difficult, so the ironist would leave that to fate or chance (CI, 282).

For the romantic ironist, actuality has no validity as such. There is no question of his adjusting himself to his environment, rather his environment must be fashioned to suit him. Thus his creative activity does not stop with himself but extends to his environment as well (CI, 283). The effect, however, of his turning his back on reality and living in a world of his own making in the imagination is that his life loses all continuity (CI, 284). As a result the ironist falls completely under the sway of his moods and feelings. His life becomes a sheer succession of moods, often of the most contradictory kinds. Thus he becomes the slave of "world irony" (CI, 284). Even here, however, he remains a poet. Thus even when he is in fact no more than "sport for the whims of world irony" he poeticizes his situation, imagining "that it is he himself who evokes the mood" (CI, 284-85). Thus moods have no reality for the ironist either and he normally expresses them only in the

---

schaft, 1972), though he fails to understand Kierkegaard.

form of their opposites. These opposites, finally, are held together in the negative unity of boredom which is the only continuity the ironist has (CI, 285).

At the root of the ironist's stance Kierkegaard discerns a fundamentally polemical attitude to actuality. This was the attitude being promulgated at the time by the Young Germany school, and he had already attacked it in *From the Papers of One Still Living*. The *Concept of Irony* continues the attack, as Kierkegaard makes explicit in a footnote, in which he explains that he not only has this movement in mind in his treatment of romantic irony but also regards the irony of the Young Germans as continuing the activity begun by Tieck and Schlegel (CI, 275).[21] Here there was no question of an aspect of given actuality being negated to make room for something new, as in the case of Socrates. Instead the whole of historical actuality was being negated to make room for "a self-created actuality" (CI, 275). There was no question of the emergence of subjectivity here either, for subjectivity was already present. Thus Kierkegaard concludes that the subjectivity of the ironist was "an exaggerated subjectivity, a subjectivity raised to the second power" (CI, 275).

The feature that Kierkegaard highlights in his discussion of Friedrich Schlegel, Tieck and Solger is precisely this rejection of historical actuality as a whole and its replacement with a self-created actuality. The essence of his critique is that despite individual differences they each fall short of reality. While they assume the existence and status of ideality, Kierkegaard argues

---

[21]The connection had already been made by Poul Møller in his essay on irony, "Om Begrebet Ironie" ("The Concept of Irony"). See Poul Martin Møller, *Efterladte Skrifter*, 2nd ed. (Copenhagen: C. A. Reitzel, 1848) 3:156. George Pattison has drawn attention to Møller's role here in an article, "Friedrich Schlegel's *Lucinde*: A Case Study of the Relation of Religion to Romanticism," *Scottish Journal of Theology* 38 (1985): 556-57 and in his *Kierkegaard: The Aesthetic and the Religious: From the Magic Theatre to the Crucifixion of the Image* (Basingstoke: Macmillan, 1992) 28. For Møller and Kierkegaard, the common factor underlying both forms of irony is their origin in Fichte. The role played by Fichte for the German romantics has been recently discussed by Michael Allen Gillespie in his *Nihilism Before Nietzsche* (Chicago: University of Chicago Press, 1995) 105-10. Gillespie also underlines the connection between Fichte and Left Hegelianism, which he characterizes as "a concealed reversion to Fichteanism" (*Nihilism* 126).

that they all fail to relate it to actuality; instead their assertion of the ideal, of the imaginary world, is always at the expense of the real one. The given world is rejected not for something higher and more perfect but for an imaginary world of dreams. The most blatant example of this Kierkegaard finds in Friedrich Schlegel's famous novel *Lucinde*,[22] which was first published in 1799 and later became, in Kierkegaard's words, "the gospel of Young Germany and the system for its *Rehabilitation des Fleisches* (rehabilitation of the flesh)" (CI, 286). The background to this remark was the fact that in 1835, when a second edition of *Lucinde* appeared, Karl Gutzkow republished Schleiermacher's defence of the novel, the *Vertraute Briefe über Schlegels Lucinde* (Confidential Letters Concerning Schlegel's *Lucinde*) with an introduction.[23] Gutzkow's interest was indeed in sexual liberation.[24] Kierkegaard is not in any doubt that *Lucinde* is obscene but, in order not to do Schlegel any injustice, he admits that there were certainly grounds for a protest against the attitudes of his age towards love, which had been reduced to something practical, domestic and totally unerotic (CI, 286).[25] His objection is that Schlegel's alternative is an illusion. Schlegel rejects an imperfect reality, but only to replace it with

---

[22]There is an English translation. Friedrich Schlegel, *"Lucinde" and the Fragments*, trans. and ed. Peter Firchow (Minneapolis: University of Minnesota Press, 1971).

[23]Kierkegaard was familiar with Schleiermacher's *Confidential Letters* as is indicated by an important entry of October 1835 (JP, 4:3846) in which he refers approvingly to the way that in that work Schleiermacher constructs personalities to represent different points of view, a technique that he himself was to develop.

[24]Gutzkow's introduction is reprinted by Gisela Dischner, *Friedrich Schlegels "Lucinde" und Materialien zu einer Theorie des Müßiggangs* (Hildesheim: Gerstenberg Verlag, 1980) 161-67. Dischner argues with justification that Gutzkow's approach to *Lucinde* was a serious misunderstanding of Schlegel's intention (*Friedrich Schlegels "Lucinde"* 147).

[25]There is more, however, to the subject of Kierkegaard and *Lucinde* than this evaluation implies. Both F. J. Billeskov Jansen in his *Studier i Søren Kierkegaards litterære Kunst* (Copenhagen: Rosenkilde & Bagger, 1951) 23-24 and Carl Roos in his *Kierkegaard og Goethe* (Copenhagen: G.E.C. Gads Forlag, 1955) 18 consider Schlegel's novel to have been one of the influences on Kierkegaard's own literary technique.

something that is not a reality at all.[26] Since, in Kierkegaard's view, Schlegel attacks the very principle of sexual morality, which is "the validity of spirit, the mastery of the spirit over the flesh" (CI, 290), the only reality he is left with is sensual reality (CI, 291), by which is meant the exclusion of the spirit. Kierkegaard, however, sees the denial of the claims of the spirit in the realm of the senses as removing the possibility of a synthesis in which both parts receive their due, which was what Schlegel actually wanted to achieve. The assertion of the subject's sovereign freedom thus paradoxically results in its enslavement "under the laws of the flesh and of drives" (CI, 301). Since, however, this sensuality is not naive but the product of an arbitrary freedom, it can at any moment give way to "an abstract and exaggerated spirituality." Thus the individual remains in the grip of "world irony" (CI, 301).

In Tieck too, whose satirical plays and lyric poetry he discusses, Kierkegaard finds the same underlying problem. Thus while readily acknowledging the value of Romanticism in an age in which "people seemed to be totally fossilized in finite social forms" (CI, 303) and the world needed desperately to be rejuvenated (CI, 304), he diagnoses as its fundamental shortcoming its failure to grasp actuality (CI, 304). The new world it discovered could only be experienced in dreams and the task of art became to conjure up this dream world, which could then be opposed to the drabness of reality. Instead of transforming a calcified reality, Romanticism merely escaped from it. According to Kierkegaard, all romantic literature moves between these two poles. On the one hand there is "the given actuality with all its paltry philistinism" and, on the other, "the ideal actuality with its dimly emerging shapes" (CI, 304-305). He sees this dichotomy of ideal and actuality as false. "In no way," he writes, "is the true ideal in the beyond—it is behind insofar as it is the propelling force; it is ahead insofar as it is the inspiring goal, but at the same time it is within us, and this is its

---

[26]That this criticism is not without foundation is shown among other things by the fact that even Schleiermacher has problems with the way that Schlegel's poetic ideals actually relate to reality. See on this issue Hans Dierkes, "Friedrich Schlegels *Lucinde*, Schleiermacher und Kierkegaard," *Deutsche Vierteljahrsschrift für Literaturwissenschaft und Geistesgeschichte* 57 (1983): 431-49, and George Pattison, "Friedrich Schlegel's *Lucinde*," 545-64.

truth" (CI, 305). According to Kierkegaard, who is here taking up one of the themes of *From the Papers of One Still Living*, the failure of the romantics to relate the ideal to reality in their literary creations robs these of genuine aesthetic value. "The very fact," he asserts, "that this poetry moves between two opposites shows that in the deeper sense it is not true poetry" (CI, 305). The standpoint of the romantic poet is "poetic arbitrariness" (CI, 305). For him the essence of the poetic consists in "the freedom in which he has everything at his disposal" (CI, 306). This freedom, however, is at the expense of the aesthetic totality. The individual elements remain separate and as a result poetic unity is impossible (CI, 306).

Kierkegaard finds the same inability to attain actuality in Solger, who treats irony philosophically. Solger's aim is "to bring about the absolute identity of the finite and the infinite" (CI, 311). But his problem, according to Kierkegaard, is that he is unable to make either concrete. Because he denies validity to the finite, which he regards as nothingness (*das Nichtige*), he finds he cannot make the infinite concrete either (CI, 312). Solger remains negative; he has the negation of the negation but cannot get from this to a positive affirmation. He thus, in Kierkegaard's view, falls victim to Hegel's positive system (CI, 323).

Controlled Irony

Irony and the Regaining of Reality

Solger provides the bridge to the final section of the dissertation, and gives Kierkegaard a neat way of signalling his divergence from Hegel on the fundamental issue. Both Kierkegaard and Hegel saw the subjectivity of the romantics as false, and both sought a remedy for it. But while for Hegel this was provided in the objectivity of the system, in which subjectivity was left behind,[27] for Kierkegaard the remedy lay rather in a deepening of the very subjectivity in question. Having established that reality was lost in romantic irony, Kierkegaard's task is now to show how it is regained in controlled irony, so that, in contrast to Hegel, for him

---

[27]On Hegel's critique of romanticism see Otto Pöggeler, *Hegels Kritik der Romantik* (Bonn: Rheinische Friedrich Wilhelms-Universität, 1956).

irony itself becomes the way to "objectivity." Here again he can point to Solger (CI, 324). For in Solger's *Lectures on Aesthetics* one of the roles of irony is to free the artist from subjective bias or personal interest, and enable him to achieve a state of "indifference" (*Gleichgültigkeit*), understood in the sense of disinterestedness, or "objectivity," as he also calls this condition.[28] Significantly, it is thus from the aesthetics of the German romantics that Kierkegaard takes the model he will use to establish the relationship between irony and objectivity understood in this sense.[29]

As an example of the relationship in action Kierkegaard chooses Shakespeare, who is justly praised, as he notes, as "the grand master of irony" (CI, 324). Yet when Shakespeare relates himself ironically to his creation, "it is precisely in order to let the objective dominate" (CI, 324). Kierkegaard identifies two ways in which irony can bring about this effect. Within the work it enables the right balance to be achieved between the disparate elements and here, as Kierkegaard notes, the greater the contrasts involved,

---

[28]See K. W. F. Solger, *Vorlesungen über Aesthetik*, ed. K. W. L. Heyse (Leipzig: F. A. Brockhaus, 1829) 199, 214.

[29]The positive value of the German romantics for Kierkegaard has been recognized by Billeskov Jansen (*Søren Kierkegaards litterære Kunst* 23-24) and Pierre Mesnard, who stresses how his conception of irony builds on their foundations (*Le Vrai Visage de Kierkegaard* 170-79). On Kierkegaard and romantic irony, see also R. L. Perkins, "Hegel and Kierkegaard." That irony could be a means for attaining "objectivity" in the literary work was, of course, one of the original ideas of Friedrich Schlegel and is expressed in his review of Goethe's *Wilhelm Meister*. A translation of this can be found in Kathleen M. Wheeler, ed., *German Aesthetic and Literary Criticism: The Romantic Ironists and Goethe* (Cambridge: Cambridge University Press, 1984) 59-73. For the German text see Friedrich Schlegel, *Kritische Ausgabe*, ed. Ernst Behler (Munich, Paderborn, Vienna: Ferdinand Schöningh; Zurich: Thomas-Verlag, 1967) 2:126-46. Kierkegaard was certainly acquainted with Schlegel: in the *Papers* from 1836-1837 there are a number of references to Schlegel's complete works in ten volumes, published in Vienna between 1822 and 1825, which we know from the auction catalogue of his library that Kierkegaard owned. Niels Thulstrup ed., *Katalog over Søren Kierkegaards Bibliotek* (Copenhagen: Munksgaard, 1957) nos. 1816-25. Carl Koch regards it as beyond doubt that Kierkegaard had read Schlegel's *Über das Studium der griechischen Poesie* (On the Study of Greek Poetry) of 1795-1797. Carl Henrik Koch, *Kierkegaard og "Det interessante"* (Copenhagen: C. A. Reitzels Forlag, 1992) 35-36. It seems natural to assume that he would also have been familiar at first hand with Schlegel's other critical works and fragments.

the greater the need there is for irony to master them (CI, 324).[30] But irony also needs to be present in the relation between the artistic work and its creator, where its task is to set the poet free from his creation, letting him float above it in Kierkegaard's image (CI, 324),[31] for the danger here is that he will become attached to it. This is the failing exhibited by the romanticist, according to Kierkegaard, for whom "the individual poetic work is either a darling favorite . . . or . . . an object that arouses his disgust" (CI, 325). For Kierkegaard, a glaring example of this fault was furnished by Hans Christian Andersen, whose activity as a novelist he had subjected to a scathing critique in *From the Papers of One Still Living*. It was Andersen's improper attachment to the characters and ideas in his novels that Kierkegaard identified there as his major weakness. Andersen provides a negative demonstration of the connection between freedom and objectivity, for the freedom aspired to here is a freedom from subjective bias. The task of the literary artist, according to Kierkegaard, is to achieve in his creation a presentation of the particular subject matter that is free of any traces of the author's "subjectivity" in the form of personal opinions and predilections that have no place in the economy of the work he is creating.[32] In *From the Papers of One Still Living* he refers to this in-

---

[30]According to Lee Capel the chief source for this imagery of contradictions as spirits to be mastered is Goethe's *Wilhelm Meister's Apprenticeship*, bk. 3, chap. 9; bk. 4, chap. 19; and bk. 5, chaps. 1 and 2 (Søren Kierkegaard, *The Concept of Irony* 425).

[31]This image calls to mind Friedrich Schlegel, for whom, in the *Lyceum Fragments*, it is a basic feature of irony that through it the artist rises above himself and his work, thereby exhibiting the freedom of self-limitation (Helmut Prang, *Die romantische Ironie* 11). Examples are fragment 108, where it is said of irony that by its means "one transcends oneself"; fragment 42, where the ironic mood "rises infinitely above all limitations"; and, above all, fragment 87, where it is stated that there are artists "who aren't free enough to raise themselves above their own greatest effort" (Friedrich Schlegel, *"Lucinde" and the Fragments*, 156, 148, 153). A further example of this stance is Schlegel's *Athenaeum* fragment 116, in which he says of romantic poetry, which he identifies with irony, that it can "hover at the midpoint between the portrayed and the portrayer, free of all real and ideal self-interest, on the wings of poetic reflection" (Friedrich Schlegel, *"Lucinde" and the Fragments*, 175).

[32]Cf. Friedrich Schlegel's *Lyceum* fragment 37: "In order to write well about something, one shouldn't be interested in it any longer. To express an idea with

appropriate material as "a residue . . . of the author's finite character, which . . . joins in the conversation at unseemly places" (FPOSL, 82).

For Kierkegaard the supreme example of a poet who had succeeded in using irony to set both his work and himself free was Goethe.[33] To be able to do this, however, as he points out, "the poet himself must be master over the irony" (CI, 324). (And he cautions that the fact that the poet may be the master of irony at the time he is writing does not necessarily mean he has succeeded in mastering it in his own life.) The greatness of Goethe for Kierkegaard consisted in the fact that "he was able to make his poet-life congruous with his actuality" (CI, 325).[34] In Goethe, Kierkegaard writes, irony was "in the strictest sense a controlled element." "On the one hand," he goes on, "the individual poem rounds itself off in itself by means of the irony in it; on the other hand, the individual poetic work emerges as an element, and thereby the whole poet-existence rounds itself off by means of irony" (CI, 325).

These considerations on literary creation have a wider significance, since for Kierkegaard the relation that the literary artist has to adopt towards his production is the model for the relation that we are all called upon to adopt to our lives. This is the basis for his declaration that it is not just the poet, but all of us who are called, as he puts it, to live poetically (CI, 325-26).[35] We may not all have literary talents, but for Kierkegaard this is not the essential

---

due circumspection, one must have relegated it wholly to one's past; one must no longer be preoccupied with it . . . " (Friedrich Schlegel, "Lucinde" and the Fragments, 146-47).

[33]Here again Kierkegaard is echoing Friedrich Schlegel. For the feature that Schlegel singled out for especial praise in his review of Goethe's Wilhelm Meister's Apprenticeship was "the irony which hovers over the entire work" (Kathleen M. Wheeler ed., German Aesthetic and Literary Criticism, 67).

[34]Despite this claim, Kierkegaard's view of Goethe even at this stage was by no means uncritical. He had already criticised Faust, and his view of Goethe as a whole was to become increasingly hostile. See on Kierkegaard's relationship with Goethe, Carl Roos, Kierkegaard og Goethe.

[35]Sylvia Walsh has stressed the importance of this notion in Kierkegaard's early work. Sylvia Walsh, Living Poetically: Kierkegaard's Existential Aesthetics (University Park: Pennsylvania State University Press, 1994) 44.

thing. As Walsh explains, "it is not the fashioning of a work of art as such but a particular way of orienting ourselves to life that constitutes the essential condition for living poetically."[36] In Kierkegaard's words: "[T]he poet does not live poetically by creating a poetic work . . . he lives poetically only when he himself . . . is positively free in the actuality to which he belongs." And for Kierkegaard, "anyone can live poetically in this way" (CI, 326).

What such a life requires, however, as the poet shows, is irony, for irony makes for "objectivity" in the sense of an undistorted appraisal of actuality. Goethe's *Wilhelm Meister's Apprenticeship*, to which reference has already been made, provides a perfect example of this in the way irony helps Wilhelm to find his true self.[37] Wilhelm is given the space to make and learn from the mistakes that are unavoidable in the process of developing to selfhood, as Goethe understood it. As Michael Beddow writes, in the conception of selfhood with which Goethe was working, aspects of which are also echoed in *The Concept of Irony*, as we shall see, a person's development depends on his successfully distinguishing "what is necessary and what is contingent for him as a particular individual in his specific historical, social and cultural circum-

---

[36]Walsh, *Living Poetically*, 60.

[37]Kierkegaard acquired a complete edition of Goethe's works in February 1836, and began at once on *Wilhelm Meister*, which he finished in March, reading the *Apprenticeship* and the much later *Years of Travel*, which are effectively two novels about the same person, one after the other (F. J. Billeskov Jansen, *Søren Kierkegaards litterære Kunst*, 22). The impression it made on him is attested by a journal entry of March 1836, in which he praises "the capacious governance which pervades the whole work, the entire Fichtean moral world-order . . . which is inherent in the whole book and gradually leads Wilhelm to the point theoretically postulated, if I may put it that way, so that by the end of the novel the view of the world the poet has advanced, but which previously existed outside of Wilhelm, now is embodied and living within him, and this explains the consummate impression of wholeness that this novel conveys perhaps more than any other. Actually, it is the whole world apprehended in a mirror, in a true microcosm" (JP, 2:1455). Billeskov Jansen points to the importance of *Wilhelm Meister* as a model for Kierkegaard's own literary activity (*Søren Kierkegaards litterære Kunst* 22-23). See also on Kierkegaard's reading of *Wilhelm Meister*, Carl Roos, *Kierkegaard og Goethe* 18-26.

stances."[38] In practice this is not always easy to do, as is illustrated by Wilhelm's conversation with the Stranger about destiny and chance early on in the novel,[39] when Wilhelm is convinced that he has found his destiny in the theatre but the stranger warns him not to confuse the hand of destiny with the direction his aspirations have taken so far.[40] This is where irony comes in. In the novel, as Beddow explains, "[t]he narrative's elucidating irony is deployed to explore the problems of a self which has not yet accomplished that distinction between the necessary and the contingent . . . which is in the arduous process of establishing by trial and error its own true priorities and a feasible mode of realising them in the available world."[41] This is the task that confronts us all according to this conception of the self. Readers of the novel are challenged to become aware of and cultivate that attitude of irony in their own lives in order to be able to abandon illusory notions of themselves, and illusory goals, as Wilhelm has to do. This is all part of the business of becoming a self.

For Kierkegaard, as for Goethe, it is axiomatic that we have to make our lives in the particular historical circumstances in which we are placed, and which we therefore have to understand and respect.[42] For the subject, as Kierkegaard puts it, historical actuality

---

[38]Michael Beddow, *The Fiction of Humanity: Studies in the Bildungsroman from Wieland to Thomas Mann* (Cambridge: Cambridge University Press, 1982) 83.

[39]Johann Wolfgang von Goethe *Wilhelm Meister's Apprenticeship*, ed. and trans. Eric A. Blackall (Princeton NJ: Princeton University Press, 1994) 38. Roos notes that although this passage, where it is stated that the texture of this world is made up of necessity and chance, is not referred to by Kierkegaard in his notes on *Wilhelm Meister*, it nevertheless finds an echo in *The Concept of Anxiety* (CA, 96-97) when fate is defined as "the unity of necessity and the accidental" (Roos, *Kierkegaard og Goethe* 21).

[40]Beddow, *The Fiction of Humanity*, 81.

[41]Beddow, *The Fiction of Humanity*, 91.

[42]This could be seen as the moral of *Wilhelm Meister*, particularly if the *Apprenticeship* and the *Years of Travel* are read in succession, as tended to be done at the time in Denmark, where the work enjoyed a wave of popularity in the 1840s. It was its ethical aspect in particular that appealed to the Danes, the way Wilhelm gives up the ideal of all-round development and commits himself to specialization in order to become a useful member of society as a surgeon. See F. J. Billeskov Jansen, *Danmarks Digtekunst* (Copenhagen: Ejnar Munksgaard, 1958) 3:299-300.

is both "a gift that refuses to be rejected," and "a task that wants
to be fulfilled" (CI, 276). In order to carry out this task, the individual must "feel himself integrated in a larger context, must feel
the earnestness of responsibility, must feel and respect every
reasonable consequence" (CI, 279). We are not free to ignore this
context and make a completely new start which, as we saw,
Kierkegaard accused the romantic ironists of attempting to do (CI,
279). We have to accept our specific reality as "gift" and work
within it. This reality sets the limits within which we are free. For
the poet, who in this respect, as we have seen, is the pattern for us
all, being "positively free in the actuality to which he belongs"
requires that he be "oriented and thus integrated in the age in
which he lives" (CI, 326). This is why he has to have "a totality-
view of the world" and thus "to be a philosopher to a certain
degree" (CI, 325). The reason this is so important for the poet is
not just that it is the way by which he can free himself from the
wrong kind of subjectivity. It is also a response to the situation of
modernity, which Kierkegaard acknowledges, in which the poet
has to operate in a fragmented world, with no underlying unified
worldview which he can simply take over. He is compelled rather
to develop his own view, to discover for himself the possibilities
and limits of his historical context. The danger here is always to
allow the uncontrolled imagination to take us beyond the limits of
the real, so that we end up living in a world of fantasy rather than
imaginatively responding to the challenges of reality, the failing
which Kierkegaard saw in the romantic ironists. Once it is
mastered, however, irony has the exactly opposite effect. Instead
of alienating the subject from his reality in dreams, it now "limits,
finitizes, and circumscribes and thereby yields truth, actuality, content; it disciplines and punishes and thereby yields balance and
consistency" (CI, 326).

Irony in this sense thus plays an essential role in the accomplishment of the human task, as Kierkegaard conceives it. It is the
condition for correctly appraising the dimension of givenness in
our situations, and for discerning the shape of the personal task
that each of us has to accept. For Christians this task has an added
dimension of seriousness since, knowing that they have reality for
God, they are responsible for trying to develop "the seeds God
himself has placed in man" (CI, 280). In this context the perspec-

tive of irony, by detaching us from any identification with the immediate, gives us a position from which to discover which of our inclinations indicate talents to be developed and which point to illusions that will prove destructive. In this way irony enables us to see our situations, our actuality, as possibility, rather than as a constriction, from which we can only seek to escape in fantasy. Irony thus enables us to live creatively in our finite circumstances, avoiding the twin dangers of on the one hand becoming overcome by the weight of reality, and on the other, getting lost in possibility, whether this is the fantasies of the romantics or the delusions of abstract thought. In thus freeing us to take responsibility for our lives, irony is the condition of our becoming selves. Without it, we are either limited to the roles society ordains for us, or condemned to live in dreams.

Irony and the Emergence of the Self

These two dangers of on the one hand getting trapped in the circumstantial and on the other getting lost in possibility anticipate the forms of despair described in *The Sickness unto Death* as necessity's despair and possibility's despair (SUD, 35-42). The conception underlying the analysis there of a self that is both situated in a specific historical reality and at the same time free in the attitude that it can take up to that reality is already present in *The Concept of Irony*. In *The Sickness unto Death* the self is defined as a relation that relates to itself (SUD, 13),[43] that is to say it is not simply a relationship between two terms, but a relating to that relationship, which means that there are three elements involved. Now it is precisely this threefold relationship that emerges in the transition from romantic irony to controlled irony.[44] For what happens in this transition is that the ironic subject itself becomes the object of irony, and with that the self emerges. The process is

---

[43]This translation, without the reflexive pronoun, is to be preferred to Hong's rendering of the Danish phrase as "a relation that relates itself to itself," which is potentially misleading. See Arnold B. Come, *Kierkegaard as Humanist* (Montreal: McGill-Queen's University Press, 1995) 8-9.

[44]Robert L. Perkins has recognized that Kierkegaard's characteristic conception of the person comes into being when irony is brought under control (Perkins, "Hegel and Kierkegaard," 250).

described as follows in a Journal entry of 1837: "[I]rony is first sur-
mounted when the individual, elevated above everything and
looking down from this position, is finally elevated beyond himself
and from this dizzy height sees himself in his nothingness. . . . The
ironical position is essentially: *nil admirari*; but irony, when it slays
itself, has *disdained* everything with humor, itself included" (JP,
2:1688).

In romantic irony, as Kierkegaard sees it, the relation is between two: a subject confronts a world "out there," as its object,
and finds it wanting. As he says, romantic irony is essentially
critical (CI, 276), and its critical stance is directed not at any particular aspect of actuality, but at actuality as a whole (CI, 276). This
position is ahistorical (CI, 279), and acosmic. It results in the loss
of the world. In controlled irony, in contrast, the subject is no
longer at the centre but gives way to the self, which is first and
foremost conscious of being in a world. The perspective is now
totally different: it is no longer a question of rejecting the real
world because it falls short of the ideal, but rather of working to
express the ideal in the circumstances of actuality, for it is in the
awareness of its situatedness that the self has to choose its possibilities and make its life. There is no longer a subject confronting
a world "out there," but a self, relating to itself and to other selves
in a world of which it is a part.[45] Thus it may be said that the
point at which irony is extended to include the subject, which
thereby loses its absoluteness and becomes a term in a relationship,
marks for Kierkegaard the emergence of the self as a self in
relation.

The implications of this are far-ranging. The ahistorical,
acosmic and withdrawing stance of the subject of romantic irony
can now give way to a movement to embrace concrete reality with
all its imperfections. The transition in question is frequently characterized as the movement from irony to humor, as indeed Kierkegaard himself refers to it in the journal entry quoted. In *The
Concept of Irony*, however, humor signifies a movement into
religious categories, as intimated in the final paragraph (CI, 329).

---

[45]Here Kierkegaard points ahead to the theme of the self-in-the-world of
Heidegger and other modern thinkers.

Although their aims are similar, the contrast with Hegel is fundamental. For Hegel the movement is from the individual (the subject of irony) to the universal; for Kierkegaard it is from the individual to the self in relation. For Hegel the supreme goal, in which irony is overcome, is the speculative understanding of reality in a philosophical system; for Kierkegaard it is authentically personal existence.

This means for Kierkegaard becoming a self. But the self is a relation, and it can only come into being when people are no longer immediately identified with particular attributes and roles, but able to relate to their situations in freedom. The condition that makes this possible is irony. This is why Kierkegaard can say that irony is the very condition, the absolute beginning, of personal life (CI, 326).

Irony and Intersubjectivity

Once existence as a self is established as the goal, however, irony does not fade into the background. Rather it takes on a new role, for authentic selfhood is a reality that has to be lived up to, and there is an ever present danger of falling back, a danger which the philosopher of personal existence in particular needs to be alive to. The task of irony is now to set people free from illusions, pretensions, fixed ideas and unconscious motivations, all of which it exposes. (The work envisaged for irony here is not entirely unlike the role assigned to the comic by George Meredith in his *Essay on Comedy* and his novels, and by Henri Bergson in his study of *Laughter*.) In this way irony is an instrument for bringing about self-knowledge, that transparency to ourselves and others, that becomes so important in Kierkegaard's subsequent work; the role it plays is thus an ethical one.[46]

---

[46]An ethical role is of course attributed to irony in the *Concluding Unscientific Postscript* (CUP, 1:502). As Perkins explains, "The ethical ironist arises when the particularities and commonplaces of finite existence are experienced under the ethical understood as universal and as a task." Robert L. Perkins, "Abraham's Silence Aesthetically Considered" in George Pattison ed., *Kierkegaard on Art and Communication* (Basingstoke: The Macmillan Press Ltd, 1992) 110-11. This condition is already present, at least in potential, in controlled irony.

This means that it will always have work to do. There will never be a point at which we can safely say that irony is no longer needed. It will always be there, ready to spring into action. Obviously if the fact that it was controlled meant that irony was mastered in any final sense it would be powerless to play its ethical role. In this respect there is an essential similarity between controlled irony and conscience.[47] Like conscience, "controlled" irony has to remain a force that we cannot dominate if it is to fulfil its role of challenging and chastening. It cannot therefore lose its edge as irony; it is just that its barbs are now seen to be necessary. And the way these barbs will come, most of the time, will be through other people. Thus controlled irony actively acknowledges our need for others. It presupposes a community. This point is worth stressing.[48] We have already seen how controlled irony, for Kierkegaard, "limits, finitizes, and circumscribes," and how it also "disciplines and punishes" (CI, 326). All these actions, however, require the involvement of other people for their accomplishment: individuals cannot realistically do them for themselves on the basis of simple self-reflection. Controlled irony is thus necessarily intersubjective.

In this respect the contrast with polemical irony, which is an essentially solitary activity, could not be greater. In this latter the ironist relishes his triumph in private, for "the source of his joy is that no one realizes his deception" (CI, 249). From this point of

---

[47]The connection between irony and conscience has been made by Gary Handwerk, who points out that in Schlegel's Cologne Lectures of 1804–1806, which represent a movement away from the position of the *Athenaeum*, the functions of irony are in fact taken over by conscience. For Handwerk this serves to underline the ethical potential of irony. See Gary J. Handwerk, *Irony and Ethics in Narrative: From Schlegel to Lacan* (New Haven and London: Yale University Press, 1985) 40-42.

[48]The intersubjective aspect of irony is the feature that Handwerk identifies as basic to ethical irony (Handwerk, *Irony and Ethics* 2-16). Handwerk is prevented by his limited view of Kierkegaard's irony, which he sees as remaining at the level of the self-enclosed individual (*Irony and Ethics* 8-10), from recognizing the connection, but in fact what he says about ethical irony also applies to Kierkegaard's controlled irony. It is fundamental to Handwerk's conception of ethical irony that the subject is not sufficient to itself, but needs others to achieve its identity.

view, as Agacinski comments,[49] the production of a wholly serious, fully objective account of irony could be the ultimate masterstroke of a brilliant ironist. That, however, was not what Kierkegaard was doing in *The Concept of Irony*, where the aim is rather to awaken people out of illusions, for which purpose the irony has to become visible. It is certainly true that by choosing the medium of an academic dissertation as the means to do this Kierkegaard was totally subverting the academic genre.[50] But perhaps that was not entirely inappropriate, for the academic dissertation is a main form for the advancement of positive knowledge, and therefore to subvert that form in a work which seeks to call into question the whole enterprise of "objectivity," when applied to personal life, is not inconsistent and serves indeed to bring form into harmony with content.

Since the role of irony is to maintain the freedom of the self, the need for it is continuing, as we have seen. It follows that controlled irony is necessarily open-ended. This also applies in the case of the poet who, in Kierkegaard's example, uses controlled irony to relate his works to his individual life, for as long as he is creating there can be no stage at which a definitive, unrevisable view of his life and production is possible. Each new work will alter the sense of the whole and call for a new perspective, and as he strives to respond to a constantly changing external situation, the poet will be involved in an ongoing dialogue. Thus he shares the common fate: for it is the case for all of us that the final meaning of our lives is always beyond us. The poet, though, is denied finality even in death, for if his work is sufficiently significant, it will constantly be interpreted anew.

Acceptance of the open-endedness of irony, and abandonment of the standpoint of a final, imposed perspective is, of course, an implication of the Socratic enterprise, as it has been presented in *The Concept of Irony*. For Socrates's role is to awaken his interlocutors out of their illusions and set them free, but the response that

---

[49] Agacinski, *Aparté*, 72.

[50] Agacinski points to the contradiction between irony and the idea of an academic thesis (Agacinski, *Aparté*, 35). Poole has taken this further, stressing that *The Concept of Irony* is primarily a piece of *writing* rather than a dissertation in any conventional sense (Poole, *Kierkegaard*, 48).

they make to their new situation is not in his control. That may have been of no concern to the Socrates of the dissertation, who remains content in his self sufficiency, but for the writer who would awaken his readers to a consciousnes of their freedom, it is the fate that he has to accept, as Kierkegaard was well aware.

In this respect, of course, Kierkegaard's controlled irony is a very long way from the Hegelian system. But it is equally far from the nihilistic irony he attacked in the romantics. As to romantic irony, however, we noted that there was more to the picture than is apparent from Kierkegaard's critique. Not only can it not be justly dismissed as subjectivism, but there is even a significant resemblance between irony as it was actually practiced by some of the romantics and Kierkegaard's controlled irony. What must always be emphasized, however, is that for Kierkegaard the subject is never infinite in itself. The self has an infinite dimension, which it is the task of irony to disclose, but this is actualized not by withdrawing from or rejecting the finite but by engaging creatively with it. And the effect of the presence of the religious in *The Concept of Irony* is precisely to accentuate the importance of the actual concrete circumstances in which the self must make its life. Here above all, in the turn to the finite (and critique of the infinitizing subject) Kierkegaard's concept of controlled irony has much to contribute to the contemporary debate.[51]

---

[51]That Kierkegaard provides material for a critique of aspects of postmodernism has been shown, for example, by Sylvia Walsh and Anthony Rudd. See Sylvia Walsh, *Living Poetically*, 243-51, and Anthony Rudd, "Kierkegaard's Critique of Pure Irony," in George Pattison and Steven Shakespeare eds., *Kierkegaard: The Self in Society* (Basingstoke: Macmillan Press, 1998) 82-96.

10

The Irony of Irony

Ronald L. Hall

I (and many others) read *The Concept of Irony* as portending Kierkegaard's philosophical, or if you will his ethical or religious (or personal?) agenda.[1] What seems to drive this first work, and what continues to drive its descendents—or better, what seems to drive Kierkegaard throughout his authorship, not to mention his life—is his passionate quest to articulate (however indirectly) and to live in accord with (however covertly) the Christian call to human beings to exist in that modality of existence he calls faith. As Kierkegaard saw it, existing in faith, if nothing else, is a decisive and radical alternative to the myriad modalities of existence he identifies with despair.

As I understand it, a modality of existence is the reflexive subjective relation that a human being can take up toward what Kierkegaard sometimes calls "the given actuality," or "the historical actuality" and sometimes simply "the world," (that is, finitude). Taking my cue from Kierkegaard, I shall refer to such a subjective relation to finitude as *an existential standpoint*. Faith is such a standpoint, despair (in its many forms) another. To exist in the existential standpoint of faith is to be transparently grounded

---

[1] On this point, I am in agreement with the Hongs, who say: "Existence as actuality, combines two opposing factors, possibility and necessity, and thereby has a paradoxical character. This view is embodied in all of his subsequent writings" (CI, xvi). "Similarly, the ramifications of other themes in *Irony*—immediacy, reflection, selfhood, subjectivity, objectivity, the esthetic, the ethical, the religious, *and the transcendence of the human*, individual and universal—are developed variously in the pseudonymous and the signed works. Thus the dissertation, although a work undertaken by Kierkegaard to some degree under external compulsion, was the seedbed of the entire authorship" (CI, xviii). Italics added.

in the (infinite) power that established (constituted) us as (finite) creatures in the world.[2] The existential standpoint of despair is of two general kinds, despair of the infinite (due to a lack of the finite), and despair of the finite (due to a lack of the infinite).[3]

In *The Concept of Irony*, Kierkegaard focuses on the existential standpoint of irony. Kierkegaard's claim is that this standpoint is utterly and absolutely negative. As such, irony as a standpoint—like all forms of despair—contrasts to faith as a standpoint insofar as faith is positive. Or as I might put this, in faith one is positively free in relation to the finite world, as opposed to despair, wherein one is either not free at all (despair of the finite due to a lack of the infinite) or only negatively free (in irony for example) in relation to the finite world (despair of the infinite due to a lack of the finite). This contrast, however, between irony and faith, or more generally between despair and faith, is radically dialectical. As such it is a tricky business to articulate clearly the nature of the relation, much less to live existentially in accord with the substance of the distinction it marks.

It is easy to see how the standpoint of irony can feed despair, since it, like despair generally, is an essentially negative existential standpoint. Again, for Kierkegaard, faith is an essentially positive existential standpoint. But as I interpret him, Kierkegaard also thinks that irony can feed, indeed must feed, faith. As Kierkegaard

---

[2]SUD, 14. In this classic definition of faith, I think of the idea of "being transparently grounded" as a kind of participation in the divine power of positive freedom. This freedom is at the very basis of the creation (the power that constituted us) and hence at the very basis of the doctrine of *imago dei*. God, the absolute infinite other, is spirit (self, subject, free agent) and, being made in this divine image, we too share something of the infinity of spirit, something most obviously seen in the human exercise of positive free action. Sharing in the power that constituted us (the power of creative positive free agency), our standpoint toward the world (finitude), is analogous to God's, with all the blessings and curses such an existential standpoint entails.

[3]SUD, 33ff. Here I am reading possibility and necessity's despair as simply a variation on finitude and infinitude's despair. For Kierkegaard, the self (in faith) is a synthesis of opposites; in despair, the opposite of faith, the synthesis collapses in one direction or the other of these opposites.

puts it, irony can be a healthiness or a sickness.[4] But how can it be
both? Well, only dialectically. The existential standpoint of irony,
like despair in general, is a sickness insofar as it is outside of faith.
Ironically, however, this sickness can be "a godsend" (SUD, 26) if
one becomes conscious of it as a sickness and wants to get cured.
We might call this a "healthy sickness"—a kind of raging fever
that dispels the germs that might just kill us. But if one is not conscious of his or her sickness, or does not want to be cured of it, or
even delights in its pain and suffering, or is hopeless of a cure,
then this sickness is merely a sickness, indeed a sickness unto
death.

In this dialectical light, it is easier to see how Kierkegaard can
both positively evaluate the standpoint of irony, as in Socratic
irony, and negatively evaluate it, as in the standpoint of Romantic
irony. The standpoint of Socratic irony is positively evaluated (that
is, justified, valid, healthy?) because it serves the existential standpoint of faith; the standpoint of Romantic irony is negatively
evaluated (that is, unjustified, invalid, a sickness?) because it serves
only despair.

Beyond this, however, there is another dialectical twist in these
matters. As Kierkegaard understands it, the existential standpoint
of faith must completely leave behind the standpoints of Socratic
and Romantic irony, despite the fact that the former served to
open to the door to faith by closing the door to its obstacles. Yet
the standpoint of faith does not leave irony behind altogether. As
I interpret him, Kierkegaard thinks that irony in some form can
(and indeed must) play an ongoing role *within* the existential
standpoint of faith. I think of this as the irony of irony—call this
the dialectical play of the negative element within the positive
standpoint of faith.

In a nutshell, I read Kierkegaard to be making the following
twofold claim: (1) the positive existential standpoint of faith must
exclude the negative standpoint of irony, despite the fact that this
negative standpoint may serve faith well, as in the case of Socratic
irony, and in accordance with the fact that, in Modernity, it most

---

[4]CI, 77-78. I cannot resist thinking of sickness in terms of despair and of health
in terms of existential faith.

often serves faith ill, as in the case of Romantic irony; and (2) the positive existential standpoint of faith must *include* the dialectical play of irony—the dialectical play of its negative qualification of subjectivity—but only as a *controlled element*.

Kierkegaard's interest in the ironic standpoint informs his subsequent development of the stages—the aesthetic, the ethical, the religious. As I have argued elsewhere,[5] Kierkegaard sees the aesthetic, and some forms of the religious, and even the ethical, as modalities of existence in which freedom is either negative, negated altogether, or at least not vested fully with its positive existential reality and power. These modalities of despair are forms of refusing positive freedom, that is, faith's positive free embrace of our actual existence in the world. *The Concept of Irony*, I claim is the seedbed where Kierkegaard begins to work out his understand-

---

[5]See my book, *The Human Embrace: The Love of Philosophy and the Philosophy of Love: Kierkegaard, Cavell, Nussbaum* (University Park: Pennsylvania State University, 1999). Here I make the controversial claim that even the ethical modality, falling short of faith as it does, is itself a form of failing existentially to embrace the world (finitude, actuality). Hence, and ironically so, the ethical modality, despite its pretensions contrariwise, does not arrive at positive freedom. Take Judge William for example. For the judge, the given actuality was as absolute, as fossilized, as the Greek state was for the Greeks of Socrates' time. In relation to the customs of his time, the judge was not free (positively or negatively); he lacked what we might call the ironic power of repudiation. For him, the idea of a teleological suspension of the ethical, something I associate with the power of repudiation, was unthinkable. As I see it, positive freedom is vested with its full rights when the concrete individual is vested with his or her rights to act. It is impossible, however, to vest the individual with his or her rights to free agency, until that individual's concrete historical embodiment is fully acknowledged and embraced (or existentially chosen). But as I see it, the historical actuality—a necessary condition for the exercise of positive freedom—cannot be embraced unless it can also be repudiated. I can do x freely only if I have the power to do otherwise. This power of repudiation I associate with irony (and humor) as well as with the negative freedom expressed by Socrates and the Romantics. Because the judge (the ethical) lacks this power of repudiation, he is not free to embrace the historical actuality. Rather it is only an absolute for him; and although he does not seem to realize it, it stands over him ready to crush his will, his cherished power of choice. For an absolutely perfect description of the judge's world— although not explicitly intended as such—I invite you, my reader, to take a look at Kierkegaard's priceless description of the world that Romanticism rightly reacted to: CI, 303-304.

ing of the dialectical contrast between these positive and negative existential standpoints.

But again, I ask you, my reader, to keep in mind that Kierkegaard was clearly interested in more than merely sorting out the differences among the various existential standpoints that human beings can bear toward the given actuality. Indeed, it is quite obvious to me that this early interest in irony served his deeper, more passionate interest, namely, his life-long interest in coming to terms with that existential standpoint that best articulates the demands of faith. He was interested in this articulation because he believed with an extraordinary tenacity that the embrace of existential faith—in particular, its positive free embrace of the world—was the absolutely necessary condition of the best possible human life, the only human life that is truly happy. No doubt, his pursuit of happiness was motivated in part by his reaction to the pervasive cultural despair around him—especially as that was manifest in the empty pretensions of the Christianity he encountered in his homeland ("the monstrous illusion"). And no doubt, it was also motivated in part by his agonizing personal fight with the monster of his own despair.

Let me introduce the body of this paper with a cryptic brief. First, I shall argue that Kierkegaard's positive evaluation of the standpoint of Socratic irony is based on Kierkegaard's appreciation of the necessity of the Socratic repudiation of Hellas. What made its destruction necessary was the fact that the Greek cosmos was no place for positive freedom (subjectivity, self, spirit) to emerge since it was thoroughly "psychically determined."[6] To live within the Greek cosmos was to live in the despair of the finite, for the infinite resources (call these the resources of historical consciousness) in which positive freedom is grounded were not available. Socrates' repudiation of the Greek cosmos was therefore a necessary (albeit negative) step to take before historical consciousness could be posited (with the positing of spirit in Christianity). Or as I might put it, Socrates' negative step away from the

---

[6]In these remarks, I am, of course, anticipating Kierkegaard's later characterization of the Greek cosmos as being "psychically qualified," in contrast to the historical actuality introduced by Christianity—a world he characterized as being "pneumatically (spiritually) qualified" ("The Immediate Erotic Stages," EO, 1).

"psychically determined" Greek cosmos—wherein spirit could not be posited *as* spirit, but only as psyche—cleared the way for spirit (self, subjectivity, positive freedom) to be vested with its full reality and power. Socrates did manage to move away from the despair of the finite, but being ignorant of spirit, he moved straight into the despair of the infinite. Yet this second despair was charged, as the first was not, with a consciousness of freedom (albeit a negative freedom, inwardness) that was absent from life in the substantial order of Greek culture. His discovery of this negative freedom—call it the human power of repudiation of, or if you like, the human power to withdraw from the conditions of finitude—constituted an advance in world-historical consciousness, for implicit in this discovery were the seeds of spirit (self, subjectivity, positive freedom). Although Socratic irony was a negative qualification of subjectivity, it nevertheless was a qualification of it, and in this sense a kind of preparation for its positive revelation (in Christ).

Second, I shall argue that Kierkegaard's negative evaluation of the standpoint of Romantic irony is based on his recognition that in this point of view, positive freedom has no place. The Romantics, like Socrates repudiated the finite world, but this repudiation turned out to be the repudiation of the very conditions positive freedom requires for its actualization, that is, historical consciousness. Socrates repudiated the substantial order of the cosmos (the psychical) that was no fit habitat for spirit; the Romantics repudiated the actuality of historical consciousness—that very actuality that spirit (the pneumatic) requires for its life of positive freedom.[7] In

---

[7]I would put the matter as follows: In the (psychically qualified) Greek cosmos the presumption to be free was sin, the sin of Oedipus for example. For the Greek, freedom (self-determination) was chaos, a threat to the metaphysical and moral order. The destruction of this cosmos by Socrates (and along with this the failure of Plato and the Medieval world to rescue and reestablish it) made it possible for the Judeo-Christian world-picture of historical consciousness to be posited. (See my *Word and Spirit: A Kierkegaardian Critique of the Modern Age* (Bloomington: University of Indiana Press, 1993). In this new (pneumatically qualified) world, sin is not the presumption to be free; rather, it is the misuse of freedom, the sin of using freedom unwisely, or the sin of not using it at all. While the Romantics were justified in repudiating these latter sins of their own day, they made the mistake of repudiating the whole of the pneumatically qualified

the end, the Romantics fell into a deeper and certainly darker despair of the infinite than Socrates suffered. Unlike Socrates, the Romantics were not ignorant of historical consciousness, spirit, and positive freedom; they simply rejected them (no doubt because they knew all too well that spirit's lifeblood, positive freedom, is too risky, too fraught with liabilities to be misused or ignored, too burdensome, and so forth). In rejecting positive freedom they were not ready to foreswear freedom, altogether; indeed, intoxicated with the (negative) power of freedom, they took flight from the world.

Finally, I shall show how Kierkegaard's positive evaluation of controlled (mastered) irony is justified. As he understands it, the negative power of irony (its negative qualification of subjectivity) is a necessary element within a healthy life (of faith?) insofar as it enables spirit (self, subjectivity) to take up its (proper) place within the (finite) world.

The Irony of Socratic Irony

Through the oracle at Delphi Socrates was told that he was the wisest man in the whole world. Certainly he must have thought: "What an irony for ignorance to be considered wisdom! How can this be true? If I am the wisest and I know nothing, how could everyone else be less wise?" So he sought to find out if what the oracle had said was true. What he found out was that his fellow Athenians suffered from an ignorance that was indeed more profound than his own. While he knew that he knew nothing, his fellow Athenians not only did not know that they also knew nothing they arrogantly thought they knew quite a lot. Socrates was thus set on his life's mission: he could not rest until he had unmasked every such pretension to know as empty and arrogant. Through dogged questioning Socrates humiliated one would-be

---

actuality, and hence the very condition for positive freedom's actualization. They threw the baby out with the bath water. The Romantics thus represent a perversion of spirit (perhaps a demonic perversion). Even though both the Romantics and Socrates suffered what Kierkegaard would later call a despair of the infinite due to a lack of the finite, there is a (demonic?) darkness in Romantic despair that is not present in Socrates.

knower after another. And can we imagine anyone better at this? No wonder his fellow Athenians wanted to, and did, silence him.

Empowered by, or driven by, or perhaps intoxicated by, this ironic knowledge of his own ignorance, Socrates suffered a kind of divine madness. His relation to the world that his fellow Athenians inhabited was like that of a god. As we might put it, he was not of their world; he was aloof from it; he hovered above it, in the clouds, as Aristophanes would put it. Alienated from their world, he was also alienated from his fellow Athenians.[8] To them, he was a mystery, perhaps a madman; to him, they were all pitiful fools.

Although Kierkegaard characterizes Socrates' ironic existence in terms of his alienation from the world, from the given actuality of Hellas, we must be careful to point out that Socrates' negative relation to this world did not entail, like its subsequent Romantic forms, that he was not interested in it at all. He did in fact have an (infinite) interest in this given actuality, but again, a wholly negative interest. His only interest in the given actuality (that is, that actuality that constituted his world, the world of Greek culture) was in destroying it. In this respect there is a sense in which the ironic standpoint of Socrates does not express a straightforward flight from the world. At the same time, he makes it clear that the world of his culture was not, or was no longer, a fit place for human habitation. In this sense, he had already abandoned it inwardly, and was now on a quest to bring his fellow Athenians to abandon it with him. As Kierkegaard puts it: "Here, then, we see irony in all its divine infinitude, which allows nothing whatever to endure. Like Samson, Socrates grasps the pillars that support knowledge and tumbles everything down into the nothingness of ignorance" (CI, 40).

---

[8]"For [Socrates], the whole given actuality had entirely lost its validity; he had become alien to the actuality of the whole substantial world. This is one side of irony, but on the other hand he used irony as he destroyed Greek culture" (CI, 264). Kierkegaard's phrases vary, but the general picture that emerges is that for him the following synonyms exist: the given actuality is, the world, the established order of Greek culture, the state, its substantial life, its customs, practices, laws, its gods, its family life, etc. To give two examples: "Socrates' [had a] completely negative relation to the established order with [regard to] religion" (CI, 164); "Just as Socrates by way of irony rose above the validity of the substantial life of the state, so also family life had no validity for him" (CI, 183).

Socrates' technique of destruction was found in the question, in the conversation, something that distinguished him from the Sophists. Again, here is what Kierkegaard says: "[Socrates practiced the] art of *asking questions* . . . the art of *conversing*. This is why Socrates so frequently and with such profound irony points out to the Sophists that indeed they do know how to speak but do not know how to converse. [The Sophists did not ask questions, they answered them; they gushed forth with answers!]. . . . [C]onversing forces the one speaking to stick to the subject—that is, when the conversation is not regarded as identical with eccentric antiphonal singing, in which everyone sings his part without regard to the other and there is a resemblance to conversation only because they do not all talk at once. . . . To ask questions denotes in part the individual's relation to the subject, in part the individual's relation to another individual (CI, 34). . . . Socrates' questioning was essentially aimed at the subject—the would-be knower—for the purpose of showing that when all is said and done they knew nothing whatever. . . . [J]ust as Socrates' philosophy began with the presupposition that he knew nothing at all, so it ended with the presupposition that human beings know nothing at all. . . . To ask questions—that is, the abstract relation between the subjective and the objective—ultimately became the primary issue for him" (CI, 37).

Questioning, its conversation of asking and answering, its call for response, and hence responsibility, has the effect of bringing forth a relation of subject to subject and of each and both to the world. Socrates' call to his fellow Athenians to justify what they claimed to know, indeed his mission to expose their pretensions to knowledge as empty, as mere pretensions, had the effect of drawing the subject out into the open. Socrates would not allow his subject of inquiry, which was as much the issue as it was his interlocutor, to be settled by recourse to external justifications. Kierkegaard learned much about this from Hegel. Quoting him, he says: "The standpoint of the Greek mind was determined in its moral aspect as natural morality. Man did not yet have the condition of reflecting into himself, of determining by himself" (CI, 163). And commenting on this Kierkegaard remarks that, "[i]n early Greek culture, the laws had for the individual the venerableness of tradition, as the laws sanctioned by the gods. Corresponding to this tradition were time-honored customs. But while the laws defined the universal, early Greek culture also demanded a decision in particular instances, both in political and private matters. The oracle served this purpose" (CI, 163). Quoting Hegel again he comes to the point: "In essence this element means that the people lacks the power of decision, that the subject is not yet ready to assume this power but can be determined by an other, by something external; and oracles are necessary wherever man does not yet know himself inwardly as being sufficiently free and independent to make a decision solely on his own—and this is a lack of subjective freedom" (CI, 163).

But we must be clear that although Socrates called upon his interlocutor to take responsibility for his or her claims to knowledge, this was something he knew that neither his interlocutor nor he himself could do. This is why he made no claims to know. But he did know something that others did not know, that he knew nothing, and that they did not either. Although he had moved beyond the externality of his fellow Athenians, he had not yet moved to inwardness, to positive subjective freedom. But at least, he had moved beyond his fellow Athenians, for he had arrived at negative freedom.[9] Kierkegaard says: "Instead of the oracle, Socrates now has his daimon. The daimonian in this case now lies in the transition from the oracle's external relation to the individual to the complete inwardness of freedom . . . " (CI, 163-64). And again, quoting Hegel: "The inwardness of the subject knows and decides by itself, but in Socrates this inwardness had a unique form. The daimon is still the unconscious, the external, that decides; yet it is also something subjective. The daimon is not Socrates himself, nor his opinion, nor his conviction, but it is something unconscious; Socrates is impelled. . . . Accordingly, the daimonian stands midway between the externality of oracles and the pure inwardness of mind; it is something inward and yet presented as a separate daimon, as distinct from human will, and

---

[9]As I see it, positive freedom is the power to do this or that, when I could have done otherwise. As such, positive freedom is necessary for action. Action requires both an inward determination and an outward—that is, a worldly—expression. Since Socrates had abandoned the world in negative freedom, he could not act in this positive sense. Instead, he hovered above the world in the clouds.

not as his own prudence and choice" (CI, 164). As Kierkegaard will understand this, Socrates has arrived at subjective freedom, but only in the negative sense of that term. He is free from a determination by externalities, but he is not yet positively free, not yet inwardly self-determined.[10]

But Kierkegaard does not take over wholesale Hegel's interpretation of Socrates. His criticism is important, and sets the stage for Kierkegaard's discussion of Romantic irony. It is Romantic irony that for Kierkegaard embodies irony's sickness, something I will turn to in the next section. For now, seeing Kierkegaard's critique of Hegel allows us to understand how Socrates' irony is different from modern Romantic irony. It also allows us to see the irony of Hegel's contempt for (Romantic) irony,[11] for his critique of Hegel's treatment of Socratic irony shows how close his (Hegel's) view of irony is to the Romantic ironists he detests. Moreover, because Hegel has contempt for irony,[12] he must refuse, as he does, to see Socrates' position as irony.[13] Certainly Hegel was correct to refuse to see Socrates' irony as Romantic. But as Kierkegaard will point out, he was incorrect to refuse to see Socrates' standpoint as essentially ironic. In this refusal, Kierkegaard points out, Hegel missed the truth of Socratic irony, as well as the truth of irony in existential faith. Or as I might also put it, Hegel could only see irony as a sickness, something that made him refuse to see Socrates as ironic; and he could not see it as healthiness, either in Socrates or in any individual. In the end then both Hegel and Kierkegaard have a positive evaluation of Socrates, but for very different reasons. Hegel saw Socrates as positive because he did not see him

---

[10]Another way to put this is to say that Socrates had not yet arrived at himself; or that he had not yet gained his self; or if you will, he had not yet had his existence qualified by spirit. On the other hand, we might say he was in paganism what John the Baptist was to Christ, a voice crying in the wilderness, a voice preparing the way.

[11]"[I]t must be said that by his one-sided attack on the post-Fichtean [Romantic] irony he has overlooked the truth of irony, and by his identifying all irony with this, he has done irony an injustice" (CI, 265).

[12]"Hegel always discusses irony in a very unsympathetic manner; in his eyes irony is anathema" (CI, 265).

[13]"Hegel declares himself against viewing Socrates position as irony" CI, 264-65).

as essentially ironic, and could not, for he had only contempt for irony. Kierkegaard is, ironically, much more dialectical than Hegel on this point. For Kierkegaard, Socrates was essentially ironic, essentially negative, and yet his standpoint of negative freedom cleared the way for positive freedom, and in this respect deserves a positive evaluation.

For Kierkegaard, Socrates is to be praised because he was preparing the ground for positive freedom (the good). But he does not think, as Hegel does, that Socrates arrived at the good. Yet, like Hegel he has high praise for Socrates. But again, unlike Hegel, Kierkegaard's praise is not based on the fact that Socrates arrived at the good, but on the basis of the fact that Socrates made such an arrival possible. Unlike Hegel, who thought of Socrates as laying new foundations for positive freedom, Kierkegaard sees him only as destroying the old foundations (paganism)—foundations that could not support a spiritually qualified positive freedom. So for Kierkegaard, Socrates is in the business of demolition, not in the business, as Hegel thought, of laying new foundations. For Kierkegaard, Socrates was no founder; rather, he was only a destroyer.

Nevertheless, Socrates was not against foundations as such; rather, he was only against the (crumbling) foundations of the Greek actuality. Indeed, his (negative) mission was simply to complete, if not hasten, the demolition of these foundations. Hegel failed to see this absolute negativity in Socrates (this irony?). Rather, he saw Socrates as essentially positive, as the one who was laying new foundations, the one who was making a new beginning. In contrast, Kierkegaard sees irony's negative qualification of subjectivity as definitive of Socrates' existential standpoint. But Kierkegaard is quick to point out that the negativity in Socratic irony is essentially different from the negativity of Romantic irony. Socrates, unlike the Romantics, was not out to destroy every foundation in actuality. Rather, Socrates repudiated only his own given actuality, not actuality in general, which is what the Romantics tried to do.

Now, it is not exactly the case that Hegel did not see the irony of Socrates. It is more accurate to say that his interpretation of Socratic irony emptied it of what is essential to irony, its absolute negativity. Hegel's high praise for Socrates is predicated on his interpretation of Socrates' mission as positive. But this turned

Socratic irony into Platonic irony. And what was Platonic irony? Well it was "a controlled element, a way of associating with people" (CI, 237). "Thus," Kierkegaard concludes, "Hegel's whole examination of Socratic irony ends in such a way that Socratic irony becomes identified with Platonic irony and both ironies become 'more a manner of conversation, sociable pleasantry, and not that pure negation, not the negative attitude . . . ' " (CI, 266). And of course, it is that "negative attitude" of (Romantic) irony that Hegel has such a negative attitude toward. So in order to rescue Socratic irony from the negative and invest his irony with a positive content, Hegel had to disassociate Socrates from (Romantic) irony. He had to make him a teacher who, via ironic techniques of conversation, lured his interlocutors into a position in which his teachings could be received with the positive earnestness with which they were delivered.

To make this case, Hegel is forced to think that Socratic irony is "pretended ignorance." As Kierkegaard puts this, Hegel thinks that "Socrates pretends to be ignorant, and in the role of being taught he teaches others" (CI, 266). According to Hegel, therefore, Socrates is out to teach his fellow Athenians something. In order to do this, however, he must disguise what he knows and pretend to be ignorant. He used this disguise as a lure, a way of drawing people into conversation, perhaps of trapping them. Once ensnared, he could teach them something. What? According to Hegel the Athenians thought they knew what reason was, what belief was, but they had only an abstract understanding of these concepts. Socrates knew what these concepts were concretely, and his mission was to bring these abstract conceptions into the clarity of concrete explication. And this, Hegel says is the truth of Socratic irony: " In saying that I know what reason is, what belief is, these remain but quite abstract conceptions; in order to become concrete, they must indeed be explicated and presupposed to be unknown in terms of what they really are. Socrates effected the explications of such conceptions, and this is the truth of Socratic irony" (CI, 267).

According to Kierkegaard, this is all wrong. First, Socrates did not pretend ignorance; he was really ignorant, even in his ironic wisdom. If there were any pretension on Socrates' part, it must have been pretended knowledge. The reality, however, is that he knew nothing. As a consequence, he could not have been trying to teach something that he knew and his fellow Athenians did not know. He was trying to bring his interlocutors to the same place where he was, that is, to an acknowledgement of utter and complete ignorance. He did not want to teach them (as clearly Plato did), but to knock them off of their horse, or even as in the case of the Sophists, to disgrace them.[14] As we might put it, there was no positive content in Socrates' irony.[15]

But didn't Socrates at least know something (positive)? Didn't he know that he did not know? This after all was the source of his wisdom. But again, what may appear to be knowledge with a positive content was actually, or should I say ironically, without positive content. For the something that he knew was in fact a nothing. So Kierkegaard argues that Hegel's attempt to "reclaim a positive content (CI, 269)" for Socrates was in vain. As he says: "If his knowledge had been a knowledge of something, his ignorance would merely have been a conversational technique. His irony, however, was complete in itself. Inasmuch, then, as his ignorance was simultaneously earnest and yet again not earnest,[16] it is on this prong Socrates must be held. To know that one is ignorant is the beginning of coming to know, but if one does not know more, it

---

[14]Kierkegaard points out an inconsistency in Hegel's treatment of this matter, when he notes that Hegel also says that Socrates' intent was to "disgrace" the Sophists. He says: "we promptly encounter a difficulty here, because in one instance he does indeed want to teach, but in the other merely to disgrace" (CI, 266). Even so, the clear impression that Kierkegaard gives is that the weight of Hegel's interpretation of Socrates falls on the side of his (positive) intent to teach.

[15]This is not to say that Socratic irony has no positive role to play, however ironic, in the positing of subjectivity in the world. Hegel could see this positive contribution only by turning Socrates' irony into something positive. As strange as it may sound, Hegel failed to grasp this because he was not dialectical enough in his conception of how the negative figures in the positive, and vice versa. For Hegel, the positive sucks the negative dry by negating it, that is, by turning it into a positive, rather than by dialectically excluding it from the positive, and hence not denying, that is, affirming, its negativity.

[16]"Therefore we can say of irony that it is earnestness about nothing—insofar as it is not earnestness about something. It continually conceives of nothing in contrast to something, and in order to free itself of earnestness about anything, it grasps the nothing. But it does not become earnestness about nothing, either, except insofar as it is not earnestness about anything" (CI, 270).

is merely a beginning. This knowledge was what kept Socrates ironically floating" (CI, 269).

Secondly, and more importantly, Hegel was confused about what Socrates' project was. As Kierkegaard sees it, Hegel thought that Socrates had undertaken to make the abstract concrete. According to Kierkegaard, Hegel, claims that "the real meaning of Socratic irony, the greatness in it, [is] that it seeks to make abstract conceptions concrete and developed" (CI, 266). But on Kierkegaard's view, this is the opposite of what Socrates was trying to do. That is, Socrates had actually undertaken to reveal the abstract; and the concrete was at most a window onto it. (And we must keep in mind here that 'abstract' was always a pejorative term for Hegel.) Or as Kierkegaard puts it: "Socrates' undertaking was by no means one of making the abstract concrete, but to let the abstract become visible through the immediately concrete" (CI, 267). So again, Hegel's reading of Socrates is entirely too positive. As Hegel would have us believe, Socrates was making a positive contribution insofar as he was making the first step toward unifying the abstract and the concrete. In contrast, Kierkegaard sees Socrates as driving a wedge between the abstract and the concrete in order to hasten his departure from the concrete actuality that defined Hellas—a departure that would take him to the new-found negative freedom he had found in hovering above actuality, in hanging as it were in the clouds in a sustained abstract detachment from the world.

In summary then, we might say that Kierkegaard and Hegel agree, Socrates deserves the highest of our praise. But there is where the agreement stops. Hegel thought that Socrates made a positive step toward the realization of positive freedom insofar as he was the first to posit subjective inwardness (in opposition to the externality of the given actuality). But for Hegel, Socrates did not go far enough. As he sees it, the inwardness of Socrates was only unconscious; it needed to be made fully conscious. In contrast, Kierkegaard thinks that Socrates did not make a positive step toward positive freedom, but only a negative step. But it was an ironic negative step. Socrates, as we might put it, destroyed the obstacles to positive freedom, but he went no further. Destroying obstacles is not the same as making a first step. Knowing that the Greek world has no place for positive freedom does not entail that he knew what a proper place for positive freedom would be (like). He was intensely aware of nothing other than the absence of such a place. At the same time, this negative awareness, and the destruction it effected, while not a positive step did have an ironically positive consequence for it made the first step toward positive freedom possible; this is what I call the irony of Socratic irony: unknown to Socrates himself, his negations were in the service of something positive, something that he himself was truly ignorant of. But I must remind you, making a first step possible is not the same as making a first step. Hegel's mistake, Kierkegaard thinks, is to think that Socrates made this first step. The beginning of knowledge need not be itself the knowledge of something, but the condition of the possibility of knowing anything.

As I might very cryptically put this, paganism had to be destroyed before positive subjectivity could take hold of human consciousness and gain its world-historical significance. Or even more cryptically, the absolute negativity of Socratic irony could be viewed as being in the service of the earnestness of Christ, who for Kierkegaard was the true founder of positive freedom. As I see it, this was the healthiness of Socratic irony. But again, it is a healthiness that is very different from the healthiness that Hegel saw in it.

Unlike the Romantic ironists, to whom we are about to turn, Socrates took nothing seriously, and so was not in earnest about anything. The Romantic ironists also take nothing seriously, but in a different sense. In contrast to Socrates, the Romantic ironists take everything ultimately to be nothing, and they are quite in earnest about this. The contrast here is between being in earnest about nothing and being in earnest that everything is nothing. The first earnestness, earnestness about nothing, Socratic irony, is a floating lightness, a liberating freedom as if from a slavery to the world; it carries in itself, I want to say, a kind of innocence. The second earnestness, the earnestness of Romantic irony, is quite different. This irony carries within itself an intoxicating fantasy that there is nothing that binds us, but ends in the disturbing nightmare that there is nothing and no one we can be bound to, for in the end, the dark truth is that there is simply nothing. This irony is far from innocence; in fact, it may just be demonic.

The Irony of Romantic Irony

At least the idealism of Kant had something of an objective side to it—what he called the *ding an sich*. Nevertheless, he made it quite clear that human knowers (limited as we are, confined within space and time) have absolutely no access to that objective noumenal world of things in themselves. For him, all we know and can know are our own constructions—what he called phenomena. ("Kant lacks the negative infinity . . . " (CI, 273)). Ironically, it was a short step for post-Kantians to turn what Kant thought of as the limitations of human construction into a liberating celebration of a god-like human power of creation. It was Fichte who led the charge toward such a full-blown idealism. In his hands, the constructing I became an omnipotent god.[17] ("Fichte [lacks] the positive" [the world] [CI, 273].)

Kierkegaard's characterizations of the irony of Fichte's idealism are worth noting: "[Fichte] wanted to construct the world. The I became the constituting entity" (CI, 273). "In Fichte, subjectivity became free, infinite, negative. . . . [His irony] was not in the service of the world spirit. . . . [I]t was all of historical actuality that it negated to make room for a self-created actuality. . . . [I]t was an exaggerated subjectivity, a subjectivity raised to the second power" (CI, 275). And further: "Irony now functioned as that for which nothing was established, as that which was finished with everything, and also as that which had the absolute power to do everything. If it allowed something to remain established, it knew it had the power to destroy it, knew it at the very same moment it let it continue. If it posited something, it knew it had the authority to annul it, knew it at the very same moment it posited it. It knew that in general it poses the absolute power to bind and to unbind . . . " (CI, 276).

---

[17]There is a sense here in which the *imago dei* has gone to seed. Or shall we say that in Romanticism the seeds of the first transgression have finally come to flower. The ironic consequence of this flowering, however, is that it marks mankind's darkest moment; it represents the fatal yielding of his spirit to the lure of divinity. Intoxicated by the power of omnipotence, he effects the complete uprooting of himself from the earth (finitude).

Post-Fichtean irony, like its Socratic distant cousin, takes aim at the given actuality. Both react to a life within finitude that keeps the infinity of freedom from being vested with its full reality and power.[18] Such obstacles to freedom include the cosmological externalities (fate, for example, or more generally the pervasive sense that life is governed by an impersonal objective natural order) that Socrates was seeking to extricate himself from; or they may be of the sort the Romantics were seeking to free themselves from, namely, the apathy, indolence, and thoughtlessness of their age that produced a world of fossilized customs and traditions; so much to the credit of both Socratic and Romantic irony. There is, however, an important—indeed an enormous—difference between the two. Unlike Socratic irony, the irony of Romanticism "was not in the service of the world spirit" (CI, 275). For Romantic irony, "it was not an element of the given actuality that must be negated and superseded by a new element, but it was all of historical actuality that it negated in order to make room for a self-created actuality" (CI, 275). Socratic negative freedom was clearing the way, as it were, for positive freedom (the positive freedom of concrete action); in contrast, the negative freedom of Romantic irony was an end in itself.

The Romantics were convinced that giving subjectivity (spirit, self, freedom) a place within the given actuality would destroy it. To tie spirit to the given finite world, in their imagination, was nothing short of tying it down, that is, nothing short of placing it in bondage to the world. In this sense, they thought that subjectivity must perpetually emancipate itself from (what is taken to be) the given actuality in order to meet the task of creating another actuality, one better suited to the infinity of spirit. Therefore, for the Romantics, the only true freedom is the negative *freedom from* the given, and it is this negative freedom that the Romantics celebrate.

The irony of such a celebration of negative freedom, of its infinite power to establish and destroy actuality, is that it ends

---

[18]I take the power of freedom to be vested with its full reality and power only insofar at it is actualized in concrete moral action. But concrete moral action needs space and time; that is, it requires the presence of others living within the continuity of a historically conscious community.

with no actuality at all. The end of the road for the Romantic ironist is worldless subjectivism, if not solipsism. The omnipotence it covets turns out to be impotence; the absolute freedom of negative freedom seems to be free to do anything, but it can, in truth, do nothing. The self, in this view, becomes, in Sartre's famous expression, a useless passion. As I would put it, the self in this Romantic delusion ends up in a desperate solitude that can only be characterized as demonic. In this negative freedom the "self" is alone with itself, haunting the world like a ghost. Far from being free, the Romantic ironist ends up, ironically, being a slave to his or her own moods; his or her original intoxication eventually degenerates into boredom; and in the end this is nothing other than despair—the deepest human sickness unto death; it is death!

As I mentioned earlier, I read the existential standpoint of irony, in either its Socratic or Romantic forms as a modality of despair, or more specifically, as a mode of the despair of the infinite (due to a lack of the finite). Let us see how this works out in the figures that Kierkegaard discusses as examples of Romantic irony, Friedrich Schlegel, Ludwig Tieck, and Karl Wilhelm Ferdinand Solger.

Schlegel saw the present given actuality of his day as dead. He was repulsed by the fact that in his world the human emotion of love, with all of its reality and power, its intense inward passion and freedom, had become "as tame, as housebroken, as sluggish, as dull, as useful and usable as any other domestic animal—in short, as unerotic as possible" (CI, 286). But is was not just that the present given actuality needed awakening from its despair of the finite (due to its lack of the infinite), it was rather, in Schlegel's imagination, that the infinite is just too powerful to be bound by any given actuality. So he sought not only to repudiate his own customs and ethics that were strangling spirit, especially the passion of love, but to repudiate any given actuality at all, save a self-created actuality. Love is too infinite to be contained in anything but a dream, a fantasy; it is too infinite to be contained within the finite, the ordinary world.[19]

---

[19]In a footnote Kierkegaard remarks: "Who would be so inhuman as not to be able to enjoy the free play of fantasy, but that does not imply that all of life

In his novel, *Lucinde,* Schlegel attempts to negate the given actuality of custom and ethics in matters of love and marriage with a fantastic, and from the common point of view of the day, an outrageous assertion of naked erotic sensuousness, a sensuousness that negated (and so was qualified negatively by) spirit. Devoid of spirit, this sensuousness lacked all content; it had no inside; it was merely the immediacy of the flesh. Note well, however, my reader, that this erotic flesh is in no way the ordinary worldly finite body of an actual person. It is an abstract, highly volatilized flesh—a kind of infinitized flesh. (Appearances notwithstanding, Schlegel does not suffer finitude's despair, due to a lack of the infinite; rather, he suffers the opposite despair, the despair of the infinite due to a lack of the (historical actuality of the) finite.

Schlegel's infinitized erotic immediacy cannot find its home in finite customs, in marriage, for example. This worldly institution is too confining, too domestic, too suffocating for the infinity of love's passion. Marriage, like any finite worldly institution and custom will inevitably douse the fire of love; it must be repudiated for the sake of love's inward freedom. Or more generally, in the name of the infinite, the finite must be repudiated lock stock and barrel. In the wake of this negation of actuality, however, life becomes but a dream. But such a life is a life without traction, without content; it is nothing else than infinitude's despair. Kierkegaard's final take on *Lucinde* is telling:

> The oddity [I would say, the irony] about *Lucinde* and the whole trend associated with it is that, by starting from the freedom and the constitutive authority of the I, one does not arrive at a still higher spirituality but comes only to sensuousness and consequently to its opposite. In ethics, the relation to spirit is implied, but because the I wants a higher freedom, it negates the ethical spirit and thereby falls under the laws of the flesh and of drives. But since this sensuousness is not naïve [as in pre-Socratic Greek culture], it follows that the same arbitrariness that installed sensuousness in its presumed rights can shift over the very next instant to assert an abstract and exaggerated spirituality [the demonic?]. (CI, 301)

---

should be abandoned to imaginative intuition. When fantasy alone gains the upper hand in this way, it exhausts and anesthetizes the soul, robs it of all moral tension" (CI, 292n).

Whereas Schlegel "turns directly away from actuality," Tieck's ironic negative withdrawal from it takes a different form. Kierkegaard characterizes Tieck's ironic standpoint as an indulgence in poetic abandon. He interprets Tieck's poetic abandonment of actuality as a token of his ironic standpoint of "indifference toward actuality" (CI, 301-302). While Kierkegaard criticizes Schlegel's rebellion and Tieck's indifference, he does recognize something beneficial in both, indeed, in Romanticism in general. As Kierkegaard points out, Romanticism's negative stance toward the world served as a wake-up call to an age "totally fossilized in finite social forms" (CI, 303). "The world was in its dotage and had to be rejuvenated. In that respect, Romanticism was beneficial" (CI, 304).

Nevertheless, Romanticism turns out to be a tragic response to the indolence and apathy of an age suffering from a despair of the finite. In the end, Romanticism does not see that if spirit (positive freedom) is to be vested with its full reality and power it must be able to find its feet in the world. Finding the given actuality to be no adequate place for spirit, the Romantic creates his own actuality. Tieck's medium for this creation is poetry, or more particularly, lyrical poetry. What he creates are beautiful, moving, sounds; or as we might put it, the dream world of spirit that Tieck's poetry creates is a world of music, for music—if it does nothing else—takes us out of the world, "far beyond the historical consciousness," as Kierkegaard puts it (CI, 307). (Kierkegaard): "The musical element in the lyric is the subjective factor. This is developed very one-sidedly. Thus everything comes to depend on the sound of the verse" (CI, 307). This sound, however, turns out to be but a tinkling cymbal, full of sound and fury to be sure, yet signifying nothing. "Such poems must now, of course, be considered the ultimate, because here mood—and mood, after all, is all important—has absolute sway and is utterly free since all content is negated" (CI, 307). Again, Tieck's ironic standpoint falls into despair; and once again, the irony of this is that he is reacting to what he takes rightly to be the despair of his own day, the despair of the finite. But to trade a despair of the finite for a despair of the infinite gets nowhere.

Finally, we turn to Solger. Unlike Schlegel and Tieck, Solger's interest in the infinite negativity of irony is not based on his repulsion at a given actuality that suffers from a despair of the finite. Kierkegaard writes: "[Solger] does not come into collision with actuality" (CI, 309). Rather his interest in irony is more speculative, or contemplative, or philosophical, even metaphysical. Indeed Kierkegaard calls him "the metaphysical knight of the negative" (CI, 309).

And what was his metaphysical agenda? He wanted "to destroy the partition that in so many ways wants to separate [the finite and the infinite]" (CI, 311). How does he do this? The short answer is that he turns to pantheism, to a view that merges the finite and the infinite. Pantheism identifies the finite and the infinite in one of two ways: either it accentuates mankind, or it accentuates God (CI, 314). In the former case mankind creates God, in the latter mankind is absorbed into God. In both cases the identity of God and mankind, the infinite and the finite, erases the conflict between them, the partition that divides them.

The problem with this, from Kierkegaard's point of view, is that it, like all pantheism, lacks a concept of creation. Implied in such a concept is what we might call the infinite absolute qualitative difference between God and mankind, Creator and creature, the infinite and the finite. Faith, for Kierkegaard finds the truth in a dialectical synthesis of these opposites, not in a destruction of their separateness via an illicit identification. Or, as I could put this, in pantheism, blurring the distinction between Creator and creature as it does, has no way of making sense of the idea that the given actuality presents itself as a gift (from the hands of the Eternal). Indeed, for Kierkegaard, Solger's pantheism just is a blur that confuses things and ultimately is disorienting.

Kierkegaard ends his discussion of Solger with an example of his confusion. He says that, "[i]n certain passages, Solger describes irony as the limiting power that specifically teaches man to remain in actuality, teaches him to seek his truth in limitation" (CI, 320). And right on the heels of this, Solger also says: "the earthly as such must be consumed if we are to recognize how the eternal and essential is present in it" (CI, 321). So in the end, Solger—who does have an intimation of "the negation of the negation" [of the given actuality]—does not see his way through to "the affirmation" [of it] (CI, 323).

To grasp this dialectical affirmation, we must turn to a different conception of irony.

The Irony of Mastered Irony

In the title of the concluding section of *The Concept of Irony*, Kierkegaard makes it clear, so obviously clear as easily to be missed, that irony has its proper (and essential) place (its truth) in the faithful and positively free affirmation of the given actuality only "as a controlled element." Please note, this is not irony as an existential standpoint; it is irony as an element. An element in what? Well, I can only speculate that Kierkegaard would answer, faith.[20] Remember that faith is a positive existential standpoint; and recall that Socratic irony and Romantic irony are also existential standpoints, but in contrast to faith, they are negative. As I see it (no doubt by reading between the lines), the claim that Kierkegaard wants to make here is simply this: *the truth of irony* is found is recognizing and acknowledging concretely its place as a necessary element within the existential standpoint of faith; *the despair of irony* is found in adopting it as an existential standpoint. But again, please remember that for Kierkegaard, despair can be an opening to faith, as it was in the case of Socrates, or an obstacle to it, as it was in the case of the Romantics.

So then, what does it mean to say that irony is a necessary element within the standpoint of faith? Well, one thing I would claim is that it does not mean that the standpoint of irony is incorporated, or transubstantiated, or synthesized within faith. Quite to the contrary: faith rejects (excludes) the standpoint of irony; and rightly so, for the standpoint of irony is despair (of the infinite). Mastered irony is not a revised version of the standpoint of Socratic irony, nor is it a transformation of its Romantic version; it is not a standpoint at all; it is merely an element, albeit a necessary one, within the standpoint of faith.

---

[20]Although Kierkegaard does not explicitly discuss faith here, he has made it clear in earlier passages that faith is an issue for him. See, for example, CI, 319. He does, however, talk about the "personal life" (CI 326). I cannot resist seeing a connection between the personal life and the life of existential faith.

So then, what do we make of Kierkegaard's contention that irony plays an indispensable role in a healthy personal life (what I would identify with the life of faith)? Again, this indispensable role of irony is as a controlled element. But what is this? In one of Kierkegaard's characterizations of it, he says that it is "a way of associating with people" (CI, 237). It is this use of irony, according to Kierkegaard, that Hegel mistakenly attributed to Socrates. On Kierkegaard's view, Hegel did not appreciate the fact that irony was much more than simply a controlled element in Socrates; indeed, irony defined Socrates' existential standpoint.

Hegel's view, in agreement with Plato, that Socratic irony was a controlled element led him, also mistakenly, to characterize Socrates as the one who pretended ignorance in order to teach something positive. Kierkegaard, as I have remarked above, shows that Hegel's interpretation of Socrates on this point is mistaken. As Kierkegaard argues, Socrates was really ignorant; he was not pretending that he knew nothing, for this is what he really knew. Socrates was not in possession of knowledge and merely masquerading this fact by pretending ignorance. And this is so, even though his interlocutors no doubt mistakenly took his claim to know nothing as a disguised pretension to know something (that they did not know). And this made them all the more suspicious of his incessant questioning.

Hegel's mistaken interpretation of Socrates aside for a moment, what are we to make of the connection that both Hegel and Kierkegaard seem to make between irony as controlled element and irony as pretended ignorance? Well, one thing that we might say is that pretending ignorance is one possible "way of associating with people." Yet we must ask, "What would such an association be like?" Would it be dishonest to pretend ignorance when you actually have knowledge? Would it betray a lack of integrity? Perhaps, but it need not. Consider the following examples.

Suppose that I know that you are contemplating suicide. I may decide to adopt the strategy of pretended ignorance (which is unlike the Socratic standpoint in which ignorance was real). I adopt this way of associating with you as a way into your agony and ultimately as a way of drawing you out of it. I will pretend that I don't know your condition when I in fact do. I may even take up your despair as my own and seek your counsel. But here is the ironic difference, I am not in despair and you are; appearances are the very opposite of what really is the case. I adopt an ironic dissemblance in order to forward my desire of bringing you back to yourself, of bringing you to see the value of embracing your life and the folly of destroying it. In no way have I adopted irony as an existential standpoint. Indeed, irony used in this way is in the service of my actual standpoint of faith. My irony serves the purpose of opening alternative possibilities for you; it offers, I might say, a space between you and the world, or what is more likely, a connection between you and the world. Offering you this space or this connection is to offer you a perspective, a condition for thoughtful and responsible action, and so constitutes an invitation to you to reconsider the value of your life.

The second example is less extraordinary; in fact it is down right ordinary. As a philosophy professor, every day I walk into class with a pedagogical agenda. But I am up against a perpetual and seemingly intractable challenge: I want my students to engage in serious philosophical criticism. They, by and large, are not interested in putting forth the effort to think—they are not used to having to. My challenge is to engage them. If I want them to think seriously and critically about, e.g. the claim that God exists, I find it pedagogically effective to take up the role of the atheist, even though I am a theist. They, of course, want to know what I really believe. If I am straight with them, however, I forfeit my (negative) freedom to take up either side of an issue. In maintaining my negative freedom by pretending to be something that I am not, I am using irony, but as a controlled element. I am merely pretending, but with a serious intent to teach something positive, call this the positive value of philosophical criticism. At the same time, I let them know that I do have a position. I don't want them to think that I merely hover, or that negative freedom, or irony, is my existential standpoint. I suspect however that I do not manage to be as convincing a believer of the things that I do not actually believe, as I am with regard to things that I do actually believe. But, I suppose this is equally true when Kierkegaard writes, as A, in praise of Mozart's *Don Giovanni*.

And here we come to the point I want to make. I suggest that in *The Concept of Irony*, Kierkegaard was already thinking about his subsequent authorship. I offer this speculation: I think that it is clear that from the beginning Kierkegaard's authorial motivation was fired by two convictions: despair is pervasive and faith is its only remedy. The problem is that despair blinds us to its remedy. So how can the eyes of despair be opened to faith? How can despair's resistance to faith be cracked? Perhaps the only way is to go undercover. And what would this mean? Well, it might mean that the best strategy for disseminating the healing truth of faith is ironically to pretend despair. And how can this be done? One might write in praise of the many life possibilities that betoken despair, in order penultimately to turn disguised despair into patent despair, and ultimately to open the back door of despair to faith. Would this not be one instance of using irony as a controlled element? I suggest so.

While I think that the above examples of "ways of associating with people" are uses of irony as a controlled element, they are not its only uses as such. I think that there are other uses that go deeper than merely ways of associating with people. The most important such use of irony is found in its role within faith's exercise of positive freedom. If we keep in mind that irony is essentially a negative element, then we might say that the role that irony as a controlled element plays within positive freedom is just the role that negation plays within it. Let me explain.

I take positive freedom to be the power of personal appropriation, the power we human beings have to make something our own. If I am positively free to do x, then I must be prepared to own that act. That is, I must be prepared to own up to it as my act, with all the responsibility that owing and owing up to entails. The obvious fact, however, is that I can act in positive freedom only if I am also negatively free to refuse to act. If, for example, my marriage is a shotgun wedding, or is arranged, or is otherwise necessary, I would not say that it is positively free in the fullest sense of the term. And what would make it free? Well, other alternatives must be open to me, really open. As I see it, I can be judged to have done x in positive freedom only if the following negative conditions apply: (1) I could have refused to do x; (2) but as a matter of fact I refused to refuse x, which is a double negation amounting to, I did x; and (3) I refused all the alternative possibilities to x that were open to me. Without these negative conditions being at play in my decisions, I am not positively free. It is mastered irony that keeps these negative conditions at play.

The differences are clear between the way that negation is at play in irony as controlled element and the way it is at play in standpoints of Socratic and Romantic irony. In Socratic irony, the given actuality of Greek culture, not actuality in general, is repudiated (negated). In Romantic irony, all actuality is repudiated (negated) in favor of a self-created "actuality." In contrast, mastered irony does not repudiate (negate) the given actuality, but tells me that I could. This momentary realization that I could repudiate the given actuality has the ironic effect of deepening my positive embrace of it. For to know that I could say "no" to actuality, deepens my capacity to say "yes" to it.

In taking up Socratic or Romantic irony as an existential standpoint is to live exclusively within the negative, that is within what is not, or if you like, within (mere) possibilities. Both turn away from actuality; neither chooses (actualizes) this or that (concrete course of action); both merely flirt with and are intoxicated by infinite possibilities; both delight in the rarefied atmosphere of nothingness. The master of irony does choose (to actualize) this or that, and knows that this choice is positively free in the fullest sense of the term, for he or she knows that each could have done otherwise. As such, controlled irony does not turn away from actuality, from positive freedom, indeed the opposite.[21]

In more theological terms, we might say this. The existential standpoint of faith understands the historical actuality as both a gift and a task (CI, 279). To see the creation as a gift is to acknowledge a Creator who is favorably disposed to his creatures. (I assume here that to call something a gift is to place a positive value on it. Certainly it would be strange to think that we could make a gift out of something utterly worthless or harmful. I may be the one who gave you the flu, but it is certainly not my gift to you.) As well, when creatures see their existence as a task, they acknowledge a primordial ethicoreligious connection (of responsi-

---

[21]"As soon as irony is controlled, it makes a movement opposite to that in which uncontrolled irony declares it life. Irony finitizes and circumscribes and thereby yields truth, actuality, content; it disciplines and punishes and thereby yields balance and consistency" (CI, 326).

bility and responsiveness) between themselves and their Creator. To accept the whole creation as a gift, but especially our own creation in the image of the Creator, and to accept our task, the responsibility of realizing our likeness to our divine source, entails the acceptance of the historical actuality (every inch) from the hands of the Eternal, as the kind of world that is appropriate for this realization. It is positive freedom alone that can appropriate the gift of actuality and fulfill the task of becoming who we are (intended to be).

I am taking it as obvious that I can accept a gift (or give one) only if I can refuse it (or to give it). Dialectically conceived, however, my acceptance of the gift requires a confrontation with the possibility of refusing it; hence, my acceptance is a refusal of this possibility of refusal. Similarly, insofar as the historical actuality also presents itself as *my* task, we realize again the implicit possibility of refusal, and dialectically that my acceptance of my task as mine, requires my existential confrontation and rejection of that negative possibility. What is mine to do, is mine also to refuse to do, otherwise it is not mine. ("[W]e have forgotten that an achievement is worthless if it is not made one's own" (CI, 327)). As we noted earlier, it is this double negation that Solger could not see as an affirmation (CI, 323).

Mastered irony tells us of our power to repudiate the historical actuality; it tells us of our power to reject it as gift and as task. Yet the irony of mastered irony is that its whisper of this alternative possibility of rejecting or refusing actuality provides an absolutely indispensable element for faith's positively free embrace of it. Irony as a controlled element continually provides me with the consciousness of my power of repudiation. And yet ironically, it is this power of repudiation that makes faith's embrace of actuality positively free. Even though mastered irony is an infinitely negative power of repudiation, it nevertheless feeds and sustains the positive existential standpoint of faith, for it provides the abyss over which faith is called to leap.

Ironically, we can live "robustly and energetically in" (CI, 326) finitude, only insofar as we can be "rescued" (CI, 326) from this life—at least from time to time. Irony as a controlled element provides the means of this rescue. But this negative power that enables us to withdraw from finitude, when it becomes "too hot and heavy" (CI, 327) is not the Romantic or even the Socratic irony of sustained withdrawal. Rather, it is only a momentary withdrawal, and perhaps only a liberating momentary possibility of withdrawal. This inward realization is "regenerating and rejuvenating" (CI, 327). But this effect of mastered irony is felt only insofar as its ultimate intention is to reaffirm finitude. Only then does mastered irony play its indispensable role in our health and happiness, only then can it be seen as an essential element within the existential standpoint of faith.

11

Beyond the Grasp of Irony

George Pattison

There has been considerable debate in recent years as to whether Kierkegaard's *magister* dissertation *The Concept of Irony* is to be taken seriously. Are we to read it as the registration-piece of an aspiring young right-wing Hegelian, taking up the Master's commission to go forth and crack the whip over the nihilistic swarm of political subversives, emancipators of the flesh and proponents of suicide who were to be regarded as the contemporary heirs of romantic irony? Such a view might still hold even if it were also to be acknowledged that by the time of the dissertation (or shortly thereafter) Kierkegaard had come to see that Hegel himself was without the authority needed to bring the left into line, since Hegel himself was, deep down, gripped by the same spirit of scepticism that motivated the ironists and their successors. Kierkegaard's turn to a more personalistic, Christianly orthodox theology would then belong to an attempt to establish a basis for the critique of irony that would be immune from ironic subversion. Or is the dissertation itself deeply ironic, so ironic, in fact, that its demonstration of the necessarily self-ironizing character of any and every attempt to master irony escaped the notice of all Kierkegaard's own contemporaries? When Kierkegaard subsequently referred to himself—with an allusion back to the degree for which the dissertation was offered—as "The Master of Irony" was this the expression of a deep satisfaction with a job well-done or an ironic recognition of the impossibility of the task?

Perhaps we could focus the question by playfully rewriting the dissertation's title, customarily translated as *The Concept of Irony*. Bearing in mind the profoundly figurative element in the Danish term *Begreb*—"grasp" (an element that is important for Hegel himself vis-a-vis the cognate German term *Begriff*)—and taking the liberty of reconstructing the grammar of the title we might rewrite it thus: *On Mastery: Irony*—i.e., a thesis demonstrating that every attempt to claim or to practice "mastery" in the world of Spirit was foredoomed to fall under the axe of irony. Certainly the opening paragraph of the Introduction to the First Part of the thesis (and every reader of Kierkegaard knows how important introductions and forewords were to him) seems to adopt what is at the very least a highly irreverent tone towards the Hegelian claim that philosophy is now able to "grasp" its phenomenon, and suggests that, all the same, it would be better not to hear too much of the jingling of the philosopher-knight's spurs or the raising of his "the voice of the master" (CI, 9). The concept (i.e., "grasping" or "mastery"), he insists, is not to be imposed on the phenomenon from without but must accompany the phenomenon's own coming to appearance: to anticipate Heidegger, it must show itself as what it is from within and by means of the phenomenon itself. Hegel could have agreed, but the bantering tone of the paragraph suggests a certain distance already from the Hegelian project. Moreover, the outcome, that the concept must be developed from the phenomenon itself, becomes something of a riddle when the concept itself is a negative concept such as irony that resists phenomenalization. Can one master a concept that does not show itself?

The question as to mastery over irony returns in the closing section of the dissertation "Irony as Controlled Moment. The Truth of Irony." The direction is set by some reflections on the mastery of irony in dramatic writing, with reference to Shakespeare, Goethe and Kierkegaard's Danish contemporary, J. L. Heiberg, and the lesson learned from the playwrights is then transferred to life in its practical and theoretical domains. The last three or four pages in which Kierkegaard makes this application are characterized by a rapid-fire succession of programmatic assertions that beg just about all the difficult questions. A prominent theme is the need to subject irony to the discipline of "actuality"—but there are, frankly, very few clues as to what this might "actually" mean. Finally Kierkegaard comes to the question of irony's "eternal validity", i.e., the question as to whether there is a legitimate place for irony in the religious life. His suggestion is that there is at least an analogue to irony here, namely, humor, but that whereas irony relates only to finitude, humor relates to sin, and does so, moreover, on the grounds of a "deeper positivity" that has to do with its "theanthropological" presuppositions, i.e., its concern with humanity's destiny to be transformed into "the God-man". The style continues to be tersely programmatic and, in any case, as Kierkegaard finally confesses, "all this lies beyond the scope of this study". However, he also adds one final recommendation: that if anyone should want food for further thought—*Stof til Eftertanke*—he would recommend them to read Professor Martensen's review of Heiberg's new poems (CI, 329).

To most Anglophone readers, and probably to most contemporary Danish readers, this is an almost entirely opaque reference. Kierkegaard's own contemporaries, however, and certainly those who attended his defense of the dissertation (including Heiberg himself), would have been aware in at least a general sense of the relevance of the review, and of the poems themselves, to Kierkegaard's topic. From this point of view alone it is, of course, worthwhile reconstructing the background of the reference. However, given the centrality of both Martensen and Heiberg to the Hegelian tendency in Danish thought, such a reconstruction may well also throw light on Kierkegaard's relation to Hegelianism at the time of the thesis, and therefore also on our contemporary question as to the irony of a thesis aimed at mastery of irony.

Johann Ludvig Heiberg (1791–1860) was a pivotal figure in Danish intellectual life in and beyond the period of Kierkegaard's youth. As director of the Theatre Royal he was largely responsible for turning the theatre away from its previous Germanic orientation and opening it up to the influence of Paris and such fashionable playwrights as Scribe, a number of whose plays Heiberg himself translated. He also embellished the theatre's repertoire with a number of his own vaudevilles, or musical comedies, many of which starred the beautiful and brilliant Johanne Luise Heiberg, his wife and the dedicatee of Kierkegaard's own feuilleton essay 'The Crisis in the Life of an Actress'. As a philosopher, however, Heiberg was also the apostle of Hegelianism in Denmark, being the author of a Hegelian-influenced course in logic as well as of a number of popularizing treatises aimed at promoting the new philosophy. Heiberg applied the principles of Hegelianism to his own practice as a literary critic, developing a complex hierarchy of genres involving the subordination of the 'merely' immediate romantic school to the more reflective, contemporary comedy that Heiberg himself cultivated. But how far could even the highest forms of art go?

Hegel himself, in the introduction to his lectures on aesthetics, had asserted that "art, considered in its highest vocation, is and remains for us a thing of the past . . . the philosophy of art is therefore a greater need in our day than it was in the days when art by itself as art yielded full satisfaction. Art invites us to intellectual consideration, and that not for the purpose of creating art again, but for knowing philosophically what art is."[1] This limitation of art in relation to philosophy—and, indeed, within the larger compass of Hegel's system in relation also to religion—does not register to anything like the same degree in Heiberg's writings. As a man of the theatre, Heiberg was not about subordinating art to philosophy, but subordinating a less adequate form and understanding of art—that of romanticism—to his own more intellectualistic practice and understanding. For Heiberg, as opposed to Hegel, the distinction between art and philosophy is narrowed to the point of collapse so that, as Paul Rubow wrote of Heiberg, poetry "is in its highest development speculative."[2] In keeping with this principle, Heiberg himself attempted to create genuinely speculative poetic works, an ambition reflected principally in the play *Fata Morgana* and in the *New Poems*, the centerpiece of which was the dramatic poem *A Soul after Death*.[3]

---

[1]G. W. F. Hegel, *Aesthetics. Lectures on Fine Art*, trans. T. M. Knox (Oxford: Oxford University Press, 1975) 11.

[2]Paul Rubow, *Heiberg og hans Skole i Kritiken* (Copenhagen: Gyldendal, 1953) 42. This, however, should not be understood as simple naivety on Heiberg's part, but in connection with his whole programme of improving Danish life and bringing it to the intellectual and cultural level of the European mainstream. If art took on a philosophical role, this was also because art, as institutionalised in Heiberg's own Royal Theatre, as an instrument of the public realm and thus had a political, moral and intellectual role in the life of the nation as a whole. Art was to reflect, but also to instruct and to elevate the public in the understanding of life that most truthfully reflected the actual level of contemporary social and intellectual development, i.e., Hegelianism itself.

[3]Although dramatic in form this was not intended by Heiberg to be staged, although this was attempted after his death, in 1891.

Before Heiberg had got round to putting his own theory into
poetic practice, however, the question of speculative poetry had
been broached by an ambitious and extremely able young
theologian, Hans Lassen Martensen. In 1837 Heiberg published in
his journal *Perseus: A Journal for the Speculative Idea* an article by
Martensen reviewing the dramatic poem *Faust* by Nicholaus
Lenau. Noting that trying to write a *Faust* after Goethe is rather
like trying to write an *Iliad* after Homer, Martensen suggests that
whether such a thing is at all possible will depend on the Faust-
idea itself and therefore we will only be able to say if Goethe's
treatment has exhausted the subject once we understand what that
idea really is. What, then, is it? At its simplest it is the idea of the
opposition between good and evil in the theoretical sphere. Now,
although the legend of Faust originated in the Middle Ages, the
medieval world could not do justice to it, since its consciousness
was bound to and constrained by externality (a view of the Middle
Ages we also find in Kierkegaard's early journals of this period).
Consciousness only developed a level of inwardness commensu-
rate with the idea of a purely theoretical treatment of the opposition between good and evil (as opposed, e.g., to good knights
slaying evil dragons, or good Christians slaying evil heathens) in
the Reformation, so that the Faust-idea could only find its adequate expression within the world of Protestantism. "Speculative
poetry knows no higher tragic object, for the content is here self-
conscious freedom, the thinking Spirit; the scene . . . is not the
tumultuous stage of events in the outer world, but the quiet realm
of thought."[4] In this "quiet realm" Faust represents "the striving
of the human race to establish a Kingdom of the Intellect without
God."[5]

Poetically, *Faust* belongs within a type of speculative poetry
that Martensen categorises as "apocalyptic," of which, after the
Book of Revelation and Dante's *Commedia* it is the third great
example. These works are all linked by a historically determined
level of ever-increasing inwardness. Thus, the Book of Revelation

[4]H. L. Martensen, "Betragtninger over Ideen af Faust," in *Perseus, Journal for
den Speculative Idee* (June 1837): 96.
[5]Martensen, "Betragtninger," 97.

"poetically" [*sic*!] portrays Christianity's triumph over Judaism and Paganism, whereas Dante's poem is situated in a world that has already been Christianised and is consequently able to focus more closely on the details of individual life—"the abstract-symbolic standpoint is left behind, and the representation becomes more individual, more visible, more painterly."[6] Nevertheless, as an expression of the medieval consciousness, the *Commedia* is still constrained by the external, and its depiction of the journey of the individual soul is staged in terms of the spatially-conceived spheres of hell, purgatory and paradise.

The imagination presupposes these spheres as given, it regards them as established in their own right, and seeks only to apprehend their content; but their own presupposition, their common midpoint, which is the ground and possibility of such "regions", remains concealed from its gaze. This midpoint in fact is nothing other than freedom itself; for hell, purgatory and paradise are themselves only the revelation of the great, universal kingdom of freedom and self-conscious thought.[7]

This is the ground on which the drama of Faust is acted out, for Faust "is the expression of thinking self-consciousness, which turns from faith to doubt, and through doubt—which has become the principle of thinking—is brought to despair."[8]

The moment of doubt, then, is crucial. "Doubt," says Martensen, "is thus the medium through which the believing intellect must pass in order to give foundation to its freedom";[9] "it is the moment of *periculum vitae* (mortal danger), for here life and freedom are themselves at stake."[10] The trial of freedom that occurs in doubt is, Martensen reminds us, a distinctively Protestant phenomenon, such that Faust is a "counter-image" to Luther. Faust resists the first two temptations of the wilderness, to turn stones into bread (one-sided materialism) and to cast himself down from the Temple (one-sided idealism), but he succumbs to the third, for he does not acknowledge the commandment to serve and to wor-

---

[6]Martensen, "Betragtninger," 102.
[7]Martensen, "Betragtninger," 103.
[8]Martensen, "Betragtninger," 108.
[9]Martensen, "Betragtninger," 109.
[10]Martensen, "Betragtninger," 111.

ship God alone. Faustian intellectuality, then, is an intellectuality free from gross externality and materialism, but unable to recognize or to accept the ultimate limitation of its own creatureliness.

Martensen concludes that this idea has not yet been adequately grasped by any of the poets who have attempted to deal with it. Finally, then

> The real poetic portrayal of the Christian myth of Faust . . . must therefore still be awaited. This will first be able to be produced when the impetus to this higher union of religion and art emerges more clearly in the consciousness of the age; when the Protestant poet, whose gaze does not merely turn outward towards nature and history but spontaneously turns towards the intellectual world itself, completely grasps this "attrait" of his genius, when, with clear self-consciousness, he feels his prophetic call, his art's universality.[11]

Six months later, in January 1838, on the occasion of the King's birthday—a fact entirely relevant to Heiberg's belief in the necessarily public office of art and of the artist's duty to give expression to the objective consciousness of the age as embodied in the State and so in the person of the monarch—Heiberg staged his own "speculative comedy", *Fata Morgana*. His reply, perhaps, to Martensen's challenge to the poet of Protestantism?

The story concerns a prince, Clotaldo, brought up as a humble fisherman's son, who falls in love with Margarita, daughter of Dionision, Duke of Palermo, in whose lands the fisherfolk's village lies. When a mirage of Palermo appears in the sky, the villagers are alarmed, ascribing it to the wicked fairy Fata Morgana, mistress of illusions. Clotaldo, who feels himself called to the life of poetry, is stirred, however. "Is there no such thing as a beautiful deception?" he asks himself,

> And is not Beauty itself a deception? And is a beautiful deception not worth more than that which the world foolishly calls truth? Oh! He who grasps only at actuality—*he* is deceived by a false appearance. The Eternal is the beautiful image which has neither flesh, nor blood, neither marrow, nor bone, but is the light

---

[11]Martensen, "Betragtninger," 163-64.

thought of the heavy world, dark actuality's clear vision in the sky. (I,1)[12]

Clotaldo, in short, is a dreamer, and the story of the play is, in a sense, his conversion from romanticism to Hegelianism. Fata Morgana, however, is eager to keep him in thrall to illusion, and gives him a magical pearl in which every person sees their deepest wish. Clotaldo sees a vision of Maragarita. But whereas Fata Morgana's plan was for this vision to bind him yet faster to his fantasy world, the plan backfires when Margarita herself appears and Clotaldo realises that the vision of the pearl is as nothing compared with the reality of her beauty: "whosoever possesses the true object praises the image no more, even if it is represented as accurately as it is here . . . my dreaming nature was chained to the image in the pearl . . . I feel myself set free in Spirit, as I offer illusions phantasm's in exchange for the true appearance" (III, 2). Naturally, Margarita feels the same about him, although, at this point, he seems to be nothing but a fisherman's son.

By way of a diversion, Heiberg introduces two burlesque characters, Harlequin and Pierrot who represent, respectively, a kind of poetic idealism that despises actuality and a kind of coarsely realist version of empiricism. Heiberg uses them to lampoon the sterile antitheses of life before speculation.

> Harlequin: There is no third position. We two are everything. That is to say, we would be if one were to put us together.
> Pierrot: What a noble thought! We two are everything. Let me embrace you.
> Harlequin: With pleasure! Let ideality kiss reality. Now we are the absolute.
> Pierrot: One moment, Signor Harlequin! Do not let your fantasy overshoot your understanding! The absolute can never be realised by finite, earthly beings; one can only approach it by an eternally maintained progress towards the unobtainable perfection. Consider that, however tightly we hold on to each other, we shall for all that never fuse into one being. We shall never become a single grey figure, despite the fact that you are black and I am white. (III, 5)

---

[12]Citations from *Fata Morgana* are my own translation and are given by act and scene. I have followed the text of vol. 2 of J. L. Heiberg, *Poetiske Skrifter* (Copenhagen: Reitzel, 1862).

But, for Hegelianism and for Heiberg, there is such a position, philosophy's "grey in grey," speculation.

Clotaldo is subsequently knighted, and, grasping the sword of his knighthood (but, we hope, without too much jingling of spurs!), declares that with it he will remind himself "of the struggle which is to be carried on on behalf of actuality; and the poet [for he is still, withal, a poet—GP] shall not be himself ensnared in his realm of images but shall struggle for the actual truth" (III, 7)—or, in other words, shall, through irony, master the poetic impulse and reduce it to rational order. However, as the plot thickens, Clotaldo is imprisoned, and, awaiting execution (in the charge of Harlequin and Pierrot) thinks again of Margarita:

> to possess you, I would have fought for and won you, you pearl of pearls, you impress of the soul, phenomenon of truth, you image of the Spirit, whose radiance is not false, not a play of the dark forces of nature, as is this false image, this pearl, which has only earthly value and yet manages to awaken hatred and discord. (IV, 5)

Seizing his sword, Clotaldo destroys the pearl, in place of which appears a rose, an image of a truth whose beauty is not external, but, like its scent, invisible. A sylph appears out of the rose bush, who tells Clotaldo of his true ancestry. So, Clotaldo now knows who he is, having broken through all errors and half-truths. Borne aloft to Fata Morgana's palace in the clouds (where Margarita is imprisoned) by Troche, Iamb and Molossos, the personified spirits of poetic technique (the ironic command of poetic form necessarily supplementing his romantic inspiration), he finally confronts the evil fairy with a few home truths.

> [Y]our "understanding" does not understand that over against the false there stands the true, the divine appearance. Your visions borrow their truth from earthly nature, from the transient being which lies behind the wall of actuality; mine take their truth from Spirit, which has impressed its image in the clay in order to lead it back to the light in which it was. Love is no delusion, though it goes in robe of clay; poetry consists of truth, even if it [also] consists of images. (V, 3)

The palace of illusion vanishes and we return to earth, to actuality, where love conquers all.

Whether the King entirely enjoyed his birthday outing to the
theatre, we do not know—but we can see even from this brief
summary that many of the crucial themes of *The Concept of Irony*
are adumbrated in it, especially the role of formal mastery in
relation to the conflict between an idealistic but fantastic poetic
longing, on the one hand, and a "merely" earthly realism, on the
other. "Actuality" is precisely to see—to speculate—the one in the
other, the ideal in the real, the truth in the image, the *true appearance*.

Martensen, at least, saw it that way. Reviewing the play he
wrote that

> Speculative poetry, like philosophy, is of an idealistic nature; it
> idealizes actuality; it continually leads reality back to ideality,
> and the poetic consciousness is the higher truth of the con-
> sciousness that belongs to and that has as its subject-matter
> actuality itself. But precisely because poetry, like philosophy, is
> the transfiguration of actuality into ideality, precisely because it
> always stands one degree higher than the consciousness of
> actuality, it always has the actual consciousness for its basis and
> presupposition.[13]

Poetry, in other words, must correspond to the inner reality or
actuality of its age. Since, as Martensen goes on to argue, the
present age is "the period of systems"[14] not only in philosophy but
also in religion, industry and trade, poetry itself must become
systematic.

> [T]he world whose thought the educated person now seeks to
> grasp, is itself a world of conflicting ideas, which have estab-
> lished their validity and are recognised *as such*, and the idea
> which is sought is therefore the central idea in all the others, i.e.,
> the speculative idea. To make this visible to us—*insofar as this is
> at all possible for art*—is poetry's highest task. Only speculative
> poetry can be the poetry in which we would be able to find a
> total and not merely a partial satisfaction, because it is not only
> a mirror which reflects the diverse ideal strivings and expressions
> of the human race, as all poetry is, but it also reflects the Ideas
> and ideals that govern life. . . . In contradiction to peripheral

---

[13]H. L. Martensen, "Fata Morgana af J. L. Heiberg," in *Maanedskrift for Literatur*
19 (1838): 362.

[14]Martensen, "Fata Morgana," 367.

poetry, which only yields a glimpse of the Idea, speculative
poetry is truly illuminating, it kindles an infinity of bright points
in the soul, which form themselves into one harmonious transparent image and transfigures the darkness of life.[15]

Speculative poetry of this kind is not merely allegorical but
symbolic, for a symbol, in the fullest sense of the word, "is image
and actuality at one and he same time."[16] Bearing in mind the
earlier discussion of the Faust-idea, it is consistent of Martensen to
emphasise that contemporary speculative poetry will not draw its
material from mythology, from the external, but from freedom,
from the depths of Spirit itself. "*This* world of appearances is . . .
the eternal essence which actuality conceals within its shell."[17] For
the same reason, such a poetry will also be comic rather than
tragic, for tragedy is tied to the external distinction between good
and evil, whereas comedy plays on the differences between essence
and phenomenon, reality and appearance: "Comedy rests on the
contrast between the true and the inverted world, which latter in
all seriousness believes in its own reality, but which, when held up
against the light of the Idea, is dissolved and evaporates as
phenomenon."[18]

Heiberg did not attempt to repeat the venture of a speculative
comedy on stage, but in 1841 published a collection of poetical
works entitled *New Poems*, comprising "Divine Service: A Spring-
time Fantasy";[19] "A Soul after Death: An Apocalyptic Comedy";
"The Newlyweds: A Romance-Cycle"; and "Protestantism in
Nature: A Mystery."

Of these "A Soul after Death" is the most significant and,
generally, the most popular. The "soul" of the title is a citizen of
Copenhagen who has just died and who duly makes his way to
Heaven's Gates. He is met there by St. Peter, who, since the soul
has not been much of a Church-goer, demands that he undertakes
a purgatorial pilgrimage, visiting all the sites named in the gospel

---

[15]Martensen, "Fata Morgana," 367-78

[16]Martensen, "Fata Morgana," 372.

[17]Martensen, "Fata Morgana," 373.

[18]Martensen, "Fata Morana," 381.

[19]Including the wonderfully bathetic line in which an angel says to a poet:
"No, we are Protestants . . . "!

narrative. The soul regards this as excessive, and says that if he has to go anywhere he'd prefer America and, anyway, he can't remember all the places concerned. Surely, he says, the important thing is not such external details but the Spirit of scripture. St. Peter asks him to explain what that Spirit is exactly. The soul demurs, for, he says, "the Spirit does not let itself be grasped in words." To which St. Peter replies "And yet the Word was God." This, however, the soul tells him is allegorical, for "the Spirit can be felt but not uttered, since the Spirit and the letter are in ceaseless conflict." St. Peter, however, says that whilst that is so on earth it is not so "in Paradise, in the presence of the Lord. The more clear the Spirit is, so much the less does it economise on the word. He who cannot express his thought in words does not enter heaven." When the soul insists that he did not seek knowledge of God in his earthly life because the one thing we know about God is that He is incomprehensible, St. Peter asks him why, then, he is so keen to get into Heaven, God's abode.[20]

After this unsatisfactory start the soul is despatched to Elysium. However, his lack of classical learning does not stand him in good stead, and so he comes, without knowing it, to the Gates of Hell. Here he is met by Mephistopheles, who assures him that there are no conditions for entry, everyone is welcome. No knowledge is necessary and, indeed, Mephistopheles congratulates him on possessing no knowledge other than that of the most recent and trivial events in local life. For, he says, "here there is surface but no depth . . . no distinction between coal and chalk, here freedom and conformity are ready-made, here everything is as new and nothing, no matter how it hurries along ever gets away from the beginning, because the brief, single moment . . . severs itself from the preceding moment . . . and begins its eternal A from which no B ever proceeds."[21] That, indeed, is why no one can ever leave once they have entered, because Hell is pure, eternal Beginning, with no before or after, nothing ever goes forward and nothing ever returns or turns back. Hell has no history. It is pure

---

[20]J. L. Heiberg, *En Sjæl Efter Døden*, 6th ed. (Copenhagen: Gyldendal, 1963) 18-19.

[21]Heiberg, *En Sjæl*, 36.

immediacy, without reflection or development. But, says Mephistopheles, "you don't need to delve into all this. It is something no one can understand."[22] No. There is nothing to understand.

A further glimpse of the meaning of Hell is opened up by one of its residents, a poet, who enters declaiming on hopeless longing as a necessary condition of poetic production.

> If I had not locked myself
> Out from goodness and from piety,
> Then my song would not have had the sound of longing,
> Then I would not have sung so beautifully
> Of the soul's craving for God,
> With a voice like that of an imprisoned bird.
>
> If my unbelief had not been so strong
> That it tore me from the Church's breast
> And cast me out of the nest,
> Then my poetic works would not have resounded
> With the tone of longing in my voice,
> With the sighing after communion.[23]

Like the soul himself, the poet believes that heaven is a matter of incommunicable and inexpressible feeling.

When the soul; asks what the place he has arrived at is called, it is Mephistopheles' turn to demur. Don't ask about such things, he advises, it's only a name anyway, just a sound without a meaning, as the language of immediacy—such as that of romantic lyricism—necessarily is. Forced to give voice to this meaningless sound, Mephistopheles quickly recovers lost ground by assuring the soul that actually this is where he has spent his whole life "only people are not so accustomed so to call that flabby phlegmatic earthly existence which puts all its trust in reality and doesn't get the slightest glimmering of . . . an Idea."[24] In any case, everything the soul likes about Copenhagen is to be found here—including his favourite newspapers and the works of H. C. Andersen and F. C. Sibbern (an early critic of Hegelianism in Denmark and chairman of examiners for *The Concept of Irony*!) and,

---

[22]Heiberg, *En Sjæl*, 38
[23]Heiberg, *En Sjæl*, 49
[24]Heiberg, *En Sjæl*, 56.

in any case, there is every probability that his wife will soon be able to join him.

Martensen is favourably impressed. In the review to which Kierkegaard refers at the end of *The Concept of Irony* he declares that "It is in fact the Spirit of the *new age* under whose guidance these poems are composed . . . what philosophy has long since whispered in the ears of its disciples, poetry now begins to preach from the roof-tops."[25] The poems, especially "A Soul After Death" (which Martensen sees as the centrepiece of the collection), are, as truly speculative, rooted in Spirit itself. In them, this world and the next become transparent to each other. Just as Dante discovered large chunks of Florence in Hell and Swedenborg wrote of finding London and Paris in the other world, so Heiberg has translated contemporary Copenhagen into the apocalyptic realm. This is of the essence of a genuinely speculative approach, for "True science and poetry, like faith, see all objects in a *double perspective*, they see them at one and the same time in the form of eternity and in the form of temporality." Heiberg is even compared favourably with Dante, whose Hell was described in moral and religious but not in metaphysical categories. Dante, as a man of the Catholic Middle Ages, therefore failed to penetrate the relationship between essence and appearance, truth and falsehood, in which comedy is at home. Characteristically his Heaven lacks the truly Christian humor. In a humorous Heaven the blessed spirits will "play with the phenomena of their temporal consciousness which, in all the detail of its empirical reality, in all its infirmity and transience, they will have with them in Heaven, because it must serve them as poetic material. . . . Their temporal, child-like concerns will now play the part of accidentalities in the substance of blessedness." In other words, the souls in paradise not only have God, they also have the world again. This is comic in the technical sense that whereas tragedy culminates in judgement and the destruction of earthly happiness, comedy goes on to affirm the good ending, that God can be all in all. Martensen thus predicts that the dialectic of

---

[25]This and following references are to H. L. Martensen "Nye Digte af J. L. Heiberg," in *Fædrelandet* 10.1.1841.

comedy and tragedy will come to rest in the concept of the humorous,

> which is not only negatively but positively comic, [it is] the speculative comedy, which relates itself to irony as profundity is related to sharp-mindedness. The "humorous" which belongs exclusively to Christianity includes not only the whole of irony, the poetic nemesis on the fallen world, but also the fullness of love and reconciliation. It comprises the pain of the whole world, but overcome in a rich depth of joy.

We can see from this the extent to which Kierkegaard's concerns in *The Concept of Irony* are extraordinarily topical, embracing issues in literature and aesthetics that were being discussed in what we might call quality newspapers in the year that saw the dissertation itself presented and defended (1841) and that marked the high-point of Heiberg's ambition to create a new paradigm of cultural Protestantism. The project of speculative comedy, culminating in the *New Poems* and Martensen's review, broached issues of essence and phenomenon, truth and appearance, romanticism and speculation, art and philosophy, irony and humour that run through the dissertation as a whole and that are brought to a point in its closing section.

At first glance, and just as Heiberg's apocalyptic comedy itself would have contained much that would appeal to Kierkegaard's own satirical view of his contemporaries, Martensen's comments on Christianity and humour might sound as if they had come from Kierkegaard's own early journals, where there are many remarks about the distinction between irony and humor and the Christian nature of the latter (especially 1837-38 and thus three or more years before the dissertation). However, there is also a single but decisive point of difference that cannot be overlooked. Although, as for Martensen, there is something essentially positive about humour—it is indissociable from joy—this positivity is itself marked by a thorough-going negativity in relation to the world. Although there is continuity in that "Humor is irony carried through to its maximum oscillations" (JP, 21699), humor is not the outcome of a dialectical development but depends on Christian revelation and the conviction that here "All is made new" (JP, 2:1711; cf. JP, 2:1690). Presupposing the utter separation of Spirit and world, the standpoint of the humorist is essentially solitary, like a beast of prey (JP, 2:1719) or like Robinson Crusoe—even when in the midst of life (JP, 2:1699). The humorist's laughter is a "son of pain", his smile like the dead man's grin "which is explained as the muscle twitch of rigor mortis, the eternally humorous smile over human wretchedness" (JP, 2:1706). The Christian humorist is like a plant whose roots alone are visible on earth, but whose flower unfolds for a higher, invisible sun (JP, 2:1690). Insofar as it is poetic at all it is "profound poetry", beyond form "and therefore crystallises in baroque forms" (JP, 2:1690). The humorous nature of Christianity is testified by its proclamation of a truth which is hidden in mystery—not a truth that is "mysterious" or "a mystery"(in the manner of, e.g., Freemasonry) but that is revealed as mystery, as hidden in mystery (JP, 2:1682). Correspondingly, a person who takes his stand on the principle of humour will have, at best, an ambiguous attitude towards writing, having "come alive to the incommensurable which the philosopher can never figure out and therefore must despise. . . . The systematizer believes that he can say everything, and that whatever cannot be said is erroneous and secondary" (JP, 2:1702).

None of these, or any of the other entries relating to humor in the journals predating *The Concept of Irony* is perhaps decisive and could be interpreted in a sense compatible with that of Martensen and Heiberg, but there is, nevertheless, a distinct difference in tone. It is, moreover, highly revealing in this connection that the epitome of the humorist is, in Kierkegaard's eyes, J. G. Hamann, whose idiosyncratic, exaggerated and polemical style and tendency was an affront to Hegelian ideals of lucidity in thought and exposition.

If, then, precisely at the point where Kierkegaard seems closest to his Danish Hegelian contemporaries, we can also see the chasm separating him from them, it becomes hard to take the "food for thought" of the closing line of *The Concept of Irony* other than ironically. But what are the implications of that for the final position arrived at in the dissertation? The question seems especially pertinent with regard to the implications of the discussion of Shakespeare, Goethe and Heiberg as "masters of irony" within the narrow boundaries of aesthetic production. This seems to be taken by Kierkegaard as a model that can be applied relatively unproblematically to life or actuality—"After all, what holds for the poet-existence holds also in some measure for every single individual's life." (CI, 325-6) But is aesthetic irony transferable in that way? Unfortunately these closing pages are fearfully condensed and, it has to be said, under-argued. One thing does seem clear in the light of this interpretation of the "food for thought", though: the claim that we might attain to an adequate theorization of such mastery by means of the concept of humor, a claim clearly made in Martensen's and Heiberg's concept of speculative comedy, is ironically punctured. Strikingly the journals say of humor itself (with specific reference, once more, to Hamann) that it "is not an aesthetic concept but life, not a hero in a controlled drama" (JP, 2:1699), and this is precisely the problem. The issue is not whether Kierkegaard is or isn't sincere in commending Heiberg's technical irony qua dramatic poet. Nor is it the correctness of the *concept* of humor. The question, however, is whether this really helps us at all in face of the actual, living questions that confront a person in their religious existence. Mastery over irony may be possible within the strictly localized sphere of aesthetic production, but mastery over irony in life is a problem of a different order of magnitude. Mastery over *life—living masterfully*—is likewise another matter. And, as some of the entries dealing with humor suggest, the way "beyond" irony is not that of mastery at all, but suffering (cf. JP, 2:1706), not knighthood in the manner of the masterful Hegelian knight invoked at the very beginning of the dissertation, but cross-bearing. The route chosen by Heiberg and Martensen, the route of aesthetic portrayal and philosophical exposition, is misdirected. Kierkegaard's ironic hint may, then, amount to an "About Turn!"—away from irony and away from mastery, a call to unburden oneself of the impossible ambition of control over one's self and accepting, instead, one's utter dependence on God's creating and saving grace. But what that "actually" means is by no means delivered in the programmatic assertions of the dissertation itself, since, as Kierkegaard himself says in the same last sentence we have been expounding, an adequate exposition of everything that belongs to such dependence lies outside the scope of the study of irony. That is the work of the authorship, pseudonymous and signed. And, of course, a task for life.

12

Kierkegaard, Socratic Irony, and Deconstruction

Merold Westphal

As any reader of Plato's *Apology* or Aristophanes' *The Clouds* knows, the Old Guard in Athens had a hard time distinguishing Socrates from the sophists. For Kierkegaard in *The Concept of Irony* and for Johannes Climacus in *Concluding Unscientific Postscript*, Socrates is a hero. Not a Christian, to be sure, but nevertheless a hero of subjectivity. In both of these texts Kierkegaard sees to it that we don't confuse him with the sophists, the distinction being explicit in the dissertation, implicit but no less powerful in *Postscript*.

In neither text is the point to identify Socrates with Plato. The distinction between Socrates and the speculative project, associated with Plato in *The Concept of Irony* and with Hegel in *Concluding Unscientific Postscript*, is just as sharply drawn as that between Socrates and the sophists. Socrates is a genuine *tertium quid*.

It is therefore important when reading *Philosophical Fragments*, where it is Socrates rather than Plato who is linked to the recollection hypothesis, not to think that the two are identified. Already in *The Concept of Irony* it is *Socrates* who "so beautifully binds men firmly to the divine by showing that all knowledge is recollection" (CI, 30). But on just this point he is distinguished from Plato.

> It would be Platonic to fortify existence by the upbuilding thought that man is not driven empty-handed out into the world, by calling to mind his abundant equipment through recollection. It is Socratic to disparage all actuality and to direct man to a recollection that continually retreats further and further back

toward a past that itself retreats as far back in time as that noble family's origin that no one could remember. (CI, 60)[1]

Thus in *Concluding Unscientific Postscript*, while immanence is tied to recollection and transcendence to revelation, neither Socratic nor Christian subjectivity, that is, neither Religiousness A nor Religiousness B can be confused with speculation.

Accordingly, one central task of *The Concept of Irony* is the dual project of distinguishing the ironic Socrates both from the sophists and from Plato.

In our own time no one is likely to identify deconstruction with the speculative task or to confuse Jacques Derrida with Plato or Hegel. But he is often confused with the sophists, that is, he is often seen as an intellectual who is a threat to the moral order of society, someone from whom our young people need to be protected. I shall argue that the space Kierkegaard opens up between speculation and sophistry, in order to understand the character of Socratic negativity properly, is the space in which we should locate Derrida in order to understand deconstructive negativity properly. Without claiming that Derrida is the reincarnation of Socrates, I want to suggest that he is a direct descendent, to suggest that by seeing how similar Kierkegaard's Socrates is to Derrida we will understand both of them better and perhaps get clearer about the sense in which "postmodernism," if there is such a thing, can have a Kierkegaardian and not only a Nietzschean inspiration. So the task is twofold: first to review Kierkegaard's portrayal of Socratic irony and then to highlight the deep kinship between it and deconstruction.

To distinguish Socrates from Plato Kierkegaard regularly presents irony as dialectical in opposition to Platonic speculation. The distinction is Hegelian. In ¶¶79-82 of *The Encyclopedia Logic*, Hegel distinguishes three moments of thought or "the *logical . . .* (α) *the side of abstraction* or *of the understanding*, (β) *the dialectical* or *negatively rational side*, [and] (γ) *the speculative* or *positively rational*

---

[1]Readers of Levinas will be reminded of the trace as the (non)sign that points to an immemorial past, a past that was never present and consequently cannot be re-presented.

one."[2] Kant, of course, had distinguished understanding, which successfully grasps the finite in its finitude, from reason, which, in its quest for the unconditioned falls into transcendental illusion. Period, so far as theoretical reason is concerned. Hegel, by contrast, treats dialectical negativity as penultimate, the legitimate critique of understanding's finite positivity and the introduction or transition to reason's infinite positivity. It plays John the Baptist, calling the understanding to repentance to prepare the way for the speculative Messiah. As we shall see, Kierkegaard has his own, very different, way of assimilating Socrates to John the Baptist.

In treating irony as dialectic, Kierkegaard emphasizes its negative character. Indeed, he borrows a phrase from Hegel to describe it as "infinite, absolute negativity" (CI, 26, 254, 261).[3] But it is the speculative Plato, not the ironical Socrates for whom this is a *via negativa* to infinite positivity (the Good, the Beautiful, the Eternal). Socrates' "dialectical vacuum pump" (CI, 178) remains a "famished" dialectic (CI, 105) which remains an "unhappy love" (CI, 108) without satisfaction. "What bears him up [at his trial] is the negativity that still [as he faces death] has engendered no positivity" (CI, 196). Thus the first book of the *Republic* "does not merely end without a conclusion . . . but rather with a negative conclusion" (CI, 111). In this irony we find the true Socrates.

In distinguishing Socrates from Plato, Kierkegaard regularly associates the mythical with the speculative. There are three things worthy of note here. First, the myths of Plato are to be understood as "the idea in a state of alienation, the ideas's externality—i.e., its immediate temporality and spatiality as such" (CI, 101). The mythical is "not so much a secondary account for younger or less gifted listeners as a presentiment of something higher" (CI, 98).[4] But while not an accommodation, as allegory might be, the mythical is

---

[2]Quoted from *The Encyclopedia Logic*, trans. T. F. Geraets, W. A. Suchting, and H. S. Harris (Indianapolis: Hackett, 1991) ¶79.

[3]For the passages from Hegel's *Aesthetics*, see CI, 475n.64.

[4]By rendering *"underordnet Fremstilling"* as "secondary account" the Hongs miss the link between *Fremstilling* and *Vorstellung* and thereby the allusion to Hegel, for whom *Vorstellungen* are always inferior to authentically speculative *Begriffe*. Capel's rendering as "inferior representation" is much to be preferred. *The Concept of Irony*, trans. Lee M. Capel (New York: Harper & Row, 1965) 130.

merely presentiment (*Ahnelse*), "the unripe fruit of speculation" (CI, 105). "Weary of the dialectical work [of negativity], the imagination begins to dream, and from this comes the mythical" (CI, 101). In Plato's myths "the poet daydreams and visualizes everything the dialectician Socrates was seeking; in the world of dreams, irony's unhappy love finds it object" (CI, 108), in other words, moves beyond irony. In this way the mythical is "the enthusiasm of imagination *in the service of speculation*" (CI, 101, emphasis added), the *Aufhebung* of irony's unhappy consciousness. When myths enter the dialogues stage right, Socrates exits stage left.

Second, this account of the mythical is very close to that expressed by Schelling in his *System of Transcendental Idealism* (1800) and especially in his lecture course, *The Philosophy of Art* (1802-1803, 1804-1805). As early as 1796 Hegel had written, in a text sometimes attributed to Schelling, "we must have a new mythology, but this mythology must be in the service of the Ideas, it must be a mythology of *Reason*."[5] In other words, while there is a romanticism that Kierkegaard will associate with the sophists, there is another romanticism he links to Plato and the speculative project.

Finally, from Plato to Rorty there have been those who have sharply opposed the literary to the philosophical in terms of rhetoric vs. logic, image vs. concept, narrative vs. argument and so forth. In contrast, Kierkegaard emphasizes the way in which the two are really up to the same thing, at least in certain modes. But while agreeing with Hegel that the literary and the philosophical, in their mythical and speculative modes, respectively, have the same goal and that the former is a happy dream but at best only a dream of having reached that goal, Kierkegaard does not buy the crucial third Hegelian claim that in speculative philosophy "irony's

---

[5]"Earliest System-Programme of German Idealism," in H. S. Harris, *Hegel's Development: Toward the Sunlight 1770-1801* (Oxford: Clarendon Press, 1972) 511. The authorship of this fragment has been disputed, but it is in Hegel's handwriting and absent further evidence to the contrary, I see no reason to dispute the view of Pöggeler and Harris that Hegel is the author, which does not mean, of course, that the ideas are uniquely his. They were doubtless shared by his friends Schelling and Hölderlin, among others.

unhappy love finds its object" (CI, 108) not as a daydream but for real.

Kierkegaard would find confirmation for his linkage of the mythical to the speculative in Camus' account of the world of myth as all answers and no questions.[6] For they see the speculative question as but a polite introduction to its answer, by contrast with the "blood-sucking questions" of Socrates,[7] "a questioning that consumes the answer" (CI, 124), that seeks "to suck out the *apparent content* by means of the question and thereby to leave an emptiness behind" (CI, 36, emphasis added).

This emptiness is not that of the cynic, who says that nothing is worthwhile, or the nihilist, who says that everything is meaningless. We can see this by noting the two ways in which it is developed. First, Socratic questioning is an acknowledgment of ignorance. Philosophies end with what they presuppose, so "just as Socrates' philosophy began with the presupposition that he knew nothing, so it ended with the presupposition that human beings know nothing at all" (CI, 37; cf. 34), that "human wisdom has little or no value" (CI, 40n.) The ironic Socrates is a Samson who "grasps the pillars that support knowledge and tumbles everything down into the nothingness of ignorance" (CI, 40). Socratic irony and Socratic ignorance are two sides of the same coin.

Ironic ignorance stands in a peculiar relation to the Idea.[8] It is dialectically negative, to be sure, but it "is *not* the dialectic of the idea" (CI, 118), the Hegelian dialectic whose natural unfolding (allegedly) yields the Idea.[9] "The particular expressions of irony here are of course *not in the service of the idea, are not its messengers who collect the scattered parts into a whole*; they do not collect but

---

[6]Albert Camus, *The Rebel*, trans. Anthony Bower (New York: Random House, 1956) 21.

[7]I follow the translation of Capel, 82. The Hongs have "squeezing-out questions" (CI, 45). Cf. CI, 49: "The ironist is the vampire who has sucked the blood of the lover. . . . "

[8]In various discourses one can substitute the Good, the Beautiful, the One, the Eternal, the Unconditioned, the Infinite, the Absolute, or simply God for the Idea.

[9]Without accepting Hegel's claim that his dialectic does in fact yield the Idea, Kierkegaard criticizes the external relation between the dialectical and the speculative in Plato. It is into this gap that the mythical enters as a *deus ex machina* (CI, 46-47).

scatter, and each new beginning . . . is not an approach to the idea, but is . . . *devoid of any relation to the idea*" (CI, 114, emphasis added).

We must restrict the meaning of "*not in the service of the idea*" and "*devoid of any relation to the idea*" to what is explicitly denied here. Dialectic is not an agent of the Absolute; it does not gather the dispersed and disseminated into Totality, but contributes to the dispersal and dissemination. For there are, other senses in which dialectic *does* stand in relation to the idea. Kierkegaard speaks of "the Socratic sensibility, which upon the most subtle and fragile contact [with the phenomenon] immediately detected the presence of the idea" and of "this unerring Socratic magnifying glass for which no subject was so compact that he did not immediately discern the idea" (CI, 17).

Realizing that the "alert reader" will suspect him of contradicting later statements like the ones we have just looked at, Kierkegaard immediately adds a note explaining that he is here distinguishing Socrates from the sophists (rather than from Plato, as in the "conflicting" passages) and that the idea whose presence Socrates detects is abstract, lacking "qualitative determinants with respect to the phenomenon's relation to the idea" (CI, 17n.) In other words, unlike the sophists, Socrates refers phenomena to the idea, but unlike Plato (and Hegel), he does not profess to be in possession of the idea, to see it clearly enough to be able to judge phenomena and guide behavior by its light. Just as Charon ferries people over to the underworld, so Socrates ferries people from reality to ideality, but because the ideality is "infinitely abstract," it only appears "in the most evanescent intimation of the slightest limitation" (CI, 236).[10] We are reminded of Augustine, striving to apprehend That Which Is, catching a momentary glimpse, and immediately falling back, unable to maintain contact.[11] By referring the phenomenon to the idea the ironist introduces the categoreal distinction between reality and ideality, for it "gets an inkling that there is something more behind the phenomenon" (CI, 257).

---

[10]"Limitation" here seems to signify determinacy of content. Capel (255) translates: "in the most fleeting suggestion of its faintest configuration."

[11]*Confessions* VII.17.

However, "it is essential for the ironist never to articulate the idea as such but only casually to suggest it" (CI, 49).[12]

There is something of the prophet about the ironist, but "he does not possess the new. He knows only that the present does not match the idea . . . he is continually pointing to something impending, but what it is he does not know" (CI, 261). For Hegel, dialectical negativity is a John the Baptist calling the understanding to repent and prepare a highway in the desert for the triumphal entry of speculation. No *via dolorosa* follows this triumphal entry, for *kenosis* is proper only to understanding and not to reason. There may be a speculative Good Friday.[13] But reason is never in danger. In its negative, dialectical mode, it is the executioner. In its positive, speculative mode it gives itself a full grant of immunity from prosecution. Socratic irony, by contrast, is the impudence that challenges that writ. It is the John the Baptist who calls speculation to repentance. To open space for what? *Je ne sais quoi.*

Socratic irony is thus a new (or rather old) critique of theoretical reason. Its ignorance, its non-possession of the idea to which it nevertheless alludes, is the emptiness left over when the radical questioning of infinite, absolute negativity has subtracted what is only apparent from the "apparent content" of our answers.

But irony is not doubt. It is not just a "philosophical position" (CI, 169) but a "qualification of personality" (CI, 220n). Thus irony is for personal life what doubt is for science (*Videnskaben* = *Wissenschaft*, CI, 326).[14] It cannot be identified with doubt for two hardly distinguishable reasons, "first, that doubt is a conceptual qualification, and irony is subjectivity's being-for-itself; second, that

---

[12]The quotation continues: "to give with one hand and take away with the other, to hold the idea as personal property. . . . " But this is only how it seems to those to whom the vampire addresses his "blood-sucking questions." Socrates knows full well that the idea is not his personal property.

[13]See Hegel, *Faith and Knowledge*, trans. Walter Cerf and H. S. Harris (Albany NY: SUNY Press, 1977) 190-91.

[14]The German equivalent is *Wissenschaft* and Hegel is insistent that philosophy be(come) *Wissenschaft*. "To help bring philosophy closer to the form of Science, to the goal where it can lay aside the title '*love* of knowing' and be *actual* knowing—that is what I have set myself to do." *Phenomenology of Spirit*, trans. A. V. Miller (Oxford: Clarendon Press, 1977) 3.

irony is essentially practical, that it is theoretical only in order to become practical again" (CI, 257).[15]

By the same token, irony cannot be reduced to a figure of speech. Saying the opposite of what is meant is only a special case of what is essential to irony, "namely, that the phenomenon is not the essence but the opposite of the essence" (CI, 247). In irony as a trope, the phenomenon is what I say, which does not correspond to what I mean. In doubt as a philosophical position, namely skepticism, it is the whole fabric of knowledge which fails to correspond to the real it intends.

But irony as "essentially practical," as a "qualification of personality," goes beyond both of these. The phenomenon (reality) which is revealed to be other than the essence (ideality) it purports to be is neither some particular statement nor even our concepts, our judgments, and our theories as a whole. It is our practices as well, and here we come to the second mode of emptiness which irony exposes. After all, although Kierkegaard sharply contrasts irony with speculation (Plato and Hegel) for his own purposes, it was not Plato who was the target of Socratic questioning, but the Established Order of a not especially theoretical Athens, as Aristophanes saw so clearly. It was the best and the brightest of the Old Guard who resented the call to repentance from this gadfly, this stingray, this hellenic John the Baptist. As our attention shifts from Platonic myths and speculation to Athenian practices, Kierkegaard expects our attention to shift from Hegel to Christendom as the Established Order he and his readers share.[16]

He suggests that the charges brought against Socrates are substantially correct. For "he was not a good citizen and certainly did not make others so." He was a revolutionary, though not the "leader of a conspiracy," and we must "admit that the state was authorized to judge Socrates" (CI, 181-82). In Hegelian language,

---

[15]Cf. PC, 81n., where Anti-Climacus insists on a similar distinction between doubt and despair.

[16]This raises the question who plays the role of Plato and Hegel for us, and who the successor to Athens and Christendom might be. Suggestion: technologically oriented science, including information sciences and a culture of entertainment and consumption embedded in the institutions of "democratic" capitalism and confident that it is the embodiment of the Good.

good citizenship is a matter *Sittlichkeit,* the social practices of a people in which their morality and their religion are embodied. The most basic and foundational of these is the family. The highest and most complete of these is the state, along with its religion. Kierkegaard, drawing on Socrates' own testimony, portrays him as a nemesis to the moral and religious *Lebenswelt* in terms of which the best and the brightest of his fellow Athenians persuaded themselves that they were the Good and the Just.

In his allegiance to his daimon, Socrates makes it clear that if he ever pledges allegiance to the state and its religion, he does so with fingers crossed. He has a private religion, which to him is higher (CI, 157-68). It is true that he is no atheist, like Anaxagoras, but he professes a radical ignorance in relation to such matters, an ignorance that can only be an offense to the state (CI, 169-78).[17]

He is equally irreverent in relation to the family. In Athenian (and Hegelian) *Sittlichkeit,*

> the state ranks higher than the family, which is within the state. But the family in turns ranks higher than the single individual, especially in regard to its own affairs. . . . Vis-à-vis the single individual, therefore, the child's relation to its parents is an absolute.
>
> Just as Socrates by way of irony rose above the validity of the substantial life of the state, so also family life had no validity for him. For him the state and the family were a sum of individuals, and therefore he related to the members of the state and the family as to individuals; any other relation was unimportant to him. Thus we see how the thesis that the most competent ought to be preferred to the less competent . . . becomes essentially immoral precisely by its total abstraction. (CI, 185)

By abstracting himself and thereby the moral and religious life from the structures of *Sittlichkeit,* Socrates empties them of the absolute authority they claim over the individual.[18]

---

[17]Capel's translation (203) of *Brøde* as "felony," is closer to the spirit of the text than the milder "offense."

[18]It is precisely these structures, not the moral law as an eternal truth apprehended by pure (Platonic or Kantian) reason, that constitutes the ethical that is teleologically suspended in *Fear and Trembling.* See esp. FT, 55 and n. 7. The Danish terms *det sædelige* and *Sædelighed* are the Danish equivalent of *Sittlichkeit,* ethical life as concretely embodied in the practices of a people. I have emphasized

At this point we can see clearly why Kierkegaard thinks that irony "is a healthiness insofar as it rescues the soul from the snares of relativity" (CI, 77). In the eyes of Socratic irony, the beliefs of Athens are not the Idea and its practices are not the Good. They are at best approximations, and as such only relatively authoritative. In posing as absolute, they are illusions at the theoretical level and idols at the practical level. Thus, for example, Socratic ignorance, like Schleiermacher's theme of absolute dependence, embodies a polemic that "dismays anyone who has found his repose in one or another finite relation to the divine" (CI, 176).

But it is also just at this point that we can most sympathize with the difficulty the Old Guard had in distinguishing Socrates from the sophists, who also lacked proper reverence for the moral and religious values of the Established Order. Especially interesting in this context is Kierkegaard's treatment of romantic irony, which he tends to assimilate to sophistry. In his discussion of Tieck he writes that "the whole romantic school stepped into or thought they were stepping into an age in which people seemed to be totally fossilized in finite social forms. . . . The glorious principles and maxims of habit and custom were the objects of a pious idolatry; everything was absolute, even the absolute" (CI, 303). Like Socratic irony, romantic irony purports to "rescue the soul from the snares of relativity" posing as something absolute.

But this passage comes almost immediately after a sustained critique of Schlegel's *Lucinde* and its scandalous refutation of marriage, which Kierkegaard sees as an immoral and irreligious attempt to free the individual, not just from finite social structures but from any spiritual constraint whatever on sensuous immediacy (CI, 286-301). Romantic irony as the critique of idolatry is but the disguise of an aestheticism beyond good and evil in which "repentance does not prick" ever again (CI, 295). This is how the Good and the Just saw Socrates. Having pried him away from Plato, can Kierkegaard keep him distinct from the sophists?

Hegel as the target of *Fear and Trembling* in "Abraham and Hegel," in *Kierkegaard's Critique of Reason and Society* (University Park: Pennsylvania State University Press, 1987).

Like Socrates, the sophists did not bow down before the phenomenon, which, in terms of practice was the Established Order. Kierkegaard defines sophistry as "the everlasting duel of knowledge [sic] with the phenomenon *in the service of egotism*" (CI, 25, emphasis added). He could neatly distinguish Socrates from the sophists if he could define irony as infinite, absolute negativity *in the service of the idea*. Unfortunately, we have already seen him deny such a claim. But—N.B.—in a very specific sense! Irony is not an ambassador of the absolute sent to gather the lost and scattered sheep into the safety of the fold. Socrates "had come not to save the world but to judge it" (CI, 173).

But is this judgment not a different way of serving the idea? Like sophistry, irony shows that the phenomenon is not the essence, that the real is not the ideal. But have we not already seen that ironic negation is a call to repentance rather than an attempt to make repentance forever unnecessary—both for the individual and for society? If so, irony's negation of the phenomenon would be in the service of something higher than the ego. It would be in the service of the idea more truly than if Socrates professed to be in possession of the idea; for in the latter case it would be all but impossible to distinguish the idea from his ego.[19] Rather than a cousin of the sophists, irony would anticipate Anti-Climacus when he writes, "Every human being is to live in fear and trembling, and likewise no established order is to be exempted from fear and trembling. . . . And fear and trembling signify that there is a God— something every human being and every established order ought not to forget for a moment" (PC, 88).

This is indeed Kierkegaard's view of the matter. The denial that irony is in the service of the idea—in the specified sense—is compatible with presenting Socrates as "a divine missionary" (CI, 236). It is compatible with seeing irony as akin to "religious devotion" (CI, 257-58) and as akin to the prophetic tradition, though the ironist, like the prophet, looks to a future in presenti-

---

[19]Perhaps this is why Climacus includes a satire of the Fichtean ego, the I-I, calling attention to the ambiguous relation between the empirical ego and the pure ego, in what is otherwise a critique of Hegelian speculation (CUP, 117; cf 190, 196-98).

ment rather than possession (CI, 260-61).[20] And if there is one prophet in particular who should be mentioned in association with Socratic irony, it is John the Baptist. For that analogy, which I have already been using, is Kierkegaard's own.

Johannine negativity has the form of law, understood by Kierkegaard in very Lutheran terms. "It was already a profound irony over the world when the law, after having declared the commandments, added the promise: If you obey these, you will be saved, since it turned out that people could not fulfill the law. . . . " John is the one who points this out. "He was not the one who was supposed to come; he did not know what was to come—and yet he destroyed Judaism. Thus he destroyed it not by means of the new [the gospel] but by means of Judaism itself [the law]. He required of Judaism what Judaism wanted to give—justice, but this it was unable to give, and thereby it foundered" (CI, 263).[21]

Elsewhere Kierkegaard suggests that what Socrates was for the Greeks, "the skepticism of the law" was for ancient Israel. It

> had to pave the way, by its negativity had to consume and cauterize, so to speak, the natural man so that grace would not be taken in vain. . . . For just like the law, irony is a demand, an enormous demand, because it rejects reality and demands ideality. (CI, 213)[22]

---

[20]This keeps prophetic and ironic discourses from being metanarratives in Lyotard's sense, whose function is to legitimize rather than delegitimize "us." His primary paradigms, the metanarratives of Hegel and of Marx, speak from a possession of the future, which turns out to be "us," bourgeois modernity in Hegel's case, the revolution in Marx's case. See Jean-François Lyotard, The Postmodern Condition, trans. Geoff Bennington and Brian Massumi (Minneapolis: University of Minnesota Press, 1984).

[21]Destroyed "Judaism" as the confidence that through moral effort the phenomenon could be adequate to the essence, the real to the ideal. Kierkegaard does not here point out that there is nothing uniquely Jewish about this confidence, which easily turns into complacency or, as Nietzsche would say, "wretched contentment." But his attack on Christendom, which already begins here in Irony, is evidence that the "phariseeism" that concerns him most is Christian.

[22]It might seem strange that in this context Kierkegaard assimilates the sophists and the Pharisees, the former holding the law in contempt and the latter practically worshiping it. What they lack in common is precisely what Socrates and John the Baptist share, a profound sense of the discrepancy between the phenomenon and the essence and of the seriousness of this discrepancy.

In other words, the prophetic reading of Jewish law helps us to understand Socrates. Irony

> disciplines and punishes and thereby yields balance and consistency. Irony is a disciplinarian feared only by those who do not know it but loved by those who do. Anyone who does not understand irony at all . . . lacks what momentarily is indispensable for personal life; he lacks the bath of regeneration and rejuvenation, irony's baptism of purification that rescues the soul from having its life in finitude even though it is living energetically and robustly in it. (CI, 326)[23]

In this passage, Kierkegaard is speaking of still another mode of irony, which he calls controlled or mastered irony. But as surely as he could not possibly have made this claim for romantic irony, he might well have made it for Socratic irony. Surely the best and the brightest of Athens, who encountered Socrates' unwelcome questioning, experienced him as a stern disciplinarian indeed.

It is precisely this awareness of the law, of the always unmet demand for justice and of the repentance and renewal that are therefore always needed, that separates Socratic irony from sophistry (including romantic irony and all forms of phariseeism). While the latter is in the service of the ego, the former is in the service of the idea, not as its ambassador, or even Messiah, but as a voice in the wilderness calling to repentance and to preparing a way for the Messiah to come. Though it insists on the relativity of the prevailing moral and religious structures, it is not the demand to free the ego of all moral and religious constraints. It speaks from a deep moral and religious passion. But, to speak once again from Kierkegaard's Lutheran perspective, it is religious as law and not as gospel.

As infinite, absolute negativity, irony is not faith, which involves the positivity of affirmation and trust. Like sophistry,

---

[23]It is not so much baptism as a means of grace that Kierkegaard here has in mind as John the Baptist's baptism of repentance. The concluding reference to living "in" but not "of" the world's finitude anticipates the description of the knight of faith as "the heir to the finite" and as one to whom "the finite tastes just as good . . . as to one who never knew anything higher"—able to "delight in it as if finitude were the surest thing of all" (FT, 50, 40).

irony is an "everlasting duel" with the phenomenon. But "faith is victory over the world, and yet it is a struggle. . . . Faith is not an eternal struggle, but it is a victory that is struggling" (CI, 319). This interpretation of faith as a victory that still struggles is a profound commentary on the relation between law and gospel. Faith affirms the gospel and trusts its Savior. In this affirmation and trust is its victory. But just as the law is the only proper preparation for faith in the gospel ("Those who are well have no need of a physician, but those who are sick; I have come to call not the righteous but sinners to repentance" Luke 5:31-32), so this preparation stays with faith as a continuous resistance to all triumphalist self-interpretation by the believer and the believing community. It is, for example, the law that precludes in advance any translation of the gospel into a speculative system whose high priest, be he Hegel or some cleric of the left or right, is in the service of the idea as its possessor and authoritative mouthpiece. It is likewise the law that insists upon the distinction between any church and any society on the one hand and the Kingdom of God on the other. Irony is not faith, but properly welcomed it can protect faith from one of its gravest temptations.

* * *

On the contemporary scene, Jacques Derrida finds himself in a situation not altogether different from that of Socrates. Deconstruction, as its very name suggests, concerns itself with "a certain negativity."[24] Suspicious that such notions as "nature" and

---

[24]So writes Thomas Dutoit, ON, ix. In Citing works of Derrida the following sigla will be used.

AT "Of an Apocalyptic Tone Newly Adopted in Philosophy," in *Derrida and Negative Theology*, ed. Harold Coward and Toby Foshay (Albany: SUNY Press, 1992).

C *Circumfession* in Geoffrey Bennington and Jacques Derrida, *Jacques Derrida* (Chicago: University of Chicago Press, 1993).

D "Différance," in *Margins of Philosophy*, trans. Alan Bass (Chicago: University of Chicago Press, 1982).

FL "Force of Law: The 'Mystical Foundation of Authority,' " in *Deconstruction and the Possibility of Justice*, ed. Drucilla Cornell, Michel Rosenfeld, and David Gray Carlson (New York: Routledge, 1992).

GD *The Gift of Death*, trans. David Wills (Chicago: University of Chicago Press, 1995).

HAS "How to Avoid Speaking: Denials," in *Derrida and Negative Theology*.

"essence" function largely to disguise the *constructed* character of our language games, and thus of our meanings, our truths, and our practices, Derrida is ever vigilant for the ways in which they *deconstruct* themselves. So much so that he has been "accused . . . of resifting the procedures of negative theology" (HAS, 74). Indeed, it would not be hard to argue that deconstruction is an infinite, absolute negativity. Derrida himself, in exploring the close connection between deconstruction and negative theology, describes the latter as "ironic" (ON, 54).

So it is no surprise that our own Old Guard, who would have hated Socrates, has trouble distinguishing Derrida from the sophists. He is a "nihilist" (HAS 75). Or, as Derrida summarizes the recurring charges of those who "denounce" deconstruction as a kind of "mafia,"

> they have no secret. They pretend to have one in order to organize themselves around a social power. . . . These obscurantists are terrorists who remind one of the Sophists. A Plato would be of use in combating them. They possess a real power. . . . Experts in the art of evasion, they know better how to negate or deny than how to say anything. They always agree to avoid speaking while speaking a lot and "splitting hairs." (HAS, 88-89)[25]

Others, however, associate Derrida with Socrates rather than sophistry. Thus John D. Caputo finds deconstruction to be "Socratically suspicious of the prestige of the ruling discourse, of the system of exclusions that is put in place when a language claims to be the language of reality itself, when a language is taken

---

M   *Monolingualism of the Other; or, The Prosthesis of Origin*, trans. Patrick Mensah (Stanford: Stanford University Press, 1998).
ON *On the Name*, ed. Thomas Dutoit (Stanford: Stanford University Press, 1995).
P   "Psyche: Inventions of the Other," in *Reading de Man Reading*, ed. Lindsay Waters and Wlad Godzich (Minneapolis: University of Minnesota Press, 1989).
[25]For a brief account of one of the uglier incidents, with references to further literature, see John D. Caputo, *Deconstruction in a Nutshell* (New York: Fordham University Press, 1997) 38-41. I was recently e-mailed a four-page essay that someone I do not know found on the Internet, explaining that if journalists ever came to take deconstruction seriously it would be the end of journalistic objectivity. Journalists would feel free to write whatever they pleased, and it would be the end to democracy, freedom, and, apparently, all things decent.

to be what being itself would say were it given a tongue."[26] For this reason, Caputo writes elsewhere, "deconstruction does not affirm what *is*, does not fall down adoringly before what is *present*, for the present is precisely what demands endless analysis, criticism, and deconstruction." But to think this way is only to continue an "old and hoary tradition—*n'est-ce pas?*—that goes back to Socrates, with whom philosophy, on some accounting, opened its doors."[27]

On this view, the negativity of deconstruction might be viewed "as a practice of its own special version of Socratic irony—which earns it about as many friends as Socrates earned in his lifetime." It is "Socratically on the alert to the gap between every existing order and justice, which, if it does not exist, calls for and solicits existence." To be sure, "Derrida's irony is not the highly Plato-nized version of Socratic irony defended by Hegel, according to which Socratic irony is said to be driven by a positive vision of the form. Derrida would never lay claim to having 'seen' the 'form' of Justice. . . . " We have just seen Kierkegaard, in an essentially anti-Hegelian move, decisively separate Socratic irony from the speculative moves of Plato (and, by implication, of Hegel). But Caputo continues by insisting, "neither is Derrida's irony the Socratic irony defended in Kierkegaard's *The Concept of Irony*, according to which the Socratic is an infinite absolute negativity, for deconstruction is through and through affirmative, a *oui*, a yes, yes, to justice."[28]

But neither is Socratic irony sheer negativity. Kierkegaard's Socrates "would never lay claim to having 'seen' the 'form' of Justice. . . . " His irony is not in the service of the idea in that way. But it is in the service of the idea as judgment in the service of justice, law in the service of gospel, John the Baptist in the service of the Messiah. Negativity is not an end in itself. It points beyond itself as a reminder that neither Socrates nor Athens has this justice, this gospel, this Messiah in their possession, captured without remainder in their conceptual paradigms and conventional

---

[26]John D. Caputo, *The Prayers and Tears of Jacques Derrida: Religion without Religion* (Bloomington: Indiana University Press, 1997) 17.
[27]Caputo, *Nutshell*, 41.
[28]Caputo, *Nutshell*, 41.

practices. So perhaps deconstruction is not just closer to Socrates than to the sophists; perhaps it is closer to Socratic irony, as presented by Kierkegaard, than it appears even on Caputo's account.[29] In any case, whatever deconstruction's contributions to literary theory may be, its linkage to irony goes well beyond reflection on a particular trope. Like John the Baptist and the prophetic tradition in which he stands, Socratic irony and deconstruction are social critique in the service of a justice not yet present, either in theory or in practice, but which calls them and their societies to self-examination, repentance, and change.

An important site of clarification about the nature of deconstructive negativity is found in Derrida's repeated attempts to respond to the "accusation" that it amounts to what is called negative theology, "sometimes erroneously . . . for essential reasons one is never certain of being able to attribute to anyone a project of negative theology as such" (HAS, 73-74). In support of this reservation, Derrida cites Jean-Luc Marion, who says that if Dionysius "speaks of 'negative theologies' in the plural, he does not separate them from the 'affirmative theologies' with which they maintain the relationship which one describes here."[30]

Earlier on,[31] Derrida seeks to distance his own thought from negative theology along several lines. "No, what I write is not 'negative theology' " (HAS, 77). First, negative theologies "are always concerned with disengaging a superessentiality beyond the finite categories of essence and existence, that is, of presence, and always hastening to recall that God is refused the predicate of existence [among other predicates], only in order to acknowledge

---

[29]In the larger context of Kierkegaard's authorship, there is more positivity associated with irony than in the case of Derrida. For Kierkegaard's faith, his gospel, and his God are much "thicker" than their very formal correlates in Derrida.

[30]One can confirm this linkage of negative with positive in the case of Dionysius himself by reading The Mystical Theology in conjunction with The Divine Names and The Celestial Hierarchy in Pseudo-Dionysius: The Complete Works, trans. Colm Luibheid and Paul Rorem (New York: Paulist Press, 1987). The Derrida citation (HAS 131n.1) is from Marion's L'idole et la distance (Paris: Grasset, 1977) 244, forthcoming as Idol and Distance from Fordham University Press.

[31]Especially in D and HAS. French original publications in 1967 and 1987 respectively.

his superior, inconceivable, and ineffable mode of being" (D, 6; cf. HAS, 74, 77-78, 101-102). Thus, *différance* is unnameable but "is not an ineffable Being which no name could approach: God, for example" (D, 26).

Accordingly, deconstruction does not relate to an unnameable God in the way the negative theologian does. On the one hand, it does not address the unnameable in prayer and hymns of praise, at least not with a prayer to the Trinity, as Dionysius begins *The Mystical Theology*.[32] On the other hand, and closely related I believe, deconstruction does not, like negative theology hope for a silent, mystical union with the hyperessential God to whom it prays. Derrida's uneasiness with Dionysius is directed "toward the promise of that presence given to intuition or vision. . . . It is doubtless the vision of a dark light . . . but still it is the immediacy of a presence. Leading to union with God." Thus unknowing is a kind of knowing, "not an adequation but an unveiling." The movement is "toward that contact or vision, that pure intuition of the ineffable, that silent union with that which remains inaccessible to speech" (HAS, 79-80).[33]

---

[32]Derrida constantly emphasizes these linkages, especially that of prayer. See HAS, 75, 79, 81, 98, 103, 108, 110-12, 116-17, 121 and ON, 51, 56, 68. The matter is complicated by the fact that while Derrida tells us "that the constancy of God in my life is called by other names, so that I quite rightly pass for an atheist," he also speaks of "the omnipresence to me of what I call God in my absolved, absolutely private language" (C, 155). He insists, "I am addressing myself here to God . . . not only do I pray, as I have never stopped doing all my life, and pray to him, but I take him here and take him as my witness" (C, 57-58). He speaks *to* the hidden god "capable each time of receiving my prayer, you are my prayer's destiny, you know everything before me, you are the god (of my) unconscious" (C, 263). Statements of this sort make it possible for Caputo to write a book entitled, *The Prayers and Tears of Jacques Derrida*.

[33]Derrida quotes Dionysius as explaining prayer to the Trinity this way: "For while it is present to us, not all are present to it. Then, when we invoke it by our most holy prayers with an unpolluted intellect which is suited for the divine union, we shall be present to it . . . by our divine remembrance and invocation we ourselves shall be guided to it and be united with it" (HAS, 112; cf. *Complete Works*, 68-69). He also cites Eckhart as aspiring to see God naked by means of negation (HAS, 114-15). In other words, negative theology seeks to accomplish the metaphysics of presence by other means.

Later on, especially in *On the Name*, Derrida seems less concerned to distance himself from negative theology. Perhaps he feels he has done that sufficiently. Or perhaps, writing in 1989-90, when he speaks of "the conversion in me" about which "they" are ignorant (C, 216), he is alerting us to some significant, though hardly total, change that took place, not on his own deathbed but during that of his mother. In any case, he seems more content to describe negative theology in ways that emphasize its kinship with deconstruction, rather than its difference from *différance*.

Already in 1987 he had described negative theology as "a certain typical attitude toward language" which affirms "that every predicative language is inadequate to the essence, in truth to the hyperessentiality (the being beyond Being) of God" (HAS, 74). Now he seems less eager to focus on the peculiar "object" of negative theology and to see it as part of what Caputo nicely calls a "general apophatics."[34] With amazing succinctness, he reprises his early critique of a semantics of pure presence—"As soon as there are words . . . direct intuition no longer has any chance" (ON, 30; cf. 50).[35]

Thus negative theology is "what questions and casts suspicion on the very essence or possibility of language" (ON, 48). It is a " 'critique' (for the moment let's not say a 'deconstruction')" of language, or better, the "*Kenōsis* of discourse" (ON, 49-50).[36] It is a

---

[34]*Prayers and Tears*, 41.

[35]Derrida tells us "I have never ceased calling into question the motif of 'purity' in all its forms (the first impulse of what is called 'deconstruction' carries it toward this 'critique' of the phantasm or the axiom of purity . . . " (M, 46). Thus the critique of the metaphysics of presence is not the denial of presence but the denial of pure or sheer or total presence. For my money the best early versions of this critique are D, esp. 9-11 and 19-21; *Speech and Phenomena and Other Essays on Husserl's Theory of Signs*, trans. David B. Allison (Evanston IL: Northwestern University Press, 1973); and *Of Grammatology*, trans. Gayatri Chakravorty Spivak (Baltimore: Johns Hopkins University Press, 1974) in conjunction with *Positions*, trans. Alan Bass (Chicago: University of Chicago Press, 1981), especially the first two interviews.

[36]*Kenōsis* is, of course, a theologically loaded term signifying not just emptiness but self-emptying. I believe the reason Derrida puts "critique" in scare quotes and follows it with a reference to *kenōsis* is to counteract the subjectivist notion that deconstruction is something we do to language. The play of *différance* that produces (not fully determinate) meanings "is not simply an activity." Meanings

language that "says the inadequation of the reference, the insufficiency or the lapse of knowing, its incompetence as to what it is said to be the knowing of." It is thus a "sweet rage against language, this jealous anger of language within itself and against itself" (ON, 59). It teaches that our assertions are intentional arrows. "But an arrow is only an arrow; it is never an end in itself. It is everything save what it aims for . . . this is what makes the arrow miss even that which it touches, which thereby remains safe" (ON, 61-62). The negativity of deconstruction is succinctly expressed in this skepticism about the adequacy of language to its object. That is why Derrida can write, "I trust no text that is not in some way contaminated with negative theology" (ON, 69).

But there is a political dimension to deconstructive negativity that means it is not just a philosophy of language in any abstract and innocent sense. As early as "Différance" Derrida links deconstruction not only to the "tomb of the proper"[37] but also to "the death of the tyrant. . . . Not only is there no kingdom of différance, but différance instigates the subversion of every kingdom." He then adds the prophetic words, "Which makes it obviously threatening and infallibly dreaded by everything within us that desires a kingdom" (D, 4, 22).

The political dimension of deconstruction for the most part lies dormant in the earliest texts. But as we move toward the present, it moves increasingly front and center. The politics of deconstruction can be read as the answer Derrida gives to a question he poses to himself at the beginning of the 1980s. In his essay on apocalyptic discourse (including, at least by implication, "postmodern" discourses on the death of God, the death of man, the death

---

are effects, to be sure, "but they are effects which do not find their cause in a subject or a substance" (D, 11). If language in its constructive mode is not an event over which the subject presides, this is true by extension of language in its deconstructive mode. This is one of the positive links between deconstruction and Hegelian dialectic. See Kenley R. Dove's analysis of dialectic as a process we watch rather than something we do, in "Hegel's Phenomenological Method," *The Review of Metaphysics* 23 (1970): 615-41.

[37]The "proper" (*le propre*) signifies a link between right and nature or essence. Like the author of *Billy Budd*, Derrida is hinting that a theory of natural or human rights built on a philosophy of nature or essence is not unambiguously in the service of justice, just because such concepts are constructions.

of the author, the death of the subject, the end of philosophy, overcoming metaphysics, etc.), Derrida notes that such discourse promises truth and he poses the question: "to what ends?" It is eager "to seduce in order to lead. . . . " By letting others in on the secret about the end, it says, "We'll be a sect. . . . They sleep, we stay awake" (AT, 53-54).

Derrida is here practicing the hermeneutics of suspicion. In response to the promise of truth, he does not ask, Is it really true? but rather, To what ends?[38] It is a question of motives (AT, 59) and of interests which "can be so dissimulated under the desire for light" that demystification turns out to be a "diversity of apocalyptic ruses" (AT, 52). Derrida knows that his own discourse is not exempt. Every discourse that does not belong to the established codes will have an apocalyptic tone, and "all language on apocalypse is also apocalyptic and cannot be excluded from its object." Is it not "in the best apocalyptic tradition" that "we, *Aufklärer* of modern times . . . denounce false apocalypses?" Even if we try, Derrida suggests, to "distinguish a deconstruction from a simple progressive demystification in the style of the Enlightenment," the inescapable question remains, "to what end . . . ?" (AT, 59-61).

In posing the question, To what end?, to his own discourse, Derrida poses the Kierkegaardian question, Negativity in the service of what? If it turns out that deconstruction is negativity in the service of the ego, Derrida will rightly be classed with the sophists, in the worst sense of the term. Derrida knows that in the final analysis he cannot be his own judge. But he does tell us what he thinks the answer to that question, To what end?, is in the case of deconstruction. Immediately after developing the question with some care and making clear that his own work is not exempt from the suspicion it expresses, he writes, "For want of time, I shall limit myself to the word, if it is a word, and to the motif 'Come' that occupies other texts written in the meantime, in particular 'Pas,' 'Living On,' and 'At This very Moment in This Work Here

---

[38]I have elaborated on this difference between skepticism and suspicion in *Suspicion and Faith: The Religious Uses of Modern Atheism* (New York: Fordham University Press, 1998) chap. 2.

I Am' " (AT, 62).[39] Whenever we ask Derrida to what end his thought is so negative, he wants us to hear the Come (*erkhou, veni, viens*) that reverberates through his work, just as it reverberates through the Apocalypse of St. John.

For my money, Derrida's best account of deconstruction's Come! is in a fourth essay, "Psyche: Inventions of the Other," in which he not only gives a deconstructive analysis of invention but presents deconstruction itself as invention (P, 42).[40] And to invent, he tells us, "would then be to 'know' how to say 'come' " (P, 56).

There is an unmistakable negativity to invention, and thus to deconstruction. It involves "breaking the rules . . . always presupposes some illegality . . . it inserts a disorder into the peaceful ordering of things, it disregards the proprieties" (P, 25). No doubt deconstruction will always be attractive to that sophomore who resents the fact that she cannot legally drink until midway through her junior year and to her teacher, the assistant professor who chafes at the code which forbids him to make her a target of sexual conquest.

But to those adolescents who love deconstruction because of its transgression theme, Derrida says "things are not so simple" (P, 41). The break with the established order, its rules and its proprieties, is not the whole story. There is a positive side as well. As inventive, deconstruction "involves an affirmation, this latter being linked to the coming—the *venire*—in event, advent, invention." This *venire* signifies "the event of a novelty that must surprise, because at the moment when it comes about, there could be no statute, no status, ready and waiting to reduce it to the same. . . . If an invention seems to have to surprise or unsettle statutory conditions, it must in turn imply or produce other statutory conditions" (P, 42-44; cf. 55).

---

[39]"Pas" and "Living On" are found in *Parages* (Paris: Galilée, 1986), the latter trans. by James Hulbert in *Deconstruction and Criticism*, ed. Harold Bloom et al. (New York: Continuum, 1979). "At This Very Moment" is found in *Re-Reading Levinas*, ed. Robert Bernasconi and Simon Critchley (Bloomington: Indiana University Press, 1991).

[40]This is possible because we do not just invent machines and technical apparatus but also stories, and thus meaning and truth (P 32, 49).

This is the dialectic of invention: it denies ultimacy to the statuses of the status quo in order to open a space for what is "brand new" (P, 27). Nor does invention just find new ways to satisfy old desires; it is willing "to dream of inventing a new desire" (P, 42). It can thus be thought as "an event through which the future (l'*avenir*) comes to us" (P, 46). It is "the inauguration for the future of a *possibility* or of a *power* that will remain at the disposal of everyone. A*d*vent there must be, because the *e*vent of an invention . . . must be valid *for the future (a-venir)*" (P, 28).

In its affirmative moment, deconstruction says come (*viens*) to the future (l'*avenir*). This future has two distinctive marks, closely intertwined: it is impossible and it is other. Elsewhere Derrida tells us he has "never loved anything but the impossible" (C, 3). Here he warns that for deconstruction "*possibility* would rather be the danger, the danger of becoming an available set of rule-governed procedures, methods, and accessible approaches. The interest of deconstruction . . . is a certain experience of the impossible: that is . . . the experience of the other as the invention of the impossible" (P, 36).[41] Thus "the only possible invention would be the invention of the impossible" (P, 60).

But if possibility is a threat to deconstruction and invention is the invention of the impossible, how can it be "the inauguration for the future of a *possibility*," as we just read? It is in terms of another category, other/same, that Derrida answers this question. There is such a thing as "the invention of the same and from the possible" in which "nothing comes to the other or from the other. For the other is not the possible" (P, 60). The possibility that belongs to the same is essentially more of the same. Its arrival surprises only superficially, for it is easily assimilated into the established order of things. In this "invention of the same" there is no "absolute surprise," nothing "entirely other" (P, 55).

It is just such a surprise for which deconstruction awaits and to which it says Come, an "unanticipatable alterity . . . for which no horizon of waiting as yet seems ready" (P, 55); for "at the moment when it comes about, there could be no statute, no status,

---

[41]Derrida also describes deconstruction as "an experience of the impossible" in FL, 15.

ready and waiting to reduce it to the same" (P, 43).[42] It is not possible within the status quo, which always limits possibility to that which conforms to the actual. Hence the only possible invention (at least so far as deconstruction is concerned) is the invention of the impossible. But the actual, which purports to contain all true possibilities, does not. To the Horatio who defines and guards the horizons of every language/power game, deconstruction says, "There are more possibilities in heaven and earth than are dreamt of in your philosophy."[43] It is these possibilities, genuinely new precisely because they are impossible within prevailing paradigms, that Derrida has in mind when he speaks of "the inauguration for the future of a *possibility* or of a *power* that will remain at the disposal of everyone" (P, 28).

This otherness so radical as to be impossible in the specified sense is clearly not at our disposal either conceptually or causally. "Yet it is necessary to prepare for it; for to allow the coming of the entirely other, passivity . . . is not suitable. Letting the other come is *not inertia open to anything whatever* . . . one gets ready for it. . . . To invent would then be to 'know' how to say 'come' and to answer the 'come' of the other" (P, 55-56, emphasis added). Not against but beyond the invention of the same, deconstruction would "offer a place for the other, would let the other come. I am careful to say 'let it come' because if the other is precisely what is not invented, the initiative or deconstructive inventiveness can consist only in opening, in uncloseting, destabilizing foreclusionary structures so as to allow for the passage toward the other. But one does not make the other come, one lets it come by preparing for its coming" (P, 60).

In other words, deconstructive negativity plays the role of John the Baptist, not in Hegelian fashion as the temporary detour of a reason that is always able to return to itself, but in Kierkegaardian

---

[42]The contrast here resembles that between normal science and the emergence of a new paradigm in a scientific revolution. See Thomas S. Kuhn, *The Structure of Scientific Revolutions* (Chicago: University of Chicago Press, 1962).
[43]With apologies to Hamlet. The refusal to restrict possibility to what the actual can accommodate is the central thrust of Herbert Marcuse in *One Dimensional Man* (Boston: Beacon Press, 1964). He presents negative thinking as the essential resistance to one-dimensionality.

fashion. His negativity was not in the service of the ego ("He was not the one who was supposed to come") nor of the Established Order ("he did not know what was to come" [CI, 263]) but of something greater than either: in biblical language, the Kingdom of God, in the language of Plato and Hegel, the Idea.

We should not be surprised, then, when Derrida introduces messianic themes into his thought. He has told us all along that deconstruction is political. Now he tells us it prepares for a future politics. Moreover, in his talk about the alterity of the future to which deconstruction says Come!, we cannot but suspect that this is not the abstract, ontological otherness of something merely different, but involves the concrete, Levinasian Other by whom I (and We) are put into question and to whom and for whom I (and We) are responsible. When, in his re-reading of *Fear and Trembling*, he tells us that every other is wholly other (*tout autre est tout autre*), this ethico-political reading is overtly confirmed (GD, ch. 3-4).

What is the content of deconstructive, messianic politics? On the one hand, since it is impossible, since it concerns the "brand new" (P, 27), the "absolute surprise" and the "entirely other" (P, 55), it falls under Derrida's "general apophatics." *Je ne sais quoi*. On the other hand, these phrases turn out to be a bit hyperbolic. "Letting the other come is not inertia open to anything whatever" (P, 55). It is especially in terms of three names that Derrida "identifies" the future for which deconstruction prepares: justice, hospitality, and the democracy to come. In works such as "Force of Law," "Back from Moscow, in the USSR," *Adieu to Emmanuel Levinas*, *The Other Heading*, *Specters of Marx*, and *The Politics of Friendship*, among others, Derrida develops these themes.[44] They are not regulative ideals, for Derrida does not purport to know just what it is we have not yet attained. But, to repeat once again, deconstruction is not "inertia open to anything whatever" (P, 55), and Derrida knows enough about the future to which he says

---

[44]For "Force of Law" and *On the Name*, see sigla above. *Adieu to Emmanuel Levinas*, trans. Pascale-Anne Brault and Michael Naas (Stanford: Stanford University Press, 1999); *The Other Heading*, trans. Pascale-Anne Brault and Michael Naas (Bloomington: Indiana University Press, 1992); *Specters of Marx*, trans. Peggy Kamuf (New York: Routledge, 1994); and *Politics of Friendship*, trans. George Collins (New York: Verso, 1997).

Come! to call it justice, hospitality, and democracy. Like Aquinas, Derrida makes bold to name the unnameable. He presupposes, but does not articulate, a doctrine of analogy to go with his "general apophatics."[45]

Derrida does not prove that democracy is better than the alternatives, nor that some form of democracy is the wave of the future. Nor does he provide any guarantees that his type of negative thinking cannot be put to libertine usage which identifies liberty with license. But the point was not to show that he fulfills the aspirations of Locke or Hegel. It was to show a certain affinity between deconstruction and Socratic irony as interpreted by our good friend Kierkegaard.

---

[45]See n. 32 above. Like Dionysius, Aquinas has a strong "negative theology," denying the adequation of our intellect to the divine reality. And like Dionysius, he nevertheless thinks it possible to speak meaningfully and appropriately about God. Similarly, while Derrida denies that we can have essential knowledge of what, for example, democracy ultimately means, he thinks it quite possible to name the politics of the future 'democracy' and not 'fascism' or 'feudalism'.

13

The Irony of Revelation:
The Young Kierkegaard Listens to the Old Schelling

Peter Fenves

Imagine this situation: a young scholar has just completed a brilliant thesis in which he sets out to prove that a particular phenomenon can, should, and must be understood in terms of a certain characteristic—call it unsystematic "negativity"—which, in turn, can be understood only in terms of its opposite, namely a "positive system." He then takes a trip to hear a once-renowned philosopher lecture about a closely related matter: the relation of negative to positive philosophy. As the young scholar begins to take meticulous take notes on these lectures, making a fair copy every night, he quickly realizes that the old philosopher calls "negative philosophy" what he, the young scholar, had previously understood as "positive philosophy," and the old philosopher proceeds to develop a "positive philosophy" that, for all its obscurity, has something in common with what the young scholar calls the "negative position" with which he is principally concerned. The young scholar could not fail to feel confused, lost, or, in any case, disoriented to the point where negativity and positivity would be reversed or—and this would be worse—lose their polar valences altogether. What an ironic situation, especially if the subject matter of the young scholar's thesis were irony. If the old philosopher has been able to reveal something about the relation of negative to positive philosophy, the thesis would not simply be ironic according to its own terms; it would turn out to be ironically ironic—which is not the same thing at all.

* * *

This story does not perfectly capture the situation in which Søren Kierkegaard found himself in the late months of 1841 and the early months of 1842, but it does describe his situation up to a point. Kierkegaard had, of course, completed a brilliant, spirited thesis in which he argues, according to the wording of its eighth thesis, "Irony, as infinite and absolute negativity, is the lightest and weakest indication of subjectivity" (CI, 5-6). And he had traveled to Berlin to hear Friedrich Schelling give his famous lectures at the University of Berlin—lectures in which the agèd philosopher and one-time friend of Hegel announces that the latter had got it all wrong: the philosophical movement that he, Schelling, had initiated under the rubric of "identity philosophy" was supposed to have developed into a "positive philosophy," not a merely into a "science of logic."[1] Identity philosophy was supposed to have issued into a mode of inquiry concerned with actual existence, not simply with being-able-to-exist or *a priori* conditions of possibility. Hegel, according to Schelling, circumvented the original task, contented himself with thought-things, not real things, and thus ironically developed a neither-nor philosophy[2]— neither strictly positive nor strictly negative—when, all along, he

---

[1]Schelling's lectures are available only in his auditors' transcriptions; the most complete transcription is the (ironically titled) one published by Heinrich Eberhard Gottlob Paulus, *Die endlich offenbar gewordene positive Philosophie der Offenbarung oder Entstehungsgeschichte, wörtliche Text, Beurtheilung und Berichtigung der v. Schellingischen Entdeckungen über Philosophie überhaupt, Mythologie und Offenbarung des dogmatischen Christenthums in Berliner Wintercursus von 1841–1842* (Darmstadt: Leske, 1843). For a readily available edition of Paulus's transcription, see Friedrich Schelling, *Philosophie der Offenbarung 1841/42*, ed. and intro. Manfred Frank (Frankfurt am Main: Suhrkamp, 1977); a translation of Kierkegaard's notes can be found in the Hongs's edition of *The Concept of Irony*. The notes themselves can be found in *Søren Kierkegaards Papirer*, ed. Niels Thulstrup (Copenhagen: Gyldendal, 1970) 13:254-329. Translations are occasionally modified to conform to the original. (The Hongs expand Kierkegaard's abbreviations and add connectives.)

[2]According to a letter Kierkegaard writes to F. C. Sibbern, the professor who signed the certificate of authentication under a misprinted date—or was this misprint itself ironic, and did Kierkegaard therefore receive his master's degree only in jest?—the opening lectures of Schelling can be summarized as an indictment of Hegel for developing a philosophy of "neither-nor": "The negative is given, but not by Hegel, for Hegel's is neither negative nor positive but is a refined Spinozism" (LD, 107; letter 55).

thought he was doing something else: making the philosophy, as the love of wisdom, into science. If, according to the young Kierkegaard, who largely relies on Hegelian schemata for the characterization of philosophical positions, Socrates is a figure of infinite and absolute negativity, so, too, strangely enough, is Hegel, according to the line of argument Schelling pursues in his Berlin lectures.[3] From this perspective, a thesis on irony could just as well have made constant reference to *Hegel* instead of Socrates—which, of course, Kierkegaard's thesis does, but only insofar as it takes Hegel to task for interpreting Socrates as a positive philosopher, albeit only a minimal one, and thereafter reiterates in an intensified, ironized form Hegel's critique of romantic irony. To cite only one particularly schematic passage in Kierkegaard's thesis: "the negative in the system corresponds to irony in historical actuality. In historical actuality, the negative exists, which is never the case in the system" (CI, 192, modified). If, however, the negative not only exists "in" the system but *would* have constituted the system as such if it had successfully accomplished its immanent goal, as Schelling argues, then all of the subsequent theses of Kierkegaard's thesis are subject to revision—at the very least. At the most, Kierkegaard's thesis would be ironic on terms other than its own. No wonder Kierkegaard writes to his closest friend, even as he registers his disappointment with Schelling's lectures: "confusion in my philosophical ideas" (LD, 134-35; letter 68 to Emil Boesen).

Kierkegaard did not manage to sit through Schelling's lectures. Like many of his contemporaries who were drawn to these lectures for a variety of reasons—from revolutionary aspirations to idle curiosity—his hopes for something exceptional were dashed, and long before Schelling began to make good on his promise to develop a "philosophy of revelation," Kierkegaard, again like many of his contemporaries, lost interest. He may have continued to attend Schelling's lectures, but his notetaking appropriately

---

[3]In an earlier work, *Papers from One Still Living*, Kierkegaard emphasizes the negativity of Hegel's system: "Like Hegel, it [the tendency] begins, not the system but existence, with nothing, and the negative element, through which and by virtue of which all the movements occur (Hegel's immanent negativity of the concept), is distrust, which undeniably has such a negative force that it—and that is the good thing about it—must end by killing itself" (EPW, 64).

breaks off on a note of opacity—as the old philosopher derives the name *Orpheus* from *orphnaios* ("the dark").[4] This well-known episode in the annals of German idealism—its last gasp, as it were—did not, however, mark the end of Kierkegaard's interest in Schelling, about whom he had written as early as 1840: "The view that Hegel is a parenthesis in Schelling seems to be more and more manifest; we are only waiting for the parenthesis to close" (CI, 440). As several commentators have noted, Kierkegaard very likely returned to the original manifesto of Schelling's late philosophy— *Philosophical Investigations into the Essence of Human Freedom*[5]—in preparation for his own inquiry into the relation of freedom to sin, an inquiry he would undertake under a title reminiscent of his master's thesis: *The Concept of Anxiety*.[6] Instead of proceeding to

---

[4]For a summary account of Kierkegaard's relation to Schelling's Berlin lectures, see Niels Thulstrup, "Kierkegaard and Schelling's Philosophy of Revelation," in *Kierkegaard and Speculative Idealism* (= *Bibliotheca Kierkegaardiana* 4), ed. N. Thulstrup (Copenhagen: Reitzel, 1979) 144-59; a slightly different version of this account can be found in the magisterial study of Thulstrup, *Kierkegaard's Relation to Hegel*, trans. George Stengren (Princeton: Princeton University Press, 1980) 267-74. It seems to me almost empirically verifiable that Thulstrup's contention that Kierkegaard's "main interest was Schelling's criticism of Hegel, that is, the negative aspect of Schelling's positive philosophy" (274) is false, since significantly more than half of Kierkegaard's notes are devoted to other matters. For a view of the relation between Kierkegaard and Schelling that resembles Thulstrup, see the introduction of Howard Hong and Edna Hong to their edition of *The Concept of Irony*, xviii-xxv. An early attempt in this same direction can be found in Anton Koktanek, *Schellings Seinslehre und Kierkegaard* (Munich: Oldenbourg, 1962).

[5]See Friedrich Schelling, *Philosophische Untersuchungen über das Wesen der menschlichen Freiheit und die damit zusammenhängenden Gegenstände* (Frankfurt am Main: Suhrkamp, 1975); *Philosophical Inquiries into the Nature of Human Freedom*, trans. James Gutmann (La Salle IL: Open Court, 1936).

[6]See esp. Vincent A. McCarthy, "Schelling and Kierkegaard on Freedom and Fall," in *International Kierkegaard Commentary: 'The Concept of Anxiety,'* ed. Robert L. Perkins (Macon GA: Mercer University Press, 1985) 89-109; Louis Dupré, "Time and Eternity," in *IKC: 'The Concept of Anxiety,'* esp. 111-15; Günter Figal, "Schellings und Kierkegaards Freiheitsbegriff," in *Kierkegaard und die deutsche Philosophie seiner Zeit* (= *Text & Kontext* 7), ed. Heinrich Anz, Peter Kemp, and Friedrich Schmöe (Copenhagen and Munich: Fink, 1980) 112-27; and Arne Grøn, "Das Transzendenzproblem bei Kierkegaard und beim späten Schelling," in *Kierkegaard und die deutsche Philosophie seiner Zeit*, 128-48. And Michael Theunissen, "Die Dialektik der Offenbarung: Zur Auseinandersetzung Schellings und

elucidate the traces of Schelling's late philosophy in this work or other, similar ones—a major project that has yet to be to carried out in full[7]—it may be worthwhile to pause and consider, in reverse, how the project undertaken in *The Concept of Irony* is made even more problematic when it is brought into relation with Schelling's so-called "positive philosophy." I say "more problematic" because, of course, *The Concept of Irony* is anything but problem-free from its opening words onward. And yet the problems it poses could in principle be solved by its own preferred method; more precisely, the master's thesis on irony could be understood as itself ironical, and this self-subverting thesis about his thesis would allow its problematical character to reveal itself—and thereby to vanish. Soon after Kierkegaard's death, a reviewer noted that the thesis was ironical, and this note has been repeated, sometimes in highly nuanced forms, numerous times since.[8] If,

---

Kierkegaards mit der Religionsphilosophie Hegels," *Philosophisches Jahrbuch* (1964): 134-60. Many of the terms of this discussion were set by Walter Schutz's *Vollendung des deutschen Idealismus in der Spätphilosophie Schellings* (Stuttgart: Kohlhammer, 1955) esp. 274-79.

[7]The words Vincent McCarthy wrote in 1985 are still true today: "the full story of Kierkegaard's encounter with Schelling's philosophy has not been told. Indeed, it has hardly begun to be told, and in great part because of a preoccupation with Hegel in Kierkegaard studies" ("Schelling and Kierkegaard on Freedom and Fall," 92).

[8]See the introduction of Howard Hong and Edna Hong to their translation of *The Concept of Anxiety*, xiv: "The review also states that the work 'not only treats irony but is irony.' " Lee Capel discusses the ironic status of the thesis on irony in the "Historical Introduction" to his translation of *The Concept of Irony*, trans. Lee M. Capel (Bloomington: Indiana University Press, 1962) esp. 31-38. For an exceptional expansion on this insight, see Sylviane Agacinski, *Aparté: Conceptions and Deaths of Søren Kierkegaard*, trans. and intro. Kevin Newmark (Tallahassee: Florida University Press, 1988) esp. 33-78; see also Kevin Newmark's introductory essay, "Taking Kierkegaard Apart," in *Aparté*, 3-30. In a lecture entitled "The Concept of Irony," Paul de Man begins by claiming that *The Concept of Irony* is "an ironic title, because irony is not a concept" (de Man, *Aesthetic Ideology*, ed. and intro. Andrzej Warminski [Minneapolis: University of Minnesota Press, 1996] 163). De Man's reason for declaring that "irony is not a concept" is a little strange: "the fact that if irony were indeed a concept it should be possible to give a definition of irony" (164). Within the context of Hegelianism—and de Man does not fail to indicate that Hegel is the one against whom Kierkegaard writes—the reverse would be closer to the truth, for abstract definitions run counter to concretion of

however, the general framework in which Kierkegaard sought to capture the phenomenon of irony—especially the framework outlined by the terms *negativity* and *positivity*—was itself fallible or even aberrant, then the ironical character of *The Concept of Irony* would not be "mastered," to use the word with which the thesis comes to a conclusion.[9] Irony would not be grasped or conceived— not even ironically. And the failure of the thesis would require a rethinking of what is to be done with the ungraspable moment of "pure irony."

The point of reading *The Concept of Irony* backwards, as it were, from the perspective of the philosophical program Kierkegaard overhears in Berlin, is not psychological; it is not to speculate on Kierkegaard's cast of mind when he hears that Hegel's system, far from being "positive" (CI, 323), as he asserts in the final words of the penultimate section of his thesis, can be summarized by the phrase "neither-nor." Still less is the point to make the thesis into an anticipation of Schelling's philosophy of revelation. Rather, the point of reading Kierkegaard's thesis in conjunction with the early sessions of Schelling's Berlin lectures is to lay out a specific philosophical-historical conjuncture in which the very ideas of "position," "positing," and "positivity" are so thoroughly shaken that a term like *irony* can carry out the ironic function of restabilization, even when it is understood at bottom as a "negative position" (CI, 269). A further thesis would be that Kierkegaard's pseudonymous authorship seeks out a more thoroughgoing, more fully fashioned response to the convulsion undergone by the idea of "position" as it organizes itself around the images of "point," discontinuity ("leap"), and "sphere," but such a thesis cannot be pursued in such a limited space. By reading *The Concept of Irony* from the perspective of Schelling's "positive philosophy," some of the problems and peculiarities of the former can be revealed in their own terms—without the trump-term *irony* having the power to bring everything ironically back into line (even if this line is, for its part, accordingly inchoate). And if this approximates some of

---

the concept.

[9]See the conclusion to the thesis, "Irony as a Controlled Element [*behersket Moment*], the Truth of Irony" (CI, 324-29).

Kierkegaard's own thoughts concerning the possibility of translating his thesis into German[10] or, more importantly, if it captures some of his reflections on the project of authorship to which he devoted himself upon returning disappointed from Berlin, so much the better; but it is not here essential. On at least two points the concerns of *The Concept of Irony* converge with those of Schelling's Berlin lectures: positivity and "divine irony." The essay discusses these two points of contact and concludes with a brief discussion of where they meet: in sin.

Positivity

If there is one overriding and underlying imperative to Hegelian thought, it consists in this: resolve all *relata*—which is to say, independent terms of a relation—into the relation itself. The relation alone is real and concrete; the *relata*, by contrast, are abstract, self-inconsistent moments. By insisting on their own reality, *relata* refute themselves, for they *are* what they are (a determinate something) only in relation to something else, more exactly, in relation to everything else, and more exactly still, in relation to the relation conceiving itself in its entirety. No *relata* can exist on their own, by definition, and the definitive, indeed the final character of Hegelian thought consists in responding in full to the imperative to define the infinite and infinitely self-mediating relation to the bitter—or comic—end: every relatum is absorbed into its relation, and the power of the relation consists in this irrepressible, expressive self-absorption, which, in turn, constitutes the essence and enactment of thought.

Each of Hegel's works contains a catalogue, so to speak, of relation terms, all of which are progressively absorbed into the relation of which they constitute determinate moments. Regardless of whether the *relata* are expressed in terms of natural philosophy, psychology, the science of spirit, or any other scientific disciplines, the imperative remains the same: no terms are positive; all are

---

[10]See Kierkegaard's letter to Professor Sibbern: "The longer I live here in Berlin the more I realize the truth of the advice your have given me again and again out of regard for both me and my dissertation: that it be translated into German. I will wait and see about that" (LD, 108; letter 55).

terms of the relation from which they are determined. Apply this imperative to the study of law, and the result is well known: outside of the state in which the relation of individuals to one another is fully mediated, individuals are nothing more than abstract entities, *persona* at best, ephemera at worst. Apply the same imperative to theology, broadly conceived, and the result is the same: there can be no God of creation, since creation is, by definition, an act in which the creator enjoys independent existence; for this reason, there can be no God other than one who would be all in all, the self-relation in which everything would express itself as absolute, divine "relativity": to cite Kierkegaard's characterization of Schelling's denunciation of Hegel in his Berlin lectures, "refined Spinozism" (LD, 107; letter 55).

Whatever else Schelling's late philosophy seeks to accomplish, it runs counter to the basic Hegelian imperative; with little guidance from either ancient or modern philosophy, almost on its own, it sets out to discover a mode of rational inquiry in which the independent existence of certain *relata* can be affirmed without this affirmation amounting to unphilosophical empiricism, abstract reflection, or baseless mysticism (although his inquiries are often confused with all three). One relation in which the *relata* must remain independent from one another to the degree that their relation defines them is, as Schelling emphasizes in his *Philosophical Investigations into the Essence of Human Freedom*, the relation of love: lovers who could not exist without those whom they love are not in reality lovers,[11] and so this relation would ironically disappear under the Hegelian imperative—ironically because the relation of love is the relation *par excellence*, the relation in which the idea of revelation alone makes sense, even as it correspondingly robs revelation of all "positive" content: revelation is the disclosure of the fact of unconditional, noncategorial, nonpredicative (and one might add, unpredictable) love. Schelling's late philosophy does not present itself so much as a corrective to Hegelian thought as

---

[11]Nowhere is Schelling more exact in this regard than in an apothegm included in his treatise *On the Nature of Human Freedom*: "this is the secret of love, that it unites such beings as could each exist for itself, and nonetheless neither is nor can be without the other" (*Wesen der menschlichen Freiheit*, 99-100; *Essence of Human Freedom*, 89; translation modified).

its antagonist, and the agon centers around this: whether it is possible for philosophy to concede a space for—and thereafter conceive of—a positive *relatum*, which is to say, something that stands in a relation but whose being is not for this reason completely absorbed therein. Such an agon turns into a philosophy of revelation for the precise reason that the relation *par excellence*—call it "love"—*is* only insofar as it reveals itself, and in order for there to be revelation, there must be someone "positive" to which someone equally "positive" is revealed: existence in the relation of love is revelation of the love in and through which the lover exists.

In his Berlin lectures, Schelling does not explicate his program in these terms, and Kierkegaard did not attend his lectures long enough to hear any part of his exposition of the "philosophy of revelation." But the lectures Kierkegaard heard were nevertheless divided into two basic parts: a presentation of the theogonic process in which revelation is supposed to make sense follows upon an inquiry into the difference between negative, which Hegel misunderstood, and positive philosophy, which Schelling would like to develop in full. Now the term "positivity" is far from neutral in the context of the philosophical initiative begun by Kant—not only the Kant of the *Critiques* but also (and this is just as important for Schelling's doctrine of potency) the Kant of the precritical *One Possible Ground of Proof for the Demonstration of God's Existence*: "being [*Dasein*] is the absolute position of a thing."[12] This programmatic principle in conjunction with a doctrine of modality according to which actuality precedes possibility serves as the basis for the young Kant's resuscitation of the ontological argument, and

---

[12]Kant, *Gesammelte Schriften*, ed. Königlich Preußische [later Deutsche] Akademie der Wissenschaften (Berlin: Reimer; later, De Gruyter, 1900–   ) 2:73; *The One Possible Demonstration*, trans. Gordon Treash (New York: Abaris, 1979) 74; §2. See also *The Critique of Pure Reason*, A:598; B:626. Cf. Martin Heidegger's essay, which also mentions Schelling in passing, "Kants These über das Sein," in *Wegmarken* (Frankfurt am Main: Klostermann, 1967), 273-307; "Kant's Thesis on Being," trans. Ted Klein, Jr. and William Pohl, *The Southwestern Journal of Philosophy* 4 (1973): 7-33. See also the investigation of "irony after Fichte" undertaken by Werner Hamacher in "Position Exposed: Friedrich Schlegel's Poetological Transposition of Fichte's Absolute Proposition," *Premises: Essays in Philosophy and Literature from Kant to Celan*, trans. P. Fenves (Stanford: Stanford University Press, 1999) 222-60.

the same principle is made into a dynamic thesis by the founder of German idealism—*as* the founding of German idealism in Fichte's various attempts at forging a *Wissenschaftslehre* (theory of science): the I posits itself absolutely, and the I alone "is there," which is to say, absolutely self-positing. With Fichte's exposition of positivity, however, Kant's contention that being is nonpredicative is annulled: *Dasein* becomes a predicate once again; more exactly, things exist only insofar as they are posited by the self-conscious I, which, in turn, consists in pure self-positing. Being, in short, is the position of pure self-consciousness. Identity philosophy takes its point of departure from the idea of absolute self-positing; but, according to Schelling's reconstruction of his (and Hegel's) philosophical path away from Fichte, the positing of the not-I on whose basis an empirical I makes itself known confuses the two senses of negation that Plato and Plutarch had clearly discerned.[13] The not-I is *relative* negativity, and so, too, is the I, which can know itself only in relation to the not-I: "This relative nonbeing is really the central point in the philosophy of identity, whereby it shows that it has abandoned the subjective orientation in Fichte" (CI, 342). With this distinction between absolute and relative negation, which Fichte misses, Schelling inadvertently touches on the central point of "pure irony" for his young Danish auditor as well: in what does absolute, infinite negativity consist? No question of irony after Fichte can ignore this question, especially since Fichte misses the distinction—and therefore the negativity—internal to the idea of negation. Identity philosophy, for Schelling, explores in full the realm of relative nonbeing, *mē on*, to use the Platonic term, and it does nothing more: it is the realm of a priori conditions of possibility, "essences," or pure being-able, without the transition of possibility into actuality that would be accomplished in a self-positing act. The task of positive philosophy, by contrast, which begins in earnest—or perhaps in irony—with Schelling's *Philosophical Investigations into the Essence of Human Freedom*, lies in coming to terms with what absolutely posits itself

---

[13]See Schelling's discussion of the distinction between *ouk on* and *mē on* that Plato makes in *The Sophist*, transcribed by Kierkegaard, *The Concept of Irony*, 342.

on the basis of an abyssal groundlessness or *Ungrund* which constitutively disposes with every positional act.

All of this is familiar to those trained in German idealism. In the Berlin lectures—for all their ponderousness—Schelling then proceeds to issue an imperative unlike the one under which Hegelian thought operates. Kierkegaard captures it in the following lines: "The philosophy of identity presupposed nature and arrived at freedom, at individual action and the individuality of history; arrived at the power that does lose itself in the process, arrived at God as the *über dem Seyn bleibende*. But this concept is not like the others. It cannot be referred to experience, and yet it does not leave us indifferent; a subjective and moral necessity [*Nødv.*] insists on finding it. The pure science of reason has no basis for going beyond itself, but this necessity will lead to a seeking outside itself for that which it does not have in itself" (CI, 353).[14] Positive philosophy stands under the "subjective and moral" imperative to discover whatever remains "beyond being," that is, over and above being understood as a position in consciousness, a moment of knowledge or science—and yet *also* remains in reflection and therefore in the realm of reason. For the "beyond being" must nevertheless, for Schelling, be *thought*; it cannot simply be presupposed, intimated in some mystical union, or claimed on the basis of unmediated "knowledge." A philosophy that remains content with the formal contents developed in the course of elaborating identity philosophy, by contrast, is only a "negative": it can never arrive at anything it has not already posited as a thing thought or a thought-thing. In short, it cannot arrive at anything positive. And this impossibility corresponds exactly to the "position" of Socratic irony as it is presented in Kierkegaard's thesis: it, too, can arrive at nothing positive—no positive doctrine, no positive relation to anything in historical actuality, no positive relation even to the negativity of death, still less a relation of love, which would at the very least suppose the singular and irreplaceable existence of the one loved. Whatever else may be said of the erotics of irony—and Kierkegaard's

---

[14]For the Paulus transcription at this point, see Schelling, *Philosophie der Offenbarung*, 134-35.

discussion of *The Symposium* in his thesis is as good a starting point as any for such a discussion—this much is clear: the one who, like Socrates, makes irony into a "position" only plays at being the lover and, interrupting the relation without revealing this interruption, turns into the beloved. Just as "pure irony or... irony as a position" (CI, 253) stops short of the idea, negative philosophy, according to Schelling, stops short of what remains "über dem Seyn." Its inventor is, for Schelling, Socrates.[15] Both negative philosophy and "pure irony" unwittingly accomplish the task of clearing a place for what they themselves are precluded from attaining—or even viewing: something positive.

This resemblance between negative philosophy and Socratic irony would be of little interest, however, if it did not issue into a complementary problem of presentation. Socratic irony cannot directly manifest itself, and the same can be said of negative philosophy. Of course, it is perfectly possible for a book to present itself as "the science of logic" without the slightest indirection. In this way, the philosophical system Schelling seeks to capture under the rubric of negative philosophy would seem to have nothing in common with Socrates, who leaves no written documents of his thought and whose "negative position" (CI, 145) can only be grasped indirectly. But such is not the case if Schelling's description of the relation of negative to positive philosophy is in any sense valid, for negative philosophy appears only in the light of positive philosophy. The following sentences are one of the very few places in Kierkegaard's notes where he goes to the trouble of underlining Schelling's point: "*Positive philosophy does not have the truth only as a conclusion, as negative philosophy does; für sich negative philosophy cannot be called philosophy; it becomes philosophy only in connection with positive philosophy....* There is, then, only one philosophy," Schelling proceeds to say and Kierkegaard stops underlining, "since negative philosophy, in becoming conscious of positive philosophy, does not in this consciousness have positive philosophy outside itself but is itself within positive philosophy"

---

[15]See Schelling, *Philosophie der Offenbarung*, 140; in the later lectures on the *Philosophy of Mythology*, Schelling calls Socrates "the true Dionysus of philosophy" (*Sämtliche Werke*, ed. Karl Friedrich August Schelling [Stuttgart-Augsburg: Cotta, 1856–1861] II/2, 284).

(CI, 365).[16] Negative philosophy presents itself as something it is not: philosophy. Negative philosophy cannot therefore fail to be ironic, and the trouble with Hegel, for Schelling, is that he forgot the ironic character of the "philosophy" he pursued and understood it as philosophy—or as "die Philosophie," to cite another of the passages Kierkegaard's emphasizes.[17] The "negative dialectic" of Socrates is the truth of Hegelian dialectics: it never arrives at anything positive and, instead, stops short with the play of mere being-able. If one wished to discover a reason for Kierkegaard's minor, perhaps only mechanical decision to take over, rewrite, and underline his account of Schelling's lectures, even as he registers his disappointment, the following remarks from The Concept of Irony might well serve the purpose: "Neither is the dialectic... a genuine philosophical dialectic... but is an entirely negative dialectic" (CI, 145).[18] A negative dialectic is not genuinely philosophical, and a fortiori an authentic philosophy not only cannot be negative; it cannot even present itself as philosophy unless it indirectly presents "the" philosophy for which it—knowingly or not—prepares a way.

But none of these "metaphilosophical" discussions about the categorial quality of dialectics or philosophy—negative or positive—amounts to much unless they open onto a program or a problem, and in this case the problem is easy to identify, the program less so: the problem is the nature of positivity "after Fichte." To be brief: when the young Kierkegaard presents a scholarly thesis organized around an athetic, absolutely nonpositive and nonposition-taking phenomenalization of "pure irony," he not only demonstrates his mastery of irony, he also registers something

---

[16]Kierkegaard's notes at this point do not closely approximate the Paulus transcription: "The science that has the true only as an end cannot be the true science, although it is not for this reason a false one. Over against the true science, which itself in the true, negative philosophy for itself [für sich] is not allowed to claim the name 'philosophy' " (Schelling, Philosophie der Offenbarung, 152; no emphasis; my translation).

[17]In Kierkegaard's first extensive notes, he underlines the following passage: "Now the question is whether it is philosophy but not "die" Philosophie—or whether it is "die" Philosophie—or whether it is not philosophy at all" (CI, 337).

[18]Kierkegaard adopts the term "negative dialectic" from Hegel's treatment of Socrates; see the discussion in the section on "Hegel's View of Socrates" (CI, 223).

else: *a crisis of positing.* A crisis of positing likewise makes itself apparent in the complicated mental maneuvers of Schelling's Berlin lectures, for the fundamental feature of these exercises in positive philosophy is the exposition of primordial being in terms of the unposited, nonpositing and especially nonself-positing. Here one might again be tempted to use the word *irony,* for the presupposition that positive philosophy seeks to capture in advance of all self-positings is contained in the thesis that primordial being is nonpositing, which, however, does not make it negative or nothingness. Schelling's preferred term for this condition is "affirmation"—a term that is doubtless misleading to the extent that "affirmation" is beyond or, more accurately, prior to any distinction between positing and negating. If positional terms would still be appropriate for the determination of the affirmative character of primary or primordial Being, it could be described in terms of a mad deposing of every position of self-consciousness. Schelling's own untranslatable terms for such Being—and Kierkegaard never ventures a Danish translation—is *das unvordenkliche Seyn*: "immemorial Being," more literally—and here I am transcribing Kierkegaard's own explanation of the strange term for a friend—*Seyn, das allem Denken zuvorkommt* [Being that precedes all thought],[19] which is to say, being prior to any positing, including and especially the self-positing of mind or spirit. By no means does Schelling champion *das unvordenkliche Seyn,* however; on the contrary, the point of the theogonic process that he proposes in the Berlin lectures is to delineate the "events" in which *das unvordenkliche Seyn* is progressively overcome—first in splendor or mastery (*Herrlichkeit*) and then again in spirit. Each of the theogonic events consists in an act of positing, which, however, is made possible by virtue of the utterly unposited, namely *das unvordenkliche Seyn.* Only against the blind and blinding background of such being can there be the light of self-positing self-consciousness. Another, more lucid, and yet cruder translation could thus be found for *das unvordenkliche Seyn*: "negative position," which, as the figure of Socrates shows, does not simply negate particular positions but blindly disposes of all positions anyone has taken—"blindly"

[19]See Kierkegaard's letter to Michael Lund (LD, 127; letter 63).

because the disposition of all theses positions has no idea of what position will overcome it. In terms of the general structure of their otherwise incomparable projects, in other words, the "negative position" of "pure irony" that Kierkegaard's thesis seeks to delineate not only bears a certain resemblance to the uncomfortable position of "negative philosophy" as it is outlined in the early, metaphilosophical sessions of Schelling's lectures; more important-ly, it corresponds to the paradoxical position of *das unvordenkliche Seyn* in the later sessions of these lectures, the ones that Kierke-gaard seems to transcribe in the greatest detail. In both cases—that of "pure irony" and that of *das unvordenkliche Seyn*—a *prius* to the *a priori* is discovered, and this disturbing, irrepressible *prius* is presented as a blind beginning, a furious "first" that has no thought as to the acts of self-positing or the doctrines of Plato that will come to overtake it.

And for precisely this reason, these two indices of the crisis of positing are impossible to present *directly*: they can be presented only in retrospect and from a point of view other than their own, for they have, strictly speaking, no "point of view" of their own, if the idea of "point of view" is understood in terms of stable positions or constant position taking. Kierkegaard's attempt to make the "view" of Socrates possible, actual, and necessary is doubtless ironic, if not outright parodic; but it also responds to a basic problem of presentation: how can one bring to light what constitutively retreats from every position? If Socrates has nothing positive to say, if he represents no position and takes no stable stance on any issue, he is bereft of those predicates that would make him identifiable in any sense other than the barest empirical one, which, in any case, would disappear with his death: "If we now say that irony constituted the substance of his [Socrates's] existence (this is, to be sure, a contradiction, but it is supposed to be that), and if we further postulate that irony is a negative concept, it is easy to see how difficult it becomes to fix the picture of him—indeed, it seems impossible or at least as difficult as to picture a nisse with the cap that makes him invisible" (CI, 12). With this image, Kierkegaard captures a problem of presentation that cannot be reduced to the merely formal one of representing what negates representation: the difficulty does not lie in the static paradox, which would in any case make the picture of the nisse impossible, not merely difficult; rather it lies in making the picture a moving one. The resolution of this difficulty lies, accordingly, in something like a *cinematic* exposition of a modality of being that remains positionless or purely dispositional. Kierkegaard goes after such a modality in *The Concept of Irony*, and so, too, does Schelling in his Berlin lectures. For *das unvordenkliche Seyn* cannot be directly presented either; on the contrary, it withdraws from presentation so completely that it might be likened to its graveyard, and the untranslatability of the term its gravestone. If there is a weakness in Schelling's lectures—and, according to all accounts, no one in the audience was unaware of their weakness[20]—it lies most clearly in their failure to respond to the problem of presentation contained in the very idea of *das unvordenkliche Seyn*. Like Socrates, according to Kierkegaard's construction, this absolute beginning can come into view only indirectly, in a cinematic process, after a self-inconsistent act of self-positing, and with the aid of a doctrine of modality.

All of the problems surrounding Schelling's project of positive philosophy as it is formulated in Kierkegaard's notes can perhaps be captured by the following sentence: "Philosophy now comprehends a posteriori the incomprehensible a priori" (CI, 373). Such is *das unvordenkliche Seyn*: incomprehensible and a priori, and incomprehensible in its a priority, not a self-illuminating axiom of reason, still less a luminous point of sense-certainty that progressively shows its inherent blindness. Only an "empirical" exercise comprehends it, and insofar as the exercise of philosophy, as love of wisdom, in contrast to sophism or *Wissenschaft*, is indeed empirical or experiential, neither the one who comprehends nor the item comprehended can be understood as *relata* superseded by the relation of rational comprehension. But the imperative under which this exercise operates corresponds to the imperative into which *The Concept of Irony* issues: the "negative position" must be "mastered." To use the phrase by which the Hongs translate "behersket Moment," *das unvordenkliche Seyn*, like irony, must become a "controlled element" (CI, 324)—controlled or mastered,

---

[20]See the documentation gathered in the third appendix to Manfred Frank's edition of *Philosophie der Offenbarung*, 419-503.

not annulled or sublated (*aufgehoben*). On January 14th, 1842, Kierkegaard makes the following note: "The *unvordenkliche Seyn* is indeed posited *ex actu*, but still not absolutely sublated [*ophævet*], for not even God is capable of that [*thi formaaer end ikke Gud*]" (CI, 383, translation modified).[21] Not even the divine act of self-positing in spirit can sublate what runs counter to positing as such. The mastering of irony by the genial poet or, more generally and more radically, by "any life that is to be called human [*humana vocetur*]" (CI, 5) is not only comparable to God's coming to mastery or becoming lord over his own *unvordenkliche Seyn*; the problem for poets, for human beings who want to call their lives human, and for God is one and the same: how to do so? How to gain mastery over what by its very nature is insubordinate, blind, and blinding—call it "pure irony" or *das unvordenkliche Seyn*?

"Divine Irony"

"*Now we come to something new*" (CI, 382). This sentence is the last of the four that Kierkegaard underlines in his notes on Schelling's lectures, and it does not follow the more detailed transcription of the lectures published by Heinrich Paulus in 1843. "Something new" consists in the posing of a question concerning "suspension": "Why," Kierkegaard asks in his record of Schelling's lectures, "does God suspend this *unvordenkliche Seyn*, why does he actualize this possibility? One could reply that it is in order to transform his blind affirmation into a conscious affirmation. But for whom, then, does he do this?" (CI, 382). In Paulus's transcription of the lectures, the question concerns the positing of that which is affirmative without having ever posited itself: "wie Gott nimmt jene entgegengesetzte Potenz an, um sein nicht-selbst-gesetztes

---

[21] According to the Paulus transcript, Schelling said "Denn das unvordenkliche Sein ist zwar ex actu gesetzt durch das konträre Sein; aber absolut can es nicht aufgehoben werden, denn es hat seine Wurzel in Ewigkeit, wohl aber kann sein actu-Sein aufgehoben werden. [For *das unvordenkliche Sein* is indeed posited from the act by contrary being, but it cannot be absolutely superseded, for it has its roots in eternity; its Being-in-act can, however, doubtless be superseded]" (Schelling, *Philosophie der Offenbarung*, 179). One wonders whether it was Schelling or Kierkegaard who came up with the striking statement "for not even God is capable of that."

Sein in ein gewolltes Sein zu verwandeln, um die blinde Affirmation seines Seins durch Negation to vermitteln. Aber *für wen* sollte
er dies tun?" [how God assumes the opposed potency in order to
transform his nonself-posited being into a willed being, in order to
mediate the blind affirmation of his being by negation. But for
whom should he do so?]."[22] With this question, Schelling comes to
the heart of the theogonic process he seeks to outline, for the
gaining mastery over "immemorial Being" is the initial event in the
coming-to-be-lord of God. The question posed by Kierkegaard's
account of "pure irony or... irony as a position" corresponds to the
one Schelling addresses at the very point Kierkegaard improvises
the sentence "*Now we come to something new*": Why would anyone
who enjoys the freedom of "pure irony" actualize any potential
and thereby take a position? Why would anyone gain mastery over
irony? Or, to use Schelling's language, "why does he [and "he"
here refers to God] actualize this possibility?" (CI, 382), which is
to say, overcome and become lord over *das unvordenkliche Seyn*. For
Schelling, the answer is clear, and this is no small favor in a lecture
series as relentlessly opaque as the one he unleashed on his largely
unsuspecting Berlin audience: it lies in a law to which even God
submits himself as proof of his own divinity: "this law is the
ultimate ground in everything," Kierkegaard notes, "this law that
nothing is to remain untried, undisclosed. This law is indeed not
above God but first places God in freedom in opposition to his
unvordenkliche Seyn" (CI, 378).[23]

Both irony and *das unvordenkliche Seyn* consist at bottom in
concealment—so much that the selfhood of this mode of being is
concealed from itself: irony is only the *beginning* of subjectivity, not
its realization, and the same is true of *das unvordenkliche Seyn*. The
fundamental affinity of "pure irony" and *das unvordenkliche Seyn*
lies in this intractable trait of self-concealment. And the imperative
under which both "pure irony" and *das unvordenkliche Seyn* fall—

---

[22]Schelling, *Philosophie der Offenbarung*, 176.

[23]For the corresponding passage in Paulus's transcription, see Schelling,
Philosophie der Offenbarung, 168: "Es gelangt dies das höchste Gesetz alles Seins,
welches will, daß nichts unversucht, Alles offen, klar und entschieden sei. Dies
Gesetz ist in dem Sinne über Gott, daß das Gesetz Gott erst in Freiheit setzt gegen
sein unvordenkliches Sein."

the imperative of trial and disclosure—cannot be expressed in the famous Hegelian law to which Kierkegaard alludes as he begins his thesis: "essence must appear [*das Wesen muß erscheinen*]."[24] For neither irony nor *das unvordenkliche Seyn* is in any sense a matter of essence. Schelling's lectures are at least clear on this point, and so, too, is Kierkegaard's thesis: irony is not an essence but at most a weak mark—"the lightest and weakest *sign* of subjectivity" (CI, 5, italics added). Insofar as both irony and *das unvordenkliche Seyn* consist in self-concealment, they constitute the necessary conditions under which the law of disclosure comes into effect, and for the very same reason, they can never fall completely under its sway. Yet the self-concealing traits of irony and *das unvordenkliche Seyn* must be overcome. Such is the imperative that makes itself known in the fifteenth and concluding thesis of his thesis and, accordingly, in its concluding section, "Irony as a Mastered Moment." And such is the imperative that Schelling formulates as "God's own law" (CI, 378).

Mastering "pure irony" and overcoming *das unvordenkliche Seyn* does not mean, however, forgetting them—or remembering them either. The precarious line of argument that Schelling and Kierkegaard pursue, each in his own way, seeks to map out a movement of overcoming, "becoming lord," or gaining mastery that neither suppresses nor sublates, neither represses nor memorializes what has been overcome, subjugated, or mastered. Only in one place in Schelling's lectures do his concerns and those of his Danish auditor perfectly coincide: it concerns this precarious line of argument in which a delicate balancing act is sketched out: *das unvordenkliche Seyn*—"immemorial being" or "being before thought"—must be overcome without being either forgotten or memorialized. God is able to accomplish this balancing act; but the same is not true of human beings. And so they trip up and fall. In his lecture notes of January 26th, 1842, Kierkegaard records Schelling's truncated recapitulation of his original inquiry into the essence of human freedom: "If creation arose *einfach*," Kierkegaard writes at the

---

[24]See the opening sentence of the section entitled "Appearance" in the so-called Lesser Logic; *Hegel's Logic*, trans. William Wallace (Oxford: Clarendon Press, 1975) 186.

beginning of these notes, "solely by the infinite causality of God, freedom cannot be saved" (CI, 395, modified).[25] Saving freedom demands a twofold account of creation in which the infinite causality of God is suspended by the possibility that God can be other than himself, other than all-in-all: in Schelling's notation, "A," the absolutely self-identical, becomes what it is not, namely "B." The distinction between creator and creature resides in the disposition of "B," the ability to be other than oneself:

> —Man possesses B [Schelling says] but possesses B only as a creature and consequently only as possibility, not as God possesses it in order to make it actual. Yet this possibility appears as the potency of a second becoming. He is commanded not to move B. In Midrash Koheleth, it says that the creator addresses newly created man: "Take care that you do not shake my world, for if you shake it, nothing (nothing new) can calm it.—This prohibition shows man the very possibility of doing it." (CI, 396)[26]

Unlike the similar place in the inquiry into the *Essence of Human Freedom*,[27] Schelling may not use the word *Angst* here; but the ironic project of grasping anxiety as a scientific concept finds its point of departure here: an incomprehensible word not only speaks of a possibility but actually makes possible what it prohibits (see CA, esp. 44-46). And Schelling then proceeds to use the master term of Kierkegaard's thesis: "What man wanted was the same turning about or turning out (*Auswendung*) of the potencies that God brought about, the same as could be called *universio*. In God's self-concept, B is the most negated and turned inward, that which in creation is most outwardly turned. This is divine irony, which thus turns out another side, therefore we must be prudent [*Dette er den gudd. Ironie, der saaledes vender en anden Side ud, hvorfor vi maa være kloge*]. The world is *unum v e r s u m, universum*: that which is turned about [*det Omvendte*]. Thus man believed he would get

---

[25] For the corresponding passage in Paulus's transcription, see Schelling, *Philosophie der Offenbarung*, 200.

[26] For the corresponding passage in Paulus's transcription, see Schelling, *Philosophie der Offenbarung*, 201.

[27] See Schelling, *Philosophische Untersuchungen über das Wesen der menschlichen Freiheit und die damit zusammenhängenden Gegenstände*, 74; *Philosophical Inquiries into the Nature of Human Freedom*, 59 (where *Angst* is translated as "terror").

eternal life by turning this principle outward. Man did not become lord over it but became mastered by it" (CI, 396).

According to Paulus's transcription of the Berlin lectures, Schelling does not say "divine irony" but only "irony": "*Gott kehrt*—und er übt diese *Ironie* schon in der Schöpfung aus—*das heraus, was seine Absicht ist*, hinein *zu kehren* [God turns—and he exercises this irony already in creation—outward what he intended to turn inward]."[28] The irony of God is not a power over which he disposes; on the contrary—and in contrast to the undisciplined talk of irony Kierkegaard associates with Solger in his thesis—irony here names a moment of unresolvable crisis: an action runs counter to its intention; the subject, in term, is no longer in a position to determine the meaning of what he or she says or does. If this is valid for the divine subject, it is all the more true of human beings, who "fall" in response to a word they cannot possibly understand until they are fallen. According to Paulus's transcription of the Berlin lectures, these reflections on divine irony serve as warrant for even greater boldness: "it is not too bold to say [*nicht zu kühn zu sagen*]: man mastered in the pretemporal act the fatherly, procreative power. But he was not given mastery over the principle that thereby became effective."[29] In Kierkegaard's notes, by contrast, Schelling issues a call for caution: "we must therefore be prudent." Nowhere else, so far as I can tell, do Kierkegaard's notes and those of Paulus contradict each other. And what a remarkable place for this contradiction: at the very moment Schelling is revealing the inner workings of the Godhead, its most inward side, according to Kierkegaard, he warns his listeners to be cautious, as if a misstep at this point might be dangerous. This warning may be Kierkegaard's ironic improvisation, or he may

---

[28]Schelling, *Philosophie der Offenbarung*, 201-202 (emphases in the original copy). There is good reason to prefer Kierkegaard's notes over Paulus's at this point, for Schelling elsewhere uses the phrase "divine irony" in similar contexts: "The potencies in their reciprocal exclusivity and their inverted opposition to each other are only God outwardly dissembled [*verstellte*] through divine irony. They are the inverted [or perverted, *verkehrte*] One insofar as, according to appearance, what is hidden, what should not be active, is apparent and what is positive, what should be apparent, is negated and in the state of potency" (Schelling, *Philosophie der Mythologie*, in *Sämtliche Werke*, II/2, 90).

[29]Schelling, *Philosophie der Offenbarung*, 203.

have misheard Schelling. Or, unlike the stenographer who took the notes Paulus publishes, he may have been directly on target—attentive the explosively ironic character of Schelling's talk of divine irony. In any case, both "therefore" and "prudence" are anything but self-evident: they point toward a certain uneasiness, perhaps even anxiety, at this point in the notes, an uneasiness that may be connected to the difference between the Kierkegaardian and Schellingian concepts of irony. For irony, according to Schelling, has nothing to do with positions or self-positings. He not only distinguishes himself from the romantics whom Kierkegaard discusses in the second part of his thesis, for whom the self-positing I was the warrant for an irresponsible display of protean personality; he also distinguishes himself from Kierkegaard, for "divine irony" is a matter of turnings, not positions—not even negative ones. Indeed, Schelling's use of the term *irony* here can be considered more exacting than that of Kierkegaard inasmuch as it aligns itself with the oldest of rhetorical traditions: irony is a turning, which is to say, a *trope*.[30] And it would make no sense to speak of a "negative" trope, since the idea of trope traverses the distinction between negativity and positivity. In *The Concept of Irony* Kierkegaard dismisses those who understand irony merely as a figure of speech, for, if a discourse is understood to be ironic, its irony disappears; it speaks directly to those "in the know," those who know that discourse is supposed to be ironic (CI, 248).

---

[30]For an illuminating account of the historical use of this term among rhetoricians, see Heinrich Lausberg, *Handbuch der literarischen Rhetorik* (Munich: Hueber, 1960) 1:302-303, 446-50. Kierkegaard does not, of course, ignore the "tropical" character of irony; on the contrary, he begins his "Observations for Orientation" by distinguishing "irony as position" from "a figure of speech with the name of irony" (CI, 247). The principal characteristic of irony in this sense is its tendency toward self-annihilation: once it is understood, it is no longer a "trope" or "turn of phrase" but *straight talk*: "The ironic figure of speech cancels itself inasmuch as the who is speaking assumes that his hearers understand him, and thus, through a negation of the immediate phenomenon, the essence becomes identical with the phenomenon" (CI, 248). The same can be said of any trope, moreover: once they are comprehended, they are no longer "turns." Instead of identifying tropes, then, Kierkegaard *enacts* them—from the beginning of the dissertation onward. These turns cannot be altogether straightened out, and for this reason, they cannot be simply understood as turns in the first place.

The "infinity" of Socratic irony, by contrast, consists in the impossibility of anyone being "in the know" about what Socrates wishes to say, for he does not wish to say anything (positive). But Kierkegaard does not then undertake a further inquiry into the nature of tropes in relation to the issue of taking-a-position, "negative position," and self-positing. Schelling, by contrast, presents irony in terms of a trope, and this trope runs counter to an intention; indeed, it operates in relative independence from consciousness: one turn gives rise to another, in an almost mechanical manner. Regardless of whether one follows Paulus's or Kierkegaard's transcription of the lectures, the point is the same: irony cannot be mastered, not even by God; indeed, irony, according to Paulus's transcription, gets the better of God, as he "turns outward what he *intended* to turn inward."

A note of caution is clearly appropriate here. What Schelling offers to his audience is more than an account of a theogonic process that makes sense of creation and a freely chosen fall. And Schelling does more than make this freely chosen fall into the case of ironic communication. For he offers to his wavering audience a way of understanding the tropological character of irony—and a way to understand what is indeed impossible to understand: the unmasterability of irony, even for God. If, for Kierkegaard, romantic irony is deficient to the extent that the romantics thought they were always in a position to posit—or reposition—themselves anew, regardless of historical actuality, the same cannot be said of the turning outward of inwardness that Schelling describes: it takes place against the intention of the one who, above all, is able to posit whatever he sees fit, namely God. By removing the problem of irony from that of self-positing and by returning the term to its tropological provenance, Schelling repeats in a minor mode the gesture by means of which he first sought to distinguish his thought from the basic Fichtean thesis: the beginning does not consist in a positional act. On the contrary, the beginning is always ironic—in at least two ways: (1) the beginning as such, *das unvordenkliches Seyn*, is ironic, for it escapes comprehension for all time, which is to say, until time comes to an end. And (2) the beginning of human life is equally ironic, for it consists in the turning outward of what is most inward—a turning outward occasioned by the desire to understand a prohibitive word that would otherwise, without this decisive and disastrous self-alteration, remain incomprehensible.

Every beginning is, therefore, ironic: this much can be learned from Schelling's account of the theogonic process. Outside of this idiosyncratic theogony, the lesson may very well stand, which means that the fifteenth thesis of the *Concept of Irony* would have to undergo a significant revision: "Just as philosophy begins in doubt, so, too, a life that can be called human begins in irony" (CI, 6). Philosophy, too, begins with irony: what it is supposed to understand from the beginning is incomprehensible, since it is *unvordenklich*—before thought and beyond memory. Every beginning is ironic and appears in the guise of irony, for, as a beginning—as an *unvordenklich* event—it cannot be grasped before it takes place; it cannot be predicted or foreseen, nor does it express any prior potentiality, a priori possibility, or "thought-thing." Everywhere one turns, there is irony—as long as one turns toward beginnings and does not simply pay attention to the supposedly continuous movements of thought or history. But the lesson of Schelling goes further: irony—and therefore beginnings—cannot be mastered; irony does not consist in the self-positing of a sovereign subject who can make itself appear under any form it chooses; and "pure irony" cannot therefore be conceived in terms of "negative position" in which all the relations are unsystematically, erratically suspended. Even the purest irony—the divine kind—turns against the subject who seeks to gain mastery over itself by a freely creative act.

The "Position" of Sin

At the end of a lengthy footnote in *The Concept of Irony* Kierkegaard lightly touches on a topic about which he otherwise remains taciturn—"nature's irony" (CI, 245). As the sole mode of irony utterly ungoverned by an intention; as mindless irony, so to speak, it has no definitive place in a discussion of irony as "negative position." At most, it is a species of "executive irony" or "dramatic irony" without further interest to the investigation into "Irony After Fichte" for which the "Observations for Orientation"—the section in which the footnote on nature's irony can be found—serves as a preparation: "This irony in nature has been placed in a footnote because only the humorous individual actually perceives it, since it is actually only through the contemplation of *sin* that the ironic interpretation of nature really emerges" (CI, 255). Thus Kierkegaard closes his footnote: nothing more will be said of a mode of irony that has nothing to do with intentions. "Divine irony," as Schelling presents this figure in his lectures, would belong to the field of "executive irony" and, more exactly, to the domain of "nature's irony," for it makes the *universum* as a whole—and everthing "in it"—ironic. And such an understanding of the universe is open only by those who are aware of sin; indeed, the awareness of the fall into sin is the sole condition for understanding the inverse character of the universe. Nature as a whole reveals its ironic character to those who are conscious of sin— which means at the very least that a *serious* investigation into the trope of irony could never begin with Socrates; it must begin much earlier and makes its own point of departure into the very problem under investigation. Thus *The Concept of Irony* turns out to be ironic after all: it is not serious about sin, the consciousness of which ironizes the universe. The problem of mastering irony, in turn, cannot be undertaken outside of another—and far more serious— problem: that of overcoming sin, which is to say, the problem of reversing the turning outward of what is inward. Insofar as every sinful act is *unvordenklich*, it is unmasterable until the end of time, and the awareness of sin opens everything in the universe, including the self-positing I, to "ironic interpretation": the position of the I is not its own, absolutely, and it is not a position mediated by its relation to the not-I; its "position" lies in sin, and none of these other terms—negativity, positivity, mediation, even relationality—can make this "position" available to a scientific inquiry, even one undertaken in the name of "positive philosophy."

Kierkegaard may very well have already been keenly interested in the problem posed by this otherwise inconspicuous footnote to *The Concept of Irony* before he heard Schelling talk about "divine irony,"[31] but the words of caution Schelling issues as he discusses the genuinely *universal* character of irony—"we must therefore be

---

[31]See the notes related to this footnote collected and translated by the Hongs, CI, 431-32.

prudent"—may also have propelled his studious auditor outside of the framework built for his own ironic elaboration of the concept of irony. Every beginning is ironic insofar as every one is *unvordenklich*. And everything in the universe is open to an ironic interpretation as soon as the interpreter is aware of sin. Such is Schelling's teaching. Kierkegaard did not have to sit through his later lectures on the philosophy of revelation to bring home with him a lesson he would elaborate into a hitherto unknown, unpredictable, and unheard-of—in short, *unvordenklich*—project of authorship.

Contributors

International Kierkegaard Commentary 2
The Concept of Irony

MARTIN ANDIC is associate professor of Philosophy at the University of Massachusetts in Boston.

ANDREW J. BURGESS is associate professor of Philosophy at the University of New Mexico in Albuquerque.

PETER FENVES is professor of German and Comparative Literature and adjunct in Philosophy and Political Science at Northwestern University, Evanston, Illinois.

RONALD L. HALL is professor of Philosophy at Stetson University, DeLand, Florida.

BRUCE H. KIRMMSE is professor of History at Connecticut College, New London, Connecticut.

TONNY AAGAARD OLESEN writes commentaries for "Søren Kierkegaards Skrifter" at the Søren Kierkegaard Research Center at the University of Copenhagen.

GEORGE PATTISON is dean of the chapel at King's College, Cambridge.

RICHARD M. SUMMERS, an independent scholar, lives in London, England.

PIA SØLTOFT is assistant professor of Theology at the University of Copenhagen and president of the Søren Kierkegaard Selskabet.

ADRIAAN VAN HEERDEN is a doctoral candidate at Cambridge University, England.

SYLVIA WALSH is a visiting associate professor of Philosophy at Stetson University, DeLand, Florida.

MEROLD WESTPHAL is distinguished professor of Philosophy at Fordham University, New York City.

ERIC ZIOLKOWSKI is professor of Religion at Lafayette College, Easton, Pennsylvania.

Editor
Robert L. Perkins, Stetson University

Advisory Board
C. Stephen Evans, Calvin College   Sylvia Walsh, Stetson University

Volume Consultant
Ronald L. Hall

International Advisory Board
Julia Watkin, Australia   Nelly Viallaneix, France
Poul Lübcke, Denmark   J. Heywood Thomas, England
Wolfdiedrich von Kloden, Federal Republic of Germany

Previous Volume Consultants

Volume 1. *Early Polemical Writings*
Julia Watkin, University of Tasmania

Volume 3. *Either/Or*. Part I
George Connell, Concordia College, Title Consultant for *Either/Or* I and II
David Gouwens, Brite Divinity School

Volume 4. *Either/Or*. Part II
Edward F. Mooney, Sonoma State University

Volume 6. *"Fear and Trembling" and "Repetition"*
Abrahim H. Kahn, University of Toronto, *Fear and Trembling*
David Goicoechea, Brock University, *Repetition*

Volume 7. *"Philosophical Fragments" and "Johannes Climacus"*
Lee Barrett, Lancaster Theological Seminary

Volume 8. *The Concept of Anxiety*
Vincent A. McCarthy, St. Joseph's University

Volume 11. *"Stages on Life's Way"*
Vincent A. McCarthy, St. Joseph's University

Volume 12. *Concluding Unscientific Postscript to "Philosophical Fragments"*
Merold Westphal, Fordham University

Volume 13. *The Corsair Affair*
Bruce H. Kirmmse, Connecticut College

Volume 14. *Two Ages*
Merold Westphal, Fordham University

Volume 16. *Works of Love*
Lee Barrett, Lancaster Theological Seminary

Volume 19. *The Sickness unto Death*
Louis Dupré, Yale University

Index

ethical, the, 141, 143, 144, 155
Euripides, 217, 216
Euripidean drama, 215n93
Evans, C. Stephen, 266
evil, 245
existence, 189, 318

faith, 318-20, 339n20, 352, 360, 377-78
Faust, 351, 352, 357
Felton, C. C., 194n11
feminist hermeneutics, 125, 139
Fenger, Henning, 3n4, 292
Fenves, Peter, 14
Ferguson, John, 199n31
Fichte, J. G., 298, 300n21, 333-34, 375n19
Figal, Günter, 394
finitude, 318
Forchhammer, Johan Georg, 54, 109, 294n15
Frank, Ann, 5n6
Freedom; 320, 351-52; negative, 142, 143, 147, 149, 156, 326n9, 327, 333; positive, 142, 143, 149, 322, 327
freedom of the press, 2
Friis, Oluf, 291n9

Garff, Joakim, 289n1
Gaves, George, 194, 204, 207
Geffken, Johannes, 200n35
Gereke, Alfred, 205n61
Gigon, Olod, 198n26
Gillespie, Michael Allen, 300n21
Gilson, Etienne, 201
Goethe, Johann Wolfgang von, 5, 13, 104, 106, 154, 155, 157, 306, 308, 348, 351, 362
Grabbe, Christian Dietrich, 291
Grane, Leif, 43, 44, 45-46, 76n95
Grote, George, 194, 204, 207

Grundtvig, Nicolai Frederik, Severin, 44, 45-45, 75
Grunnet, Sanne Elisa, 149
Grøn, Arne, 394
guilt, consciousness of, 158
Gutzkow, Karl, 301

Hall, Ronald L., 13
Halliäj, al-, 201
Halperin, David M., 131n7
Hamacher, Werner, 399
Hamann, Johann Georg, 200n37, 202, 210-12, 293, 296n18, 362, 363
Hamlet (and *Hamlet*), 93, 94-95, 98, 224n124
Hammerich, Martin, 58, 59-60, 61, 67-69
See also Latin requirement
Handwerk, Gary, 313nn47-48
Harnack, Adolf, 199n35, 200n36
Harris, H. S., 368n5
heaven, 357, 358, 360
Hegel, Georg Wilhelm Friedrich (and Hegelianism), 10, 11, 14, 46, 47, 50, 56-58, 59, 74, 77-80, 83, 95-95, 105, 108, 109m 110, 119, 124, 141, 142, 146, 148, 149, 150, 151, 152, 153, 156, 186-88, 195, 198, 203-204, 206-207, 209-10, 212-14, 216, 217, 218, 219-21, 222-23, 225-26, 232, 235-63, 265, 270-73, 276, 279, 291, 293, 294, 296, 298, 300n21, 303, 312, 347-48, 349, 350, 354-55, 359, 366-67, 368n5, 369, 392, 393, 394, 397-98, 401, 409
Heiberg, Johan Ludwig, 13, 14, 46, 62-63, 74, 79, 104, 106, 152, 154, 155, 157, 221, 259, 348, 349-60
Heiberg, Johanne Luise, 349
Heidegger, Martin, 311n45, 348, 399
Heine, Heinrich, 291

Jesus, 189n46, 199-202, 203
Joël, Karl, 204n57
Johansen, Karsten Friis, 115
John the Baptist, 327n10, 372, 376,
    379n23, 380-91, 388
Judah, Halevi, 201
Judge William, 157, 320n5
justice, 390
Justin Martyr, 10, 200

Kant, Immanuel, 202, 246, 253, 255,
    265, 298, 399
Keeley, Louise Carroll, 265
Keicher, Otto, 202n44
Kidd, I. G., 201n39
Kierkegaard, Michael Pedersen, 37,
    92-93
Kierkegaard, Søren A., 212
    as Christian-Socratic moral phi-
        losopher, 236, 261, 263
    "Another Defense of Woman's
        Great Abilities," 1, 2
    "The Battle between the Old and
        the New Soap Cellars," 6-7
    Christian Discourses, 159, 212
    Concluding Unscientific Postscript
        to "Philosophical Fragments,"
        121-22, 158, 159-60, 224
    Early Polemical Writings, 212,
        222-23
    Eighteen Upbuilding Discourses,
        158-59
    Either/Or I, 226
    Either/Or II, 157, 158, 159, 224
    Fear and Trembling, 196
    For Self-Examination, 232-33
    From the Papers of One Still Liv-
        ing, 300, 303, 305, 393
    "Gilleleie Journal," 3-4, 7
    Johannes Climacus, 145

Journals and Papers, 196n17, 210,
    212, 213, 215n92, 215n94, 223-
    25, 227-33, 361-62
    "Literary Quicksilver," 227n127
    Philosophical Fragments, 121-22,
        236
    Point of View, 232
    Stages on Life's Way, 224
    The Concept of Anxiety, 138,
        308n39, 394
    The Concept of Irony
        composition of, 101-108
        first evaluation of, 103-105
        methodology of, 101-108, 395-
            97, 403, 45-46, 409, 412,
            414-15
    The "Corsair" Affair, 120-21,
        195n15, 227n127, 228-31
    The Sickness unto Death, 224, 310
    Two Ages, 228, 261
    Works of Love, 159, 236, 261
Kirmmse, Bruce H., 1n1, 5n6, 8, 276
Kleve, Knut, 114
Kloden, Wolfdietrich von, 109
Knox, T. M., 243
Koch, Carl, 304n29
Koktanek, Anton, 394
Kuhn, Thomas, 388n42

Lactanius, 200n37
Lange, Frederik O., 145
Latin requirement, 42-43, 50, 52-53,
    54
    Adolph Peter Adler's case, 54,
        59-60
    Martin Hammerich's case, 53-56
    Hans Lassen Martensen's case,
        57-57
    K. W. Wiborg's case, 61
Law, David R., 6n10, 222n118
Ledger, Gerald, 162n1
Lenau, Nikolaus, 291, 351